EL Education

Your Curriculum Companion

The Essential Guide to Teaching the EL Education 6–8 Language Arts Curriculum (Second Edition)

Libby Woodfin, Suzanne Nathan Plaut, and Sarah Boddy Norris

EL Education
247 West 35th St., 8th Floor
New York, NY 10001
212-239-4455

Design by Mike Kelly

Entypo pictograms by Daniel Bruce — www.entypo.com

Art on page 20 by students at Launch Expeditionary Learning Charter School,
a NYC Outward Bound School

Photo on page 235 by João Silas on Unsplash

Photo on page 289 by Angelina Litvin on Unsplash

Photo on page 369 by Jamie Passinault

All other photos EL Education

Table of Contents

Table of Contents

Video Table of Contents

All videos listed here can also be accessed from the Your Curriculum Companion, 6–8 Video Collection on our website (https://ELeducation.org/resources/collections/your-curriculum-companion-6-8-videos). As new videos are created to support the EL Education 6–8 Language Arts Curriculum, they will be added to the collection. Check back periodically.

Video Table of Contents

---

1. This video was created by Edutopia and is not included in the Your Curriculum Companion, 6–8 Video Collection on the EL Education website.

Video Table of Contents

Preface

The EL Education 6–8 Language Arts Curriculum offers teachers, schools, and districts a truly comprehensive approach: it is content-based and standards-aligned; it is designed based on the principles of Universal Design for Learning to support all students to succeed within heterogeneous classrooms; it provides explicit lesson-level support for English language learners; and it weaves character development into every lesson.

We built the curriculum based on the research of experts in the field of literacy, joined with the wisdom and experience of practicing teachers who were with us through every step of the design process. At the heart of everything we do is our commitment to equipping educators— new and veteran alike—with resources and professional learning opportunities to help them learn and grow. We see our curriculum as a powerful resource that provides teachers with the tools they need and students with the great instruction they deserve.

Our public education system has the power to be an engine for equity, justice, and opportunity. However, all too often it serves instead to perpetuate inequity. Academic outcomes correlate almost exactly with levels of poverty, and race continues disproportionately to predict student outcomes, in school and in life. Instead of empowering and elevating all students as capable citizens and leaders, schooling too often reflects existing inequality and privilege, entrenching the divisions of our society.

Premised on the dream of equal opportunity, the reality of today's education system remains one of disparity and unfulfilled potential. It enables advantaged students to benefit from schools that challenge, stimulate, and engage them. Meanwhile, others, typically students of color from low income communities, must settle for schools with a narrow approach to education focused on compliance and lacking in intellectually challenging work. Neither traditional school approaches nor decades of school reform have overcome this two-tiered system to produce equitable, excellent outcomes for students of all backgrounds.

EL Education's K–8 Language Arts Curriculum is a key component of our vision for a transformed education system where race and background have no predictive power with respect to student outcomes. This vision of education is grounded in an integrated view of learning and achievement—of a system preparing young people to thrive in college, at work, and in community, with the commitment and capacity to create a better world.

Nearly a decade ago, we decided to test a big idea: that we can transform student outcomes by creating a content-rich curriculum and giving teachers the support to fully engage with it. And now we have increasing evidence—from multiple rigorous studies covering grades K–8— that the EL Education curriculum results in higher ELA achievement for students, and shifts in teacher practice (go to ELeducation.org for more information).

By choosing EL Education's Language Arts curriculum, you can feel confident that you have chosen a content-based, research-aligned curriculum that challenges, engages, and empowers every student to succeed. In addition to this evidence of academic achievement, we're proud that our curriculum prioritizes character and high-quality student work as key dimensions of student achievement. Developing students' capacities to succeed in all three dimensions of achievement has always been at the core of our work at EL Education and is a reminder that we can provide the kind of education every child deserves—one that results in academic excellence, character, and high-quality work.

EL Education's strong evidence of impact reflects the power of an instructional approach that has been honed over a quarter-century of work in thousands of schools. Our language arts curriculum is now extending our reach beyond individual schools to district partnerships that inspire educators with an approach that brings joy into their classrooms and transforms the achievement of all children.

Scott Hartl
President and CEO, EL Education
New York, NY
February, 2020

Acknowledgments

The real heroes of this project are the EL Education staff, teachers, and expert consultants who wrote the EL Education 6–8 Language Arts Curriculum, as well as those who help us bring it to teachers, schools, and districts across the United States. They are rarely publicly acknowledged, but they deserve our gratitude, particularly Christina Riley, EL Education's director of curriculum design, who shepherded the second edition of the curriculum from start to finish. The result is a rigorous, compelling, and justice-oriented curriculum that is good for kids, teachers, and the world, thanks to Christina and her team.

We also want to give special shout-outs to Mike Kelly, the graphic designer for this book who worked patiently with us to get everything just right, and to Cheryl Dobbertin, who was instrumental in bringing to life the first edition of the Grades 3–8 curriculum. And, to members of EL Education's senior leadership team who ensure that our organization can continue to bring these resources to educators and students across the United States, thank you Scott Hartl, Kathleen Schwille, Kemi Akinsanya-Rose, Ron Berger, and Beth Miller.

All the people listed here played an important role with the curriculum or this book and we owe them all a debt of gratitude.

EL Education Curriculum Design Team

Kevin Jepson
Monica Lewis

Christina Riley
Katie Shenk

Corey VanHuystee

Teachers and Consultant Curriculum Designers

Deb Griffith
Anthony Holley
Breah Johnson and
Amana Academy
Dominique Johnson
Stephanie Kane-Mainier

Eleanor Kashmar Wolf
Susan Leeming
Jessica Madsen
Kathleen McCormack
Ali Morgan and
Odyssey School of Denver

Emma Samuels Ezzell and
Grass Valley Charter School
Jen Soalt
Chrissy Thuli

Expert Advisors to the Curriculum Design Team

Rebecca Blum-Martinez
Joseph Bruchac
Carlisle Indian School
Digital Resource Center

Steve DelVecchio
Joey Hawkins
Diana Leddy
Auddie Mastroleo

Allison Posey and CAST
Smithsonian Museum
of the American Indian
Yoo Kyung Sung

EL Education Curriculum Development and Production Team

Ananda Grant
Madison Kamakas

Rupa Mohan
Lloyetta Walls

Emily Williams

Curriculum Review Panel

Kristen Briggs
Sandra Calderon
Sucia Dhillon
Rebecca Feder
Tiffany Fick
Karina Flores
Paul Gerber

Ashley Goggins
Jenny Henderson
Kari Horn Lehman
Staci Intriligator
Stephanie Jakimczyk
Monica Lewis
Shanta Lightfoot

Sarah Metzler
Briana Nurse
Michelle Pinta
Adrianna Riccio
Natalie Schnorr
Jessica Seessel
Melissa Wilhelmi

EL Education Staff Who Supported Schools and Districts during the 2019-2020 Soft Launch of the Second Edition Curriculum

Laurel Davis
Staci Intrilagator
Kevin Jepson
Wanda McClure

Caitlin McKenzie
Carrie Moore
Janey Stoddard
Tarika Sullivan

Erin Vaughn
Melissa Wilhelmi

West Ed Staff Who Conducted Focus Groups and Research during the 2018-2019 Pilot

Lauren Agnew
Candice Bocala

Karen Melchior
Cerelle Morrow

EL Education Staff Who Reviewed Portions of *Your Curriculum Companion*

Amy Bailey
Ron Berger
Kristen Briggs

Kevin Jepson
Monica Lewis
Kate Palumbo

Christina Riley
Katie Shenk
Anne Vilen

Educators Who Appear in *Your Curriculum Companion's* Videos

Jodi Arellano
Kaitlyn Billops
Stephanie Clayton
Monet Cooper
Jennifer Dauphinais

Anne Gillyard
Peter Hill
Pamela Hornbuckle
Tawana Jordan
Sarah Mitchell

Rich Richardson
Jason Shiroff
Sheela Webster
Jessica Wood
Sloane Young

Videographers

Sebastian Buffa
Casey Couser

Rosa Gaia
David Grant

Greg Marasso
Katie Schneider

Teachers Who Contributed Work or Stories from their Classrooms to *Your Curriculum Companion*

Erin Harvell
Sarah Mitchell

Jamie Passinault
Bess Pinson

Lindsay Slabich
Emily Zutz

And finally, thank you to the schools and teachers who participated in the 2018 pilot and 2019-2020 soft launch of the Grades 6–8 (second edition) Language Arts Curriculum. Your feedback and partnership was invaluable to our development process.

About the Authors

Libby Woodfin

Libby Woodfin is the director of publications for EL Education. She started her career as a fifth- and sixth-grade teacher at the original lab school for the Responsive Classroom in Greenfield, Massachusetts, and went on to become a counselor at a large comprehensive high school. Libby started with EL Education in 2007 while completing graduate work at the Harvard Graduate School of Education in Education Policy and Management.

Throughout her career, Libby has written articles, blogs, chapters, and books about important issues in education. Her previous books include *The Leaders of Their Own Learning Companion: New Tools and Tips for Tackling the Common Challenges of Student Engaged Assessment; Your Curriculum Companion: The Essential Guide to Teaching the EL Education K–5 Language Arts Curriculum; Learning That Lasts: Challenging, Engaging, and Empowering Students with Deeper Instruction; Management in the Active Classroom; Transformational Literacy: Making the Common Core Shift with Work That Matters; Leaders of Their Own Learning: Transforming Schools through Student-Engaged Assessment;* and *Familiar Ground: Traditions That Build School Community.*

Suzanne Nathan Plaut

Suzanne Nathan Plaut, former director of curriculum design for EL Education, is now the managing director of program for EL Education. She previously served as the vice president of education at the Public Education & Business Coalition in Denver, overseeing professional development, evaluation, and publications. Suzanne holds a doctorate from the Harvard Graduate School of Education, where she served on the editorial board for the Harvard Educational Review. Her previous books include *Your Curriculum Companion: The Essential Guide to Teaching the EL Education K–5 Language Arts Curriculum; Transformational Literacy: Making the Common Core Shift with Work That Matters* and *The Right to Literacy in Secondary Schools.* She also has been published in EdWeek. Suzanne worked as a literacy coach and director of literacy in several Boston public schools and taught high school English in Colorado and New Zealand. She lives in Lafayette, Colorado, with her husband and two children.

Sarah Boddy Norris

Sarah Boddy Norris is the associate director of program development for EL Education. In previous work as an EL Education school designer, she coached teachers and administrators in schools all over the southeast United States. Sarah came to EL Education after being a New York City middle school teacher, and has taught English to multilingual learners in Palau, Corsica, and Georgia. Sarah has taught in K-12 settings, technical colleges, community education centers, and universities. Sarah holds degrees from Reed College and Teachers College, Columbia University. Her writing on educational equity has appeared in EdWeek and elsewhere. This is her first book.

About EL Education

"There is more in us than we know. If we can be made to see it, perhaps, for the rest of our lives, we will be unwilling to settle for less."

Kurt Hahn

EL Education is redefining student achievement in diverse communities across the United States, ensuring that all students master rigorous content, develop positive character, and produce high-quality work. We create great public schools where they are needed most, inspiring teachers and students to achieve more than they thought possible.

EL Education's portfolio of instructional materials and coaching services draws on decades of deep partnership with schools and districts in our national school network—those implementing our school model—and in our family of literacy partners—those implementing our Language Arts curriculum.

Based on our founding principles of meaningful work, character, and respect for teachers, EL Education's offerings transform teaching and learning to promote habits of scholarship and character that lead to high student achievement. In addition to success on standardized tests, EL Education students demonstrate critical thinking, intellectual courage, and emotional resilience; they possess the passion and the capacity to contribute to a better world.

EL Education's curriculum is a comprehensive, standards-based core literacy program that engages teachers and students through compelling, real-world content by diverse authors. The curriculum has received the highest marks from EdReports.org and Educators Evaluating the Quality of Instructional Products (EQuIP). Rigorous impact studies by Mathematica Policy Research demonstrate that teachers significantly improve their craft and students achieve more, regardless of background.

EL Education, a 501c(3) nonprofit, was founded in 1992 by Outward Bound USA in collaboration with the Harvard Graduate School of Education. The ideas of Kurt Hahn, a founder of Outward Bound USA, have inspired and animated EL Education's work with schools since our founding. Hahn believed in the genius in every child, and in the power of education to help children develop academic courage and ethical character.

Your Curriculum Companion

The Essential Guide to Teaching the EL Education 6–8 Language Arts Curriculum (Second Edition)

Introduction

EL Education's Grades 6–8 Language Arts curriculum is a comprehensive, standards-based core literacy program that engages teachers and diverse learners through compelling, real-world content. Through the curriculum we address an expanded definition of student achievement that builds students' academic knowledge and skills, habits of character, and capacity to create high-quality work. Our approach infuses rigor and joy and embodies a focus on equity and closing learning opportunity gaps.

Originally designed and developed with a team of teachers in 2012, the national interest in our Grades 6–8 Language Arts curriculum is inspiring. The first edition was originally commissioned by New York State, which required a total of six modules per grade and alignment to the state's Social Studies and Science Standards. Though initially designed with New York teachers as the primary audience, the curriculum has found a home with a national audience of educators who are seeking out curriculum that uses authentic texts and is directly aligned to the standards. To meet this need, we have created a second edition that broadens the curriculum's relevance to schools nationally and incorporates feedback from teachers across the country.

Your Curriculum Companion is designed to accompany the second edition of the curriculum.

▶ What's New in the Second Edition?

Overall Design and Structure

» Four modules per grade level for a complete year of study (no longer A and B module options)

» New topics and texts for three out of the four modules at each grade level for national relevance. Anchor texts remain the same in the following modules:

- Grade 6: Module 1 (*The Lightning Thief* by Rick Riordan)

- Grade 7: Module 1 (*A Long Walk to Water* by Linda Sue Park)

- Grade 8: Module 2 (*The Omnivore's Dilemma* by Michael Pollan)

» Explicit supports for English language learners (ELLs), including differentiated materials, Conversation Cues, and Language Dives, which are 10- to 20-minute teacher-guided conversations in which students deconstruct and analyze language structures in a single sentence

» Design informed by the Universal Design for Learning framework to increase meaningful access and reduce barriers to learning for students with diverse learning needs

» Explicit integration of EL Education's habits of character: Work to Become an Effective Learner, Work to Become an Ethical Person, and Work to Contribute to a Better World

» Explicit integration of academic mindsets through reflection

» Streamlined Teacher Guides to support navigability and accessibility

» More authentic performance tasks that support the creation of high-quality work and integrate twenty-first-century digital skills

» Each section of the lesson is now assigned a standard in the subheading, and teaching notes describe how this standard is taught and/or practiced in this section of the lesson.

We have also refined our approach to addressing the standards with more explicit writing and language instruction, more progress monitoring tools, and more differentiated learning materials.

Reading

- » Pacing: Students now preread the chapter for homework, and reread a 10- to 15-minute excerpt in the lesson.

- » Text Guides for teachers outline the sensitive issues in an anchor text and describe how to handle them.

Writing

- » Explicit and consistent writing instruction using the Painted Essay® structure, developed by Diana Leddy at the Vermont Writing Collaborative, which uses color to help students visualize the parts of an essay and organize their information

- » Models for student analysis and for use as teacher exemplars

Speaking and Listening

- » Conversation Cues: Questions teachers can ask students and students can ask one another to promote productive and equitable conversation

- » Enhanced informal speaking and listening assessment materials, such as checklists

- » Formal speaking and listening assessments

Language

- » Explicit vocabulary, grammar, and punctuation instruction aligned to the requirements of the Language standards

Assessments

- » Differentiated student materials used for ongoing assessment

- » Writing rubrics (for W.1 argument, W.2 informative/explanatory, and W.3 narrative)

- » Improved alignment between standards, texts, and assessment questions

- » Standards identified with each assessment question

- » Improved support for students to track and assess their own progress

- » More time within lesson plans allotted for assessments

Materials

- » More diverse and inclusive texts and topics

- » A new unit-level teacher guide outlines considerations for ELLs, including suggestions for lighter and heavier supports for each lesson.

- » Information about each unit for families

- » Answer keys for everything, including homework

▶ What Makes the Curriculum Unique and Valuable?

This brief introduction provides key information about how the curriculum is designed and built, and describes the principles that underlie it. It will give you a good summary of what makes this curriculum unique and valuable. Much more detail about these principles and practices, along with rich examples from the curriculum, will be provided throughout this book.

How Is the Curriculum Structured?

The four modules fully teach and assess the literacy standards as students build important content knowledge based on a compelling topic related to science, social studies, or literature. Each module uses rich, authentic text throughout.

» Four modules per year

» Each module is eight to nine weeks long

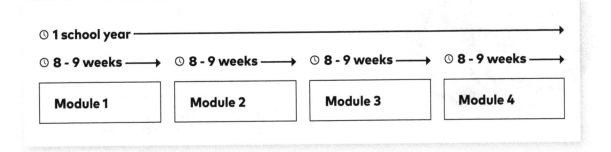

Module Lessons and Assessment Structure

» Three units per module

» Two curriculum-based assessments per unit: mid-unit and end of unit

» Forty-five minutes of instruction each day

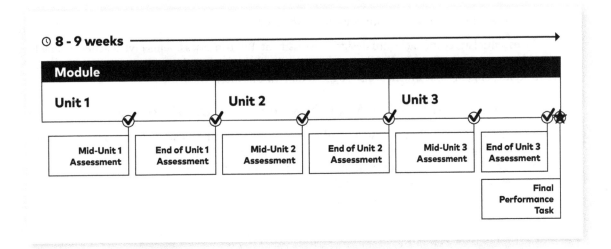

Performance Task

Unit 3 includes a performance task—an extended, supported writing task or presentation where students bring together their knowledge of the module topic to celebrate learning.

What Principles Underlie the Grades 6–8 Curriculum?

Equity Matters

EL Education is fiercely focused on equity for all children. All children deserve schools that foster their unique abilities, give them real opportunities to achieve high academic standards, and help them take their full place in a society for which they are well prepared when they leave school. Equity is the foundation on which the entire curriculum rests. From this foundation of equity comes what EL Education calls the Dimensions of Student Achievement.

» **Mastery of knowledge and skills:** Students demonstrate proficiency and deeper understanding, apply their learning, think critically, and communicate clearly.

» **Character:** Students work to become effective learners, to become ethical people, and to contribute to a better world.

» **High-quality work:** Students demonstrate craftsmanship and create complex, authentic work.

These three dimensions are the aspirational outcomes for the entire Grades 6–8 Language Arts curriculum. Achievement is more than mastery of knowledge and skills, or students' scores on a test. Habits of character and high-quality work are also taught and prized. The Dimensions of Student Achievement are detailed in Chapter 1A (see Figure 1.2) You can also learn more on our website at: http://eled.org/character-framework.

Backward Design Means Planning with the End in Mind and Assessing All along the Way

The guiding principle of backward design is straightforward. Designers must consider three questions:

» At the end of a sequence of instruction, what will students know and be able to do?

» What will proficiency look and sound like?

» How will we know when students are proficient?

An essential aspect of backward design is assessment. Built-in assessments give teachers valuable information and reflect the key literacy learning that students have been acquiring in the lessons. Specific, ongoing assessment is also suggested in the daily lessons.

Early Adolescents Need What They Learn to Have Emotional Resonance

Their well-developed limbic systems and sensitivity to dopamine mean that early adolescents are deeply compelled by content that stimulates their emotions. If content and instruction are not emotionally resonant, students will seek other means to fill this need—perhaps to the frustration of their peers and teachers. However, this can also be viewed as a capacity for deep investment in what they are learning. To increase the chances that a student will find an emotionally resonant point of entry, the EL Education Grades 6–8 Language Arts curriculum modules are centered around diverse and current topical issues and texts. (For more information about "The Characteristics of Middle School Learners," see Chapter 1A).

Students Excel in Diverse and Inclusive Settings

The EL Education Grades 6–8 Language Arts curriculum recognizes that students learn from one another—and learn to respect one another—when they learn together in the same classroom. At the same time, students sometimes have needs that require various types of differentiation. Module lessons provide tools and scaffolding to support and engage all learners. In addition, the lessons give flexibility in how information is presented, how students may respond, and how students are engaged (based on the Universal Design for Learning framework).

Language minority students and ELLs bring a wealth of diverse experience and wisdom to the classroom. In EL Education's curriculum, ELLs are presumed to be fully participating members of a diverse and heterogeneous classroom structure. The curriculum honors the fact that ELLs need targeted instruction within each lesson and additional supports to be successful.

Specific scaffolds have been integrated into each module lesson, so the classroom teacher can provide myriad supports for students, particularly for those classified as long-term ELLs. These resources take a variety of forms. Two specific areas of emphasis are the Language Dive (conversations that teach students to unpack the structure and meaning of complex sentences) and Conversation Cues. (For more information, see Chapter 5: Supporting All Students).

Protocols and Conversation Cues Promote Student Thinking, Collaboration, and Respect

Between the childhood attachment to home and family and the self-definition that comes in one's twenties lies a period where young people form their identities in relation to their peers. This means they want to spend time with one another, and this interaction is of service to their development. Because adolescents take one another's opinions seriously and act accordingly, collaborative conversation—frequent, focused, exploratory—is a key tool for deep learning. Clear and simple protocols make collaborative conversation rich and purposeful to students. Through collaborative conversation, students deepen their learning and come to appreciate the value of one another as individuals with diverse perspectives. Conversation Cues (questions that teachers can ask, such as "Can you say more about that?" or "Can you figure out why?") encourage productive and equitable conversation. These simple cues help students extend their thinking. (Conversation Cues are explored in depth in Chapter 5C.)

Students Own Their Learning

Early adolescents develop through cycles of action and reflection. As they become more independent, form their identities in relation to peers, and solidify the mindsets that shape their approach to the world, they need rich experiences around which to exercise these new capacities. They also need support to reflect on what happened and what they learned in order to integrate that learning. Students using EL Education's curriculum learn to see themselves as active learners with agency in their own education. With teachers' guidance, they articulate specific learning targets ("I can...") for every lesson. They learn to set goals, assess their own learning, and use feedback from peers, themselves, and their teachers to make progress.

Families and Guardians Are Partners

EL Education's curriculum welcomes students' families and guardians as partners in education. Students learn best when families have the opportunity to be part of the educational journey. The curriculum includes sample letters teachers can send home that describe what students will learn during a given module, how guardians can support that learning, and specific homework assignments. Students are encouraged to share what they are learning with their family and, sometimes, to interview family members about their expertise and experiences.

Curriculum as Powerful Professional Development

This curriculum helps teachers build on their existing expertise and continue to improve their ability to make strong instructional decisions during planning and while teaching. Teachers are provided rich resources and opportunities to make sound and specific instructional decisions based on their students' needs.

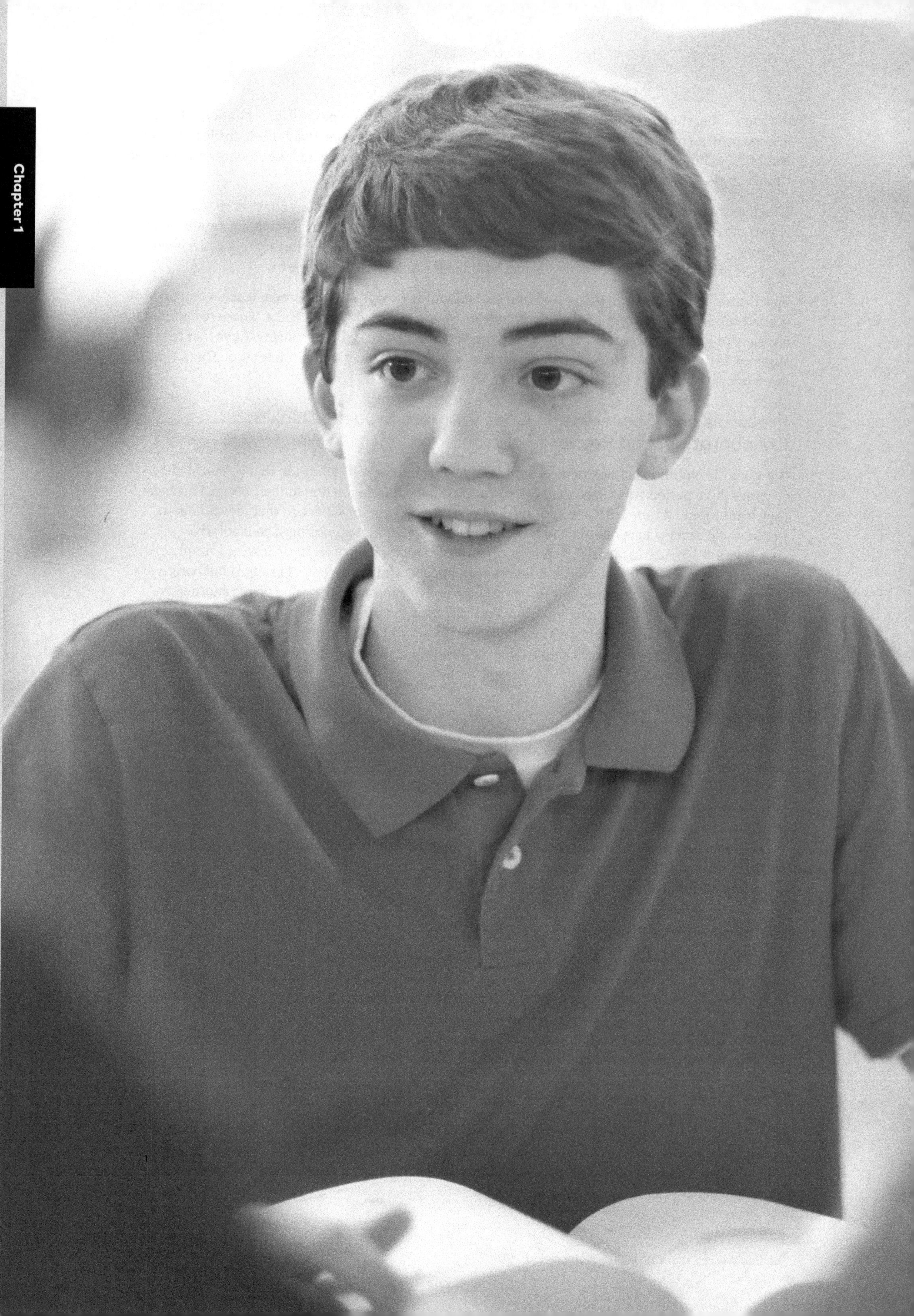

Chapter 1:
Before You Begin: The Foundations of the Curriculum

Chapter 1A:
What Makes This Curriculum the Right Choice for Me and My Students?

By now you have probably encountered the EL Education Language Arts curriculum in some form or fashion. You may have found it online and downloaded modules or lessons to explore. Your school or district may have adopted it and delivered boxes of books and materials to your classroom. You may have attended school or district trainings to support you in using it, or even have had some experience teaching the first edition, which was published in 2012.

You may feel excited about its potential to help your students and be eager to get started. Or, you may feel overwhelmed.

For all of you, in all of these categories, this book is for you. It was written partly to provide you with an orientation to the curriculum, partly to be a guide to the instructional practices embedded in the curriculum, and, perhaps most important, partly to act as a coach. We hope it will alleviate your stress, address your questions, enable you to use the curriculum most effectively, and help you understand it deeply enough to decide whether, when, and how to make adjustments given your context and needs.

Our curriculum is fundamentally different from most published curricula. It was created to support your students to build skills and content knowledge, to meet college- and career-ready standards, and, at the same time, to become more confident and collaborative learners. It also was created to help you become a stronger teacher:

» **Our curriculum was written by teachers, for teachers.** It is not the product of a for-profit publishing company. Former teachers working at EL Education—a nonprofit school improvement organization—and current teachers in public schools across the country joined together in this work. Many teacher-authors of this curriculum are practicing teachers who used their own classrooms to test and improve the practices and structures of the curriculum.

» **Our curriculum is offered as a free, open resource.** All elements of the curriculum, K–8, are hosted online. It is intended for you to "own" and make wise changes to once you understand the design fully. Our curriculum is not designed to be "teacher-proof" (a term that is disrespectful to the professionalism of teachers and represents a misguided and impossible goal). If you need to make changes, this book provides the knowledge and tools to do so in a way that maintains the integrity of the purpose, principles, structure, and intended outcomes of the curriculum.

» Our curriculum is designed to help teachers become even better in their practice. We hope that using the curriculum will be a form of professional learning for you, building instructional wisdom and providing strategies and tools that will help you hone your practice, whether you are a new or veteran teacher. Unlike most published curricula, which primarily consist of student-facing materials, ours consists primarily of teacher-facing materials. We provide extensive teaching notes, guidance for using new instructional techniques and protocols, suggestions for supporting students needing scaffolds or extensions, differentiated materials and guidance for English language learners (ELLs), and step-by-step training in practices such as leading students in close and careful reading of complex text or citing evidence in writing.

> *"The curriculum as a whole... it's almost like this equal composition of learning how to become a better teacher... and watching your students become better learners. I feel like this is the roadmap to being a good teacher."*

Richard Finn
Teacher, Boston

Our curriculum has been judged by independent experts[1] to be the best in the country in its alignment to college- and career-ready English language arts (ELA) standards used in almost every state. And, a rigorous evaluation by Mathematica Policy Research[2] finds that higher student literacy achievement results from combining our curriculum with actionable professional learning for teachers. Teaching our curriculum has been a transformational learning experience for many teachers across the country, reinvigorating their passion for teaching, deepening their expertise, and making their classrooms more respectful, energized, and effective. *But none of that means anything if it doesn't work well for you.*

▶▶ Video Spotlight 1.1

This video overviews the EL Education K–8 Language Arts curriculum, which was written for teachers by teachers. Our curriculum is fundamentally different from most published curricula. It was created to support students to build skills and content knowledge, to meet college- and career-ready standards, and, at the same time, to become more confident and collaborative learners. It was also created to help teachers develop stronger practice.

https://vimeo.com/341351270

---

1. Edreports.org
2. Mathematica.org

▶ HOW WILL I MAKE THIS CURRICULUM MY OWN?

A curriculum is not effective on its own. It requires a teacher who understands it, trusts it, and teaches it with integrity, creativity, and professional judgment. This means both knowing the curriculum well and knowing your students well so that you can make decisions that serve them best: speeding up, slowing down, reviewing or skipping a step, adding a resource, or innovating with extensions. Our curriculum is not meant to be simply delivered. It is a tool to be used, with your professional expertise, to accelerate literacy learning and excellence for all of your students.

We designed our curriculum based on what teachers told us they needed: a curriculum that is comprehensive, that provides everything you need to teach and assess ELA standards; that engages students in meaningful content; that helps students become strong learners and people; that empowers them to create high-quality work that matters; and that is compelling, engaging, and joyful. We provide detailed lessons for almost every single day of the year that fit this bill, and we offer guidance for how to execute those lessons effectively.

When you first encounter our curriculum, you may incorrectly assume that it is prescriptive, since every lesson is described down to the smallest detail. It is descriptive, but it is not intended to be prescriptive. *It is a thinking teacher's curriculum*; it is not designed to be followed mindlessly.

Using Creativity and Professional Judgment

We encourage you to use your creativity and professional judgment to make the curriculum your own. You may wish to enhance and enrich a module by adding in local connections and resources, for example, or to slow down lessons to make sure all students understand the content. We also encourage you to weigh the pros and cons of any changes you are inclined to make. Because the various components of the curriculum are carefully constructed to ensure that students achieve mastery on every college- and career-ready ELA standard in the course of the year, any changes you wish to make should be done with care. This book will give you an "insider's" view into the *what, why*, and *how* of the curriculum's design so that you can make *informed* decisions about customization.

▷ This book will give you an "insider's" view into the *what, why*, and *how* of the curriculum's design so that you can make *informed* decisions about customization.

Counting on the Curriculum

For more than twenty-five years, EL Education has equipped teachers in our network schools across the country to design their own curriculum using an interdisciplinary project-based curricular structure we call learning expeditions. Thousands of teachers have used this structure to create powerfully engaging and effective curriculum for their students. From that work, we know that not all teachers, within and beyond our network, have the time, support, and expertise to design their own curricula while simultaneously attending to meeting the needs of every student with strong instruction and effective classroom management. As standards have gotten more challenging, it has been especially difficult to ensure that curricula support all students to meet those standards.

By creating this ELA curriculum, we provide you with a foundation of texts, lessons, and assessments that you can count on. We hope that those of you who have been creating your own curricula and struggling to meet all standards can now use this curriculum as a solid base for your teaching. By giving you these resources, we empower you to spend more of your time thinking through the nuances of your instruction and how best to support your particular students. For those of you more accustomed to using published curricula, we hope that ours will give you all that you need to support your students to succeed and will also help you learn and grow as a teacher.

In the first year or two of using our curriculum, you may find that you adhere to it quite closely. Over time, we hope all teachers will learn to effectively customize and expand upon it to create powerful lessons and projects on their own. Designing curriculum is some of the most creative and rewarding work a teacher can do, but it's certainly not easy. We hope our curriculum, in combination with this book, will provide you with the tools you need to create powerful learning experiences that challenge, engage, and empower students equitably and hit standards sharply.

▶ WHAT ARE THE FUNDAMENTAL QUESTIONS ABOUT TEACHING AND LEARNING THAT THIS CURRICULUM WILL HELP ME ANSWER?

Our curriculum was created with founding principles designed to address *these fundamental teacher questions:*

 » How can I motivate students to take on challenges and succeed?

 » How can I ensure that *all* students have access to equitable high-level work?

 » How can I elevate student achievement beyond just test scores?

 » How will content-based literacy benefit my students?

 » How do I help all students stay active, engaged, and excited to learn?

How Can I Motivate Students to Take On Challenges and Succeed?

In a number of urban public schools in the EL Education network, school begins in an unusual way. During the first month of school, students leave the building, sometimes for multiple days, to engage in a wilderness experience. The challenge for these students is to work together as a team to get every person to the top of the mountain. Many have never been in this kind of environment before, and there is a wide range of physical, emotional, and social abilities among students and teachers. But they have a few important things in common: they are all outside of their comfort zone, they are all facing a worthy challenge, and they all have to depend on and support one another if they hope to succeed.

The students and teachers will tell you right away that it isn't all fun. It's a long, hard journey. They get exhausted, sweaty, and filthy. They grow discouraged and overwhelmed. They argue sometimes and want to give up. But they stick together and eventually reach the summit—proud, exhausted, and amazed. They drop their backpacks and cheer and hug and drink cool water and sit down and take in the beautiful view together, on top of the world.

Back in school, "climbing the mountain together" is the memory and metaphor that guides learning. School may be overwhelming and discouraging at times, but the job of students and teachers is to work together as a team to make sure everyone gets to the summit. It won't be easy, but if they stick together and work hard, they can make it.

Though we are focused here on our Grades 6–8 ELA curriculum, it is important to keep in mind that our goal is for students to leave high school college- and career-ready. Graduation and college acceptance is the looming peak. In many EL Education high schools in low-income urban communities, one hundred percent of graduates have been accepted to college—every graduate, every year for almost a decade. That success is built on the strong literacy skills and habits of character students develop throughout their K–12 education.

A primary challenge for students in schools across America is building the literacy skills to succeed—not just during ELA lessons, but across all subjects. In the wilderness, the challenges may be rough weather, confusing trails, and steep climbs. In school, the challenges are likely to be complex text to read and difficult written tasks to complete. For the vast majority of students, the mountain is a metaphor—it represents the real challenges that students face. However, whether facing an actual mountain or a metaphorical one, the approach is the same: to embrace challenge, together; to not be afraid to stumble and fail at times; to take risks; and to push and support one another.

Providing Worthy Challenges

A founding principle of this curriculum is to provide worthy challenges for all students and to provide structures for them to work together as a team to support one another to succeed. If the curriculum feels daunting at first, to you and your students, that's by design. We believe that worthy challenges, carefully scaffolded and supported, lead to deeper learning.

By way of example, consider the story of how a middle school teacher in Boston skillfully walked her students up and over the mountain of a very complex text. The text, "Substrate Determinants and Developmental Rate of Claw Asymmetry in American Lobsters, *Homarus Americanus,*" was first published in the *Journal of Crustacean Biology* (see Figure 1.1 for an excerpt). The students' initial reaction was similar to what you're likely thinking right now: "This is crazy! I'll never understand this!"

Figure 1.1: Excerpt from Lobster Text

SUBSTRATE DETERMINANTS AND DEVELOPMENTAL RATE OF CLAW ASYMMETRY IN AMERICAN LOBSTERS, *HOMARUS AMERICANUS*

Jason S. Goldstein and Michael F. Tlusty

(JG) Old Dominion University, Department of Biological Sciences, Hampton Boulevard, Norfolk, Virginia 23529 U.S.A. (jgoldste@odu.edu);
(MT, correspondence), New England Aquarium, Edgerton Research Laboratory, Lobster Rearing and Research Facility, 1 Central Wharf, Boston, Massachusetts 02110-3399 U.S.A. (mtlusty@neaq.org)

The North American lobster (*Homarus americanus* H. Milne Edwards, 1837) exhibits the largest chelipeds (claws) of any known crustacean. The "Great Chelae," as published by Herrick (1909), exemplifies just one of many early studies examining the structure and function of American lobster claws (also see Smith, 1873, and Templeman, 1935). Although they may comprise less than 5% of the total body weight of early-staged juvenile lobsters, contour containing faster responding muscles that yield a significantly reduced strength (Govind and Pearce, 1992). The fourth (post-larval) and fifth (early benthic phase juvenile) developmental stages are essential critical periods for determining claw asymmetry (Emmel, 1908; Govind and Pearce, 1989). Once a crusher claw has been determined, the asymmetric pattern becomes fixed for life, regardless of any future claw autonomy or

Source: Goldstein, J.S. & Tlusty, M.F. (2003). Substrate Determinants and Developmental Rate of Claw Asymmetry in American Lobsters, Homarus americanus. Journal of Crustacean Biology, 23(4), 890-896. By permission of Oxford University Press.

"Most students approach text expecting to understand it right away—they plow through and do their best to understand it after reading it once. If they struggle too much, they may begin to practice avoidance strategies, believing that the text is simply too hard for them. Too many experiences like these can affect students' confidence as readers" (Berger, Woodfin, Plaut, and Dobbertin, 2014, p. 85). But the teacher in this case approached the challenge with a different mindset, and she slowly but surely helped her students put one foot in front of the other to start making their way through the text.

Here's what she said:

> *"This is a great scientific paper by one of the world experts on lobsters. It has important information that will inform our study of Boston Harbor. But almost no one in the world has read it and few people can understand it. Even your parents may not be able to understand it. Some of the teachers here may not understand it. At least not right away. But together, we can make sense of it. We are in no rush. Today we are just going to tackle the first page. We will start with the words we know and the sentences that make sense to us. And we will keep going until it all makes sense. I'll bet there are many words you see right now that you understand, and parts of sentences, too. You will start alone, making sense of what you can, then you will work with two partners to share what you discover. Then all the triads will come together and share what they think. By the end of the period, we will understand this whole first page."*

This teacher set a new expectation for students that disrupted their instinct to attempt to read quickly through something she knew would frustrate them and, ultimately, fail to teach them anything. She helped them see that they could each contribute to a shared understanding of a text they were unlikely to be able to read independently. She also chose an article that had information they wanted and needed for their research on Boston Harbor, so by the time she had reset their expectations about what their reading process would look like, they were eager to take on the challenge and poised to succeed. They left the class having learned a lot about lobsters, but most importantly, they left with a positive mindset about the challenge of complex text. They were proud, and they really did feel like they had climbed a metaphorical mountain together.

Minding Student Mindsets (and Your Own)

At EL Education, when we refer to mindsets, we are referring to a set of four academic mindsets. The term "growth mindset," which will be familiar to many educators, is one of the four academic mindsets (number 3 in the following list). Academic mindsets refer to the motivational components that influence students' desire and their will to engage in learning. Research shows that academic mindsets are a better predictor of student success than any other determining factor (Farrington et al, 2012). The four academic mindsets are:

1. I belong in this academic community.

2. I can succeed at this.

3. My ability and competence grow with my effort.

4. This work has value for me.

When students can say affirmatively that they belong in their academic community, that they believe they can succeed, that their ability and competence grow with their effort, and that their work has value to them, they have a far greater chance of academic success than if those statements have no resonance or if they actively deny them.

Through frequent reflection and scaffolding, we intentionally support students to affirm each of these academic mindset statements. In the curriculum, students develop an understanding of and reflect upon all four academic mindsets throughout each module. In nearly every lesson, teachers are cued to help students consider how their mindsets influence their learning and overall experience in school. For example, in Grade 6, Module 1, Lesson 2, *empathy* and *respect* are two of the vocabulary words students encounter in the lesson. At the end of the lesson, students reflect on how empathy and respect help them feel a sense of belonging in their learning community.

Because a new curriculum may present new challenges for your students, and for you, it's worth taking a closer look at growth mindset in particular. Consider the example from the lobster text in the preceding section. Perhaps you have witnessed students feeling intimidated by challenging text like that in Figure 1.1. You have also likely witnessed the pride that comes with overcoming a challenge like this. Perhaps more than any other challenge students and teachers face when striving to meet rigorous college- and career-ready standards, reading complex texts is the greatest. The teacher who taught this lesson on lobsters was not using our curriculum—this was many years ago—but she knew from experience that helping students climb the mountain together would allow them to succeed.

Fostering your students' growth mindset means encouraging and supporting them to take on meaningful challenges. Just as they would when reaching the peaks of mountains, students will feel pride in their success with challenging texts and tasks and build the muscles they need to push on and do more than they think possible. As you embark on your adventure with our curriculum, we urge you to consider your mindset as well; yours may be a figurative adventure, rather than a literal one, but that doesn't make the journey any less significant. You will encounter challenges, even if you are a veteran teacher, and your willingness to take them on with a spirit of growth and learning will help you and your students meet success.

> *"We have to believe that students can be successful with academic challenges the same way they are with character and physical challenges... We can't wait until they are 'ready,' because what happens is that students in poverty and students at risk never even get to attempt that kind of work. All students need the same access to academics that will prepare them for college and beyond."*

Laurie Godwin
Principal, Aurora, Colorado

The metaphor of getting all students up the mountain is not meant to be intimidating. But it is meant to signal one of the key philosophical beliefs upon which our curriculum rests: All students deserve the opportunity and access to the tools they need to read and write proficiently. Equity for *all* students drives the EL Education curriculum.

How Can I Ensure that *All* Students Have Equitable Access to High-Level Work?

All children deserve schools that foster their unique abilities, give them a real opportunity to achieve high academic standards, and help them take their full place in a society for which they are well prepared when they leave school. In our curriculum, all students are given the opportunity and the tools they need to read complex texts that are at or above grade level, compose high-quality writing, and engage in sophisticated high-level discourse.

Preparing students for the duties of work and citizenship has always been at the core of public education in the United States. Preparing students for the rigors of college, on the other hand, has historically been limited to a privileged minority. Despite centuries of restriction regarding who has access to college, the boundaries are beginning to crumble. More and more, college readiness is seen as a goal for all students. Certainly this doesn't mean that all students will go to college, but it does mean that all students must be prepared so that the choice is available to them when they graduate from high school. As author and activist bell hooks reminds us: "Being oppressed means the absence of choices" (2000, p. 5).

Students can and should be reading more challenging texts, presenting opinions and arguments with evidence, challenging ideas, and considering divergent perspectives. They should be engaged in high-level thinking and discourse, analysis, and synthesis. This shouldn't be the aim of education only for elite scholars; all students deserve an education that gives them a chance to reach their full potential. Historically underserved populations of students have experienced less rigorous curricula and instruction, which has limited their educational opportunities. Our curriculum is designed to provide all students, from all backgrounds, with the skills and knowledge they need to be literate and confident students.

Embracing the Highest Aspirations of the Standards

Ever since the Common Core ELA/literacy standards were introduced, EL Education has embraced them. Despite the controversy that has swirled around their implementation, we believe that they represent a real opportunity to create more equitable educational opportunities for students most in need. "We believe the standards invite us to build in our students critical skills for life—for career success and civic contribution. What is important is not just what the standards say, but how they are used. The standards can be used to build classrooms where students are active, reflective critical thinkers, not passive recipients of content. The standards can be used to build in students the dispositions and skills to do work that matters to them and their communities" (Berger, Woodfin, Plaut, and Dobbertin, 2014, p. 5). Our curriculum is built upon this expansive interpretation of the standards; if the standards were designed to level the playing field for all students, then our curriculum was designed to give all students the equipment they need to get in the game and win.

★ **A Word about the Common Core State Standards**

When the Common Core standards were first introduced in 2010, almost every state adopted them. A decade later, most states have accommodated the changing political climate by customizing and renaming them. Despite new names, most states' college- and career-ready ELA standards closely resemble Common Core standards. We have built our curriculum around the Common Core standards because they allow us to have a common reference point in states across the country. If you teach in a state that doesn't use Common Core standards, this curriculum is still going to help you meet your state's standards. However, you may need to match the numbers or names of the Common Core standards to those in your state.

Honoring the Diversity of Learners

Our aspirations are not always easy to achieve, or even imagine, when students come to school with such a wide variety of strengths and needs, but we believe strongly that students excel in diverse and inclusive settings. Students learn from one another—and learn to respect one another—when they learn together in the same classroom. At the same time, students sometimes have needs that require varied approaches. Our curriculum provides supports and resources for differentiated instruction, which allows teachers to provide for students who need additional support as well as those who may need academic extensions. Tools and scaffolding that support all learners and flexibility in the ways information is presented, the ways students respond, and the ways students are engaged are embedded throughout the curriculum based on Universal Design for Learning (UDL). (The principles of UDL are explored in Chapter 5A).

ELLs and multilingual students also deserve to have their assets honored and their needs supported. These students bring a wealth of experience and wisdom to the classroom. In our curriculum, these language learners are presumed to be fully participating members of a diverse and heterogeneous classroom structure. We also honor the fact that language learners need targeted instruction within each lesson and additional supports if they are to be successful.

Specific scaffolds have been integrated into lessons so teachers can provide myriad supports for these students, particularly for those classified as "long-term English learners," those students who have been enrolled in U.S. schools for six years or longer, and who have not made academic progress due to gaps and deficiencies in the rigor of their education (Olsen, 2010). Additional designated time beyond that held by our curriculum may be needed for students who are new to learning English. (Supports for ELLs are explored in Chapter 5C).

Elevating Student Thinking, Voice, and Work

Our curriculum also prizes and elevates original student thinking, student voice, and student work. We ask students to grapple with worthy texts and tasks, participate in scholarly discourse, and engage in critique of their written work to build quality and ownership. We support them to become leaders of their own learning, rather than simply obedient task completers.

▷ Our curriculum also prizes and elevates original student thinking, student voice, and student work. We ask students to grapple with worthy texts and tasks, participate in scholarly discourse, and engage in critique of their written work to build quality and ownership. We support them to become leaders of their own learning, rather than simply obedient task completers.

Building these capacities in students has always been something we have believed in at EL Education and is what led us to rethink what student achievement really means. While we believe that college- and career-ready standards represent an opportunity to address inequity, raise expectations, and increase opportunities and excellence for all students, we are also aware of the ways in which standards have polarized the debate about education in the United States. Reducing the success or failure of students and teachers to a single measure of mastery of standards does not allow anyone to live up to the promise of what standards *could* mean for students and communities. We have chosen to define student achievement more expansively, recognizing the fullness of what it means to succeed in school and life, and we have built our curriculum to reflect this more expansive definition.

How Can I Elevate Student Achievement Beyond Just Test Scores?

Our nation's education system has focused too narrowly for too long on a single dimension of achievement, resulting in too many disengaged students and teachers and, often, poor and inequitable student outcomes. The reality is that educators, parents, and students themselves care about much more than just the traditional view of what mastering knowledge and skills looks like on a test. We want students to also learn to be deep thinkers and good people who care about the quality of their work, and who are determined to contribute to a better world.

Promoting a Multi-Dimensional View of Student Achievement

We promote a three-dimensional view of student achievement—including mastery of knowledge and skills, character, and high-quality student work—that offers a vision for education we would want for every child and provides the "north star" for all of our work (see Figure 1.2).

EL Education

Dimensions of Student Achievement

Dimension of Achievement	Students	Teachers and Leaders
Mastery of Knowledge and Skills	• **Demonstrate proficiency and deeper understanding:** show mastery in a body of knowledge and skills within each discipline • **Apply their learning:** transfer knowledge and skills to novel, meaningful tasks • **Think critically:** analyze, evaluate, and synthesize complex ideas and consider multiple perspectives • **Communicate clearly:** write, speak, and present ideas effectively in a variety of media within and across disciplines	• Ensure that curriculum, instruction, and assessments are **rigorous, meaningful, and aligned with standards** • Use **assessment practices** that position students as leaders of their own learning • Use **meaningful data for both teachers and students to track progress** toward learning goals • **Engage all students in daily lessons that require critical thinking** about complex, worthy ideas, texts, and problems
Character	• **Work to become effective learners:** develop the mindsets and skills for success in college, career, and life (e.g., initiative, responsibility, perseverance, collaboration) • **Work to become ethical people:** treat others well and stand up for what is right (e.g., empathy, integrity, respect, compassion) • **Contribute to a better world:** put their learning to use to improve communities (e.g., citizenship, service)	• **Elevate student voice and leadership** in classrooms and across the school • **Make habits of scholarship visible** across the school and in daily instruction • Model a **school-wide culture of respect and compassion** • **Prioritize social and emotional learning**, along with academic learning, across the school
High-Quality Student Work	• **Create complex work:** demonstrate higher-order thinking, multiple perspectives and transfer of understanding • **Demonstrate craftsmanship:** create work that is accurate and beautiful in conception and execution • **Create authentic work:** demonstrate original thinking and voice, connect to real-world issues and formats, and when possible, create work that is meaningful to the community beyond the school	• **Design tasks that ask students to apply, analyze, evaluate and create** as part of their work • **Use models of excellence, critique, and multiple drafts** to support all students to produce work of exceptional quality • **Connect students to the world beyond school** through meaningful fieldwork, expert collaborators, research, and service learning

Mastery of Knowledge and Skills

Mastery of knowledge and skills is the dimension of student achievement that most schools are already fairly familiar and comfortable with. Held within this dimension are state tests and other high-stakes assessments that are a required part of public schooling. High-stakes achievement tests have an important role to play in shining a light on inequities in public schooling. However, our nation's hyper-focus on these kinds of assessments in recent years has led to a reductionist view of what mastery of knowledge and skills means and how students should be taught.

When interpreted and applied as intended, the new standards are also asking teachers to focus on critical thinking, effective communication, and deeper learning. Our curriculum compels students to demonstrate deep understanding of concepts and content, analyze, evaluate, and synthesize their content knowledge, and demonstrate that they can transfer their understanding to novel tasks. When building knowledge of the world, students must consider multiple perspectives and viewpoints. They must present their thinking in multiple ways—informal and formal writing, conversation, and formal presentations—which builds strong communication skills. Our curriculum gives students opportunities to develop these skills, and the assessments and performance tasks are designed to evaluate them in authentic ways.

Character

A central goal of our curriculum is to give students the tools to become effective, ethical learners who work to make the world a better place. We have our own language and approach to fostering what we call "habits of character," which are a part of daily lessons at all grade levels. Our habits of character can and should complement, not replace, any existing frameworks, language, or routines for promoting social-emotional learning in your school. If another framework for character is in place at your school (e.g., Second Step; RULER; CASEL's five core competencies), it will be important for you to help your students make connections between that framework and ours. In practice, this means helping students understand the meanings of specific words (e.g., if *tenacity* is used at your school, help students see the connection to *perseverance,* which is used in our curriculum). This unpacking is a great opportunity to teach academic vocabulary and for students to see how words that define character are connected to, not separate from, academic tasks.

Promoting character development is not new in schools. What makes our curriculum distinct is that it integrates an intentional focus on developing students' habits of character within the context of academic lessons (e.g., *persevering* as they work on multiple drafts of their performance task). Character is not "preached" through admonishments; rather, it is learned through authentic experiences and ongoing reflection on those experiences. *How children learn and the environment in which they learn is as important as what they learn.*

High-Quality Student Work

When students complete their formal schooling, with few exceptions they will no longer be assessed by tests. Instead, they will be assessed by the quality of their character and their work. Preparing students to be successful in these areas is one of the reasons we are so focused on a broader definition of student achievement.

High-quality student work—work that demonstrates complexity, craftsmanship, and authenticity—not only has the power to assess aspects of learning that can be elusive, such as communication skills and conceptual understanding, but can also motivate students. Models of high-quality work give students something to aspire to and can answer some of their most timeless questions: *Why do we have to do this? How will we use this?* High-quality work, especially when modeled after real-world work and embedding the knowledge and skills students are currently learning, can engage students in ways that little else can.

In the curriculum, a commitment to quality shows up in all kinds of ways—from scaffolded, and often collaborative, high-quality performance tasks to the everyday craftsmanship of precisely color-coding a Painted Essay®. Helping students commit themselves to quality work and being leaders of their own learning is a thread throughout all components of the curriculum. (In Chapter 6A, we explore looking at student work as one source of evidence to assess student progress.)

Of note, one key aspect of high-quality work, as it is defined in Figure 1.2—authenticity—was not always possible to build into our curriculum. Authenticity means original student thinking, which we do prioritize in the curriculum, *and* it also often means that student work is connected to a real community need. Within a nationwide curriculum like ours, it's a challenge to make local connections that will have relevance across the country. This is one area ripe for enrichment, where your experience and creativity as a teacher can bring greater authenticity to students' work. For example, sixth-grade teachers with self-contained classrooms might use science time to research how the contributions of "hidden figures" of mathematics and space science are visible in their own daily lives, and share their knowledge with their communities. Seventh-grade ELA teachers may find that studying plastic pollution galvanizes their students into locally focused action, and that science teachers are ready to collaborate when standards align. (Much more on helping students connect module topics to community need through extensions is offered in Chapter 5B.)

*Students persevere through multiple drafts to produce work they can be proud of.**

How Will Content-Based Literacy Benefit My Students?

The design of our curriculum reflects compelling research showing that students learn best to become effective readers, writers, thinkers, and speakers when literacy instruction is content-based. Content-based literacy is an approach to helping students build literacy as they learn about the world.

Content knowledge and literacy skills are inextricably linked. Common Core ELA standards state: "Building knowledge systematically in English Language Arts is like giving children various pieces of a puzzle in each grade that, over time, will form one big picture. At a curricular or instructional level, texts—within and across grade levels—need to be selected around topics or themes that systematically develop the knowledge base of students" (National Governors Association Center for Best Practices & Council of Chief State School Officers, 2010, p. 33).

Research shows that the deeper the content knowledge students have, the more they are able to understand what they read, and the more they are able to speak and write clearly about that content. In fact, remarkably, research shows that they are even more able to successfully read about and understand *new* content. This proficiency and knowledge transfers to the next occasion for reading and learning, creating an upward surge that builds on itself and is both highly rewarding and motivating (Baldwin, Peleg-Bruckner, and McClintock (1985); Cervetti, Jaynes, and Heibert (2009); Kintsch and Hampton (2009); McNamara and O'Reilly (2009)).

Content-based literacy is similar to, yet distinct from, what many educators refer to as "reading to learn." The approaches are similar in that the goal is for students to learn about the world and build literacy skills; however, there are important differences. Reading to learn means that students first build strong literacy skills so that they can access texts, which allows them to build their knowledge of the world. By contrast, content-based literacy means students build their knowledge of the world by reading multiple texts on a topic—some with structured support and some independently—which allows them to read even more sophisticated texts and build more knowledge, which builds their literacy skills.

---

* This piece of student work is from Grade 6–7, but is not related to the curriculum.
You can find it at modelsofexcellence.ELeducation.org.

Turning On Students' Curiosity Motors

Content-based literacy is highly engaging for students and, often, inspiring for teachers. You are probably familiar with adolescents, either in your classroom or your own family, who find that a controversy in the news or the science behind a favorite fantasy series sparks an obsessive need for more and more information, which they devour both in long stretches curled up in a chair and in surreptitious moments of class time. Their interests push them into texts or to online sources that may be much more complex than they would choose if their own curiosity weren't driving them like a motor. When students get into this zone, they can really dig in, even when the going gets tough. They can read and research and talk about their topics for hours.

Too often school isn't the place where these interests are nurtured. Texts are disconnected or treated shallowly, and topics may shift from week to week. In our curriculum, we walk students into the content with the intention of turning on those curiosity motors. We build curiosity through high-interest topics, texts, and collaborative tasks, all designed to work with instead of against the increased sociability and emotionality of early adolescents. We find that once students are hooked, they engage much more deeply in both the content and the key literacy standards of reading, writing, speaking, and listening. For example, what follows is a sampling of some of the high-interest topics in the curriculum, which students are immersed in for eight to nine weeks:

» American Indian Boarding Schools

» The Lost Children of Sudan

» Epidemics

» Plastic Polution

» Folklore of Latin America

» Voices of the Holocaust

Our curriculum proves that a *both/and* approach to content and skills is possible and preferable. Research and experience have shown us that students need both content *and* skills and, beyond that, both should be woven together in ways that turn on those curiosity motors that keep driving students forward. Students learn best when they are engaged, and it's hard to be engaged when learning skills in a vacuum, particularly for middle schoolers no longer motivated by pleasing their teachers. Building knowledge of the world is an important arrow in our quiver as we strive to accelerate literacy learning and excellence for all students.

How Do I Help Middle School Students Stay Active, Engaged, and Excited to Learn?

Few people have fond memories of middle school. One of the reasons that middle schools have the unfortunate reputation they do is that much of the education offered to adolescent learners is designed with adult preferences—rather than learner needs—in mind. Tests, worksheets, and sitting in rows are prioritized over emotional resonance, the chance to interact meaningfully with peers, and opportunities to engage deeply with the real issues students see in their communities and the wider world. The result is, too often, disengaged students.

Our curriculum was designed with the needs of adolescent learners in mind. We have balanced the need for students to be challenged academically and to advance on pace with grade-level peers with engaging instructional strategies and—yes—emotional resonance, meaningful peer interaction, and deep engagement with issues that matter to them. Students will learn to read challenging texts and produce high-quality writing while at the same time collaborating with their classmates, taking academic risks in sharing their thinking and reasoning about topics they care about, and connecting their learning to issues of social justice and community need. Nearly every day, students will engage with protocols that allow them to work together, co-construct meaning, and take charge of their learning. We prioritize active learning, not passive listening.

We recognize that early adolescent learners have a unique set of developmental needs, and we have designed our Grades 6–8 curriculum with those needs in mind. Our work in this area is guided by an EL Education document called "The Characteristics of Middle School Learners." This document, which is excerpted here, is research-based, experience-tested wisdom on what it takes to meet the needs of young people at the beginning of a major transition in their lives.

Designing Curriculum with the Characteristics of Middle School Learners in Mind

Our brains begin a round of tremendous change starting in early adolescence (defined as ages 11–14), and these changes impact how young people engage with their parents, teachers, and one another. What follows are eight key characteristics of early adolescent learners. Each of these characteristics is based on the research of experts like psychologist Camille Farrington and her colleagues at The University of Chicago (Nagaoka et al., 2015) and neuroscientist Sarah Jayne Blakemore (2018), as well as the experience of middle school educators in the EL Education network.

Early adolescents are intensely oriented toward their peers

Between the childhood attachment to home and family and the self-definition that comes in one's twenties lies a period where young people form their identities in relation to their peers. This means they want to spend time with one aother, and indeed such contact is in service of their development. Adolescents are measurably influenced by one another; while they have a reputation as being highly likely to take risks, they are actually just highly likely to take more risks in the presence of peers. Because adolescents take one another's opinions seriously and act accordingly, adults can partner with students in shaping the culture of a school or classroom, making norms explicit and intentional. Adolescents look for frequent opportunities to collaborate and construct meaning together and adults can establish structures and opportunities to do this successfully.

Early adolescents benefit from collaborative, supportive relationships with caring adults...

... *who aren't their primary caregivers.* They are becoming ever more independent from the adults who care for them at home, as they are ever more influenced by the opinions and behavior of their peers. However, they continue to crave care from adults who accept them and who can support them as they pursue what matters to them. Schools can design time for this—many schools have an "advisory" period, and the EL Education model includes a structure for social and academic support called "Crew"—but any adult who sees an early adolescent as a developing being rather than a problem to be solved can be a source of important, subtle guidance.

Early adolescents are developing their executive function skills and metacognitive capacities.

Part of what generates the behavior that can so confound adults is that early adolescents have limbic systems that already work well, but have prefrontal cortices that are still very much under construction. This means that while adolescents are exquisitely and emotionally sensitive to rewards, they are not commensurately able to inhibit impulses, reflect, and plan. These fledgling abilities are further impacted by forces beyond their control: a new circadian rhythm means that students' bodies try to stay awake later and rise later as well, resulting in decreased attentional resources earlier in the morning. Childhood experiences of trauma can slow the development of the prefrontal cortex, moving the starting blocks back for students who may already be struggling.

This tricky developmental period, though, is exactly when early adolescents can make remarkable progress in executive function skills that will serve them well their whole lives. Their burgeoning metacognitive abilities are strengthened by practice. As they reflect on how different ways of learning work for them (or don't), they both get better at reflecting, and also gain information about what will serve them. Teachers can infuse required content with opportunities for adolescents to learn, apply, and reflect on strategies for self-regulation; consider how actions impact the future and impact others, and how predictions do or do not hold; and better understand what kinds of learning modalities are most effective for them as individuals.

Early adolescents need meaningful choices in what they learn.

As they begin to apply their agency to interests outside the home, and as they begin to identify themselves as "someone who loves ___," early adolescents benefit when they are invited to incorporate what they care about into their school day. Teachers can plan both short- and longer-term tasks to incorporate individual student preference and passion, while maintaining class-wide progress toward excellence through common learning targets, tasks, and high-quality work.

Early adolescents need what they learn to have emotional resonance.

Their well-developed limbic systems and sensitivity to dopamine mean that early adolescents are deeply compelled by content that stimulates their emotions. If content and instruction are not emotionally resonant, students will seek other means to fill this need—perhaps to the frustration of their peers and teachers. However, this can also be viewed as a capacity for deep investment in what they are learning. To increase the chances that a student will find an emotionally resonant point of entry, teachers can plan interdisciplinary curriculum, with attention to current, topical issues in a given field of study.

Early adolescents develop through cycles of action and reflection.

As they become more independent, form their identities in relation to peers, and solidify the mindsets that will shape their approach to the world, they need rich experiences around which to exercise these new capacities. They also need support to reflect on what happened and what they learned in order to integrate that learning. Schools can be a lever for equity here, designing curriculum and instruction to ensure that all students have opportunities to encounter models, tinker and explore, practice with feedback, make choices, and use what they've learned to contribute. They can support all students in meaningful reflection: to describe and evaluate, connect what they learned with what they already knew, envision their future, and ultimately integrate their insights into their larger senses of self.

Early adolescents find physical and social differences interesting and meaningful.

At a time when their bodies are undergoing significant visible and invisible changes, on highly individual timetables, early adolescents are also very sensitive to comparison. Their self-esteem can fluctuate wildly on a day-to-day basis. One implication is that early adolescents are particularly aware of the equitability of classroom dynamics. If certain students are given more positive attention than other students, and if this is predictable according to student identity (i.e., in terms of such things as race, class, gender, ability, immigration status, appearance, etc.), early adolescents will register and assign meaning to it. They may take it as evidence of the teacher's bias, and/or they make take it as evidence of some immutable characteristic about students who identify that way (including themselves). Teachers can keep an eye out for students whose differences may be getting outsize attention, and subtly and separately check in with them, letting them know they are seen and valued and asking what support they might want. Teachers can strengthen their own self-awareness, reflecting and asking for feedback from trusted colleagues or students themselves on how they distribute their positive and negative attention across the classroom community.

Early adolescents prioritize the attainment of rewards (rather than the avoidance of punishment).

While adults sometimes interpret early adolescent decisions as evidence that young people do not understand the risks attached to their behaviors, evidence shows that early adolescents are well aware of risk, but make internal calculations in favor of reward. Because their brains produce less dopamine, and the receptors are more sensitive to whatever dopamine does come along, good things are really good, and *immediate* good things are best. This, combined with their newfound attachment to peers, means that they are particularly drawn to immediate social rewards. A remark that gets the class to laugh has a high reward in the peer-sensitive adolescent brain—a reward weighing far more on balance than a potential consequence. To honor this need, teachers and leaders can foster a school culture where students are socially rewarded for behaviors that support learning but that can be socially risky (e.g., sharing thinking publicly).

Each of these characteristics of middle school learners has deep implications for teachers and certainly had a big influence on the design of our Grades 6–8 curriculum. In some ways, the needs of these students are no different from those of any age: the need to belong, to express themselves, and to engage in challenging, meaningful work. In others ways, early adolescents require an approach that emphasizes certain practices, adapts others in developmentally appropriate ways, or creates unique structures and tools to provide the foundation that will support cognitive and social flourishing as they mature. Brain plasticity—the brain's ability to create new connections—is higher in adolescence than at any other time since the first years of life, meaning that the brain is primed to adapt to the environment it finds itself in, and the connections it makes during this time will govern its later function.

As caring adults, it is not ours to struggle against what's new—the pulling away from home and family, the running toward peers, the sensitivity to everything social, the wish for quick gratification, the perceived disregard for short- or long-term negative impacts. It is ours to make a world where adolescents can safely practice all that they are newly driven to do. If we approach this period in our students' lives with an asset-based mindset, the peculiarities of this age are not a problem to be solved, but a chance to support young people in a way that can positively influence the rest of their lives.

Chapter 1B:
How Did Research Impact the Design of the Curriculum, and What Difference Will It Make to My Students?

Due to pervasive learning opportunity gaps, students often begin their K–12 schooling at different starting points. Children enter kindergarten with varying levels of readiness for reading and writing, and those who start behind too often stay behind as they move through school. These differences are too often predictable by socioeconomic status, zip code, and race. This predictability reflects the failure of our institutions to nurture all people well, rather than a failure of children or their families. Systemic inequities throughout our social institutions, including schools, mean that many children do not have an equal opportunity to achieve, resulting in what has sometimes been termed an "achievement gap." Our curriculum is driven by a simple mission: give *all* students access to a challenging, engaging, and empowering curriculum built on best practices in literacy instruction in order to accelerate their achievement.

The research is sobering. Before entering school, learners who have experienced systemic inequities suffer from a chain breaking at every link. Opportunity gaps result in many children starting school with less access to

» vocabulary,

» content knowledge, and

» complex syntax (including practice responding to questions and making inferences).

These differences are exacerbated by what is known as the Matthew Effect (Stanovich, 1986, 1992; Stanovich and Cunningham, 1993): "The rich get richer; the poor get poorer." In school, this means that proficient readers start at a higher level than non-proficient readers and move faster each year relative to non-proficient readers. Gloria Ladson-Billings (2006) uses the term "education debt" to reframe the problem as a need to repair the accumulated harm done to historically underserved students. Given the reality of this debt, research tells us that schools must stay laser-focused on certain elements of literacy instruction—vocabulary, knowledge-building, syntax, fluency, and decoding—to close the gap.

► HOW WILL THE CURRICULUM HELP ME ACCELERATE LITERACY LEARNING AND EXCELLENCE FOR ALL OF MY STUDENTS?

Research has helped us learn a great deal about the problems borne of learning opportunity gaps. Thankfully, it also offers many strategies to intervene at the level we can control: what happens in the ELA classroom. In Table 1.1, we look at the four elements of literacy instruction most critical for addressing opportunity gaps at the middle school level—vocabulary, knowledge-building, syntax, and fluency—and how our curriculum addresses each[3]. We view literacy as a civil right, and believe that literacy research and the strategies it points to are key levers in ensuring all students in all schools are afforded instruction that will accelerate their achievement.

Table 1.1: Research and Strategies for Accelerating Literacy Learning[4]

Vocabulary Students need to know a lot of words. They particularly need to learn academic vocabulary (or "Tier 2 words") (e.g., community, relate) that they'll encounter across contexts and content.	
What We Know from the Research	**How Our Curriculum Addresses It**
» Nearly a century of research shows that word knowledge is critical for reading comprehension (Whipple, 1925; National Center for Education Statistics, 2012). » When reading complex text, unfamiliar words are the feature with which students typically have the most difficulty (Nelson, Perfetti, Liben, and Liben, 2012). » Students' scores on first-grade vocabulary assessments predict thirty percent of Grade 11 comprehension (Cunningham and Stanovich, 1997). » Reading or listening to a series of texts on the same topic can yield as much as four times the vocabulary growth as the same amount of text on different topics (Landauer and Dumais, 1997; Adams, 2009; Cervetti and Hiebert, 2015).	» Lessons at all grade levels feature a heavy focus on volume of reading and close reading of complex text. » Students read multiple texts on a topic. At least half of the texts students read are related to the specific topic of study. » Students learn to analyze the morphology of words (i.e., roots, affixes, suffixes), which is taught explicitly in earlier modules and becomes a habit in later modules. This helps them learn word-learning strategies, rather than just learning specific words. » Explicit vocabulary instruction occurs in almost every lesson (e.g., unpacking academic vocabulary in a learning target, focusing on vocabulary words in text, incorporating new vocabulary into writing). » In addition to addressing specific standards related to vocabulary, we paid as much, if not more, attention to choosing rich texts and designing meaningful activities that build students' knowledge and academic vocabulary.

---

3. Our K–5 curriculum, particularly the EL Education K–2 Reading Foundations Skills Block, addresses decoding.
4. Based on a presentation by David Liben, Student Achievement Partners, July 2015; adapted with permission

Knowledge-Building

Students need not just "word" knowledge but also "world knowledge." They must develop knowledge about important topics in science, social studies, arts, and technology.

What We Know from the Research	How Our Curriculum Addresses It
» Reading or listening to a series of texts on the same topic can yield as much as four times the vocabulary growth as the same amount of text on different topics (Landauer and Dumais, 1997; Adams, 2009; Cervetti and Hiebert, 2015). » Knowledge builds knowledge. The more one knows about a topic, the more one is able to read and understand about that topic (e.g., children who have been dinosaur fanatics from age two and who have read many increasingly complex texts on that topic over the years can read really sophisticated texts about dinosaurs by age six) (Adams, 2009). » In a research study, seventh- and eighth-grade students were asked to read a text about baseball. Students reading at "lower reading ability" (approximately third- to fourth-grade reading level) who had some knowledge about baseball did better than students with "high reading ability" but low knowledge about baseball (Recht and Leslie, 1988).	» The curriculum is based on topics (e.g., hidden figures in space science) rather than more abstract "themes" (e.g., the struggle for civil rights) or decontextualized "skills." Students read multiple texts on that topic. This is what we mean when we refer to content-based literacy. » Structures are built in for independent reading on the same topic. » Students study the same topic over many weeks in many ways (e.g., reading; writing; discussing; creating multimedia representations of learning, including websites, podcasts, and infographics). » Students have many opportunities to talk about the topic.

Syntax

Syntax is the grammatical structure of a sentence. Research has shown that the ability to parse complex syntax is a critical skill for proficient readers to develop.

What We Know from the Research	How Our Curriculum Addresses It
» Multiple studies (Gilkerson and Richardson, 2008; Gilkerson et al, 2017), suggest that interactions between child and caregiver are crucial to learning the kind of speech that supports school readiness; in particular, more "conversational turns" invite students to think, talk, and make inferences.	» Students are exposed to complex sentence structures in written and spoken language. » Students do close, careful reading of complex text; they don't just read it once. Students work not only with the text's meaning (basic comprehension), but also its vocabulary, syntax, and author's craft.

What We Know from the Research	How Our Curriculum Addresses It
» Much research has shown that the ability to parse complex syntax is a critical skill for proficient readers to develop. For example, only students who obtained nearly perfect scores (35 out of 36) on the 2006 ACT tests did as well on complex text as they did on the less challenging text, indicating that a significant number of students who met the benchmark still scored relatively poorly on complex text (ACT, 2006). » Text that students read in school has become less complex. Between 1963–1991, the average length of sentences in K–8 reading textbooks (basals) was shorter than in books published between 1946–62 (Hayes, Wolfer, and Wolfer, 1996); in seventh- and eighth-grade "readers" (usually anthologies, which are widely used), the mean length of sentences decreased from twenty to fourteen words. Vocabulary also declined. The vocabulary level of eighth-grade basal readers after 1963 was equivalent to fifth-grade readers before 1963; twelfth-grade literary anthologies after 1963 were equivalent to seventh-grade readers before 1963.	» Students engage in frequent Language Dives: 10- to 20-minute conversations between teacher and students about the meaning and purpose of a compelling sentence from a complex text, followed by frequent practice using the language structures from the sentence. (See Chapter 5C for more on Language Dives).

Fluency

Fluency is defined as reading grade-level, complex text accurately, at a rate appropriate to the text, and with proper expression (Rasinski, 2004). Over one hundred studies have connected fluency to comprehension at all grades (see achievethecore.org).

What We Know from the Research	How Our Curriculum Addresses It
» Fluency does not guarantee comprehension, but lack of fluency guarantees lack of comprehension, especially with complex text. » Average scores of students not fluent were "below basic" on the Grade 4 National Assessment of Educational Progress (NAEP) (Chall, 2005). » Sixty-one percent of ninth-graders in urban sections of Miami-Dade County are unable to read eighth-grade text fluently (Rasinski et al., 2005).	» Close reading builds fluency as students often work with the same passage multiple times, either reading themselves or hearing it read aloud. » Students follow along in the text while a fluent reader reads aloud to model fluency. » Students partner-read aloud. » Students sometimes read as part of a performance (e.g., podcasts, documentary voiceover, audio museum).

What We Know from the Research	How Our Curriculum Addresses It
» Fluency problems compound vocabulary and knowledge gaps.	
» Most vocabulary is learned by reading after Grade 2 and especially after Grade 5 (Nagy and Anderson, 1984; Nagy, Anderson, and Herman, 1987).	
» Reading is the most efficient way to grow knowledge.	
» If you comprehend less of what you read, you will gain less knowledge and will learn fewer new words.	
» Disfluent readers are less motivated to read.	

▶ HOW WILL THE CURRICULUM HELP ME ADDRESS COLLEGE- AND CAREER-READY STANDARDS?

Much of the research base on the critical areas of need explored in Table 1.1 informed the creation of the Common Core State Standards and other college- and career-ready standards, and the identification of three big instructional shifts that focus teachers on addressing these needs.

The three main shifts in English language arts (ELA)/literacy instruction focus on:

» Building knowledge through content-rich nonfiction

» Reading, writing, and speaking grounded in evidence from literary and informational text

» Regular practice with complex text and its academic language

The instructional shifts have attempted to bring into balance the disconnect between the research on best practice and previous *common* practice in ELA instruction in the United States. Prior to the widespread adoption of college- and career-ready standards, the majority of reading instruction involved fictional text; the majority of writing centered on personal narratives and personal opinions; and, in all subjects in school, too many students were not being challenged to read complex text. In some schools and districts, these shifts have taken deep root and no longer feel much like "shifts" at all; in others, the pace of change has been slower. We continue to refer to "the shifts" as a shorthand, and to acknowledge that even as these practices become a more routine component of ELA instruction, they are still quite different from the way many of us learned to teach and what we experienced ourselves as students.

Shift 1: Building Knowledge through Content-Rich Nonfiction

Previous practice: The majority of reading instruction in school involved literary texts.

Instructional shift: Content-rich nonfiction (informational text) must be balanced with literary texts. In Grades K–5, teachers should strive for a 50:50 balance, but as students move through secondary school, the balance should shift to seventy percent informational text and thirty percent literary. A greater proportion of informational texts better prepares students for the kinds of reading that will be required of them in college, careers, and life. The content-based literacy components of our curriculum feature a mix of high-quality texts—both literary and informational—that deepens students' understanding of the content. Informational texts give students an opportunity to build world knowledge (e.g., about epidemics or mythology). And related literary texts—with engaging stories and characters—help them connect with the content more deeply.

Shift 2: Reading, Writing, and Speaking Grounded in Evidence from Literary and Informational Text

Previous practice: The majority of writing in school centered on personal narratives and personal opinions.

Instructional shift: Reading standards require that students read for and write with evidence. Students must read texts with care so that they can understand a topic deeply and then present clear analyses, well-defended claims, and clear information based on evidence in the text. Rather than asking questions that students can answer from prior knowledge or experience, teachers should ask text-dependent questions that point students back to the text for evidence to support their opinions and claims. The questions should require not only literal comprehension, but also inferences based on careful attention to the text. Narrative writing is still called for by the standards, and students still write stories and poetry. But there is a greater focus on the sequence and detail that are so important in argument and informational writing. Our curriculum features frequent opportunities for students to gather and talk about evidence so that they can use it skillfully in all kinds of writing. We use the Writing for Understanding framework developed by the Vermont Writing Collaborative to ensure that students have plenty of opportunities to learn about a topic and strong scaffolding to communicate their learning, usually through writing.

Shift 3: Regular Practice with Complex Text and Its Academic Language

Previous practice: In all subjects in school, too many students were not challenged to read complex text.

Instructional shift: The standards call for students to read texts of increasing complexity as they move through their K–12 schooling so that they are ready for college- and career-ready reading by the time they graduate. Our 6–8 curriculum prioritizes high-quality, complex texts related to compelling content that students are eager to dig into. Close reading helps them unpeel the layers of text so that they can comprehend it deeply. Also key to this shift is a greater focus on academic, or Tier 2, vocabulary: words that appear in a variety of content areas (e.g., ignite, commit). In our curriculum, students grow their vocabularies through a mix of structures and strategies that involve reading complex texts, engaging in academic conversation and discourse, and direct instruction. In addition to building students' knowledge and vocabulary, complex texts help students become more facile with syntax (the arrangement of words and phrases).

Addressing Specific Aspects of the Standards

The college- and career-ready standards themselves, based in research on best practices in literacy, were a strong and steady guide when designing this curriculum. This was layered on top of our commitment to providing students with worthy challenges, elevating achievement beyond test scores, content-based literacy, and student engagement. Our focus on meaning, joy, and collaboration is always in service of meeting standards and helping students be better readers, writers, and communicators. For every instance when we ask students to re-imagine a myth or to take a position on where their food should come from, we are clear about what standards they are working toward and how these experiences, combined with reading worthy texts, help students build their knowledge of the world. Table 1.2 describes how the curriculum addresses specific aspects of the standards.

Table 1.2: Addressing College- and Career-Ready English Language Arts/Literacy Standards

Reading

Aspect of Reading	How Our Curriculum Addresses It
Text complexity	Frequent use of grade-appropriate complex text at all grade levels for all students; scaffolds so all students are successful
Vocabulary	Intentional vocabulary-building from content-based text aligned to Language standards
Close reading	Teacher-led close reading of content-based texts; carefully developed text-dependent questions; multiple reads for deepening comprehension
Volume of reading	Accountable independent reading at individual student's level; reading to deepen and expand content knowledge and vocabulary
Research	Frequent research projects aligned to the Writing standards result in high-quality writing; accountable independent reading on the topic; gathering evidence to build knowledge before writing

Writing

Aspect of Writing	How Our Curriculum Addresses It
Writing reflects content understanding	All writing explores specific content knowledge and synthesizes knowledge of the topic.
Specific instruction in aspects of writing	Writing skills (e.g., use of introductions, transitions) and approaches (e.g., gathering evidence to support a statement) scaffolded specifically for particular writing types in each module
Writing fluency, ease with writing	Frequent short writing tasks as well as developed pieces
Writing process (plan, draft, revise, edit)	Instruction and scaffolding in each aspect of writing process

Speaking and Listening

Aspect of Speaking and Listening	How Our Curriculum Addresses It
Participation in discussion, building on others' ideas	Collaborative protocols; small group discussion; Socratic Seminars; frequent opportunities for students to orally rehearse ideas and thinking before writing, including structured conversations and Language Dives
Presentation of ideas in a style appropriate to audience	Presentation of students' work, both formally and informally, to an audience of their peers
Standard grammar and usage	Short and fully developed writing; Language Dives; embedded grammar and usage instruction within tasks
Standard writing conventions, including spelling	Short and fully developed writing; Language Dives
Academic and domain-specific vocabulary	Multiple reads of complex text; short and fully developed writing; Language Dives

► HOW CAN UNDERSTANDING THE BACKWARD DESIGN OF THE CURRICULUM HELP ME TEACH IT MORE EFFECTIVELY OR ADAPT IT IF NECESSARY?

We designed this curriculum using the guiding principles of backward design, which require curriculum designers to consider three questions:

» At the end of a sequence of instruction, what will students know and be able to do?

» What will proficiency look and sound like?

» How will we know when students are proficient?

Designing Curriculum with the Four T's: Topic, Tasks, Targets, and Texts

We employed the principles of backward design using a framework we call the Four T's. We started the process of designing every module, unit, and lesson asking ourselves the question: how can we best combine *topic, tasks, targets,* and *texts* to engage students with worthy content in a way that compels them to meet the standards? The Four T's interact dynamically at every level of the curriculum—for the module as a whole, for each unit, and even for discrete lessons—to support students to learn about the world, master standards, become proficient and confident readers and writers, and produce work that matters. Table 1.3 describes each of the Four T's. Following the table, we describe in greater detail how the Four T's interact in each module of our Grades 6–8 curriculum.

What Do the Four T's Look Like in Each Module in the Curriculum?

You may have heard our advice: "Whatever you do, keep the Four T's intact." We deeply respect teachers as creative agents in their classrooms, and we know anyone teaching a curriculum needs to make it their own. So our advice comes not from a wish for uniformity, but from a sense of the magnitude of what a change to the Four T's would mean: we know how much intention went into every aspect of the design, how carefully every text was evaluated in light of targets, how purposefully each lesson builds to the assessments, and how many times the materials, such as the assessments themselves, were test-driven to ensure that they are doable and will guide students to meet standards.

We also know that the volume of materials available can be overwhelming. This is understandable; it's important that teachers can find the answers they need, and we know that teachers will save their deepest focus for the materials that best enable them to teach the students in front of them.

In acknowledgement of those realities, in the pages that follow we offer two perspectives on each of the twelve modules in the Grades 6–8 band. One includes the nitty-gritty technical details of the Four T's for that module—all the guiding questions that invite students into the topics, all the tasks, all the texts, and all the standards (which show up as targets). All of that information is available in the curricular materials themselves, of course, and in much greater detail, but we know it can be helpful to have it compiled in one place for quick reference, and to be able to see how learning unfolds over the course of the three years.

Along with those technical details, we share some "behind the scenes" perspective on how the Four T's intertwine to create the remarkable learning in each module. Much of what's here comes from interviews with the designers themselves; their stories reveal how much thought, literacy expertise, and love for students and teachers went into each decision they made. These pages also include excerpts from the Notes from the Designers that are included in each Module Overview, and the Anchor Text Guidance resource for each grade level, which is available on our website at http://eled.org/tools.

Table 1.3: The Four T's: Topic, Tasks, Targets, Texts

Topic	Tasks
The compelling topic that brings the content to life; almost always based on priority content standards that students are expected to meet	*The culminating task—a scaffolded product or performance task—and the on-demand assessments to gauge students' independent mastery of content and literacy*
The topic gives cohesiveness to the unit of study. It is the "what" students are learning about, often connected to specific content knowledge. Although students may be able to meet standards without an engaging topic, a compelling, relevant topic helps them develop their reading and writing skills more deeply as they engage with increasingly complex text. The best topics teach standards through real-world issues, original research, primary source documents, and the opportunity to engage with the community, and they lend themselves to the creation of authentic tasks/products.	The culminating task gives students the opportunity to read for and write with specific textual evidence and to meaningfully apply standards (targets). This is different from just writing "about" what one has read. The best tasks give students the opportunity to address authentic need and an authentic audience related to the topic. This task is always scaffolded and leads to high-quality student work. Also essential are on-demand tasks (assessments) so that students can demonstrate independent mastery of content and ELA standards.

Targets	Texts
The learning targets derived from the specific language and rigor of grade-level ELA standards that students are expected to meet; contextualized based on the topic	*The complex texts (e.g., books/articles) that students will read closely and additional texts to ensure students read a "volume of reading" on the topic at their independent reading level*
In the context of the Four T's framework, "targets" refers to the ELA standards. Attention to the specific language of the grade-level demands of the standards is paramount, as is an analysis of how a given standard is typically assessed. (Some say, "The standard is not the standard; the assessment of the standard is the standard.") The standards are then turned into long-term targets, contextualized to the topic, which prepare students for and guide the task and ensure proper, deep analysis of the text. The types of texts students would need to read to master specific standards is a highly interrelated consideration.	The text is the main vehicle through which the topic is taught. Carefully selected texts within the text complexity band for a given grade level give students access to the topic/content standards through close and careful reading. Attention to text selection ensures that students can practice specific ELA standards *and* learn content deeply. Text must be chosen judiciously to ensure that it is "worthy" in terms of the world knowledge it will help students build and the opportunities it presents for students to master specific standards (based on the text's content, language, or structure). Less is more.

Grade 6, Module 1: The Four T's*

TOPIC: Greek Mythology

Guiding Questions and Big Ideas

» What is mythology, and what is the value of studying mythology from other cultures?

» Why have stories from Greek mythology remained popular?

» How does point of view change with experience?

TASKS

Unit 1: Build Background Knowledge: Greek Mythology

» Read a new chapter of *The Lightning Thief* and analyze and determine the meaning of unfamiliar vocabulary and phrases, including figurative language; explain how an author develops the point of view of the narrator in a new chapter of *The Lightning Thief* (mid-unit assessment).

» Prepare for a text-based discussion with peers in a Socratic Seminar, answering the prompt: How does Percy respond to challenges? What can we infer about his character from these responses? (end of unit assessment)

Unit 2: Write to Inform: Compare and Contrast Text and Film of *The Lightning Thief*

» Read several Greek myths featured and identify their themes; compare and contrast select scenes from the film version of *The Lightning Thief* to the novel (mid-unit assessment).

» Write an informational essay using a compare and contrast structure; follow a Peer Critique protocol to revise writing (end of unit assessment).

Unit 3: Research to Create a New Character and Write a Narrative

» Read another Greek myth to determine a central idea and write a summary of the text; determine the meaning of unfamiliar vocabulary (mid-unit assessment).

» Write a narrative inserting a newly created demigod character into a scene from *The Lightning Thief*; revise narratives for sentence patterns and consistency in style and tone (end of unit assessment).

Performance Task: Presentation: Revised Scene of *The Lightning Thief*

TARGETS (Standards explicitly taught and formally assessed)

» **Unit 1:** RL.6.1, RL.6.3, RL.6.4, RL.6.6, L.6.4a, L.6.4b, L.6.4c, L.6.4d, L.6.5, L.6.6, SL.6.1
» **Unit 2:** RL.6.1, RL.6.2, RL.6.7, RL.6.9, W.6.2, W.6.5, W.6.6, W.6.9a, W.6.10, L.6.2b, L.6.6
» **Unit 3:** RI.6.1, RI.6.2, RI.6.4, W.6.3, W.6.4, W.6.5, W.6.6, W.6.10, L.6.3, L.6.4, L.6.6

TEXTS

Throughout the Module: *Percy Jackson and the Olympians: The Lightning Thief* by Rick Riordan

Additionally:

» **Unit 1:** "Why Ancient Greek Mythology Is Still Relevant Today"
» **Unit 2:** Greek Myths: "Theseus and the Minotaur," "Cronus," "Medusa," and "Hestia"
» **Unit 3:** Greek Myths: "Prometheus" and "Helios"

* Note: Four T's boxes are found in the Unit Overviews for each module and may contain more detail than this module-level summary.

Grade 6, Module 1 Overview

In *The Lightning Thief*, students meet figures from ancient Greek mythology who are placed in a contemporary setting and evaluate how stories from a different time and place continue to resonate today. Students use their understanding to plan, write, and revise a scene from the book and create a multimedia presentation explaining their narrative choices. Students present their slideshow to a live audience, including reading aloud their revised scene.

How do the Four T's interact in Grade 6, Module 1?

A TEXT that draws students into the TOPIC

The Lightning Thief is a book many sixth-graders already have some familiarity with, and they tend to love it. Starting with this text and using it as the context for specific Greek myths draws students right in. It gives them a compelling reason to do the work of understanding the sometimes subtle themes of myths, and a clear (and funny!) model for how those themes relate to the world they live in today.

TARGETS to empower students, and a TASK that can be customized

One thing this module and text show is that there can be a conflict between texts that are popular and likeable, and texts that are sensitive to difference and the varied nature of human experience. Students might have a reaction to passages in *The Lightning Thief* that are not inclusive—for example, that discuss people with larger bodies as less worthy of respect, or that privilege Western civilization over others—and they may not have the tools to process them responsibly. Central to the design and learning of this module is an emphasis on guiding students to be ethical people. Due to its inclusion of alternative perspectives, this module facilitates regular opportunities for students to practice showing respect, empathy, and compassion for the attitudes and worldviews of their classmates. This focus, combined with a grounding in the targets from standards like CCSS RL.6.4: *Determine the meaning of words and phrases as they are used in a text, including figurative and connotative meanings; analyze the impact of a specific word choice on meaning and tone* empowers students to be critical readers who can use the language of a text as a way to understand the worldview it portrays.

The Lightning Thief also incorporates many figures from Greek mythology into the plot, including gods, goddesses, and monsters, and some students may be surprised or offended by the relationship depicted between gods and humans. In Unit 3, students use first-person point of view to rewrite a scene of *The Lightning Thief* inserting a new character, a child of a Greek god or goddess of their choosing. Some students and their families may find this exercise in conflict with their religious views. To account for this possibility, we provide the option of basing it on another major figure, someone like a superhero, fictional protagonists from beloved novels, important figures in history, or important religious figures from their own tradition. If students struggle with how reading mythology aligns with their own beliefs, the lessons help students take on these questions as anthropologists: studying what might have been believed at the time, rather than having them try on what it would like to believe something themselves.

The compelling TEXT and TOPIC push students to master TARGETS

This module uses a popular text to build a grade-appropriate, foundational set of critical reading skills that will support students across the academic year, and equips teachers with the critical eye and attention to sensitive issues that will become more and more important as they move into texts around other sensitive topics. Doing this through standards on figurative language, but also theme (CCSS RL6.2) and narrative writing (CCSS W6.3), means that by the time students are working with texts on famine and racism later in the year, they are better equipped to be critical readers and writers, and teachers are better equipped to support them.

The popularity and familiarity of *The Lightning Thief* allows immediate buy-in and connection, but the module doesn't end with that. Students get to enjoy reading through appreciation of a funny narrator, and they also begin to recognize that stories tell more than what's on the page—reading well involves reading between the lines. These are the most nascent steps of critical thinking that will be important to them throughout their lives.

Grade 6, Module 2: The Four T's*

TOPIC: Critical Problems and Design Solutions

Guiding Questions and Big Ideas

» How can design thinking help solve a critical problem?

» What habits of character can help solve a critical problem to contribute to a better community?

TASKS

Unit 1: Build Background: William Kamkwamba and Design Thinking

» Read a new excerpt of *The Boy Who Harnessed the Wind* and answer selected response questions about vocabulary in context, central idea, and methods used by the writers to develop the readers' understanding of William's character (mid-unit assessment).

» Read a new excerpt of *The Boy Who Harnessed the Wind* and answer selected response and constructed response questions about figurative language in context, central idea and summary, chapter structure and the contribution of single sentences to the development of ideas, and methods used by the writers to develop the readers' understanding of William's character (end of unit assessment).

Unit 2: Research to Discover Innovative Designers

» Read a new informational text, "The Hippo Roller," and answer selected response and constructed response questions about figurative language, connotative meanings, and vocabulary in context; central idea; methods used to introduce and develop our understanding of the ideas in the text; and how structure and particular sentences contribute to the development of ideas. Students also write a brief summary of the text (mid-unit assessment).

» Answer selected response and constructed response items to demonstrate research skills, such as the ability to choose the most relevant search results, understanding how the quality and specificity of search terms impacts search results, identifying types of sources, assessing reliability and credibility of possible sources, evaluating paraphrasing, paraphrasing information from a source, and gathering bibliographic information from a source (end of unit assessment).

Unit 3: Write to Inform: Problem-Solution Essay

» Write a problem-solution essay about the innovator researched in Unit 2 and how that person applied the design thinking process and habits of character to develop a solution to a critical problem (mid-unit assessment).

» Engage in a Fishbowl discussion about how habits of character help people solve critical problems using details and examples from *The Boy Who Harnessed the Wind*, student research, and the Solution Symposium note-catcher (end of unit assessment).

Performance Task: Presentation: Solution Symposium

TARGETS (Standards explicitly taught and formally assessed)

» **Unit 1:** RI.6.1, RI.6.2, RI.6.3, RI.6.4, RI.6.5, W.6.7, W.6.8, W.6.10, L.6.4a, L.6.5a, L.6.5c
» **Unit 2:** RI.6.1, RI.6.2, RI.6.3, RI.6.4, RI.6.5, W.6.7, W.6.8, W.6.10, L.6.4a, L.6.5a
» **Unit 3:** RI.6.1, RI.6.7, W.6.2, W.6.4, W.6.8, W.6.9b, W.6.10, SL.6.1, SL.6.2, L.6.6

TEXTS

Throughout the Module: *The Boy Who Harnessed the Wind* (Young Readers' Edition) by William Kamkwamba and Bryan Mealer

Additionally:

» **Unit 1:** "William Kamkwamba's Electric Wind"
» **Unit 1:** "How I Built a Windmill" TedTalk
» **Unit 2:** Model Problem-Solution Essay

* Note: Four T's boxes are found in the Unit Overviews for each module and may contain more detail than this module-level summary.

Grade 6, Module 2 Overview

Students read the true story of William Kamkwamba in *The Boy Who Harnessed the Wind* and how he used design thinking to confront the devastating effects of famine on his country, Malawi. Throughout Units 2 and 3, students research an innovator who created a solution designed to address a crucial issue. For the performance task, students present in a Solution Symposium, interacting with their audience to explain how science, reading, and habits of character led to the successful implementation of the solution.

How do the Four T's interact in Grade 6, Module 2?

TEXT, TOPIC, AND TASK keep students moving toward TARGETS

In this module, the interplay among the topic, text, and task ends up offering students a compelling outlet for engaging with problems they personally care about. Reading about a real-life person who uses design thinking and habits of character to solve problems is inspiring for students. The module builds on that inspiration by allowing students to demonstrate similar habits in the major tasks of the module. They reflect the protagonist's questions and the spirit of an inquisitive researcher. William Kamkwamba embodies a growth mindset and was interested in finding answers to questions around him. In digging into research tasks, students get to try on and embody some of those same qualities, and this gives them context and motivation for mastering targets grounded in research standards: CCSS W.6.7: *Conduct short research projects to answer a question, drawing on several sources and refocusing the inquiry when appropriate,* and *CCSS* W.6.8: *Gather relevant information from multiple print and digital sources; assess the credibility of each source; and quote or paraphrase the data and conclusions of others while avoiding plagiarism and providing basic bibliographic information for sources.*

TARGETS support students with the complexities of TEXT and TOPIC

To work responsibly with the concept of "critical problems," teachers must strike a few balances. They must nurture students' empathetic reactions as they read, while simultaneously equipping students with the literacy skills necessary to interpret the writers' choices. They must help students see a community's problems clearly, while simultaneously avoiding reductive stereotyping. The challenges of drought in a resources-limited community is not something most students in the United States have direct experience with, but the module helps students build empathy without direct experience.

In emphasizing the impact of the famine faced by William and his Malawian community, this text features occasional passages that may be difficult for students to read, as they detail the suffering felt by William and others in his village. Other elements of the text may also require heightened attention and sensitivity; for instance, told through the eyes of William as he grows up in an impoverished village, *The Boy Who Harnessed the Wind* presents a somewhat singular picture of Africa as poor, rather than as the diverse, heterogeneous continent that it is. Across lessons, notes emphasize specific passages that may require special attention and offer suggestions to help students interpret and process the text's content with strength, empathy, and a questioning spirit.

TARGETS and TOPIC show up seamlessly in the performance TASK

The performance task of the module is a Solution Symposium, which is supported by students having written a problem/solution essay in Unit 3. This, in turn, is supported by the research into critical problems and design solutions begun in Unit 2. Students study and unpack a particular framework—Design Thinking—for thinking about problems and solutions. This framework is in fact the topic of the module, more than the particulars of William's story.

Grade 6, Module 3: The Four T's*

TOPIC: American Indian Boarding Schools

Guiding Questions and Big Ideas

» Why were American Indian boarding schools first established?

» What kind of experiences did students have at American Indian boarding schools? How did these experiences impact students?

» What factors influence our identities?

TASKS

Unit 1: Build Background Knowledge: Analyze Points of View toward American Indian Boarding Schools

» Read a new excerpt, "The Cutting of My Long Hair," of Zitkala-Sa's first-person account of her time at the White's Indiana Manual Labor Institute and answer selected response questions about vocabulary in context, as well as the author's point of view and how it is conveyed in the text. Answer a short constructed response question to integrate their interpretations of two photos related to the ideas of the text (mid-unit assessment).

» Read a new chapter of *Two Roads* and answer selected response and short constructed response questions about the use of intensive pronouns, the impact of dialect in the text, and how Cal's point of view is developed by the author (end of unit assessment).

Unit 2: Confront Challenges: Characters' Responses and Emerging Themes

» Read a new chapter of *Two Roads* and answer selected response and short constructed response questions about Cal's point of view, how Cal is responding and changing throughout the plot, and what themes are emerging in the text (mid-unit assessment).

» Write a narrative letter and revise based on pronoun case, pronoun number and person, vague pronouns, and sentence variety (end of unit assessment).

Unit 3: Literary Argument Writing: Gather Evidence and Reflect on Multiple Perspectives

» Write a literary argument essay about whether or not Cal should return to Challagi Indian School, using reasons and evidence to defend a claim (mid-unit assessment).

» Record a performance task contribution and then reflect on and self-assess for volume, pronunciation, and language use. Provide feedback on a peer's recording (end of unit assessment).

Performance Task: Audio Museum: Voices of American Indian Boarding Schools Audio Museum

TARGETS (Standards explicitly taught and formally assessed)

» **Unit 1:** RL.6.1, RL.6.5, RL.6.6, RI.6.1, RI.6.4, RI.6.6, RI.6.7, L.6.1b, L.6.1e L.6.4

» **Unit 2:** RL.6.1, RL.6.2, RL.6.3, RL.6.6, RL.6.10, W.6.5, W.6.10, L.6.1a, L.6.1c, L.6.1d, L.6.3a

» **Unit 3:** RL.6.1, RL.6.3, RL.6.10, RI.6.1, RI.6.6, W.6.1, W.6.4, W.6.5, W.6.6, W.6.9a, W.6.10, SL.6.1d, SL.6.4, SL.6.6, L.6.2, L.6.3, L.6.6 (optional: L.6.1)

TEXTS

Throughout the module: *Two Roads* by Joseph Bruchac

Additionally:

» **Unit 1:** "The Cutting of My Long Hair"; *The Problem of Indian Administration: Report of a Survey made at the Request of Honorable Hubert Work, Secretary of the Interior, and Submitted to Him, February 21, 1928*; "The Advantage of Mingling Indians with Whites"

» **Unit 3:** *Land of the Spotted Eagle*

* Note: Four T's boxes are found in the Unit Overviews for each module and may contain more detail than this module-level summary.

Grade 6, Module 3 Overview

Through their reading of the historical fictional narrative *Two Roads* by Joseph Bruchac and several supplemental primary texts, students uncover an often unacknowledged aspect of U.S. history—the forced acculturation of American Indians through boarding schools. To honor those who experienced this injustice, students create listening stations for an Audio Museum as their performance task: students select a meaningful text (e.g., a poem, personal narrative) written by a survivor of the boarding schools and write a preface and reflection based on their chosen text. Students record themselves sharing their reading, acting as witnesses to this unrecognized time period in U.S. history.

How do the Four T's interact in Grade 6, Module 3?

The TOPIC fires students up, and the TASK gives them an outlet

Middle school students want and need to explore questions of justice and fairness, and this topic activates and channels that readiness. American Indian boarding schools and the experiences of those who were sent there aren't well known or frequently talked about, so students may end up more informed about this aspect of U.S. history than many adults in their lives. They also have a chance to do something about it through the performance task, an audio museum, which highlights, centers, empowers, and amplifies the voices of those who lived through it. At the same time, we were wary of trying to provoke empathy in students by asking "how would you feel if this happened to you?" and didn't want to take students' focus away from the actual experiences of those who lived them. Instead, students are asked to practice *empathy* by being the medium through which voices from the past can be heard more widely, through the audio museum.

The TARGETS give students access to the nuances of TEXT

One of the standards addressed in this module is CCSS L61.e: *Recognize variations from standard English in their own and others' writing and speaking, and identify and use strategies to improve expression in conventional language.* While we don't accept the idea that one variation of English is inherently better than another, we do recognize that speakers need to be able to skillfully move between variations. We include language dives that focus on the main character's best friend, Possum, who regularly code-switches into and out of dialectical varieties. As a nimble user of language, Possum changes his to suit a particular time or person. Zeroing in on Possum's dialogue invites students to think of variations as strategic choices, rather than something in need of correction.

The TARGETS give students a way to process the TOPIC

The anchor text in this module is frank about the role that race and identity play in the narrator's experience, and supplemental texts are clear about the culturally destructive motivation for establishing American Indian boarding schools in the first place. The module gives teachers tools to help students process all of this responsibly, which leads to authentic opportunities to include meaningful point-of-view work. Digging deeply into the points of view of the characters in the literary anchor text and of the authors in supplemental text is useful in its own right, and also helps students process challenging issues. When students read something painful, point-of-view work allows them to "assign it" to a person they are reading about and not have to internalize it in order to understand it.

The extensive work on point of view feeds one of the main assessments, a literary argument essay. The task poses questions that require students to analyze choices of characters, and this is much more helpful with sensitive topics than asking students to create an argument about American Indian boarding schools in general. It avoids asking students to write as moral authorities in ways they might not be prepared for.

Grade 6, Module 4: The Four T's*

TOPIC: Remarkable Accomplishments in Space Science

Guiding Questions and Big Ideas

» What were the main events of the Space Race, and in what scientific, political, and social context did it take place?

» What were the accomplishments of the "hidden figures" at NASA, and why were they remarkable?

» Why is it important to study the accomplishments of the "hidden figures" and of others whose stories have gone unrecognized?

TASKS

Unit 1: Remarkable Accomplishments in the Space Race

» Read a new informational article, "An Account of the Moon Landing." Answer constructed response questions about vocabulary and figurative language in the text and about the author's point of view and how it is conveyed in the text (mid-unit assessment).

» Read the opinion article "An Argument against the Moon Mission." Answer constructed response questions about the author's point of view and how it is conveyed in the text. Trace the author's argument, identifying a claim, reasons, evidence, and reasoning (end of unit assessment).

Unit 2: Remarkable Accomplishments of the Hidden Figures

» Read two short sections of chapter 9 in the anchor text, *Hidden Figures*, and answer selected response and short answer questions about the argument the author makes in the text, as well as the author's point of view toward Dorothy (mid-unit assessment).

» Reread an excerpt from the anchor text, *Hidden Figures*, about Katherine Johnson and then read an excerpt from "Katherine Johnson: A Lifetime of STEM" that describes the same events as the anchor text. Respond to selected response and short constructed response questions to compare and contrast each author's presentation of those events in terms of content, author's methods, and point of view (end of unit assessment).

Unit 3: Remarkable Accomplishments in Space Science

» Write an argument essay about why the researched focus figure's accomplishments are remarkable, using reasons, evidence, and reasoning to defend a claim (mid-unit assessment).

» Present the narrative nonfiction picture book pages developed for the performance task, and trace the arguments presented by classmates. Participate in a culminating discussion to summarize and reflect upon learning across the module (end of unit assessment).

Performance Task: Children's Picture Book: Hidden Figures in Space Science Picture Book

TARGETS (Standards explicitly taught and formally assessed)

» **Unit 1:** RI.6.1, RI.6.4, RI.6.6, RI.6.8, RI.6.10, W.6.10, L.6.5c
» **Unit 2:** RI.6.1, RI.6.3, RI.6.6, RI.6.8, RI.6.9, RI.6.10, W.6.1b, W.6.10
» **Unit 3:** RI.6.1, RI.6.3, RI.6.10, W.6.1, W.6.4, W.6.5, W.6.6, W.6.7, W.6.8, W.6.9b, W.6.10, SL.6.1, SL.6.3, SL.6.4, SL.6.5, SL.6.6, L.6.2, L.6.3, L.6.6

TEXTS

Throughout the module: *Hidden Figures: The True Story of Four Black Women and the Space Race* children's picture book by Margot Lee; *Hidden Figures* (Young Readers' Edition) by Margot Lee Shetterly

» **Unit 1:** "The Space Race"; "Special Message to the Congress on Urgent National Needs"; "Benefits of NASA's Space Technology on Earth"; "This Is How the Space Race Changed the Great Power Rivalry Forever"; "An Account of the Moon Landing"; "An Argument against the Moon Mission"

» **Unit 2:** "Moon Dust and Black Disgust"; "From Moton to NASA"; "Mary Winston Jackson"; "July 20, 1969: One Giant Leap For Mankind"; "Katherine Johnson: A Lifetime of STEM"

* Note: Four T's boxes are found in the Unit Overviews for each module and may contain more detail than this module-level summary.

Grade 6, Module 4 Overview

Students study the contributions and celebrate the accomplishments of key "hidden figures" in space science. They start with the "West Computers," the first black women hired by NASA whose talents helped land human beings on the moon, and eventually research other under-recognized hidden figures in space science. Working in groups of three, students create a picture book devoted to the stories of the focus figures they chose to research. Students uplift the mostly unknown stories of these other hidden figures and distill information about them into simpler language that can be shared with younger students.

How do the Four T's interact in Grade 6, Module 4?

The way TEXTS are sequenced gives students experiential insight into the TOPIC

This module is carefully designed to have an experiential component to it. To help students understand and feel the impact of the West Computers being unknown and unheralded for so long, all the texts they read about space science and the social forces of the 1960s in Unit 1 intentionally leave them out. When the women appear in Unit 2 and the extent of their contribution becomes clear, students can *feel* the injustice of their absence. This builds students' need to uplift the stories in a way no assignment, even a great performance task, can do on its own.

TARGETS support students to process the TOPIC's complexities

Understanding the racist world in which the West Computers lived is critical for understanding their professional and societal legacy and impact. Still, reading descriptions of the discrimination against the West Computers may be painful for students. Across lessons, Teaching Notes call out specific passages that may be especially upsetting for students and offer suggestions for helping students process the content of these passages respectfully and compassionately. Instructional decisions based on the learning targets throughout the module also equip students with the literacy skills necessary to interpret and process the content of the text and contribute meaningfully to class discussions.

The TASK gives students a way to respond to the TOPIC

One of the ways this module harnesses student indignation at how uncelebrated the West Computers were is to give them a chance to research and tell the stories of other hidden figures in space science, and to offer some choice. Even as this presents an additional layer of meaning for students, it can present an additional layer of preparation for teachers, and so part of what we offer is a thoughtfully curated set of options for the individual research component.

Grade 7, Module 1: The Four T's*

TOPIC: The Lost Children of Sudan

Guiding Questions and Big Ideas

» Who are the Lost Children of Sudan, and what is their story?

» What are the habits of character the Lost Children used to survive?

TASKS

Unit 1: Build Background Knowledge: The Lost Boys of Sudan

» Read a new chapter from *A Long Walk to Water* and answer selected and constructed response questions to analyze how setting shapes plot and characters and how the author develops and contrasts points of view (mid-unit assessment).

» Participate in text-based discussion about the development of themes in *A Long Walk to Water* (end of unit assessment).

Unit 2: Write to Inform: The Lost Children of South Sudan

» Watch a clip of *God Grew Tired of Us* and answer selected response questions related to the main ideas and supporting details. Research online to answer a question about *A Long Walk to Water* (mid-unit assessment).

» Write an essay to compare and contrast the novel *A Long Walk to Water* and the informational article "The 'Lost Girls' of Sudan" to analyze how the author of the novel uses or alters history (end of unit assessment).

Unit 3: Write to Raise Awareness: The Lost Children of South Sudan

» Answer selected and constructed response questions to contrast the effects of the techniques in the audio and text versions of *A Long Walk to Water* (mid-unit assessment).

» Draft a children's book narrative that showcases the habits of character that a Lost Boy or Girl of Sudan demonstrated in his or her journey (end of unit assessment).

Performance Task: Illustrated Ebook: Lost Boys and Girls of Sudan

TARGETS (Standards explicitly taught and formally assessed)

» **Unit 1:** RL.7.2, RL.7.3, RL.7.4, RL.7.6, RL.7.10, SL.7.1, SL.7.1a, SL.7.1b, SL.7.1c, L.7.4, L.7.4a, L.7.4b, L.7.4c, L.7.4d, L.7.6

» **Unit 2:** RL.7.1, RL.7.9, RI.7.1, RI.7.2, W.7.2, W.7.2a, W.7.2b, W.7.2c, W.7.2d, W.7.2e, W.7.2f, W.7.4, W.7.6, W.7.7, W.7.8, W.7.9a, W.7.9b, SL.7.2

» **Unit 3:** RL.7.1, RL.7.7, W.7.3, W.7.3a, W.7.3b, W.7.3c, W.7.3e, W.7.4, W.7.6, W.7.10

TEXTS

Throughout the module: *A Long Walk to Water* by Linda Sue Park

Additionally:

» **Unit 1:** "The Lost Boys of Sudan"

» **Unit 2:** *God Grew Tired of Us*; "The 'Lost Girls' of Sudan"; "The Need"

» **Unit 3:** "The Lost Boys of Sudan"; "The Lost Girls of Sudan"; *God Grew Tired of Us*; "The Need"; *A Long Walk to Water* audio version; "One Day I Had to Run"

* Note: Four T's boxes are found in the Unit Overviews for each module and may contain more detail than this module-level summary.

Grade 7, Module 1 Overview

Students launch the year developing their ability to analyze narratives about the Lost Children of Sudan. Students conduct research and develop first their informative writing skills by comparing a fictional to a historical account. Then, for the performance task, students develop their narrative writing skills to create their own stories about a lost child of Sudan and the lessons revealed through their journeys. Students refine their narratives and convert them into ebooks to publish and share with others, especially elementary school children.

How do the Four T's interact in Grade 7, Module 1?

The TASK activates adolescent learners' expertise and supports TARGETS for narrative writing

The performance task involves writing a book about a sensitive topic to educate younger students, and seventh-graders jump at the chance to be the experts, get creative, and communicate the information in a way that's appropriate for younger students. The task is a great start to the year for students—it includes art, and because the writing is for an audience of younger students, it takes the pressure off of seventh-graders to sound erudite and academic, while still learning the content deeply and working toward targets grounded in CCSS W.7.3: *Write narratives to develop real or imagined experiences or events using effective technique, relevant descriptive details, and well-structured event sequences.*

Careful work with the TEXT supports a nuanced understanding of the TOPIC

A Long Walk to Water deals with topics such as war (including the violent death of family members and children), displacement, family separation, hunger, dehydration (including death from lack of water), refugee camps, violent deaths from wild animals, and serious illness of family members. These issues must be carefully and sensitively discussed to give students context as they read the story. It is important for students to understand that while this is *an* African story, this is not *the* African story, and it is also not the only way to think of Sudan itself.

Throughout the module, students have opportunities to learn about Africa beyond a "single story." They do a picture walk through the places one character goes in Sudan and South Sudan, to show clearly that there are cities, hotels, and modern buildings. One of the characters describes his part of South Sudan, before the war, as having been lush and beautiful. His family had been able to grow whatever they wanted, and owned cattle. The module makes time for students to reflect on how their new learning is different from the "single story" of Africa that they may have had previously.

The TARGETS support a high-quality TASK in this module and beyond

This module brings in CCSS RL7.7: *Compare and contrast a written story, drama, or poem to its audio, filmed, staged, or multimedia version, analyzing the effects of techniques unique to each medium (e.g., lighting, sound, color, or camera focus and angles in a film)* in a way that's both helpful for teaching it well, and that lays important, strategic groundwork for later modules. Students analyze the audio version of selected chapters of *A Long Walk to Water* then look at how techniques like sound effects, music, pauses, and actors—with emotion in their voices—add to or change their experience of the story. This is good preparation for Module 3, when students will revisit CCSS RL7.7, and Module 4, when they work on CCSS RI.7 and deeply analyze techniques for documentary.

Grade 7, Module 2: The Four T's*

TOPIC: Epidemics

Guiding Questions and Big Ideas

» What are epidemics? How do they develop?

» How do people respond to an epidemic?

» What is the role of character and mindset in solving epidemic crises?

» What methods and tools help people to solve epidemics?

TASKS

Unit 1: Build Background Knowledge: Solving Medical Epidemics

» Read pages 41–44 in *Patient Zero* and answer selected and constructed response questions to analyze how the author structures the text (mid-unit assessment).

» Read final excerpt of chapter 4 of *Patient Zero* and answer selected and constructed response questions to analyze how individuals, events, and ideas interact in the text (end of unit assessment).

Unit 2: Write to Inform: Are Social Epidemics Real?

» Read a new informational text, "Are Social Epidemics Real?" and engage in a text-based discussion about the strength of the article's argument (mid-unit assessment).

» Write an informative essay about how social scientists use ideas from the study of epidemics to explain human behavior (end of unit assessment).

Unit 3: Spread the Message: How to Respond to Epidemics

» Read the informational text "Disease Detectives" and answer selected and constructed response questions to analyze how individuals, events, and ideas interact in the text; and conduct research to answer a question (mid-unit assessment).

» Present a podcast script, focusing on coherence and organization of information, volume, clarity, and formal English (end of unit assessment).

Performance Task: A Podcast of an Epidemic

TARGETS (Standards explicitly taught and formally assessed)

» **Unit 1:** RI.7.1, RI.7.3, RI.7.4, RI.7.5, RI.7.10, L.7.4, L.7.6
» **Unit 2:** RI.7.1, RI.7.2, RI.7.8, RI.7.10, W.7.2, W.7.2a, W.7.2b, W.7.2c, W.7.2d, W.7.2e, W.7.2f, W.7.4, W.7.5, W.7.6, W.7.10, SL.7.1, SL.7.1a, SL.7.1b, SL.7.1c, SL.7.1d, L.7.1, L.7.2, L.7.6
» **Unit 3:** RI.7.1, RI.7.3, RI.7.4, W.7.7, W.7.8, SL.7.4, SL.7.6, L.7.3a, L.7.4, L.7.6

TEXTS

Throughout the Module: *Patient Zero: Solving the Mysteries of Deadly Epidemics* by Marilee Peters

Additionally:

» **Units 2 and 3:** "Kindness Contagion"; "Social Contagion: Conflicting Ideas"; "Are Social Epidemics Real?"
» **Unit 3:** "Disease Detective"

Note: Four T's boxes are found in the Unit Overviews for each module and may contain more detail than this module-level summary.

Grade 7, Module 2 Overview

Students read to develop background knowledge about epidemics in many forms: historical and current, medical and social. While students learn about the scientific investigation and medical intervention in these outbreaks, they also focus on the social and cultural responses to develop a model of how best to respond to challenging circumstances. Students research and develop a podcast about an epidemic that concerns them or their community, sharing the dynamic podcast—complete with sound effects and music—with others beyond the classroom.

How do the Four T's interact in Grade 7, Module 2?

The TEXT draws students in to a "gross" TOPIC and a social lens on medicine

The anchor text *Patient Zero* is, in a word, gross. It's gross in just the right way to make history compelling and lively for seventh-graders. The lens the module brings to that history is also one that matters to adolescents: when students begin exploring the history of medical epidemics, they focus on people's mindsets and contributions, and how they behaved differently from those around them. Then in Unit 2, students are introduced to the topic of social epidemics and get grounded in the basic terms and theories behind social and emotional contagion. Because there is some genuine debate in the field of epidemiology about the applicability of medical concepts to social contagion, students also get to engage with these real questions and come to their own conclusions about whether the authors of an article have provided sufficient evidence and reasoning for their claims connecting social and disease epidemics.

The TEXT raises complexities, and TARGETS help students make meaning

Along with the grossness that generates energy for students, the anchor text contains references to sensitive topics such as disease and death as well as the unsanitary conditions that contribute to disease. One way students process all their learning is through a note-catcher that invites them to consider what ideas people held before the epidemic, and how those changed because of events and individuals involved with the epidemic. By the time they get to those questions, students have already done a great deal of work on how text features and structure contribute to the overall meaning of the text, and are able to look beyond the gross factor to these important questions about how societies deal with contagion.

A potentially intimidating TASK is deeply supported for teachers and students

The resources provided to support students in creating the performance task podcast allow teachers to guide students in making something really cool without having to create or curate all the models themselves. In Unit 3, students begin by listening to exemplar podcasts and reading a model podcast script about epidemics and how people responded to them. They analyze what makes these podcasts strong and build criteria for success based off of their observations. Using these models as a template, students embark on researching an epidemic of their choosing. In triads, students plan, write, and revise a narrative nonfiction podcast script. For their end of unit assessment, students present their script, focusing on coherence and organization of information, volume, eye contact, clarity, and formal English. Next, they find sound effects, and then finally, they record and splice together the podcast. In the end, they have a podcast created with craftsmanship to publish for their classmates, school, or even the world.

Grade 7, Module 3: The Four T's*

TOPIC: Harlem Renaissance

Guiding Questions and Big Ideas

» How does collaboration influence an artistic renaissance?

» What are some of the historical factors surrounding and contributing to the Harlem Renaissance?

» What are some of the lasting legacies of the Harlem Renaissance?

TASKS

Unit 1: Collaboration in the Harlem Renaissance

» Read the lyrics to "Lift Every Voice and Sing" by James Weldon Johnson and answer selected and constructed response questions to analyze and compare literary and musical techniques and their effects on meaning (mid-unit assessment).

» Read the poem "I Shall Return" by Claude McKay and answer selected and constructed response questions to analyze structure, figurative language, and theme (end of unit assessment).

Unit 2: The Context of the Harlem Renaissance

» Read the last part of the short story "The Boy and the Bayonet" by Paul Laurence Dunbar and answer selected and constructed response questions to analyze story elements, language, and theme (mid-unit assessment).

» Write a literary argument essay connecting three works by theme (end of unit assessment).

Unit 3: The Legacy of the Harlem Renaissance

» Read "The Sculptor" by Nikki Grimes and answer selected and constructed response questions to analyze the structure, language, and theme of poetry (mid-unit assessment).

» Present a curator's statement, one piece, and its associated label from their Harlem Renaissance museum exhibit (end of unit assessment).

Performance Task: Harlem Renaissance Museum Collection

TARGETS (Standards explicitly taught and formally assessed)

» **Unit 1:** RL.7.1, RL.7.2, RL.7.4, RL.7.5, RL.7.7, L.7.4, L.7.5, L.7.5a, L.7.5c

» **Unit 2:** RL.7.1, RL.7.3, RL.7.6, RL.7.10, W.7.1, W.7.1a, W.7.1b, W.7.1c, W.7.1d, W.7.1e, W.7.5, W.7.6, W.7.9, W.7.9a, W.7.10, L.7.1, L.7.1a, L.7.1b, L.7.4

» **Unit 3:** RL.7.2, RL.7.4, RL.7.5, SL.7.4, SL.7.5, SL.7.6, L.7.4

TEXTS

Throughout the Module: *One Last Word: Wisdom from the Harlem Renaissance* by Nikki Grimes

Additionally:

» **Unit 1:** *Shuffle Along*; "Lift Every Voice and Sing"; "The Negro Speaks of Rivers"; "Calling Dreams"; "Hope"; "I Shall Return"; *Ethiopia Awakening*; *African Phantasy: Awakening*

» **Unit 2:** "Under Jim Crow's Thumb"; "A Call to Move"; "The Harlem Renaissance: A Cultural Rebirth"; "His Motto"; "The Boy and the Bayonet"

» **Unit 3:** Preface in *One Last Word*; "Emergency Measures"; *"Emergency Measures"* artwork; "Uptown" video of Alvin Ailey Dance Company; "Uptown" podcast; "On Bully Patrol"; "Hope"; "David's Old Soul"; "A Negro Speaks of Rivers"; "The Sculptor"; "Calling Dreams"

* Note: Four T's boxes are found in the Unit Overviews for each module and may contain more detail than this module-level summary.

Grade 7, Module 3 Overview

Students explore drama, poetry, song, art, stories, and dance to understand and appreciate the significance of the Harlem Renaissance. Students read articles and short biographies to build knowledge about the collaboration among writers, musicians, and artists; the social and political context of the 1900s for black Americans; and the legacy of the Harlem Renaissance. Students write literary argument essays about themes across several works from the period. Then, they develop a Harlem Renaissance exhibit of several works correlated by theme and including one contemporary work that students chose or created themselves.

How do the Four T's interact in Grade 7, Module 3?

An array of TEXTS brings the TOPIC to life

This module was designed so that students can really feel the explosion and confluence of art, music, and literature that defined the Harlem Renaissance. Instead of one anchor text and a few supplementary texts, this module brings in poems, plays, artwork, and songs. Part of what's significant about these choices is how these works and these artists were all in rich conversation with one another, both contemporaneously and across time. Unit 1 is an exploration of those works that saturates students with the artistry and genius of the Harlem Renaissance, which they have a chance to put in vital historical context in Unit 2. Once they get to Unit 3, students are equipped to curate a museum exhibit, which includes three pieces from the Harlem Renaissance and one contemporary piece that they have studied or created themselves.

The complexities of the TOPIC show up in the TEXTS

In Unit 2, students explore the social and political context of the Harlem Renaissance by reading short informational texts and examining visual art. Students learn how the Harlem Renaissance occurred during the era of the Great Migration, Jim Crow laws, and the racial violence of post-Civil War America. In tackling issues of racial oppression, the texts examined across this module raise issues that may be upsetting, painful, or confusing for students. The design of the module aims to support students as they process sensitive or challenging passages. Across lessons, Teaching Notes call attention to specific passages that may be especially troubling for students and offer suggestions for helping students process the content of these passages with strength and compassion.

TARGETS reflect professional formats and standards of the TASK

The way that the Speaking and Listening standards show up in the curator's statement that students write in Unit 3 is exciting and was carefully designed. Students must learn formal speech in order to speak as a museum curator. Using a museum advice column as a support, students write labels as professionals in the field do. This task was refined by designers over the course of multiple "test-drives"; just as we recommend teachers "test drive" assessments, test-driving everything from exit-tickets to performance tasks is part of our design process. The first versions of the task called for students to write a lot of text for the labels, but designers realized that was addressing Writing standards rather than Speaking and Listening. Through a process of refining and revising, with expert feedback, the task now requires one sentence for the label and one paragraph for the curator's statement—just right for the genre, and for the standards.

Grade 7, Module 4: The Four T's*

TOPIC: Plastic Pollution

Guiding Questions and Big Ideas

» Where and how does plastic pollute?

» What can be done about plastic pollution?

» What is being done about plastic pollution?

» What can I do about plastic pollution?

TASKS

Unit 1: Build Background Knowledge: What Is Plastic Pollution?

» Watch a clip of *A Plastic Ocean* and answer selected and constructed response questions to compare portrayals of subjects in the film and transcript and to evaluate speakers' argument (mid-unit assessment).

» Read an excerpt from *Trash Vortex* and answer selected and constructed response questions to analyze central ideas as well as the author's point of view and purpose (end of unit assessment).

Unit 2: Take a Stand: Ways to Reduce Plastic Pollution

» Read the informational text "Boyan Slat: The Great Pacific Garbage Patch Kid" and answer selected and constructed response questions to analyze an author's point of view as well as how authors shape their interpretations about the same topic (mid-unit assessment).

» Write an argument essay using evidence from the texts to defend a claim about which part of the plastic life cycle is the best place to intervene to reduce plastic pollution (end of unit assessment).

Unit 3: Spread the Message: We Can Make a Difference!

» Revise a section of the documentary film script (mid-unit assessment).

» Present the documentary film pitch (end of unit assessment).

Performance Task: Plastic Pollution Documentary Clip

TARGETS (Standards explicitly taught and formally assessed)

» **Unit 1:** RI.7.1, RI.7.2, RI.7.6, RI.7.7, RI.7.10, SL.7.2, SL.7.3, L.7.4
» **Unit 2:** RI.7.2, RI.7.4, RI.7.6, RI.7.9, RI.7.10, W.7.1, W.7.1a, W.7.1b, W.7.1c, W.7.1d, W.7.1e, W.7.5, W.7.6, W.7.9, W.7.9b, W.7.10, L.7.1, L.7.1c, L.7.2, L.7.2a, L.7.2b, L.7.4, L.7.5, L.7.5b
» **Unit 3:** W.7.5, SL.7.4, SL.7.5, SL.7.6, L.7.6

TEXTS

Throughout the Module: *A Plastic Ocean; Trash Vortex: How Plastic Pollution Is Choking the World's Oceans* by Danielle Smith-Llera

Additionally:

» **Units 2 and 3:** "Five Weird Materials That Could Replace Plastic"; "Five Things You Can Do to End Plastic Pollution"; "Boyan Slat: The Great Pacific Garbage Patch Kid"

* Note: Four T's boxes are found in the Unit Overviews for each module and may contain more detail than this module-level summary.

Grade 7, Module 4 Overview

Seventh-graders close the year by reading about and researching plastic pollution in an informational film, text, articles, and online resources. Through these media, students explore solutions for plastic pollution at different points in the life cycle of plastic. Students write an argument essay about which point in the plastic life cycle is most effective for addressing plastic pollution. Then, students develop an action plan they can enact through research, advocacy, or personal commitment. They conclude the module and year by creating a documentary film clip that conveys their argument, action plan solution, and conclusions about plastic pollution which they can share with their community and the world beyond.

How do the Four T's interact in Grade 7, Module 4?

The TASKS connect to adolescent learners' instincts to dig into an important TOPIC

In this module, seventh-graders get to do something they deeply desire: tell others what they should do! They learn deeply about plastic pollution, and the thread throughout is that there are multiple points in the plastic life cycle at which we can intervene to make change: how plastic is made, how it's used, and how it's disposed of. Students debate which points of intervention and methods will matter most, based on the evidence they gather through research and the perspective they gain through action-planning. The documentary film clip that students create for the performance task ties it all together.

The TOPIC evokes emotion, and the sequence of TEXTS and TASKS supports students to channel it toward action

Throughout the documentary *A Plastic Ocean* and the book *Trash Vortex*, the producers and authors present evidence about the harms that plastic pollution can cause to the environment and wildlife. To help students process this information, Teaching Notes provide suggestions about specific questions and activities to contextualize the subject matter and empower students to identify the habits of character of the people addressing these problems and relate them to their own lives. Some students will be deeply affected by images and discussion of the suffering and harm that plastic pollution can cause. Throughout the module, students have opportunities to discuss and react to these issues through engaging literacy tasks. Additionally, Teaching Notes are included throughout the module to help students navigate these issues. Despite learning so deeply about content that can be dispiriting, by Unit 3 it's clear to students that people are taking action, and that they can take action, too.

The sequence of assessments makes the performance TASK powerful

One of the ways the module builds toward the performance task is by getting students' arguments in good shape, so that their documentary clips can pack a punch. In Unit 2, students read three articles and revisit their anchor texts to understand what interventions can be taken at each stage of the plastic life cycle: beginning, middle, and end. In this unit, students build their understanding of and skills for debate in a highly supported way. By the middle of the unit, students take a stand about which part of the plastic life cycle would be most effective to target and have the opportunity to defend their position in a debate with their classmates.

Although this debate is not assessed, students' preparation and participation in the debate continues to prepare them for their End of Unit 2 Assessment and performance task in Unit 3. In the second half of Unit 2, students use the evidence and reasoning they've collected and organized from their reading to practice an on-demand argument essay about which point in the plastic life cycle is the best place to target to reduce pollution. That in turn forms the basis for the documentary film script and pitch in Unit 3, which will convey their argument, solution, and conclusions.

Grade 8, Module 1: The Four T's*

TOPIC: Folklore of Latin America

Guiding Questions and Big Ideas

» Why do we see evidence of myths and traditional stories in modern narratives?

» How and why can we modernize myths and traditional stories to be meaningful to today's audiences?

TASKS

Unit 1: Build Background Knowledge: Read and Analyze *Summer of the Mariposas*

» Read a new chapter from *Summer of the Mariposas* and answer selected and short constructed response questions to analyze the impact of point of view and figurative language (mid-unit assessment).

» Read Chapter 12 of *Summer of the Mariposas* and complete a graphic organizer and answer selected response questions to analyze aspects of character revealed through events in the text (end of unit assessment).

Unit 2: Theme and Summary in *Summer of the Mariposas*: Narrative Writing

» Read Chapter 16 of *Summer of the Mariposas* and answer selected response and short constructed response questions to track the development of theme in *Summer of the Mariposas* and write summary paragraphs (mid-unit assessment).

» Research a "monster" from Latin American folklore and write an additional chapter for *Summer of the Mariposas* in which the Garza girls encounter a modernized version of this "monster" (end of unit assessment).

Unit 3: Compare and Contrast Essay: *Summer of the Mariposas* and Latin American Folklore

» Read an essay and determine the central idea of the text (mid-unit assessment).

» Write an essay comparing the original depiction of another "monster" from Latin American folklore with a modernized depiction from Unit 2 narrative essays (end of unit assessment).

Performance Task: Class Website: Folklore of Latin America

TARGETS (Standards explicitly taught and formally assessed)

» **Unit 1:** RL.8.1, RL.8.3, RL.8.4, RL.8.6, RL.8.10, L.8.4a, L.8.5b, L.8.4c, L.8.4d, L.8.5a, L.8.6
» **Unit 2:** RL.8.1, RL.8.2, RL.8.4, RL.8.9, RL.8.10, W.8.3, W.8.4, W.8.6, W.8.10, L.8.4
» **Unit 3:** RL.8.1, RL.8.9, RI.8.1, RI.8.4, RI.8.10, W.8.2, W.8.4, W.8.5, W.8.9, W.8.10, L.8.4

TEXTS

Throughout the Module: *Summer of the Mariposas* by Guadalupe Garcia McCall

Additionally:

» **Unit 1:** Excerpt from *The Latin American Story Finder*
» **Unit 2:** "The Peuchen"
» **Unit 3:** *La Llorona*

* Note: Four T's boxes are found in the Unit Overviews for each module and may contain more detail than this module-level summary.

Grade 8, Module 1 Overview

Why do we see evidence of myths and traditional stories in modern narratives? How and why can we modernize myths and traditional stories to be meaningful to today's audiences? In this module, students read *Summer of the Mariposas* and analyze theme, point of view, and characterization. Students write their own narrative scene in which they modernize a character from Latin American folklore. Finally, students write expository essays about the modernization of Latin American folklore and create a website to house their narratives and essays.

How do the Four T's interact in Grade 8, Module 1?

A welcoming TEXT embodies a powerful TOPIC

Summer of the Mariposas is a genuinely engaging book. The story involves cross-cultural experiences and an exploration of identity that is a powerful way to start the year. The characters are relatable, and students connect with them. The module invites students to think about identity, culture, and family, and how we bring those aspects of ourselves to the experiences we have, and, in turn, how we are shaped by our experiences. Folklore is a vehicle for students to think about how our own traditions and cultures shape who we are and play a role in our identities. Eighth-graders are ready to consider themselves and their contexts in this way, and the module supports them with skills they need as they prepare for the work ahead in Modules 2, 3, and 4.

A worthy TEXT for eighth-graders doesn't shy away from sensitive TOPICS

Part of what is compelling and relatable about *Summer of the Mariposas* is also what can make it tough. The way that family relationships unfold in the text—including a parent being distant from the sisters, and unkind to the other parent—may connect to difficult situations that students are also dealing with. The text also mentions a murder and children's discovery of the corpse, illegal crossing of the border between the United States and Mexico, and Latin American folklore that includes references to magic, spells, witchcraft, and monsters. As always, Teaching Notes will support teachers to carefully and sensitively discuss these topics, and give students context as they read the story. Texts can provide both positive models from which to learn, and also negative lessons on which students can reflect in order to consider the "right" thing or the most effective/safe/legal course of action. The Teaching Notes throughout the module describe strategies teachers can employ to help students process the choices made by characters within the text.

The TARGETS support foundational work on theme

As a building block for the entire year, the skills students learn in Module 1 are foundational for the grade. Students do a lot with summarizing and thinking about theme. The Language standards focused on in this module work in service of the Reading and Writing standards. Students do a lot of work with vocabulary, figurative language, and connotation, all to help them unpack a fictional text, particularly toward meeting CCSS RL8.2: *Determine a theme or central idea of a text and analyze its development over the course of the text, including its relationship to the characters, setting, and plot; provide an objective summary of the text.*

As ELA teachers know, *theme* is a nuanced concept. It is a big idea, a message that develops over the course of the text, emerging from the events and character responses in the text itself. In *Summer of the Mariposas*, as in other literary works, several notable and thought-provoking themes develop over the course of the text. This module emphasizes two prominent and important themes ("Being kind and pure of heart can help people live fuller, more meaningful lives" and "Things are not always as they appear") and supports students to track their development in the text. This not only helps students deeply understand this particular text—it also allows students to better understand the concept of theme development, so it can become one of the capacities they bring to any rich literary text.

Grade 8, Module 2: The Four T's*

TOPIC: Food Choices

Guiding Questions and Big Ideas

» Where does our food come from?

» How do we analyze arguments about how food should be grown and processed?

» What factors influence our access to healthy food? How do we research this?

» What factors should we prioritize when making choices about our food? How do we share these recommendations with others?

TASKS

Unit 1: Build Background: Food Choices

» Watch the video clip "Why Eat Local" and read an excerpt from *Chew on This* to answer selected and constructed response questions to analyze the author's point of view and perspective; analyze the structure the author uses and how it contributes to key points; and evaluate arguments, considering whether or not the evidence is sound and sufficient (mid-unit assessment).

» Read the informational text "Is Eating Healthy Really More Expensive?" and watch the video clip "No Free Lunch." Answer selected and constructed response questions to analyze the purpose and motive behind information presented in these different mediums, evaluate the advantages and disadvantages of using different mediums to present information, and analyze cases in which two sources disagree (end of unit assessment).

Unit 2:

» Research to answer the question "How might climate change contribute to a food shortage?" (mid-unit assessment).

» Participate in a Desktop Teaching protocol to share with classmates research findings about how the topic of choice impacts access to healthy food (end of unit assessment).

Unit 3:

» Read a new excerpt from *The Omnivore's Dilemma* and answer selected response and short constructed response questions to analyze language in *The Omnivore's Dilemma* (mid-unit assessment).

» Write an argument essay to defend a claim about how communities can make healthy food choices (end of unit assessment).

Performance Task: Roundtable Presentations of Food Choices

TARGETS (Standards explicitly taught and formally assessed)

» **Unit 1:** RI.8.5, RI.8.6, RI.8.7, RI.8.8, RI.8.9, RI.8.10, SL.8.2, SL.8.3
» **Unit 2:** RI.8.1, W.8.7, W.8.8, SL.8.4, SL.8.5, L.8.6
» **Unit 3:** W.8.1, W.8.4, W.8.6, L.8.2, L.8.2a, L.8.4, L.8.4a, L.8.4b, L.8.5, L.8.5b, L.8.5c, L.8.6

TEXTS

Throughout the Module: *The Omnivore's Dilemma* by Michael Pollan

Additionally:

» **Unit 1:** *Chew on This: Everything You Don't Want to Know about Fast Food*; "Is Eating Healthy Really More Expensive?"; *Nourish: Short Films: 54 Bite-Sized Videos about the Story of Your Food*
» **Unit 2:** "Sticking Up for Coke, Sort Of"; "The Advantages and Disadvantages of Pesticides"; "To GMO or NOT to GMO"; "Food Desert"; "Organic Food"; "A Shock to the Food System"

* Note: Four T's boxes are found in the Unit Overviews for each module and may contain more detail than this module-level summary.

Grade 8, Module 2 Overview

In this module, Students read *The Omnivore's Dilemma* and watch related video clips from *NourishLife*. Students then evaluate the authors' motives, purposes, and points of view, including whether and how conflicting viewpoints are addressed. Additionally, students evaluate the advantages and disadvantages of using different mediums to convey information, write an argumentative essay about the food choices they think would most benefit their community, and present their claim to an audience.

How do the Four T's interact in Grade 8, Module 2?

A TOPIC that honors student agency

At the heart of this module is the idea that choices we make as individuals impact our world and the people in it. Eighth-graders are in the midst of developing more and more autonomy, and they are ready to genuinely consider questions like "How do the choices I make about food help me contribute to a better world?" and "How can I make responsible choices?"

A TEXT that may illuminate different points of view, and TARGETS to give students a process

Each student will come to the text from different circumstances, and some of what is in *The Omnivore's Dilemma* and other module texts may bring these differences to the fore. Some students may be upset or may find their values conflict with descriptions of poor treatment of cows in feedlots, or of chickens on free-range farms. Students may be sensitive to the topic of access to food based on their own access to food. Students may also be sensitive to the way the texts discuss fast food, high-fructose corn syrup, and obesity, especially if they don't have much control over the food they eat or if they or others they know are experiencing situations similar to those in the text.

Throughout the module, the targets students are working toward build their skills for encountering information that bears on their life, and that may activate their sensitivities. Students follow a process of exploring a topic, researching, and getting information first before making a judgement. Only then do students start trying to make a strong argument. Students are learning to make sense of the information they receive about the world, and, through standards-based targets, this module equips them with a container and a process for that important work. Once they have developed an informed argument, students build the essay out into an infographic based on an analysis of different media, the ways point of view is communicated, and the advantages and disadvantages and what's effective in the format. Putting their skills in making an argument and presenting it to use helps students see more value in building their content knowledge.

A TEXT that models the TASK as well as informs about the TOPIC

The Omnivore's Dilemma is a high-leverage anchor text because it serves a dual purpose: as a source of information, and also a model. Michael Pollan starts by posing a question, and sets the tone for a spirit of inquiry throughout the module. He makes specific arguments about food choices in a way that is grounded in objective, verifiable information. Eighth-graders do their first argument writing in this module, and the text is a place for them to start building knowledge about the topic grounded in a model of what argumentation looks like.

Grade 8, Module 3: The Four T's*

TOPIC: Voices of the Holocaust

Guiding Questions and Big Ideas

» What was the Holocaust, and how did it occur? Why do we remember it?

» How did victims and survivors respond, and how can we honor their voices?

» How did upstanders respond, and what can we learn from their voices?

TASKS

Unit 1: The Holocaust: Build Background Knowledge

» Read a chapter of *Maus I* and answer selected and constructed response questions about language, dialogue, tone, and character (mid-unit assessment).

» Write a summary of of *Maus I*, including a theme statement (end of unit assessment).

Unit 2: The Holocaust: Voices of Victims and Survivors

» Answer selected and constructed response questions to compare and contrast the structure and theme of "The Action in the Ghetto of Rohatyn, March 1942" and *Maus I* (mid-unit assessment).

» Read a summary paragraph of an excerpt of the memoir *The Boy on the Wooden Box* and answer selected and constructed response questions about verb conjugation, voice, and mood (end of unit assessment).

Unit 3: The Holocaust: Voices of Upstanders

» Read a text reflection on how Nicolas Winton was an upstander and edit paragraphs for punctuation and verb voice and mood (mid-unit assessment).

» Write a narrative depicting a fictional interview with an imaginary upstander during the Holocaust (end of unit assessment).

Performance Task: Create and Present a Graphic Panel Depiction of a Fictional Holocaust Upstander

TARGETS (Standards explicitly taught and formally assessed)

» **Unit 1:** RL.8.1, RL.8.2, RL.8.3, RL.8.4, RL.8.10, W.8.4, W.8.5, W.8.10, L8.1b, L8.3a
» **Unit 2:** RL.8.1, RL.8.2, RL.8.4, RL.8.5, RL.8.10, L.8.1, L.8.1a, L.8.1b, L.8.1c, L.8.1d, L.8.3, L.8.3a, L.8.5, L.8.5a, L.8.5b
» **Unit 3:** W.8.3, W.8.4, W.8.6, W.8.10, L.8.1, L.8.1b, L.8.1c, L.8.1d, L.8.2, L.8.2a, L.8.2b

TEXTS

Throughout the Module: *Maus I* by Art Spiegelman

Additionally:

» **Unit 1:** "The Holocaust: An Introductory History"
» **Unit 2:** "Often a Minute"; Excerpt from "Abe's Story: Excerpts & Synopsis"; Excerpts from *Night*; Excerpts from *The Other Victims: First-Person Stories of Non-Jews Persecuted by the Nazis*
» **Unit 3:** "Johtje Vos, 97; Sheltered Jews in Her Home in WWII Holland, Saving 36"; "The Forgotten Swiss Diplomat Who Rescued Thousands from Holocaust"; "Marek Edelman Obituary"; "1994, Miep Gies"

* Note: Four T's boxes are found in the Unit Overviews for each module and may contain more detail than this module-level summary.

Grade 8, Module 3 Overview

In this module, students read *Maus I* and analyze dialogue, tone, characterization, and theme. They write literary analysis essays to compare the structure and meaning of two texts. Students read accounts of victims and survivors of the Holocaust, analyze language, and write summaries. Students read accounts of upstanders during the Holocaust and write reflections on what qualities and actions made them upstanders. Students write a narrative interview about a fictional upstander, create a graphic panel based on this narrative, and present it to an audience.

How do the Four T's interact in Grade 8, Module 3?

<u>A careful sequence to support the TOPIC and the TARGETS</u>

This module starts in Unit 1 with a deep dive into one survivor's experience, then expands into exploring other experiences in Unit 2 using poetry and memoir. Then in Unit 3, students move into thinking about upstanders. This sequence was carefully designed to be a supportive way to help students build understanding about this topic—reckoning with the horror and suffering of this time, while keeping clear sight on the agency and humanity of victims, survivors, and upstanders.

Students engage in two sequences of close reading in this module—the first is with *Maus I* in the beginning of Unit 1. In most modules, typically students don't do close reading right away; but it was important to help students get acclimated to graphic novel format. This module includes CCSS RL8.5, the standard about text structure, so we built in support in accessing formats like graphic novels and poetry.

<u>Honoring voices through TARGETS about habits of character</u>

Any curricula about the Holocaust must truly honor the experiences of victims, survivors, and upstanders. The upstander component in our curriculum ties the topic to habits of character and makes it more real for students. The Holocaust is a difficult topic that we know will be difficult for students to work through—they are processing lessons about why it's dangerous when groups of people are targeted, and thinking through issues of large-scale power. Studying upstanders helps students find something positive that they can learn and apply from this dark time.

<u>TARGETS help students understand TEXT structure</u>

The work students do in Unit 2 is to compare the respective structures of *Maus I* and of a poem by Magdalena Klein. They are well prepared to do this work by the Language standards they study in Unit 1. In fact, this module has more Language standards than any other in Grade 8, which builds students' understanding of the structure of a text. Teachers are able to support students in using language to understand that bigger structural picture. This module also asks students to work with literary elements, which contributes to their big-picture understanding of each text.

The performance task for this module is to create a graphic panel, based on the fictional upstander interviews students write. This serves as a culminating experience: it's built directly on the narrative interviews, so there is an especially clear connection for students. *Maus I* is a graphic novel—when students come to the end of the module, they come full circle and use that format themselves to convey information about what they've learned.

Grade 8, Module 4: The Four T's*

TOPIC: Lessons from Japanese Internment

Guiding Questions and Big Ideas

» What were the causes and impacts of Japanese American internment camps?

» What are the main lessons that can be learned from Japanese American internment?

» How can people effectively apply the lessons of internment to their own communities?

TASKS

Unit 1: Build Background Knowledge: Lessons from Japanese American Internment

» Read chapter 5 in *Farewell to Manzanar* and answer selected response and short constructed response questions about vocabulary and how connections and distinctions are made between individuals, ideas, and events (mid-unit assessment).

» Use textual evidence and follow discussion norms to participate in an academic discussion centered on the first module guiding question: "What were the causes and impacts of Japanese American internment camps?" (end of unit assessment).

Unit 2: Write a Literary Argument: Significant Ideas in *Farewell to Manzanar*

» Read the Part 3 epigraph and a portion of Chapter 22 in *Farewell to Manzanar* and answer selected response and short constructed response questions about point of view, vocabulary, and how connections and distinctions are made among individuals, ideas, and events in *Farewell to Manzanar* (mid-unit assessment).

» Write a literary argument essay to evaluate the effectiveness of the choices made in the film *Farewell to Manzanar* in conveying the text using points, evidence, and reasoning to support a claim and to address a counterclaim (end of unit assessment).

Unit 3: Investigate, Discover, and Apply Lessons from Japanese American Internment

» Participate in a collaborative discussion to discuss what overarching lessons can be learned from Japanese American internment and how these lessons have been embodied in the redress movement (mid-unit assessment).

» Deliver a presentation as triads to share findings from research into how a community organization embodies lessons from Japanese American internment today (end of unit assessment).

Performance Task: Activists Assembly: Focus Group on Applying Lessons from Japanese Internment

TARGETS (Standards explicitly taught and formally assessed)

» **Unit 1:** RI.8.1, RI.8.3, RI.8.4, RI.8.10, W.8.10, SL.8.1a, SL.8.1b, L.8.4a, L.8.4b, L.8.5a, L.8.5c

» **Unit 2:** RL.8.1, RL.8.7, RI.8.1, RI.8.3, RI.8.4, RI.8.6, RI.8.10, W.8.1, W.8.4, W.8.5, W.8.6, W.8.9b, W.8.10, L.8.2c, L.8.5a, L.8.6 (L.8.1 and L.8.3 optional)

» **Unit 3:** SL.8.1c, SL.8.1d, SL.8.5, SL.8.6, L.8.6

TEXTS

Throughout the Module: *Farewell to Manzanar* by James D. Houston and Jeanne Wakatsuki Houston (book and film)

Additionally:

» **Unit 1:** Excerpt from the "Power of Words Handbook"; "Japanese Relocation During World War II"; "Surviving Poston's Desert Heat: Cellars, Fans, Ponds, and Gardens"; "Life in the Camp": excerpts from the Clara Breed Collection; "In Response to Executive Order 9066: All Americans of Japanese Descent Must Report to Relocation Centers"

» **Unit 3:** "Seeking Redress"; "Japanese Internment Camp Survivors Protest Ft. Sill Migrant Detention Center"; "Psychological Effects of Camp"; "Editorial: 75 Years Later, Looking Back at The Times' Shameful Response to the Japanese Internment"

* Note: Four T's boxes are found in the Unit Overviews for each module and may contain more detail than this module-level summary.

Grade 8, Module 4 Overview

Students read *Farewell to Manzanar* and analyze connections and distinctions among individuals, ideas, and events in the text. Students watch the film adaptation of *Farewell to Manzanar* and analyze how the film stays faithful to or departs from the text. Students write a literary argument essay to evaluate the filmmakers' choices. Additionally, students generate lessons from Japanese internment from their reading of *Farewell to Manzanar* and other informational texts. Finally, they research how community organizations are applying these lessons from Japanese internment today and present their findings to an audience.

How do the Four T's interact in Grade 8, Module 4?

A TOPIC students care about and a TASK to channel their care into their community

As students read the anchor text and the powerful supplementary texts, including one on modern internment, they are asking again and again: "What are the lessons from internment? Why do we still learn about it? Why do we still read *Farewell to Manzanar?*"

When it is time to work on the performance task, students have done a great deal of work to synthesize what they think those lessons are. They are then ready to research an organization in their community that embodies the lessons from internment, which may or may not be directly connected to Japanese internment. Students make contact with the organization via email or phone and use what they learn to make a presentation at an activist assembly. At the assembly, students make their presentations and then facilitate a discussion about the lessons from internment, how they are being applied, and how others can get involved.

A set of TEXTS that creates a nuanced understanding of TOPIC

Farewell to Manzanar conveys the first-hand experiences of young Jeanne Wakatsuki, who was imprisoned with her family at an internment camp for Japanese Americans. The experiences described may be upsetting or challenging for students to process. Wakatsuki is honest about her experience as a child. She grew up in the camp and so she made it her own, as a way to survive. One of the harder parts for her is what the experience did to her parents, and, in turn, what their parenting did to her. The last chapter is her realizing she'd never been able to get over having been unjustly imprisoned as a child.

At the same time, the text as a whole is largely upbeat, and offers only one very personal perspective on internment. In Unit 1 students do additional reading to complicate the story. In a "building background knowledge" (BBK) lesson, students are flooded with different perspectives and different genres: poetry, images, articles that offer more specifics about how many people were in the camps, and a narrative detailing the day-to-day physical aspects of life in a camp. This process gives them a broader sense of internment, so that when they are asked to trace significant ideas through the *Farewell to Manzanar* text and film in Unit 2, they have a sense of the context in which Wakatsuki is telling her story.

A thoughtful TASK and TARGETS that bring in interesting standards

A key consideration for the designers was how students should take notes when watching the film. The standard demands that their work center on how faithful the film was to the book, rather than about film techniques. Designers test-drove multiple versions of the note-catcher to ensure it was meaningful, doable, and would get the students to the skill of the standard.

The performance task was similarly well-planned by designers. It depends on contact with outside organizations, and that means teachers need support for the practicalities. Although students don't start getting in touch with organizations until Unit 3, teachers will start to see notes about the process in Unit 2, such as suggestions for pre-vetting local organizations, and reaching out to a few beforehand as well. So, while students are doing research, one of the three organizations they look into will have been teacher-chosen to ensure no one is scrambling in the end.

The "Fifth T": Time

The truth about this curriculum, and any curriculum, is that no matter how good it is, its success relies heavily on the Fifth T: *time*. Without your time spent learning deeply about the purpose of the curriculum as a whole and the practices embedded within it, the potential of the curriculum to accelerate literacy learning and equity for all students may not be fully realized. We focus on time a lot in Chapter 2A. There we'll give you some tools and techniques for unpacking and analyzing each part of the curriculum to help you feel ready to teach it.

Chapter 1C:
What Will It Take to Lead Schoolwide Change?

Whether you are a district leader, principal, instructional coach, or teacher who is leading the charge with this curriculum in your school, you know that change of this nature is not easy. You may find yourself supporting new teachers who are already feeling overwhelmed by learning how to manage a classroom alongside veteran teachers who may feel that what they are already doing is working just fine.

In almost every school, there will be some who are eager to get started with a new curriculum and some who are reluctant. This is a common dynamic in schools and districts; usually everyone can agree that they want students to succeed, but not everyone can agree on how to get there. This reality is actually quite healthy—neither teachers nor students are automatons, and our curriculum, like any curriculum, will root itself in the real conditions of your school and the people who interact with it. Helping everyone in your school community, including families, understand how the curriculum will accelerate literacy learning and excellence for all students is key to its success. For all of these reasons, strong and focused leadership is critical to the success of this work.

▶ AS A SCHOOL LEADER, HOW CAN I MAXIMIZE THE POTENTIAL OF THE CURRICULUM TO HELP STUDENTS AND TEACHERS SUCCEED?

No curriculum, no matter how comprehensive, is a panacea. Like a lot of things, you'll get out of it what you put into it. We feel confident that ours is a great curriculum; otherwise we wouldn't have published it. The principles it is built on and its focus on accelerating literacy learning and excellence for all will give students a strong foundation for success as readers, writers, and thinkers. While the curriculum itself has been highly rated by independent reviewers,[5] it will be most powerful when it is combined with strong and consistent professional learning opportunities for teachers.

A 2019 report by Mathematica Policy Research studied the positive impact our curriculum had on the instructional practices of teachers using the curriculum as part of our Teacher Potential

---

5. Edreports.org

Project (TPP)[6] and their students' subsequent achievement in ELA. One year after adopting TPP, the teachers participating in the study showed significant growth in their general instructional practices and in specific skills that research shows are key to higher student achievement, such as engaging students in reading, writing, and speaking about texts; supporting students' higher-order thinking; and increasing students' use of textual evidence. The researchers found that the students of TPP teachers (including those who received one year and those who received two years of professional learning support) demonstrated significantly higher ELA achievement than students in the control group. Not surprisingly, the students whose teachers had two years of direct professional learning support from TPP demonstrated even higher performance, with their growth equivalent to an added 1.4 months in just one school year.

We're proud of those achievements, but it probably doesn't matter to you what the researchers say! What matters is how it takes root in your school. Your efforts to create the conditions for success can make the difference between the curriculum living up to all that it can be and the potential for it to be just one more change for teachers to adjust to. You have a pulse on the needs of your teachers and students and deep knowledge of both strengths and areas of needed growth among your staff. Experience tells us that at the heart of the work we do is a need to tend to the people who are most deeply impacted by the changes that are on the horizon:

» How will you support them and set them up for success?

» How will you make space for risk-taking?

» How will you ensure that teachers have time to talk and plan together to make sense of all that they are learning?

» How will you articulate your encouragement of them and assure them that they are on the right path?

At its best, this curriculum is about reimagining what learning can look like for students. You may find that you and your staff will need to examine your current thinking about long-held instructional practices or your approach to student engagement. At the same time, you will likely see how the deep study of compelling, relevant topics will start to transform your students. As teachers begin to examine their practice and take risks, you will see them grow and transform as well. But, like a lot of journeys, it won't necessarily be a linear process for everyone, and it will take time. In the pages that follow, we offer suggestions, specifically for those in leadership roles, for where to start, how to dig deep, and how to find additional resources from EL Education.

> *"The core of our reform has to happen in the classroom or you aren't going to see a difference in [academic] outcomes. There is nothing more important than providing teachers with the right tools to be successful and a curriculum that is highly aligned to the standards and engaging for students."*[7]

Nikolai Vitti
Superintendent, Detroit Public Schools Community District

---

6. Teachers in the study were a part of EL Education's Teacher Potential Project, through which they participated in a variety of activities, including on-site institutes, coaching from EL Education professionals, interactive webinars, lesson studies, classroom observations, and professional learning communities within their schools. In addition, the project provided professional learning for school leaders and instructional coaches.
7. From the Detroit News, July 22, 2018

Managing Complex Change

Because every school is different, the most important first step for managing complex change is to find entry points that will be effective within the culture of your school.

Lay the Groundwork

» Be the lead learner. Though you may believe in the need for this change, it will be hard for you to help teachers navigate the implementation of the curriculum if you do not understand it well. We encourage leaders to actively participate in the change as much as possible. Consider adopting a classroom or two as case study classrooms that you can visit often, or consider doing some teaching yourself so that you better understand the instructional practices in the curriculum. Use the Unit-at-a-Glance charts, found in the Teacher Guide for each module, to maintain a sense of what's happening in classrooms and give yourself context for the lessons you'll see in the classrooms you visit.

» Form a team to help you lead this change and to maximize the support you are able to offer teachers.

» Build shared commitment to the need for change. In some schools, an examination of achievement data, combined with the research on the learning opportunity gap explored in Table 1.1, is a helpful place to start. In other schools, teachers may feel drawn to the compelling topics and active pedagogy in the curriculum. It's important that teachers see the curriculum as a solution to a problem they are having and not a top-down mandate. (See box: Tools for Managing Complex Change for change-management models we recommend.)

» Articulate for staff the ways in which the choice of curriculum can be a lever for equity. Take a stance that it is a priority for your school to ensure that *all* students have access to high-quality core instruction and that you will use the school's resources (i.e., time and people, primarily) to ensure that this can happen in the core classroom.

» Include staff in the strategic planning. Work together to set goals, gather data (e.g., student work, teacher observations), and make clear the relationship between the actions of adults in the building and the expected outcomes for students.

» Seriously consider what you should *stop* doing. As a leader, you can see the big picture of all that is happening across the school and district. As you plan for implementation of this curriculum, look around at other changes and new initiatives, and ask yourself, "What *must* we stop doing (because it's incompatible or redundant with this new curriculum)? What *can* we stop doing (to ensure we aren't doing too many things)?" This process isn't easy, but what we know for sure is that you are unlikely to be able to continue all that you have been doing *and* add this curriculum into the mix. You may need to rethink your approach to grammar instruction, the teaching of novels instead of teaching skills in the context of novels, and other long-held literacy practices. Importantly, you'll also need to include your teachers in these discussions and decisions so that they feel like changes are happening *with* and *in support of* them and not to them.

» Establish and intentionally nurture a schoolwide growth mindset. Acknowledge and celebrate that everyone is learning something new—administrators, teachers, and students—and no one has all the answers. Hard work and effort will make the difference.

» Attend to the language you use to message change to the school community. Messages that connote tackling a worthy challenge together will be supportive of teachers who may need inspiration and motivation.

» Examine current class grouping and scheduling practices. This curriculum is designed to work—and works best—in heterogeneous classrooms. We have seen that when students are grouped by ability, teachers struggle more with implementation, partially because they are needing to prepare very different versions of the lessons for each group they see, and partially because the design of the lessons presumes a heterogeneous group. When students are clustered at one level, powerful elements like protocols can't do what they are meant to do. (For more on the power of heterogeneous classrooms see Chapter 5A.)

» Be the lead listener. There will be bumps in the road along the way. It's important to listen to concerns and to approach each one with a collaborative, problem-solving spirit.

🔦 Tools for Managing Complex Change

Adopting our curriculum may mean a big change for your school. Consider using an existing model for managing complex change to guide you and your staff through this work. Here are a few that we recommend:

» The Beckhard and Harris Change Equation (Dissatisfaction x Desirability x Practicality > Resistance to change) may be a useful place for you to start to assess your school's readiness for change of this nature.

» The Knoster Model can help you assess the conditions and climate at your school against the five elements required for effective change: vision + skills + incentives + resources + a plan = sustainable change.

» The Concerns-Based Adoption Model (CBAM) can help you and your staff identify concerns as you progress through the stages of implementing something new. The seven stages of concern include awareness, informational, personal, management, consequence, collaboration, and refocusing.

Be an Instructional and Operational Leader

» Be ready to support teachers with the learning required to teach the curriculum. There's a lot to learn, and you'll need a plan. You know your school best and have a sense of the amount of change affecting teachers in your building and, in some cases, across the district. Look carefully at current literacy curricula and programs in your school. Ask yourself honestly how much change will be required of teachers and how much you think they can handle.

» Set up a schedule and structures for professional learning and collaboration, or consider how to use existing structures to meet teachers' new needs. This may include whole-staff meetings, team meetings, professional learning communities, book groups, and the like. This book, along with many of the resources listed at the end of this chapter, are good resources for this professional learning. You may also consider bringing in staff from EL Education for professional learning and/or coaching. Suggested topics for professional learning include:

- Managing change/coaching for change (for coaches and teacher leaders)

- The structure and content of the specific modules teachers will use (including the Four T's)

- How to approach the materials and prepare well (what's there, how to find it, and when to look at what)

- Management in the active classroom (addressing an increase in student engagement and activity in the classroom)

- Protocols (addressing what they are and why they are important)

- Academic mindsets, character, and social-emotional learning in the curriculum

- Student-engaged assessment in the curriculum (particularly learning targets)

- Differentiation (what's built in, and how to differentiate further when necessary)

- Close reading

- Strengthening writing with models, critique, and descriptive feedback

- When relevant: supporting English language learners

- Supporting students to meet grade-level expectations or who need additional challenges

» Teachers also will need dedicated time together to talk through what they are trying and how it's going. Ensure that in addition to structured learning on topics like those listed above, they have regular opportunities for reflection, sharing practices, discussions about each module's texts, and collaborative problem-solving.

» Set up effective feedback loops. Teachers will benefit from coaching support and feedback from leaders as well as opportunities to observe and learn from one another. Gather real-time data and celebrate success, gains, and early wins. If you have a team to support curriculum implementation, distribute leadership for this work.

» Take care of the logistics so that teachers can focus on their instruction. Setting up the daily schedule, scheduling professional learning for training and coaching, and communicating with families are all steps you can take that will shrink the change for teachers.

» Order (or designate someone to order) all of the materials teachers will need, including student texts. (If possible, support teachers even more by designating someone to organize and manage the materials.)

Assessing Your Readiness to Offer Support

Your role as an instructional leader also may need to change. Depending on existing practices in your school, what you see in classrooms using the curriculum may be different from what you are used to. Classrooms will buzz with activity. If your existing observation checklist rewards teachers with very quiet classrooms, for example, you may need to create a new one. Because you won't experience the same changes and eurekas that your teachers will on a daily basis, it's important that you learn as much as you can about the curriculum and the practices designed to help students be leaders of their own learning. We have many video and print resources on our curriculum website at http://eled.org/tools to support your exploration, and it's also important that you spend as much time as possible in classrooms so that you are as close to the experience of your teachers and students as you can be.

As you think about your role in making the curriculum a success in your school, consider the following questions and assess your readiness to offer support to teachers.

» Consider the schoolwide logistical implications of adopting a new curriculum:

- What do you need to do before you start using the curriculum?

- Do you need to change your master schedule?

- Do you need to reexamine staffing?

- What do you need to stop doing to give yourselves the best chance of success? This may involve letting go of some existing programs to protect time for the curriculum.

» What data do you have or should you collect to understand teachers' needs in teaching this curriculum?

» How well do you understand the research behind college- and career-ready standards and instructional shifts? How well aligned is your school to those standards?

» What professional learning do you personally need to best support implementation of the curriculum? Where might you need the help of other teachers, leaders, or outside experts to provide quality support to teachers?

» How can you adjust your personal schedule to maximize your availability to support the teachers in your building? Do you have a system in place to put classroom walk-throughs and observations on your calendar as "sacred" time?

» How can you gather evidence and provide growth-producing feedback to teachers?

» How can you assist teachers in looking at student work and assessments to guide instructional decisions and plan for future professional learning?

» How do you currently use time in the following areas? If it's not already, can any of this time be used for literacy-focused professional learning?

- Early release days

- Grade-level meetings

- Team meetings

- Whole-faculty meetings

- Curriculum committee meetings

- District and school administrator meetings

- Other structures

» What would a plan for support look like? Try mapping out a schedule of professional learning that meets your teachers' needs and takes advantage of structures already in place. Consider what additional structures could be put in place to offer greater support.

» What resources from EL Education can you use to support your work (see possible resources in the Instructional Leadership section at the end of this chapter)?

Proactively Addressing the Complexities You Will Encounter

As with any new curriculum adoption, you can expect complexities and challenges to arise. In Table 1.4, we highlight some of the complexities that you and your teachers will likely face. Proactively acknowledging these complexities with teachers is one way to build a sense that you are all working together to overcome challenges. This can go a long way in helping teachers not feel isolated with their struggles. In addition to highlighting several complexities and noting the reasons why they might occur, we also offer strategies that you might use to support problem-solving for each complexity.

Table 1.4: Implementation Complexities

Implementation Complexity #1
Managing Complex Change: You may face resistance from teachers.

Reasons This May Occur

» Change is hard, and some resistance is normal, especially within schools, which are highly complex systems with many moving parts.

» Teachers may not have enough information about the curriculum to see its value.

» Teachers have not been included in the process and feel that change is happening *to* them and not *with* them.

» Teachers don't have enough time to learn the curriculum's practices and structures or to collaborate with one another.

Leadership Strategies to Support Teachers

» "Go slow to go fast." In other words, invest time in the process of change so that resistance doesn't derail it. Spend time with staff analyzing student needs, learning about the curriculum, and identifying the ways that it can be a solution to a problem teachers are having. Build a vision and a plan for its implementation and hoped-for impact *together* with teachers.

» Communicate with staff transparently about the process of adopting and implementing the curriculum.

» Provide professional learning opportunities for teachers to learn the structures and practices in the curriculum, as well as time for them to collaborate and learn from one another.

» Help teachers see that the curriculum is an opportunity for them to learn and grow as teachers—it is not a script to follow, but a tool to use.

» Consider using a tried-and-true model for managing change (see box: Tools for Managing Complex Change).

Implementation Complexity #2
Pacing: Teachers may struggle to match the curriculum's suggested pacing.

Reasons This May Occur

» Teachers are learning a new curriculum; effective and efficacious implementation takes time. In the beginning of the year it is particularly common for teachers to use more time than is suggested for some components of the lessons (e.g., giving students much more time than is suggested to work with complex text, which can often lead to frustration and be counterproductive to the success of the lesson).

» Teachers are hanging on to existing practices that are comfortable and feel important to them and sometimes supplement or substitute these practices into lessons. This "mixing and matching" often slows the pacing.

» The curriculum promotes a higher ratio of student talk to teacher talk. Depending on current practices, teachers may need to work at not talking as much because it can slow pacing.

» There is a built-in intensity to the curriculum that requires students and teachers to work at a pace that may seem initially uncomfortable. Students have lots to do! Our experience tells us that in most cases, students and teachers rise, over time, to this level of rigor.

» Teachers may stretch one lesson out over multiple days because they are afraid students did not master the content.

» Teachers are not prepared ahead of time with the various materials needed in lessons, units, and modules (e.g., anchor charts, note-catchers).

Leadership Strategies to Support Teachers

» Offer empathy and encouragement to teachers. Saying, "Yes, pacing is an issue. You are learning something new" invites teachers to more safely engage in the productive struggle needed when they are first starting out.

» Remember that teachers are shifting their instructional practice. This happens to varying degrees and at different rates depending on multiple variables (e.g., a teacher's length of time teaching, the degree to which the curriculum requires teachers to shift their practice). Some teachers will need to unlearn old practices; as they embrace these changes, their pacing will improve and their confidence in the curriculum will grow. Newer teachers may not be as challenged by pacing as veteran teachers, as they have less to unlearn.

» Encourage teachers to ask, "When will students talk, and when will I talk?" as they prepare for lessons. This will help them be mindful of not talking too much.

» Ensure that teachers have common planning time to discuss pacing and other complexities of practice that emerge in the implementation of the curriculum. Looking ahead through lessons, units, and modules will also support them with materials management. Guidance on planning, including task cards for teachers, can be found in Chapter 2A.

» Help teachers understand that the curriculum spirals through Reading, Writing, and Speaking and Listening standards over time; they are repeated in multiple lessons and various components of the curriculum. Reassure teachers that if students do not meet standards the first time around, they will have several more opportunities to do so. For this reason, encourage teachers not to stretch lessons over multiple days.

» Encourage teachers to use a timer.

» Emphasize that students are not expected to understand one hundred percent of all complex texts, including every academic vocabulary word. They are refining their understanding of a topic *over time*. As they build content-related vocabulary and background knowledge, students' understanding of texts will increase.

Implementation Complexity #3

Classroom Management: Teachers may struggle to adapt to managing an increased activity level in their classroom.

Reasons This May Occur

» The curriculum depends on students collaborating and becoming leaders of their own learning. This often means an increase in student activity and talk in the classroom.

» There are multiple student engagement strategies used throughout the curriculum, including protocols. Protocols can appear to be messy and unorganized at first.

» There are natural management issues in active classrooms.

Leadership Strategies to Support Teachers

» Promote active classrooms where students are collaborating, talking, and moving. Celebrate and honor teachers who are courageous in implementing new strategies; it can take multiple tries to feel comfortable.

» When teachers ask, "Can I just skip the protocols?" encourage them to keep at it. Protocols need to be taught, rehearsed, and reinforced multiple times; they are worth the effort because during protocols students are challenged, engaged, and empowered to learn more deeply. Protocols ensure equal participation and accountability in learning.

» Encourage teachers trying a new protocol with students to be very clear initially with their expectations. The following steps can be done fairly quickly; however, some pre-planning may be necessary each time a new protocol is introduced. When teaching a new protocol for the first time, some adjustments to the timing of other lesson sections may be necessary so that you and your students have five or ten extra minutes to learn the ropes:

- Provide a model and unpack success criteria with students.

- Give students real-time feedback during the protocol, based on success criteria.

- Facilitate student reflection and goal-setting around success criteria for subsequent uses of the protocol.

» Choose a few protocols to use in staff meetings and professional learning so you and your staff become more accustomed to them. Ask teachers which they recommend.

» For additional reading, see Chapter 2 of this book and the Classroom Protocols section of our curriculum website (http://eled.org/tools). You may also wish to purchase the EL Education book *Management in the Active Classroom* or view its accompanying videos, which can also be found on our website, at: https://eleducation.org/resources/collections/management-in-the-active-classroom-videos

Implementation Complexity #4

Mindset: Teachers and/or students may describe the curriculum as "too hard."

Reasons This May Occur

» Students and teachers are often engaging in new and unfamiliar tasks. Students are reading text that is complex in language, structure, and content. It is hard!

» Students are asked to write for multiple purposes, with higher expectations and in higher volumes than they may be accustomed to.

» Students may be asked to embrace greater levels of independence, perseverance, and personal ownership of learning than they are used to.

» Teachers are finding that students score lower on curriculum assessments than on assessments they gave in the past.

» If students are grouped into class sections based on previous assessments, teachers may say the work is fine for some classes but too hard for others.

» The curriculum moves slowly in places to build deep conceptual understanding and encourage higher-level thinking. Occasionally teachers may feel that the curriculum is "easier" than what they have done in the past because some components don't move as fast as what they are accustomed to. In these cases, the hard work for teachers may be trusting the process of slowing down and going deeper.

Leadership Strategies to Support Teachers

» Remind teachers that getting used to the rigor of the curriculum will take time. Implementing the curriculum is a process of change that all are engaging in together over the course of the year.

» Remind teachers that as they raise expectations, students may find tasks and texts "too hard." Teachers will need to coach students on habits of character such as *perseverance*, *collaboration*, and *productive struggle*.

» Ensure that classes are as heterogeneous as possible.

» Provide reassurance to teachers that they will begin to grow more confident and comfortable with each module.

» Ensure that teachers have clear guidance about the school's grading policies and how the mid- and end of unit assessment results should be reported. (see Complexity #6)

» Talk to teachers about having a growth mindset about themselves as professionals and about their students as learners.

» Unify teachers around a central message that curricular choices are made to support students in building stronger literacy skills and more word and world knowledge and, ultimately, to prepare them for the world that awaits them. The curriculum is designed to compel and support students to work together to tackle challenging materials and solve difficult problems.

» Highlight that this curriculum is a core curriculum for all students. Students should not be given less complex text as a replacement for grade-level text. More on scaffolding texts and tasks for students is provided in Chapter 5 of this book, and plenty of guidance is offered in the lessons themselves.

Implementation Complexity #5

Curriculum Purpose/Use: Leaders and/or teachers may misperceive that this curriculum is the only literacy instruction that students need.

Reasons This May Occur

» Because the EL Education Grades 6–8 Language Arts Curriculum is a comprehensive curriculum that addresses all college- and career-ready ELA standards, and because it is designed for 45 minutes of instructional time every day for an entire year, it is easy to assume that it will "cover" all ELA needs for students. However, students who are not meeting grade-level expectations may still need additional support.

Leadership Strategies to Support Teachers

» Plan for the fact that students who are not meeting grade-level expectations, especially in reading, will require additional instructional time and interventions that meet their unique needs. Our curriculum is one component in a well-balanced system of instruction that should also include independent reading time and, for some students, foundational or remedial skill work.

» Promote the adoption of additional materials and curricular resources for use beyond the 45 minutes of instruction dedicated to the modules in order to meet the unique challenges of the population of students served in your school or district.

» Examine your master schedule and scheduling practices to ensure that the maximum time for literacy instruction is allotted in the school day.

» Promote dialogue with teachers in all content areas about approaching literacy instruction in their classrooms. Literacy should be taught across all content areas.

» Utilize a multidisciplinary team meeting approach to analyze student needs and best instructional practices. These meetings could include staff from one school or staff from across multiple sites in the district. Ensure that there is representation from a variety of staff with specialization in the following areas: reading, special education/students with disabilities, intervention, differentiation, and ELLs to discuss how best to meet student needs.

» Ensure that adequate staff/parent/community support is in place to meet the diverse needs of the population of students served in your school or district.

Implementation Complexity #6

Grading: Leaders and/or teachers seek guidance on grading student work and reporting on student progress.

Reasons This May Occur

» The curriculum does not specifically provide guidance on how to assign grades on individual components of the curriculum (e.g., point value, letter grades).

» Student work often is assessed using standards-aligned rubrics, rather than letter grades (which may be unfamiliar for some teachers).

Leadership Strategies to Support Teachers

» Provide time for grade-level teams to calibrate regarding grading practices, and ensure grade-level decisions align with schoolwide policy.

» Give teachers specific time to examine the Assessment Overview and Resources found in the Teacher Supporting Materials for the module. These materials include sample student responses and scoring guidance (e.g., rubrics, checklists) that show teachers what proficiency looks like for a given standard or set of standards at a particular grade level.

» Give teachers time to analyze and calibrate the writing rubrics (opinion, informative/explanatory, and narrative) as well as various checklists (for Speaking and Listening standards, Language standards, and some ongoing assessment of reading) that are used in the Grades 6–8 modules.

» Use a process or protocol that promotes looking at student work as a way to assess student progress on standards (see Chapter 6 for more information).

» Remind teachers that every lesson includes Ongoing Assessment. Teachers need not collect or record all this data, but there are specific suggestions for formative assessment.

» Promote conversations about using learning targets as a way for students to self-assess progress toward standards. (Note: Learning targets are discussed in more detail in Chapter 2B.)

» Ensure that time is spent creating a common vision for how student achievement is measured. See the EL Education Dimensions of Student Achievement in Figure 1.2.

» Assure teachers that as long as grading and reporting aligns with the school's policies, you will support them in conversations with parents who have questions about assessments or scores.

Chapter 1:
Instructional Leadership

We believe that impactful instructional leadership involves cycles of action and reflection. Here we offer questions for reflection, indicators of progress, and resources for the *planning phases of implementation*.

Table 1.5: Chapter 1 Quick Guide for Instructional Leaders: Planning for Implementation

Questions for Reflection
» How do you currently define student achievement?
• Now that you've read about EL Education's three Dimensions of Student Achievement (see Figure 1.2), what are your next steps as a school to identify and celebrate achievement in all three dimensions?
• What steps have you taken to cultivate students' academic mindsets—that they belong in the academic community, that they believe they can succeed, that their ability and competence grow with effort, and that their work has value to them?
• What do you already do to foster a spirit of equity in the school—that all students deserve and can be successful with challenging work? What more can you do to foster success?
» What bridges can you build between what the curriculum offers and areas of need identified by teachers or by school-level data?
• How will you share the research behind the design of the curriculum to build understanding and support for its adoption in your school?
• Do you and your teachers understand the "deep logic" of the curriculum's design (i.e., the Four T's) well enough to know when and how to customize it if necessary?
» Have you and your staff developed a vision for change and a plan for how to get there?
• Do teachers feel included in the vision (i.e., it's being done *with* them and not *to* them)? How do you know?
• Have you ensured that your school schedule will accommodate this curriculum? Are teachers and leaders clear about what they may need to stop doing as they implement the curriculum?

- What complexities or challenges have you already identified? Who can help you see what you might be missing? What is your strategy for managing change of this nature?

- How does your school cultivate a culture of risk-taking and trust?

Indicators of Progress

» Teachers demonstrate a growth mindset with regards to their own professional learning and student achievement.

Not Yet True   *Somewhat True*   *Very True*

» Teachers express a belief that all students deserve the opportunity to do challenging work and that they can provide them with the tools they need to do it.

Not Yet True   *Somewhat True*   *Very True*

» Teachers understand the research behind the curriculum design.

Not Yet True   *Somewhat True*   *Very True*

» Teachers see the value of a curriculum grounded in content-based literacy.

Not Yet True   *Somewhat True*   *Very True*

» The district/school consistently provides teachers time, structures, and supports for planning and professional learning.

Not Yet True   *Somewhat True*   *Very True*

» Professional learning time is devoted to learning about the curriculum: its design, the research that supports it, and its potential impact on student learning and teacher growth.

Not Yet True   *Somewhat True*   *Very True*

» Leaders have a clear vision and action plan for successful implementation that will lead to student achievement and educator impact.

Not Yet True   *Somewhat True*   *Very True*

» School staff feel that they have a voice in developing the vision and process for adopting the curriculum. Structures are in place for staff to share successes and voice concerns or questions, and they trust that they will be heard respectfully. Leaders have outlined a plan for progress monitoring (e.g., walk-throughs are to be conducted by the Implementation Team three times in the implementation year).

Not Yet True   *Somewhat True*   *Very True*

» Teachers are supplied with necessary texts and curricular and supplemental materials (e.g., chart paper). The potential challenges teachers may face have been addressed through professional learning and logistical support so that teachers can focus on quality instruction.

Not Yet True   *Somewhat True*   *Very True*

» Successful curriculum implementation is a priority in this district/school with no competing literacy initiatives.

Not Yet True   *Somewhat True*   *Very True*

» The school schedule supports successful implementation of 45-minute lessons, and includes additional intervention time within or beyond ELA class (see Chapter 5).

Not Yet True   *Somewhat True*   *Very True*

Resources and Suggestions

» The curriculum itself, along with a full suite of companion resources and tools, can be found at: Curriculum.ELeducation.org. Resources include:

- Curriculum Plans (zoomed-out overview of the entire Grades 6–8 band)

- Curriculum Maps (zoomed-in module-by-module details for each grade)

- Grades 6–8 Required Trade Book Procurement List

- Grades 6–8 Recommended Texts and Other Resources

- Classroom Protocols

- Why Use Books to Teach Literacy?

- Topic and Text Selection Rationale for Grades 6–8

- Welcome Letters to Families for Grades 6–8

» Additional resources can be found on the main EL Education website (ELeducation.org):

- Online Canvas Course: Introduction to the EL Education Grades 6–8 Language Arts Curriculum (second edition)

- Videos: https://eleducation.org/resources/collections/your-curriculum-companion-6-8-videos

- PD Packs

  ○ Culture of Growth

  ○ Coaching for Change

- Professional Development Opportunities (or email pd@eleducation.org)

» Books by EL Education that deepen understanding of practices in the curriculum:

- *Management in the Active Classroom*

- *Leaders of Their Own Learning: Transforming Schools through Student-Engaged Assessment*

- *The Leaders of Their Own Learning Companion: New Tools and Tips for Tackling the Common Challenges of Student-Engaged Assessment*

- *Transformational Literacy: Making the Common Core Shift with Work That Matters*

- *Learning That Lasts: Challenging, Engaging, and Empowering Students with Deeper Instruction*

- *Your Curriculum Companion: The Essential Guide to Teaching the EL Education K–5 Language Arts Curriculum*

» Website: achievethecore.org (Common Core resources)

Chapter 1: Before You Begin: The Foundations of the Curriculum

Chapter 1A: What Makes This Curriculum the Right Choice for Me and My Students?

Chapter 1B: How Did Research Impact the Design of the Curriculum, and What Difference Will It Make to My Students?

Chapter 1C: What Will It Take to Lead Schoolwide Change?

Instructional Leadership

▶ Frequently Asked Questions

Chapter 1:
Frequently Asked Questions

I recognize that this curriculum has a lot to offer my students, but I'm going to miss designing my own. What opportunities are there to put my own stamp on it?

Depending on your teaching experience and your comfort level with the instructional practices embedded in this curriculum, you may feel ready to begin enhancing or customizing some elements of it right away. However, we strongly recommend that you spend at least a year teaching the curriculum and getting used to the rhythm and flow before making too many changes.

Some components of the curriculum are easier to put your stamp on than others. You may have favorite discussion protocols or total participation techniques, for example, that you have been using for years. There's no reason that you can't continue to use those old favorites as long as they achieve the same purpose as the ones written into the curriculum. In terms of the modules, one of the best enhancements is to find local connections for your module topics, particularly related to the performance tasks. Is there additional fieldwork that students can do to deepen their learning? Can experts in the field visit your classroom? Can you provide a service learning component related to the module topic? (See Chapter 5B for much more information on challenging students through work with experts, fieldwork, service, and extensions). Though many ELA teachers at the Grades 6–8 level will be limited to one period a day with our curriculum, your school may be structured into teams, and this is a good opportunity to work with science or social studies teachers to consider how the content of the ELA modules can be enhanced in their classes. We do not recommend making changes to the texts, tasks, topics, or targets (the Four T's) of a module.

I'm nervous that this curriculum is going to be too hard for some of my students. Are there ways I can adapt it for students who may struggle?

Our approach to supporting students who may struggle is not to adapt, but to scaffold. We want all students to have access to rigorous content, engaging texts, and opportunities for sophisticated thinking and discourse. Rather than denying students these opportunities, the curriculum offers scaffolds that give them the support they need to succeed. Throughout the curriculum, you will find extensive guidance in the Teaching Notes section of each lesson—look for the subheading "Support All Students." There is also a Teacher's Guide for English Language Learners that accompanies each module. This book offers guidance for lighter and heavier support for English language learners for every lesson of every module as well as numerous scaffolded materials that can be used with any of your students, not just ELLs. We urge you to nurture your own growth mindset as a teacher and to embark on this journey with a belief that your students can do it and that you can give them the support they need.

You talk a lot about content-based literacy. Does this mean there's less time for skills work?

Content-based literacy means that students are learning key literacy skills (e.g., determining the main idea in a text) as they learn compelling science and social studies content. Content-based curriculum isn't in opposition to skills—it's more like a vehicle for skills. Learning literacy skills in the context of learning important content actually accelerates literacy learning (refer to the research in Table 1.1). In our curriculum, there's not less time for teaching skills, but time is used differently; skills work is woven into student learning about content. Instead of teaching discrete literacy skills with a random assortment of materials that aren't connected to one topic (e.g., practicing determining the main idea in articles about dolphins, then Argentina, then the water cycle), we connect them through compelling content (e.g., as seventh-graders learn about how the Lost Children of Sudan overcame tremendous challenges on their journey through Southern Sudan, Ethiopia, and Kenya in search of safe haven, they also are developing their ability to analyze narratives and to create their own stories).

I know I'm going to have to answer a lot of questions from parents and guardians about why we chose this curriculum. What's the best resource for explaining the why behind the what?

There are different resources you can choose from based on the level of interest of your community. The Welcome Letter to Families for your grade level is a great place to start. If families are eager to go a litter deeper, Chapter 1A of this book can provide an overview of the principles on which the curriculum is built. For those eager to read more about the research, Table 1.1 is a good summary. In fact, all of Chapter 1B makes a compelling case for the design of the curriculum, based on research. For those who want a more general, easy-to-access overview, we suggest directing them to our website to explore videos and other resources and to learn more about the compelling content in the curriculum (Curriculum.ELeducation.org).

We don't use the Common Core State Standards in my state. Is this curriculum still going to work for us?

If your state is not using the Common Core State Standards, there's a good chance that it is using college- and career-ready standards that closely resemble them. You or your school or district leaders may need to do some mapping of the standards we use onto yours. We can't speak for every possible context, but we are pretty confident that this curriculum addresses ELA/literacy standards in most locations. We have also chosen module topics that address science and social studies content that is commonly taught in states across the country.

The curriculum doesn't give us any time for additional skills/grammar work or writers' or readers' workshop. When will we fit those in?

Our curriculum is comprehensive, designed to help students achieve mastery on all grade-level college- and career-ready standards during a 45-minute per day ELA period for a full school year. If your school schedule allows for only one 45-minute ELA period, the curriculum may be the only ELA curricula you offer. This may be frustrating for you as a teacher who feels that your students need additional support. Finding a solution will require the support and collaboration of school leadership. If one 45-minute period is insufficient to meet the needs of most students, can creative scheduling solutions be considered? Can an additional period be offered for interventions? Can block scheduling be considered? This is not something that any individual teacher can solve on their own. It may require some innovation and creativity on the part of school leaders.

I'm familiar with the first edition of EL Education's 6–8 curriculum. How does this new edition compare? Are there overlaps, or is it all new?

Originally designed and developed with a team of teachers in 2012, the national interest in our Grades 6–8 Language Arts curriculum has been inspiring. The first edition was originally commissioned by New York State, which required a total of six modules per grade and alignment to the state's Social Studies and Science Standards. Though initially designed with New York teachers as the primary audience, the curriculum has found a home with a national audience of educators who are seeking out curriculum that uses authentic texts and is directly aligned to the standards. To meet this need, we have created a second edition that broadens the curriculum's relevance to schools nationally and incorporates feedback from teachers across the country.

For a full accounting of all the very specific second-edition enhancements, see the introduction to this book and/or the first few pages of every module Teacher Guide.

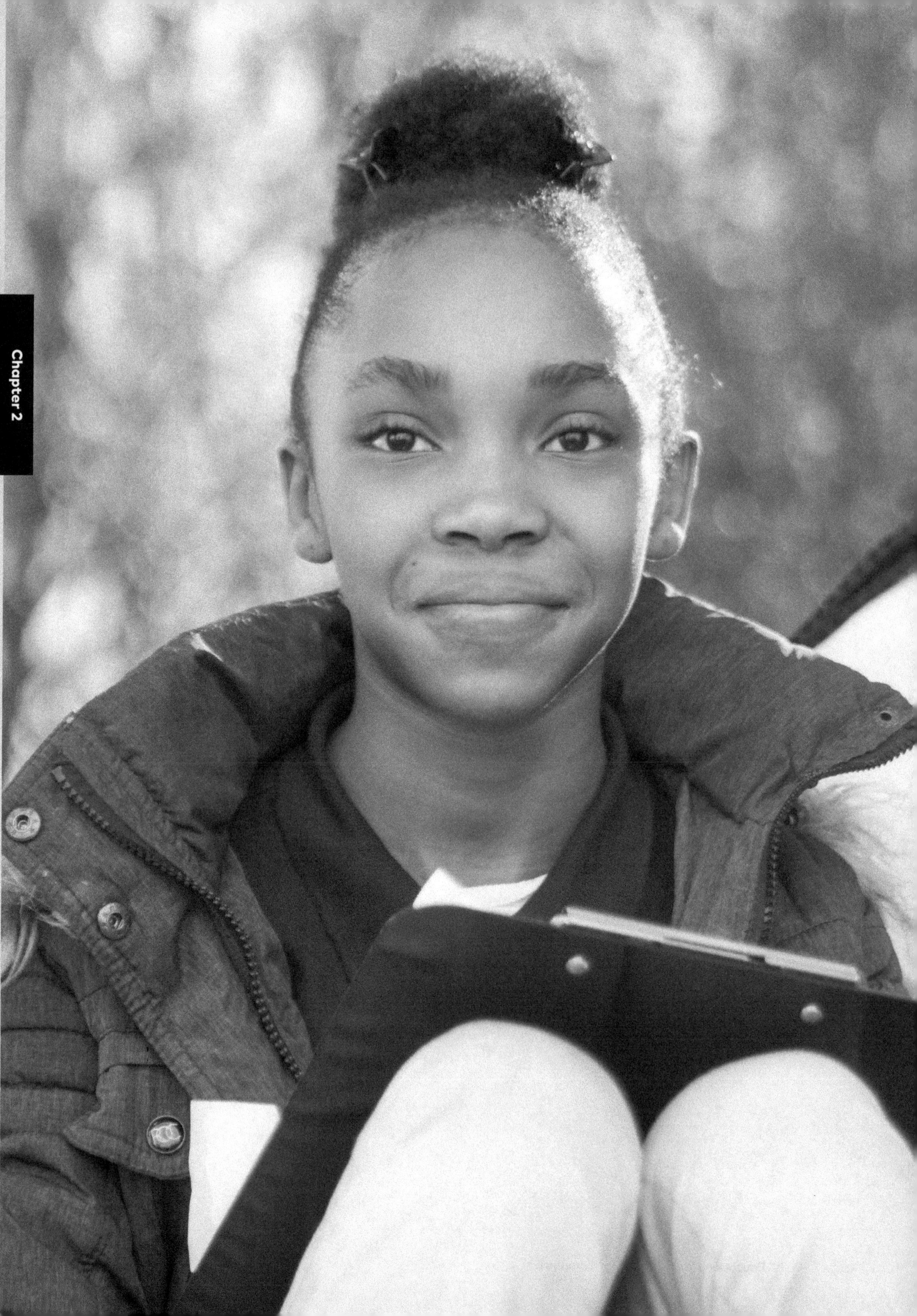

Chapter 2:
Preparing to Teach: Planning for Challenge, Engagement, and Empowerment

Chapter 2A:
How Do I Plan When the Planning Has Been Done for Me?

Our curriculum is comprehensive. It includes everything you need to teach and assess college- and career-ready English language arts (ELA) standards. It is also compelling, built around topics we know middle school students will be interested in, full of books that are worth reading and proven strategies to help them become better readers, writers, speakers, listeners, and thinkers. As you and your students dig into and become accustomed to these new materials and practices, we feel confident that they will grow as readers, writers, and thinkers and that you will grow as a teacher, too—you will undoubtedly learn new things, no matter how much experience you have in the classroom.

It may be tempting to think that such a comprehensive and detailed curriculum means that you won't have to do much planning. After all, hasn't the planning already been done for you? Yes and no. The answer to that question is more complex than you might think.

▷ This is a thinking teacher's curriculum. It is not a script. Our goal is for teachers to be less concerned with *fidelity* to the words on the page and more concerned with upholding the *integrity* of the purpose of the curriculum.

Teaching our curriculum will require a different kind of planning than you may be used to. You'll need to look out across units and modules to understand the flow of the year. And, although you won't need to plan a lesson from scratch, you will need to plan for each lesson to make it your own and the best it can be for your students. This is a thinking teacher's curriculum. It is not a script. Our goal is for teachers to be less concerned with fidelity to the words on the page and more concerned with upholding the integrity of the purpose of the curriculum.

Conducting lessons exactly as they are written and adhering strictly to the timing, language, and suggestions provided is possible, but it's not necessarily typical, nor is it recommended.

This *fidelity* to the way the curriculum is written doesn't account for the dynamic and unpredictable ways in which a classroom full of students interacts with the material. A question from a student may take the class in an unpredictable, but worthwhile, new direction; students may struggle to find the answer you want them to find in the text or need a robust discussion of norms before engaging in a protocol; or the mundane realities of life in school—from fire alarms to snow delays—can disrupt, delay, or redirect a lesson. These "hiccups" to the best-laid plans are actually the most predictable part of teaching.

Knowing this, our goal is to help you teach the curriculum with *integrity*. This means understanding the deep logic of the design, as well as our commitment to challenging, engaging, and empowering all students, so that making changes to accommodate the living, breathing organism of the classroom still results in students meeting standards and achieving at high levels. Understanding, for example, that grappling with challenging text is a purposeful feature of close reads and serves an important role in developing students' literacy muscles may help you consider how best to scaffold the lesson for particular students to ensure that they have access to the same challenging text and can feel successful reading it. Similarly, understanding the purposes and benefits of protocols will help you avoid the temptation to skip them or, if necessary, to swap one protocol for another with a similar purpose. Just as students start each module by building background knowledge of their topics, this book is designed to help you build background knowledge of the curriculum so that you can make the most of it in your classroom.

★ A Coach's Perspective on Teaching with Integrity

EL Education coaches often explain "teaching with integrity" as "keeping the Four T's intact." The Four T's interrelate so closely that changing one would mean changing all of them; at that point, you would no longer be teaching the curriculum.

» The TOPIC is the driver for what texts were selected, how targets are written, and what tasks the students will complete.

» TASKS: Everything students do throughout the first half of a unit builds up to the mid-unit assessment; likewise, the second half of a unit builds to the end of unit assessment. The task is always written to reflect the features and demands of a particular text.

» TARGETS are how the standards show up; the sequence of lessons in the module build up to the assessments, and the standards themselves were selected to be a tight match with the texts.

» The TEXTS were carefully selected to best teach the relevant targets (standards) in a way that engages students with the topic.

Attending to the Four T's, i.e., keeping them intact, will allow you to be more nimble with lessons when necessary.

(See Chapter 1B for extensive details about the interplay of the Four T's in each module of the Grades 6–8 curriculum.)

▶ WHAT KIND OF PLANNING WILL HELP ME TEACH THE CURRICULUM WITH INTEGRITY (NOT JUST FIDELITY)?

Teaching this curriculum with integrity requires deep knowledge of it. Knowing where you are headed over the long term allows you to make more informed decisions in the short term. If you are not sure what's coming tomorrow or next week, you may find yourself feeling unsure of how to make informed decisions to best support your students' learning today. This can sometimes lead to an overreliance on fidelity to the words on the page of any given lesson, as if it were a script.

On the other hand, if you have looked ahead and understand how standards spiral in and out of lessons over days and weeks, and you have analyzed the assessments and the ways in which students prepare for those assessments, you'll be able to use your wisdom and experience as a teacher to be responsive to the needs of your students within your fast-paced, always changing classroom environment.

Zooming in: From Wide-Angle to Close-Up

With teaching with integrity as the goal, it will be important for you to engage in both a yearlong "wide-angle" unpacking of the curriculum and a lesson-level "close-up" unpacking.

Wide Angle Planning

Looking over the year with a wide-angle lens will help you get a feel for the flow of the four modules, including how standards are taught and assessed across the year. In addition to the wide-angle, yearlong view, it will also be important to engage in a slightly zoomed-in, midrange module- and unit-level analysis four times a year, well before you start teaching a new module.

Close-Up Planning

The close-up lesson-level view, which occurs weekly and daily, will ensure that you understand each lesson fully and that you have a chance to consider the needs of your particular students, including the supports and materials they may need above and beyond what's included in the lesson. This is your time to think through the logistics of each lesson. How will you make it your own? How will you keep your notes to stay organized? How will you prepare for the inevitable distractions or account for the fact that your students have lately needed extra time with things like transitions and paper management?

Refining Lessons

You might be starting to think that that's a lot of unpacking to do! It is; however, it's the kind of preparation that allows you to spend your time taking a lesson you know is already solid and making it the best you can for your students. It may help to think of the process more as refining than as planning. Rather than running around looking for a good text or being forced to improvise because you ran out of time to plan, you can instead spend your time considering the best grouping strategies for your English language learners (ELLs), for example. Or, perhaps you can spend time preparing the materials in such a way that the students you see after lunch, who have been struggling to begin work promptly, will have just what they need to begin right at their seats when they walk in. Reading ahead, taking notes, and making the lesson your own will help you attend to these kinds of small details because they matter a lot, especially to your students, and they can make a big difference in both what and how students learn.

> *"This is why it's called a thinking teacher's curriculum, because you do have to make those difficult decisions to scaffold your students to success, to know what to help your students dig into and what to let go of."*

Breah Johnson
Teacher, Alpharetta, Georgia

For the remainder of Chapter 2A, we're going to walk you through the process of unpacking the entire curriculum, starting with the wide-angle lens (the yearlong view) and working our way to the close-ups (the daily lessons). We will provide brief descriptions of the documents you'll need to reference, followed by task cards that will help you and your colleagues dig in.

★ **A Word about Unpacking the Curriculum**

Since the first edition of our curriculum was released in 2012, it has been downloaded more than ten million times. Some schools and teachers have used it on their own, along with our publicly available tools, and some have sought support from EL Education directly. We've "unpacked" this curriculum at the year, module, unit, and lesson level with thousands of teachers at this point, and what we can say for sure is that there truly is no *one* way to do it. There are, however, certain questions that we know are important for teachers to answer for themselves as they go through the process. And, as they seek these answers, it's important that they learn the materials well enough to move through them with ease. It can be a bit of a treasure hunt!

One set of tools we offer are the task cards on the following pages. The Long-Range (Year-Level), Mid-Range (Module-Level), and Short-Range (Unit-Level) task cards are completed infrequently. We expect you'll work with these during summer planning time or periodic professional learning days at your school. They are designed for a deep review of how the curriculum unfolds over the course of the year, and it's important to analyze them carefully.

The Up-Close (Lesson-Level) task card offers the same deep review, but of just a single day's worth of instruction and materials. While it is powerful to look at a lesson this way, it isn't practical to look at *every* lesson this way. We recommend using it several times at the beginning of the year, and internalizing the questions that serve you and your students best. Most teachers end up landing on a process for lesson preparation that incorporates some combination of deep questions about what will best meet their students' learning needs, along with the necessary logistics that make the lesson run smoothly. EL Education coaches have collaborated with teachers to write these processes down, and design simple preparation tools in addition to the task cards (a few examples of these tools follow the task cards at the end of Chapter 2A).

As you get used to how the lessons work, you will judge what's most helpful to you and, if it makes your life easier, create your own preparation tool that best meets your needs. You may find that 20 to 30 minutes gives you plenty of time to read the lessons, think through the needs of your students, and prepare your materials.

The task cards that follow, as well as detailed planning templates, can be found on our website (http://eled.org/tools). You can download them and either print them or work from digital copies.

Orienting to the Year

There are two documents that will give you the widest view of the curriculum: the **Curriculum Plan** (which includes Grades 6–8) and the **Curriculum Map** (one for each grade level). These documents will orient you to the big picture of the skills and content focus of the modules.

The Curriculum Plan, which is the widest-angle lens, will orient you to how the four modules will unfold across the year at your grade level, as well as the full Grades 6–8 band. One thing you will notice when reading the Curriculum Plan is that the high-level focus of each module is the same for each grade. Students in each grade will experience the same general flow in terms of the skills they will build in each module.

The focus of the Grades 6–8 modules:

» Module 1: Reading, Writing, and Speaking Grounded in Evidence

» Module 2: Researching to Build and Present Knowledge

» Module 3: Analyzing, Interpreting, and Evaluating Text

» Module 4: Researching to Write and Present Arguments

The Curriculum Map zooms a little closer into the four modules for your grade level, detailing the texts, assessments, performance tasks and standards across the entire year. This document is critical to your understanding of the flow of the modules, how each module builds on the preceding module, and when and how often each standard is assessed. As you read, consider how the modules connect to other requirements in your school or district. For example, if your school or district has curriculum maps in place for science and social studies content, how can standards covered in each module fit into that agreed-upon scope and sequence? The Year-Level Planning Task Card that follows will help you see the big picture of how the curriculum unfolds across the year.

LONG-RANGE (YEAR-LEVEL) PLANNING TASK CARD

Key Resources and Tasks:

» Read the Curriculum Plan for the Grades 6–8 grade band.

» Read the Curriculum Map for the grade.

Suggested frequency: Once in summer; revisit as needed

Suggested people: Teachers, coaches, and building leaders

School structures needed: One or two hours of collaborative or individual planning time, supported by a coach when possible, with as much lead time as possible before school starts.

In each task card we offer questions that will help teachers, coaches, and building leaders get to the heart of the curriculum. We ask: "Why" (big-picture student engagement); "What" (the content and skills students will learn); "When" (flow and timing considerations); and "How" (key instructional moves).

Table 2.1: Long-Range (Year-Level) Planning Task Card

Why: Big-Picture Engagement	Response
» What are you looking forward to over the course of the year? What do you think your students will most enjoy? How will they benefit from this curriculum?	

What: Content and Skills	Response
» How might you describe the literacy work in your classroom this year to your students or their families? » What will be true about students' knowledge and skill mastery by the end of this year?	

When: Flow and Timing	Response
» How does the curriculum spiral the ELA standards throughout the year? » What implications does the standards grid in the Curriculum Map have for your pacing? (e.g., "If my seventh-graders are struggling with CCSS L.7.2 in Module 2, I should look for it again on the Curriculum Map; that standard shows up strongly in Module 4, so I don't necessarily need to slow down in Module 2.")	

How: Key Instructional Moves	Response
» What implications does the standards grid have for your planning? (e.g., "Based on their standardized test scores from last year, I'm thinking that my students may struggle with CCSS L.8.1a. I can plan to adjust my instruction by...")	

Orienting to a Module

There are several key documents that will orient you to each module: the **Module Overview** and the **Assessment Overview** will offer a high-level look, and the three **Unit Overviews** taken as a whole will reveal how the "story" unfolds over the course of the module. If you teach ELLs, the Teaching Notes for each unit in the **Teacher's Guide for English Language Learners** will offer a high-level sense of the supports available for the module.

The Unit and Assessment Overviews will give you a good sense of the specific skills students are building as they gear up for the performance task at the conclusion of the module. Test-driving assessments and performance tasks is one of the highest-leverage planning moves you can make. We recommend that you take the mid- and end of unit assessments well before students do, which you can do now or as part of unit-level preparation. We also recommend that you attempt the performance task. Naturally, you will not have the benefit of all the lessons and materials that will support students, but making even a rudimentary mock-up will teach you something valuable about what is required for an excellent podcast, museum exhibit, or graphic panel.

In order to really understand what you are planning for, you will also need to read the texts of the module. In our experience, reading just enough to keep slightly ahead of students ends up making planning much harder, and so we recommend that before beginning Unit 1, you read all the module's required texts.

The familiarity you build with these texts, in the big-picture context of the content and skills addressed in the module, will be much more impactful if you know how your students are stepping in. For this reason, we recommend analyzing student work and/or data from the previous module (or previous year), particularly on standards that you know will be repeated, so that you can take best advantage of the options you'll see in the Teaching Notes for each lesson.

MID-RANGE (MODULE-LEVEL) PLANNING TASK CARD

Key Resources and Tasks:

» Analyze student work or data from the previous year (or relevant current data; see Chapter 6 for more information).

» Read the Module Overview.

» Skim the three Unit Overviews (you will read them closely later).

» Read the Assessment Overview.

» Read the Performance Task Overview and complete the performance task yourself.

» Read all texts in the module.

Note: It is important that you read each text in its entirety; however, students won't necessarily read every page of every book during the course of a module. As you read, do not be too concerned about whether your students will be able to access the entire text; the lessons are designed to support them to master standards as they focus deeply on short sections.

Suggested frequency: Once a quarter; at least two weeks before starting each module

Suggested people: Teachers and coaches

School structures needed: 2–3 hours of collaborative or individual planning time; support in analyzing student data; additional time to read module texts (will vary by grade level)

In each task card we offer questions that will help teachers, coaches, and building leaders get to the heart of the curriculum. We ask: "Why" (big-picture student engagement); "What" (the content and skills students will learn); "When" (flow and timing considerations); and "How" (key instructional moves).

Table 2.2: Mid-Range (Module-Level) Planning Task Card

Why: Big-Picture Engagement	Response
» Consider the guiding questions, big ideas, and anchor texts. What's most exciting to you, and what do you think will be most exciting for your students?	
» In addition to the anchor text(s), what do students read? What will your students like best about these texts?	
» What is intriguing, surprising, or confusing about the topic or texts? How might the topic and/or texts be challenging for you or your students? What issues might come up?	
» If you have taught the module before: Consider the optional experts, fieldwork, service, and extensions. How might you incorporate one of these additions to enhance the authenticity of the performance task?	
» How might extensions be added into the workflow of the module/unit without extending *too far* or requiring major curriculum shifts?	
What: Content and Skills	**Response**
» Describe in your own words what this module is mostly about, in terms of both the content students are learning and literacy skills they are building.	

When: Flow and Timing	Response
» How do the three units and their assessments build toward the performance task?	

How: Key Instructional Moves	Response
» Look at the standards explicitly taught and formally assessed in this module. Do you anticipate needing to provide any additional support for particular students? » Based on your students' needs, where might you embed additional support into the existing lessons? (e.g., "I know that my students struggled with CCSS L.8.1a on the end of unit assessment, so I can plan to adjust my instruction by inviting students to keep a log identifying gerunds, participles, and infinitives in their complex texts before the next module's L.8.1a ongoing and summative assessments.") » If you teach subjects beyond ELA, where else in the day can you reinforce the standards on which students need additional support? » Where might you have to prioritize or expand instruction for ELLs in this module?	

Orienting to a Unit

Each unit contributes to the story of the module by focusing instruction around the specific literacy skills necessary to holistically study the module topic. Reviewing the **Unit Overviews** will bring more of the details into focus as you continue the process of "zooming in" closer and closer to daily lessons. If you teach ELLs, you will also want to refer to the Teaching Notes for the unit in the **Teacher's Guide for English Language Learners** for the module and peruse the materials for the unit.

In each Unit Overview, there is a small box called the Four T's (see Figure 2.1 for an example). This box will give you a quick snapshot of the topic, tasks, targets, and texts of the unit. If you have time, we recommend covering this box up with sticky notes (no peeking!) and grappling with the Four T's on your own or as a team as you examine the documents. Grappling is good for students; it's also good for you. Searching for this information will likely make it stick a bit more than just reading it.

It is important to read all three Unit Overviews to get a sense of the big picture of how the three units build on one another and how they fit together to tell the story of the module. The Unit-at-a-Glance charts are an especially important component of the Unit Overviews. Most teachers reference these charts frequently to understand the arc of each unit, how lessons build toward assessments, the recommended scaffolding (including key anchor charts), the protocols used across the unit, and when each text is introduced and how much time is recommended to spend on each. When reviewing the Unit Overviews, it is also a good idea to refer to the **Recommended Text and Other Resources List** to ensure that your classroom has the materials students will need to build their knowledge of the module topic.

The highest-leverage move you can make in preparing to teach a unit is to take the mid- and end of unit assessments yourself. Go to the Unit-at-a-Glance chart, find which lessons contain the assessments, and flip to the Supporting Materials for those lessons. Taking the assessments will give you a deeper sense not only of what students are working toward, but what kinds of answers correspond with various levels of mastery of the relevant standards.

You will want to analyze all three units of a module; however, you may opt to take a collaborative approach to this work, and you don't have to analyze all three before beginning the first. For example, with your grade-level team and/or other support specialists who are involved with your class (e.g., English as a second language teachers), you might consider a "jigsaw" structure to divide and conquer the analysis of the three units, with each teacher completing one of the Unit-Level Planning Task Cards on the following pages. Build in time to share information with one another and revisit this information on your own before teaching. Whether reviewing the Unit Overviews on your own or as a team, if your time is limited:

» Prioritize analyzing how the units work together to create the arc of the entire module.

» Chunk the unit into two halves, and focus on how the lessons in each half scaffold toward the assessments: what is expected of students, and how do the lessons get them there?

Figure 2.1: Sample Four T's Box from the Grade 7, Module 2, Unit 3 Overview

The 4 Ts

TOPIC

Epidemics: Spread the Message: How to Respond to Epidemics

TASK

Read a new article; answer selected and constructed response questions to analyze how individuals, events, and ideas interact in the text; and conduct research to answer a question.

Present a podcast script, focusing on coherence and organization of information, volume, clarity, and formal, conventional English.

TARGETS

RI.7.1, RI.7.3, RI.7.4, W.7.7, W.7.8, SL.7.4, SL.7.6, L.7.3a, L.7.4, L.7.6

TEXTS

Patient Zero

"Kindness Contagion"

"Social Contagion: Conflicting Ideas"

Various Research Texts

"Are Social Epidemics Real?"

SHORT-RANGE (UNIT-LEVEL) PLANNING TASK CARD

Key Resources and Tasks:

» Read the Unit Overview.

» Read the Unit-at-a-Glance chart.

» Take the unit assessments (or divide among team members). We know it's tempting to skip this step; don't skip it!

Suggested frequency: About every two weeks; at least a week before the beginning of each unit

Suggested people: Teachers

School structures needed: 1–2 hours of collaborative or individual planning time; ~45 minutes to take the unit assessments

In each task card we offer questions that will help teachers, coaches, and building leaders get to the heart of the curriculum. We ask: "Why" (big-picture student engagement); "What" (the content and skills students will learn); "When" (flow and timing considerations); and "How" (key instructional moves).

Table 2.3: Short-Range (Unit-Level) Planning Task Card

Why: Big-Picture Engagement	Response
» How does this unit connect to previous learning, and build toward future learning? » What do you think students will like about the particular task and/or texts of this unit?	
What: Content and Skills	**Response**
» Describe in your own words what this unit is mostly about, in terms of both the content students are learning and literacy skills they are building. » Once you've taken the assessments, examine the scoring tools (e.g., rubrics, sample student responses, checklists) found in the Assessment Overview and Resources section of the Teacher Supporting Materials for the module. What standard(s) are being assessed? How will you know if students are proficient?	

When: Flow and Timing	Response
» Looking at the Unit-At-A-Glance Chart in the Unit Overview: • Considering the pattern of learning for the first five lessons, what is the main skill(s) students are being asked to learn and master? • What patterns of instruction and learning do you find? What are students being asked to learn and master over these lessons? • Scan through the Ongoing Assessment column of the chart, and choose a few to look at in the Teacher Supporting Materials. How do these formative assessments build toward the mid- and end of unit assessments?	

How: Key Instructional Moves	Response
» Look at the standards explicitly taught and formally assessed in this unit. Do you anticipate needing to provide any additional support for particular students? » When you look at the rubrics, checklists, and sample student responses for the unit's assessments, what do you conclude about the support/scaffolding students will need to be successful on the assessments?	

Orienting to the Lessons

The primary document you'll reference at this stage—the "close-up" stage—is the specific **Lesson** you are preparing to teach.

Like most teachers, your lesson planning process most likely involves toggling between looking out over the week or weeks ahead and then focusing in on what's right in front of you—tomorrow (or even today!). The process with our curriculum is no different. To prepare well for what's coming tomorrow, it's important to situate individual lessons within the module and unit, and it's *critical* to spend focused time understanding and preparing for individual lessons and the arcs of lessons that may occur over the course of several days.

Each lesson in our curriculum provides detailed descriptions of everything from the purpose of the lesson, as stated in the learning targets, to the materials you will need, to suggested language for introducing new vocabulary, text-dependent questions, and myriad other "moments" in the lesson. Extensive Teaching Notes are provided to help you think through the key parts of the lesson and how each connects to previous and future lessons.

As curriculum designers, we've put tremendous thought into every part of every lesson, and we hope that they will come alive as you apply your own wisdom and expertise to delivering them. But the lessons need your input to be the best they can be, and not all the information we provide will be critical to your daily preparation. This is why analyzing each lesson and understanding its greater purpose is so important. Because all the basics for a strong lesson are already there, you can spend your prep time really thinking through how to make it most effective and engaging for your particular students and, importantly, how you are going to deliver it. (We offer advice on delivering your lessons in the section titled "How Can I Stay on Track and on Target with My Pacing?" which follows the task cards and planning tools.)

The Lesson-Level Task Card on the following pages will help you analyze and gain comfort with the lessons. Use this task card often when you're first starting out. Over time, you may find that you need it less and less.

UP-CLOSE (LESSON-LEVEL) TASK CARD

Key Resources and Tasks:

» Keep the Unit-at-a-Glance chart handy, as well as any other task cards you've completed.

» Read the lesson or series of lessons in the Teacher Guide.

» Review the lesson's Supporting Materials.

» If applicable, review the ELL-specific materials in the Teacher's Guide for English Language Learners (e.g., differentiated note-catchers).

Suggested frequency: We recommend using a task card like this several times at the beginning of the year, and then again for the first couple of lessons in a module, to give yourself a chance to notice key design features and use them to greatest effect. After that, it's most typical that teachers develop their own daily/weekly planning process; we've included some examples on the pages that follow.

Suggested people: Teachers

School structures needed: Collaborative or individual planning time; time and/or support for preparing lesson materials

In each task card we offer questions that will help teachers, coaches, and building leaders get to the heart of the curriculum. We ask: "Why" (big-picture student engagement); "What" (the content and skills students will learn); "When" (flow and timing considerations); and "How" (key instructional moves).

Table 2.4: Up-Close (Lesson-Level) Task Card

Why: Big-Picture Engagement	Response
» Look at the Teaching Notes, paying close attention to the Building on Previous Lessons and Down the Road sections. How does this lesson connect to previous lessons and build to future ones? » What forms of assessment are in this lesson, and when do they appear (e.g., checklists, note-catcher)? » How does the assessment connect to the learning targets for the lesson? » How does this assessment build toward the mid-unit assessment, end of unit assessment, and/or performance task? » What will your students most enjoy about the lesson? What might be challenging for them (or for you as a teacher)? » How will you help students understand the purpose of their work (including how each section of the lesson connects to learning targets)?	
What: Content and Skills	**Response**
» What cognitive work will students be doing during this lesson? (Hint: look at the verbs in the learning targets.) » What will students be reading, thinking, talking, and writing about in this lesson? » What will students be learning and what are the tasks for each portion of the lesson? » Read the Purpose of the Lesson section of the Teaching Notes. Is the purpose for each section of the lesson connected to the main skill of the learning target, or is it to build the routine of a protocol? » How do the graphic organizers or note-catchers scaffold students toward learning targets?	

When: Flow and Timing	Response
» How will you know if students need additional support? » When do protocols and anchor charts appear in the lesson? » How do the protocols and anchor charts help students achieve mastery of the intended learning? » What other parts of the lesson might need to be tightly timed in order to ensure you have time for the protocols?	

How: Key Instructional Moves	Response
» What materials do you need to prepare, for yourself (e.g., slides or a "Cliff's Notes" version of the lesson)? » What materials do you need to prepare for students? Are there already differentiated materials? Will they work for your students as is, or do they need further customization? » How will student reading, thinking, talking, and/or writing be scaffolded in this lesson? » What suggested questions in the lesson (or additional questions) are most important for student understanding? What is the purpose for asking these questions? » What additional questions could you ask when students get stuck with the question(s) provided in the lesson? How might you scaffold your questions to deepen understanding? » What kinds of collaborative work will happen in this lesson? What is your grouping strategy? » What planning is necessary to make transitions successful? » How will you ensure that you protect time for the closing reflection?	

Summary: Next Steps	
» What do you most want to remember as you are teaching? » What questions from this task card, or the others, most helped you feel well-prepared to teach a lesson?	

Simple Daily Lesson Preparation Tool

Purpose: This template is designed to support teachers as they prepare to deliver lessons from EL Education's Language Arts Curriculum. A digital version of this tool is available at https://eled.org/tools

Directions: EL Education's lesson plans are comprehensive. As you read through your lesson plans in preparation for teaching, consider completing this simple form as a more concise lesson plan that you can use both before and during your lessons to guide your instruction.

Date:

Module: **Unit:**   **Lesson:**

Daily Learning Targets	How is this assessed in the lesson?

Notes for preparation:

To Do Ahead of Time		To Do Ahead of Time	
Materials to Copy/Locate		Charts to Make/Directions to Write on Board	
Student Work to Grade/Distribute		Scaffolds/Supports to Prepare	

Skeletal lesson agenda:

Section	Time	What is the teacher doing? What are the students doing?	Scaffolds/Supports
Opening			
Work Time A			
Work Time B			
Closing and Assessment			

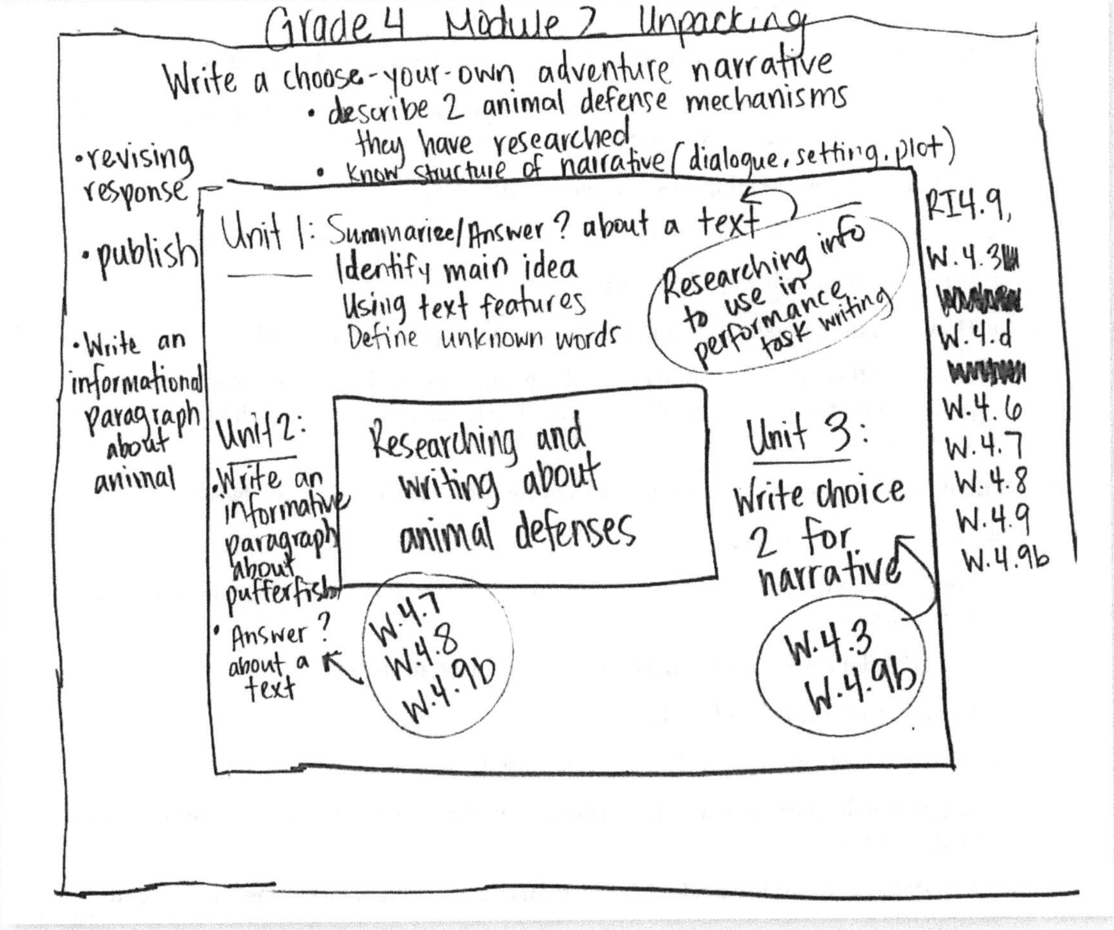
Grade 4 Module 2 Unpacking
Write a choose-your-own adventure narrative
• describe 2 animal defense mechanisms they have researched
• know structure of narrative (dialogue, setting, plot)
• revising response
• publish
• Write an informational paragraph about animal
Unit 1: Summarize/Answer ? about a text
Identify main idea
Using text features
Define unknown words
Researching info to use in performance task writing
Unit 2:
• Write an informative paragraph about pufferfish
• Answer ? about a text
Researching and writing about animal defenses
W.4.7
W.4.8
W.4.9b
Unit 3:
Write choice 2 for narrative
W.4.3
W.4.9b
RI4.9,
W.4.3
W.4.d
W.4.6
W.4.7
W.4.8
W.4.9
W.4.9b

The Boxing protocol is a way for teachers to collaboratively explore module or unit materials as they prepare to teach. Kristen, an EL Education coach, led teachers in an unpacking process with this chart that they can refer back to all year. The center box is the story of the module; the middle box is a snapshot of the unit assessments and their connections to the performance task; and the outer box is a synopsis of the performance task and the key learning students will need to do throughout the module to master it. The Boxing protocol can be done with curriculum materials at any grade level. For details on this process, and more tools like it, visit http://eled.org/tools.

Janey's Lesson Planning Steps

Janey, a coach for EL Education, developed this process based on her observations of what teachers seemed to need most when planning at the daily/weekly level. The task cards on the previous pages will help you deeply understand the structure of the curriculum, which will help you teach it more impactfully. And, at the same time, every teacher needs a way to efficiently internalize the most relevant details to get ready to teach *tomorrow*. That's what Janey's Lesson Planning Steps do best.

STEP 1: Look at the Unit Overview.

» Skim all learning targets for the week.

» Look for patterns of instruction and learning. What are students being asked to do this week?

STEP 2: Look at Learning Targets for your first lesson.

» What do we want students to learn by then end of this lesson (intended outcome)?

» Write down a few words to describe this outcome next to your learning target(s) (e.g., Purpose = how to have a collaborative discussion).

STEP 3: Look at the Ongoing Assessment for the lesson.

» Look at any materials used in the assessment (e.g., checklist, note-catcher).

» What are students being asked to do?

» How does the assessment connect to the learning targets for the day?

» How does this assessment build toward the mid- or end of unit assessment, and/or performance task? (e.g., scaffolds the structure for summary paragraph in mid-unit assessment)

STEP 4: Read Purpose of Lesson and Down the Road in the Teaching Notes.

» Look for key purposes.

» Look for how future lessons build off of this one. What materials will you use spanning several lessons?

STEP 5: Highlight Protocols and Anchor Charts used in the lesson.

» Skim through the body of the lesson.

» Highlight every protocol and anchor chart used.

» Determine the purpose of each protocol and anchor chart. Write a short purpose note next to each one.

STEP 6: Read each section of the Lesson Plan (i.e., Opening, Work Time, Closing and Assessment).

» For each section, THINK: Is this connected to the **Main Skill** of the learning target or is it a **Routine**?

» Connected to the **Main Skill**?

- If yes, STAR IT! *

- THINK: How do the anchor charts and protocols help students achieve mastery of this skill? (Reminder: protocols and anchor charts are about putting students in the driver's seat of the thinking and learning.)

- THINK: Which text-dependent questions are <u>most important</u> for student understanding? What is the purpose for asking each question?

» **OR** is this section teaching a **Routine**?

- If yes, write an R by it.

- How does this routine (e.g., protocol) support the main learning of the lesson? What supports and practice will your students need to be successful with this routine?

- You may consider introducing the routine or protocol prior to the lesson as a support to students.

▶ HOW CAN I STAY ON TRACK AND ON TARGET WITH MY PACING?

Maintaining the suggested pacing when teaching the curriculum is likely to be challenging, especially your first time through and especially over the course of Module 1, when the structures and routines of the curriculum are newest to students and possibly newest to you. With practice, the minute-to-minute pacing decisions about where to linger and where to zoom will become second nature, and you'll feel increasing confidence about how to "fit it all in." The steps laid out in the preceding pages will help ground you in the big picture of where you're headed and can allow you enough foresight to adjust if necessary. As you plan for specific lessons, consider the following steps to guide wise, carefully considered pacing decisions.

Before the Lesson

» Study the lesson in advance individually or with your grade-level team, using the task card or another template for unpacking a lesson. The more familiar you are with the lesson, the easier it will be to move through the components with fluidity.

» As you analyze the lesson, ask yourself: "When will students talk?" and "When will I talk?" Consider inviting a colleague into your classroom to take note of when you are talking and when students are talking, or invite them to videotape you. Often it's too much teacher talk that leads to the lesson getting off track in terms of pacing. It takes practice to get the balance right.

» Consider one or more of the following strategies to prepare you to deliver the lesson:

- If you have a printed version of the lesson, use it as is, but mark it up with a highlighter or use sticky notes to keep yourself focused and to aid a smooth delivery.

- Create a "Cliff's Notes" synthesized version of the lesson with the main chunks to cue you for the flow. Within each chunk, highlight in large text specific phrasing, questions, or instructions. Consider using or adapting the Simple Daily Lesson Preparation Tool found earlier in the chapter or on our website (https://eled.org/tools) to help you create these notes and customize your delivery of the lesson.

- Create a PowerPoint or Smartboard Notes that will guide you through the lesson with visuals of the learning targets, directions for protocols, text-dependent questions, images, vocabulary words, or other lesson elements that will be helpful cues for you and your students. You can also use the notes section of the PowerPoint to include specific questions and other things you want to remember to say in a particular way.

- Write the agenda out on the whiteboard with key words to cue you about the contents of each part of the agenda. Use the lesson itself to reference as needed, with things you want to say highlighted or pointed to with sticky notes for easy visual reference.

» Talk to your colleagues. Is another teacher in your building a few lessons ahead of your class? Can you talk with them about successes and challenges? Are there any barriers to avoid? Make note of their suggestions and consider whether they would be helpful in your class.

During the Lesson

» Use a timer. Setting a timer sends a message to students that there is a sense of urgency and that staying on task is important. The timer is likely to help you maintain the pacing of the lesson; it will also be appreciated by many students.

» Stay on topic and aligned with the learning targets. Students may be interested in learning more, but before being led astray by their many questions, consider alternatives for exploring additional topics. Some teachers have offered students extra credit or offered individual research opportunities in areas of interest. Explain to students why it's important to stay on topic. Study the flow of the module ahead of you so you know if the things students have questions about will be the topic of a future lesson.

» Balance briskness and thoroughness as you unpack the learning targets. The lesson will offer specific suggestions for how to unpack the learning targets, which frequently include a focus on vocabulary. It's important to be thorough, but don't linger there too long. The average time you should spend unpacking the learning targets is 3–5 minutes. When more than the recommended amount of time is spent on the learning targets, this segment is likely to turn into a mini lesson, which is not the intention.

» Pay attention to when students will talk and when you will talk during the lesson. It's easy to unintentionally use up a lot of time explaining things to students. The lessons are designed to let students figure things out on their own. Try to keep your teacher talk aligned to the facilitation and guidance they need.

"For daily planning, I make sure I know where we are heading for the week and then I condense the lessons into my own personal planning document using trigger words from the curriculum to help me remember where to go next in the lesson. I always make sure I have the materials prepared the day before so that everything is on hand when I need it."

Sara Metz
Teacher, Denver

» During work time, catch students' attention to clarify misconceptions or answer questions and then release them back to the task as soon as you can.

» Plan for and practice transitions. Moving from one section of a lesson to another can be a time waster. Have materials ready in advance, and spend time at the beginning of the year practicing with students. It will pay off to "go slow to go fast" with transitions—front-load students' attention on efficient transitions early in the year to save time later. This kind of attention may mean that Module 1 takes ten weeks instead of eight to nine, and that is okay.

» When teaching a new protocol for the first time, some adjustments to the timing of other lesson sections may be necessary so that you and your students have 5 or 10 extra minutes to learn the ropes:

• Provide a model, and unpack success criteria with students.

• Give students real-time feedback during the protocol, based on success criteria.

• Facilitate student reflection and goal-setting around success criteria for subsequent uses of the protocol.

» When using protocols you have already taught and practiced, maintain the recommended timing noted in the lesson. If you are running short on time, use your discretion—you may be able to substitute one protocol for another as long as it serves the same purpose. Once you have taught a protocol, it may be signaled as a "Repeated routine" in the lesson. This signal assumes that you are familiar enough with the protocol to proceed without any written instructions in the lesson. This gives you discretion, but may also mean that you'll need to be extra vigilant about your pacing and timing.

» Be very cautious about cutting a portion of the lesson. Remember to maintain the integrity of the lesson and consider its greater purpose in terms of the intended content and skills students are meant to learn. It's also important to know where the lesson is leading; look at the Down the Road section of the lesson's Teaching Notes, the Four T's for the modules, and the mid- and end of unit assessments to understand if a missed lesson component will end up impacting later lessons (e.g., students won't have a note-catcher they need to show their learning on an assessment, or the class won't be able to reference an anchor chart as part of a protocol).

After the Lesson

» Keeping in mind that this curriculum spirals, so skills will be revisited again and again over the course of the year, consider whether some students would still benefit from the re-teaching of certain pieces of the lesson at another time. If so, when could this small group instruction take place?

» Jot down any thoughts or notes about the timing of the lesson for the following year. Were there sections that could be condensed? Were there sections that needed more time than the lesson allotted?

» Save samples of student work to use as models next year. Strong models of work help teachers "show, not tell" students what they are aiming for, decreasing the amount of time needed to get students headed in the right direction.

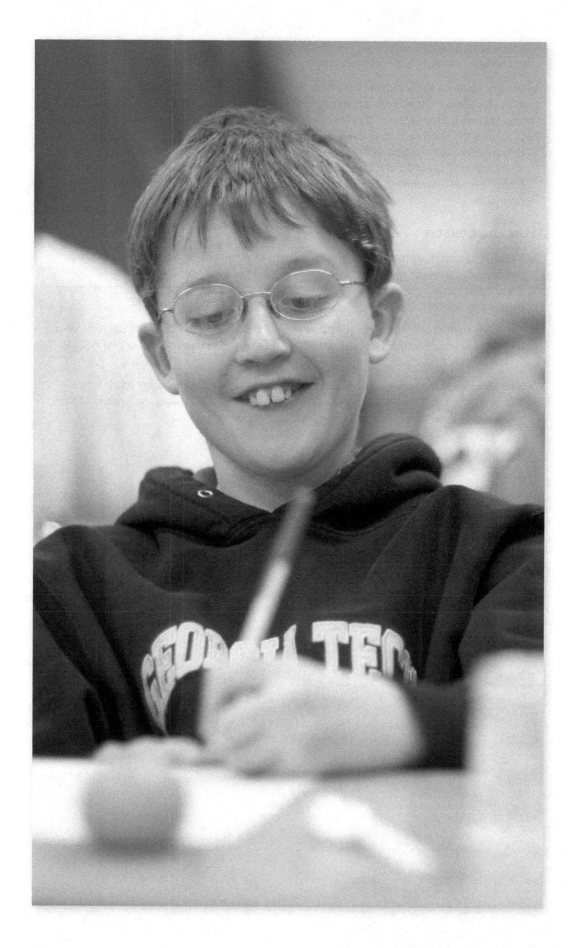

Chapter 2B:
How Will the Curriculum Empower My Students to Own Their Learning?

On the surface, this curriculum might look like *just* an ELA curriculum. It certainly is that. *And* it's also full of powerful practices designed to empower students to own their learning that can be lifted out of our ELA curriculum and into all parts of the school day. From the learning targets that start every lesson, to protocols that engage students in academic discourse, to debriefs that ask students to reflect on their learning and habits of character, you can see our commitment to teaching much more than just literacy skills. This commitment is a part of our heritage and our work in schools over more than two decades.

Though this curriculum may be your first introduction to EL Education, we have actually been around for a long time—more than twenty-five years—working with K–12 schools and teachers. We have always focused on combining challenging work with the joy of discovery and pride in mastery, and on preparing students to become contributing citizens with both the skills and character necessary for success throughout college, work, and life.

To use our ELA curriculum requires no familiarity with EL Education, our model, or our network of schools. It stands alone and can be used in any school. That said, our experience working with schools and teachers has helped us develop a set of practices and approaches to teaching and learning that may be new to you. When you encounter high-leverage practices like discussion protocols or total participation techniques for the first time, for example, we think it will help to have a little background on why we use those practices, how they can be used in other parts of your school day, and, most important, their impact on student learning.

Table 2.5 describes high-leverage instructional practices that are not necessarily specific to literacy but that empower students to be leaders of their learning across the school day, building the skills they need to be engaged and self-directed learners. The practices are highly transferable; their consistent use in the curriculum will allow you to gain mastery with them so that they can be used throughout the school day. Following this table, each practice is detailed in greater depth for the remainder of Chapter 2B.

Table 2.5: High-Leverage Instructional Practices that Empower Students to Own Their Learning

Instructional Practice	Impact on Student Learning
Using learning targets *Learning targets translate standards into student learning goals for lessons. They are written in student-friendly language that is concrete and understandable, beginning with the stem "I can." Learning targets are posted, discussed, and tracked by students and teachers.*	» Learning targets set a course for learning: students know where they are headed during the course of the lesson. » Learning targets contain embedded vocabulary. Unpacking the targets with students is an opportunity to teach new words, particularly academic vocabulary. » When learning targets are used actively during lessons, students gain valuable skills in setting goals, taking ownership of their learning, and reflecting on their progress. » Beyond mastery of standards, student ownership of and engagement with their learning is a higher-level goal of the curriculum.
Checking for understanding *Checking for understanding goes hand in hand with using learning targets. Quick and frequent formative assessments allow you to adapt instruction quickly and respond to students' needs in real time so that you can move forward if they are ready and help them get back on track if necessary.*	» Frequent formative assessments of student progress allow you to adapt instruction to meet students' needs. » Getting students back on track quickly helps them sustain their confidence and effort, which leads to new learning. » Asking students to frequently self-assess their progress keeps them tuned in to their learning targets and further develops their ownership of their learning.
Employing total participation techniques *The total participation techniques in the curriculum are used to solicit answers to questions or prompts from a wide variety of students. Rather than just calling on those students who may have their hands raised, these total participation techniques (e.g., Turn and Talk) challenge and hold accountable all students.*	» Total participation techniques demand accountability and attention from all students because anyone can be selected to offer their ideas at any time. » Especially when a positive classroom culture has been established, students who otherwise may have remained quiet have the chance to share ideas with a peer, small group, or the whole class. » Total participation techniques establish a sense of fairness for students: rather than the "smart kids" or the "struggling kids" always being prioritized to be called on, all students have the same chance, voice, and expectation of active engagement.
Fostering a culture of grappling *A culture of grappling is one in which students are supported to make meaning on their own or with peers, rather than being taught by a teacher first. In the curriculum, students often have a "first go" at something, particularly complex text, before teacher instruction or intervention. The idea is not to "give" students information or understandings that they can figure out on their own.*	» Students learn best when they can grapple with challenges that are within reach (i.e., productive struggle). If they are "spoon-fed" information, they won't experience the joy that comes from figuring things out on their own, and they often won't learn the concepts deeply. » Productive struggle supports students to build a growth mindset and take academic risks.

Using questions to promote—not just assess—student learning *In the curriculum, we view questions as a way to help students learn, not just as a way to assess their learning. Strategic questions can help "lift" students to an understanding of a challenging text or make sense of a tricky concept.*	» Asking open-ended questions, rather than those with "right" answers, gives students a chance to come up with their own ideas, individually or in collaboration with peers, and defend them with evidence. » Strategic questions can engage students more deeply in the lesson content, help them make connections, and require them to articulate their learning in their own words. » Strategic questions demand that students think deeply and critically, not just that they remember or relate to their own experience.
Engaging students with protocols *The protocols in the curriculum are one of the key ways that students are engaged in discussion, inquiry, critical thinking, and sophisticated communication. There are a variety of protocols in the curriculum, and all offer a structure and a set of steps to help students talk to one another and dig deeper into text or ideas. Protocols can be used throughout the school day, in any classroom, to promote student engagement and discussion.*	» Protocols are one of the best ways we know to help students be leaders of their own learning. » Making meaning together enhances learning. Rather than looking to the teacher for answers and information, protocols help students learn to find those answers themselves and with the help of their peers. » Protocols are a great way for students to learn and practice speaking and listening skills and to build their habits of character.
Deepening student discourse *Perhaps the best measure of an effective classroom is the quality of student conversation. With teacher modeling, Conversation Cues, sentence frames, consistent use of academic vocabulary, and a commitment by the teacher to draw out and celebrate student ideas, students can learn to have powerful analytical conversations at all grade levels.*	» When students recognize that their ideas and opinions will be taken seriously by you and their peers—analyzed, critiqued, and built upon—it lifts their commitment to sharing their best thinking. » Simple sentence frames can transform discussion in a classroom (e.g., "I would like to build on Chantelle's idea"; "I appreciate that idea, but I respectfully disagree"; "Can you offer some evidence?"). » Prioritizing discourse in the classroom elevates student voice, develops their oral processing skills, and deepens their learning.
Co-constructing anchor charts with students *Anchor charts make student thinking visible by recording content, strategies, processes, cues, and guidelines during the learning process. Students add ideas to posted anchor charts as they apply new learning, develop new understandings, and expand their knowledge of the topic. These charts reflect the current learning in the classroom, contain only the most relevant or important information, and are neat and organized, with simple icons and wording.*	» Posting anchor charts keeps relevant information easily accessible for all students, reminds them of prior learning, and enables them to add to their learning as it changes and expands. » Posting anchor charts provides students with support when answering questions, adding to discussions, and problem-solving in class. » English language learners and students who may need additional support with perception and information processing benefit from this kind of visual display as a varied means of representation. » Providing individual copies of anchor charts to students and/or customizing the display (e.g., enlarging the font; adding simple icons, definitions, or translations next to important words or ideas) also provides students with additional support.

Using Learning Targets

We start here with learning targets because that's where we start nearly every lesson in our curriculum. Learning targets anchor students and teachers in a common understanding of where they are headed with their learning. When students know where they are headed, they can take more ownership of getting there.

> *"Learning targets are goals for lessons, projects, units, and courses. They are derived from standards and used to assess growth and achievement. They are written in concrete, student-friendly language—beginning with the stem 'I can'—shared with students, posted in the classroom, and tracked carefully by students and teachers during the process of learning."*

> *"Rather than the teacher taking on all of the responsibility for meeting a lesson's objectives, learning targets, written in student-friendly language and frequently reflected on, transfer ownership for meeting objectives from the teacher to the student. The seemingly simple work of reframing objectives written for teachers to learning targets, written for—and owned by—students, turns assessment on its head. The student becomes the main actor in assessing and improving his or her learning."*

> *"The term target is significant. It emphasizes that students are aiming for something specific. Learning targets are meant to focus students in this way, directing their efforts and attention, as would a physical target. Every day, students discuss, reflect, track their progress, and assess their work in relation to learning targets. Learning targets build investment in learning by giving students the language to discuss what they know and what they need to learn. As an eighth-grader at the Odyssey School (in Denver) remarked, 'The teacher will take time to break down the target, so we know where we're going with the learning'"* (Berger, Rugen, and Woodfin, 2014, pp. 21–22).

In our curriculum, we use daily learning targets, which are reviewed with students at the beginning of lessons. Sometimes learning targets are also reviewed later in the lesson following a new chunk of cognitive work (e.g., the first part of a lesson may have a learning target related to speaking; later, when students dig into a writing task, there may be a second learning target related to writing). Often, we think of reviewing learning targets as *unpacking* or *dissecting* them. This should not take much time, but it is an important opportunity to look carefully with students at the words in the learning target and make sure they know what they actually will be learning (not just what activity they will be "doing") and why (i.e., how it might connect to previous learning or guiding questions).

Unpacking Learning Targets

Using one of the first learning targets students will see in Grade 6 as an example—*I can explain Percy's point of view toward Mr. Brunner in Chapter 1 of* The Lightning Thief—let's start with the verb *explain*. The verbs in learning targets are important because they dictate what students will be doing and give an indication of the cognitive rigor of the lesson. *Synthesizing* will be more cognitively rigorous for students than *explaining; evaluating* more so than *labeling*. No matter the verb or the rigor it signals, the first step is to make sure students know what the verb means and what it's going to look like and sound like for them to do that work.

Reviewing, or unpacking, learning targets is an excellent way to teach academic vocabulary: "What does it mean to *explain*?" Often—and we'll get to this later in this chapter—the curriculum will suggest a total participation technique, such as Turn and Talk, to give all students a chance to think and talk about what it will mean for them to explain (or synthesize or evaluate or label, or whatever the verb is). This engages all students in beginning to take aim at the learning target; it sets a course for their learning throughout the lesson.

But verbs aren't the only important words in learning targets. Using our example again, the next question might be: "What other words in this learning target seem most important to guide our learning today?" Students might come up with *point of view* as the thing they'll be learning about and *Percy* and *Mr. Brunner* to indicate that two characters are involved in what they'll be explaining.

Often the lessons in the curriculum will cue you to add words from the learning targets to the class academic word wall or to have students add them to vocabulary logs. In this way, unpacking learning targets is important instructional time.

All of this unpacking should happen quickly in the lessons in our curriculum, usually 5 minutes or less. The goal is to make sure that students know what they are aiming for and to set purpose, not to belabor every word. This is why vocabulary is so often the focus of this process. It will be hard for students to take aim at the target if they are not sure of what it means. The first few lessons of Module 1 explicitly unpack learning targets. Because it's something that you are likely to pick up quickly, thereafter you will see instructions to follow the same routine as in previous lessons (i.e., "Repeated routine"). We want to emphasize, however, that although unpacking learning targets is a *routine*, it should not become *routinized*. It's important not to just go through the motions or you may miss an opportunity to truly engage students. There's no one right way to unpack learning targets; what really matters is that students are crystal clear on their intended learning so they can take ownership of their progress.

▶▶ Video Spotlight 2.1

In the video, "Students Unpack a Learning Target," see how fourth- and fifth-grade teacher Jason Shiroff, at Odyssey School of Denver, ensures that his students understand exactly what their learning target—*I can use transition words (or phrases) to connect my paragraphs*—means before they begin the lesson. Students grapple with what the word *phrase* means, and they look together at a model to see what happens when paragraphs are put together without a transition. Shiroff uses checking for understanding and total participation techniques to engage all students.

https://vimeo.com/44052219

Using a Learning Target throughout a Lesson

Unpacking learning targets during the lesson opening is just the first step. It is critical that learning targets are used *throughout* a lesson. "Even well-written learning targets will contribute little to engaging, supporting, and holding students accountable for their learning if they are not referred to and used actively during the lesson. For this reason, teachers must use techniques to check for understanding and mark progress toward learning targets. Students must have the opportunity to reflect on their progress; this is key to student ownership of their learning" (Berger, Rugen, and Woodfin, 2014, p. 29).

Going back to our example, *I can explain Percy's point of view toward Mr. Brunner in Chapter 1 of The Lightning Thief*, how will you know how students are progressing in their effort to explain Percy's point of view? The lessons in our curriculum will cue students to self-assess as you check their understanding in a variety of ways. Sometimes you will listen in to student conversations as they assess their progress; other times you might stop the class, read aloud the learning target, and ask students to give you a self-assessment, such as a thumbs-up, thumbs-sideways, or thumbs-down, so that you know with whom you might need to spend extra time to help them reach the target. Other times students may write an exit ticket that you will collect and assess. (We will explore self-assessment and checking for understanding in the next section.)

There are numerous ways to keep the learning target alive during the lesson and to check for understanding. And, just as with the process of unpacking learning targets, there's no one right way to actively use them throughout a lesson. What's important is that you find ways to do so that are appropriate to the target. Not every assessment of progress is appropriate to the target. For example, if students are *labeling* a diagram, you won't be looking for progress in a written paragraph. If they are *collaborating* with partners, you won't be looking for individual responses.

Our curriculum will give you plenty of good strategies to help students self-assess in order to keep the learning target front and center in students' minds. Based on the way your students respond and your assessment of their needs on any given day (e.g., they need more movement), you will likely find your own favorite ways to keep the learning targets alive during lessons.

Going Deeper with Learning Targets

First and foremost, learning targets must help students understand what their intended learning is, which is driven by standards. This is something we took deeply to heart when crafting the learning targets you see in the curriculum. We always started with what the standards require, what mastery will look and sound like, and what scaffolding students will need to get there. This drove all of the downstream creation of daily learning targets.

When using our curriculum, there is no need for you to create your own learning targets. They are "baked in" to every lesson. However, learning to analyze the learning targets that are provided will help ground you in the greater purpose of any given lesson. If a target states, for example, that students will determine a character's motivations *using details from the text*, you and your students have some clues about the work of the lesson. Know, too, that all of our targets were carefully derived from the Common Core standards; if you are ever in doubt about the intent of a lesson, go back to the language in the standards themselves.

We have already pointed to the importance of the verbs in learning targets. The framework of knowledge, skill, and reasoning as three types of learning targets—which are largely determined by what verbs are used—can offer further precision for your analysis. Based on the work of Rick Stiggins and colleagues (2006), Table 2.6 describes each type, along with a sampling of accompanying verbs that will make it clear to you and your students what the intended learning is. Throughout the curriculum, you will notice all three types of learning targets. Attending to a balance of all three types is one way that we ensured that the cognitive rigor of student tasks is varied throughout the curriculum.

Table 2.6: Attending to Cognitive Rigor: Knowledge, Skills, and Reasoning Learning Targets

	Knowledge	**Skill**	**Reasoning**
Explanation	Learning (or using reference materials to retrieve) knowledge, facts, concepts	Using knowledge and reasoning to perform an action (with an emphasis on demonstration)	Using knowledge to solve a problem, or to make a decision or plan
Sample verbs	explain, describe, identify, tell, name, list, define, label, match, choose, recall, recognize, select	observe, listen, perform, conduct, read, speak, write, assemble, operate, use, demonstrate, measure, model, collect, dramatize	analyze, compare and contrast, synthesize, classify, infer, evaluate

Deriving Your Own Quality Learning Targets

The learning targets in our curriculum are derived from multiple sources. The primary source is the Common Core State Standards (CCSS). Other sources include the Next Generation Science Standards and the National Council for Social Studies 3C framework. While we have strived to select a variety of content topics that meet grade-level content standards in states across the country, we know that we haven't met them all. Depending on your school, district, or state, you may be compelled to adapt or enhance the curriculum further to meet your local context.

Further, once you see the power of learning targets to empower your students to take more ownership of their learning, you may feel motivated to create learning targets for other lessons that you teach, beyond our curriculum; or, if you don't have the opportunity to teach lessons beyond our ELA curriculum, you may wish to support members of your teaching team (e.g., science, social studies teachers) in this work. We wholeheartedly endorse this. Using learning targets is truly a high-leverage instructional practice that can be lifted out of the curriculum and into any other lessons you are creating. For this reason, we offer some guidance here on how to create your own learning targets. If you don't foresee any opportunities to create your own learning targets, you may want to skip the rest of the Learning Targets section and pick back up at the Checking for Understanding section.

Making Learning Targets Student-Friendly

One of the first things to remember about creating quality learning targets is to avoid the temptation to tack the words "I can" onto a standard. Learning targets must be written in student-friendly language that students will understand and can take ownership of. For example, in Grade 8, Module 1, Unit 2, Lesson 9, the learning target is: *I can plan the plot of my new scene for* Summer of the Mariposas *that results in the same outcome as the original scene.* This learning target is derived, in part, from CCSS W.8.3a. If we were to tack the words "I can" onto that standard, it would read like this: "I can engage and orient the reader by establishing a context and point of view and introducing a narrator and/or characters; I can organize an event sequence that unfolds naturally and logically." That would not be a student-friendly learning target. It would have more than one verb, which makes it difficult to assess (i.e., students wouldn't easily be able to assess when they have met the target), and it would not be contextualized to the content at hand (e.g., *Summer of the Mariposas*). Overall, it is too broad and too big to be a quality learning target.

Learning targets must focus on one thing at a time so that students can focus on the intended learning and monitor their progress most effectively. Let's look at an example from a Grade 7 module in our curriculum. CCSS W.7.5 appears in an arc of lessons (Module 2, Unit 2, Lessons 13–15): *With some guidance and support from peers and adults, develop and strengthen writing as needed by planning, revising, editing, rewriting, or trying a new approach, focusing on how well purpose and audience have been addressed.* This standard requires students to demonstrate mastery of two skills in their writing process: 1) developing and strengthening their writing and 2) attending to purpose and audience. These two skills are combined in the standard because students have to consider their purpose and audience in order to effectively plan and revise their writing; however, leaving the skills together in one learning target would be a lot for students to take aim at. As a result, across these three lessons, there are two learning targets to help students focus on one skill at a time:

1. *I can plan an informative essay.*

2. *I can revise my essay focusing on evidence and elaboration.*

Since this is an informative essay about social and medical epidemics, evidence and elaboration are key to students being able to meet the part of the standard that asks them to focus on purpose and audience—evidence and elaboration are important for this audience. It is also important to note that this isn't the only arc of lessons in which CCSS W.7.5 appears. Standards and their associated learning targets spiral in and out of lessons, giving students the opportunity to truly master them.

Preparing for the Common Challenges of Writing Learning Targets

If you decide to dive into writing learning targets yourself, be aware that there are many common challenges to the practice, including:

» Learning targets that are actually *doing* targets (e.g., *I can make a poster* vs. *I can describe X in poster format*)

» Learning targets that are too complex

» Learning targets that require all lower-level cognitive work

» Learning targets that are mismatched to assessments

If you want to start creating your own learning targets, we encourage you to collaborate with other teachers to help one another critique and revise the targets. You can find more information in our 2014 book *Leaders of Their Own Learning: Transforming Schools through Student-Engaged Assessment* and our 2020 book *The Leaders of Their Own Learning Companion: New Tools and Tips for Tackling the Common Challenges of Student Engaged Assessment.* The box on the next page: Crafting High-Quality Learning Targets Checklist, which is a set of criteria to support your work writing learning targets, comes from *The Leaders of Thier Own Learning Companion.*

Crafting High-Quality Learning Targets Checklist

For each learning target, check all that apply:

☐ The learning target begins with "I can."

☐ The verb in the learning target makes clear to students the intended learning.

☐ The learning target contains only one verb. If students need to focus on more than one thing during a lesson, there is more than one learning target, each with only one verb.

☐ The target is a learning target, not a doing target (unless the learning target is purposefully written to take aim at a craftsmanship skill).

☐ The learning target is contextualized to the specific topic, text, or task in the lesson—it is not a general learning target that could be used for any old lesson.

☐ Multiple learning targets during a lesson or across more than one day fall into a variety of categories on a cognitive rigor tool (e.g., the Knowledge, Reasoning, and Skills Framework; Bloom's Revised Taxonomy; Hess's Cognitive Rigor Matrix).

☐ When appropriate, the learning target uses playful, engaging language.

Checking for Understanding

Checking for understanding goes hand in hand with using learning targets, and a variety of strategies are used throughout the curriculum to formatively assess students' progress. There are many ways to check for understanding, including summative assessments like tests, essays, and performance tasks. These more in-depth checks for understanding are certainly a part of our curriculum, but we will explore them fully in Chapter 6. Here we focus on techniques used during the flow of daily lessons throughout the curriculum:

» Writing and reflection

» Strategic observation and listening

» Debriefs

There are two sections of every lesson that will cue you to the assessments in the lesson: the Ongoing Assessment section at the beginning of the lesson and the Assessment Guidance section within the Teaching Notes[1]. These sections will orient you to the kinds of data you can collect on student progress during the lesson (e.g., entrance ticket; Informative Writing Plan graphic).

These quick and frequent assessments allow you to adapt instruction quickly and respond to students' needs in real time so that you can help them get back on track if necessary. And, importantly, checking for understanding helps students check in with themselves as they self-assess their progress and take ownership of their learning.

Writing and Reflection

Writing is an effective way for students to articulate and reflect on their developing understanding of a topic. Writing is often overlooked as a quick formative assessment technique, perhaps because it's not as quick as eliciting verbal responses. However, many writing techniques, especially once students grow accustomed to them, can be done quite quickly, and they appeal to students' diverse learning styles. Writing also requires that students commit to

---

1. Another important part of the assessment picture is the Assessment Overview and Resources, which can be found in the Teacher Supporting Materials; here you'll find the summative assessments for each unit along with tools such as rubrics, sample student responses, and checklists.

a response, revealing evidence of progress that is quite useful as a formative assessment. In general, the written response techniques we're talking about here are short and informal. They are completed and checked quickly. Table 2.7 describes a few techniques that you will find in the curriculum.

Table 2.7: Checking for Understanding: Writing and Reflection Techniques

Technique	Description
Summary writing	Students summarize what they have learned. This technique gives them valuable practice in condensing information and provides you with a window into student learning.
Note-catchers	Students record facts, observations, and insights on a note-catcher template as they work.
Entrance and exit tickets	As an opening or closing activity, students write a reflection on their learning in the class that day or the previous day in response to a specific prompt. The writing serves as evidence of student understanding to help shape subsequent lessons.

Strategic Observation and Listening

Circulating and listening in while students are engaged in conversation and group work is an effective and efficient way for you to assess progress and confer with students. In fact, in nearly every lesson in our curriculum you will find something like this: "As students work, circulate and look/listen for... " Also, throughout the curriculum we use parentheses to cue you to what you should listen for after asking a question or giving a prompt. For example, from Grade 6, Module 1, Unit 1, Lesson 3:

> Turn and Talk:
>
> » "Which word best defines the word *vaporized* in the excerpt given from Chapter 1 of The Lightning Thief?" (destroyed)
>
> » "What strategy did you use to determine your answer?" (Responses will vary, but may include: using context clues, drawing on prior knowledge, replacing each option into the sentence.)

Of course, this means that students must have plenty of opportunities to work with and talk with one another. In our curriculum, protocols are often used to give students this chance for discourse. (Protocols will be discussed later in this chapter.)

Each module in the Grades 6–8 curriculum includes a set of checklists, including several speaking and listening checklists, which allow you to track students' progress toward Speaking and Listening standards. You will be cued in the Assessment Guidance section of the Teaching Notes as to how the checklist can be used. Sometimes it will be used informally, other times it will be used during a mid- or end of unit assessment. Speaking and listening checklists may also be used by students as a tool to assess one another's progress, as in Grade 6, Module 1, Unit 3, Lessons 10–11; students conduct presentations and work with a partner to provide feedback on the Speaking and Listening Informal Assessment: Presentation of Knowledge and Ideas checklist.

Checklists will not only help you stay focused on particular standards, which are tied to daily learning targets, but they also help you track how many and which students you have observed or conferred with, make decisions about any further support that may be needed, and determine next steps for instruction. (Using checklists as formative and summative assessments is explored in Chapter 6).

Debriefs

"An effective debrief is the last chance during a daily lesson for a teacher to check for understanding, help students synthesize learning, and promote reflection so that students can monitor their own progress. It is an essential component of each lesson" (Berger, Rugen, and Woodfin, 2014, p. 74). Each lesson in our curriculum includes a Closing and Assessment, which typically lasts for 5 to 10 minutes. This is when the debrief occurs. During this time, students often reflect on their progress toward the learning targets, using a technique like the Thumb-O-Meter to indicate their current mastery of a literacy skill (e.g., their ability to analyze how the setting of Sudan during two time periods shapes character and plot in *A Long Walk to Water*). They also reflect on their habits of character and academic mindsets (e.g., "How does collaboration help you feel a sense of belonging in this classroom community? During this lesson, how did you help others to feel they belong in this community?").

After the first few lessons in a module, the Closing and Assessment section of lessons will cue you to use a "Repeated routine" to reflect with students. As with any repeated routine in the curriculum, it will be important for you to have some questions or protocols at the ready, but for the process not to become routinized to the point that students are just going through the motions. The debrief is an opportunity to help students reflect not only on *what* they learned during the lesson, but also on *how* they learned. During the debrief, and at any point in a lesson, you can build students' ability to be metacognitive by helping them analyze their thinking and the logic of their reasoning, or giving them opportunities to apply their learning to novel situations. Probing questions may include the following:

» Why do you think this?

» How do you know?

» What evidence supports your thinking?

» How has your thinking changed, and what changed your ideas?

» How might your thinking change if... ?

It's hard to fit everything in when you're teaching. When time is short, as it often is at the end of a lesson, resist the temptation to skip the debrief. Invite students to answer synthesis or reflection questions in pairs, trios, or quads, or employ a quick protocol or total participation technique so that all students have a chance to talk with one another, rather than asking a few to raise their hands to answer questions. This will save time *and* engage all students. Or you may be able to employ a quick written check for understanding (e.g., exit ticket) that can save you time.

Also, remember that giving students the chance to reflect on *what* and *how* they learned keeps them tuned in to their progress and builds ownership in their learning. Character is one of our three Dimensions of Student Achievement (Figure 1.2). It was a priority for us to build habits of character into the curriculum, and we hope it will be a priority for you, too. This is something you can build into anything you teach, not just the lessons in our curriculum, to equip your students with powerful tools for learning. Chapter 6 will provide you with more information about using formative and summative assessments to monitor student progress.

In the video, "Instructional Strategies that Support Learning—Checking for Understanding," teacher Jessica Wood at the Springfield Renaissance School in Springfield, Massachusetts, uses a variety of checking for understanding strategies to keep her students focused on their learning target throughout the lesson.

https://vimeo.com/43990520

Employing Total Participation Techniques

Total participation techniques[2] are a way to engage all students—not just your "frequent fliers"—in responding to questions and prompts. They are checking for understanding techniques that have the additional purpose of engaging all students. For example, rather than asking a question and looking for raised hands, employing a total participation technique would require you to ask the question and then engage all students in answering it. Turn and Talk is a common example: in response to a question, students pair up and each takes a turn answering the question. As students talk to each other, you can walk around and listen in to their conversations.

Total participation techniques play an important role in an equitable classroom. They give all students a voice, and they allow for students who may need additional processing time the ability to work out their thoughts with a peer or in writing rather than being asked to share in front of the whole class.

> *"With total participation techniques, I really try to have them in my back pocket, like a handful that I know I can pull out at any time. That way when I get to a question that I know I'm going to ask, I can gauge the room. Do they need to move?"*

Sara Metz
Teacher, Denver

You will be invited to use a variety of total participation techniques in the curriculum. You may find that your class develops a favorite or that one is more effective than another with your students. You may use techniques from the curriculum or develop your own. Table 2.8 describes some, but not all, of the total participation techniques that you will find in the curriculum.

---

2. From the book *Total Participation Techniques: Making Every Student an Active Learner* (2011) by Persida Himmele and William Himmele

Table 2.8: A Sampling of Total Participation Techniques

Technique	Description
Turn and Talk	Turn and Talk is one of the easiest, quickest, and most efficient total participation techniques. It can be used practically at any time, anywhere, in a lesson in any content area. 1. When prompted, students turn to an elbow partner. 2. In a set amount of time, students share their ideas about a prompt or question posed by the teacher or other students. 3. Depending on the goals of the lesson and the nature of the Turn and Talk, students may share some key ideas from their paired discussions with the whole class.
Think-Pair-Share	This practice promotes productive and equitable conversations, in which all students are given the time and space to think, share, and consider the ideas of others. It ensures that all students simultaneously engage with the same text or topic, while promoting synthesis and the social construction of knowledge. 1. Move students into pairs, and invite them to label themselves A and B. 2. Pose the question, and give students time to think independently and silently about their answer to the question. 3. Invite partner A to ask partner B the question. 4. Give partner B a specified time frame (e.g., 30 seconds, 1 minute) to share their response. 5. Have partners reverse roles and repeat steps 3–4. 6. Using another total participation technique (e.g., cold calling, equity sticks), invite students to share their responses with the whole group. 7. Repeat this process with remaining questions.
Write-Pair-Share	This is a variation on Think-Pair-Share where students think *and* write before they share with their partner.
Cold Call	Cold Call serves as an engaging and challenging, yet supportive, way to hold students accountable for answering oral questions the teacher poses, regardless of whether a hand is raised. Cold Call requires students to think and interact with the question at hand, even if they're not sure of the answer. It also promotes equity in the classroom; students who normally dominate the discourse step back and allow other students to demonstrate their knowledge and expertise. 1. Name a question before identifying students to answer it. 2. Call on students regardless of whether they have hands raised (often using equity sticks). 3. Scaffold questions from simple to increasingly complex, probing for deeper explanations. 4. Connect thinking threads by returning to previous comments and connecting them to current ones; model this for students and teach them to do it, too.

Equity Sticks	Equity sticks are true to their name: They ensure academic equity by allowing teachers to physically track who they have called on or interacted with during the course of the class. This is especially useful during whole class discussions or while working with large groups of students.
	Using Popsicle sticks or something similar—one per student:
	1. Pose a question to the class.
	2. After giving students some think time, pick an equity stick and call on the student whose name is on the stick for an answer. At times you may want to move the equity stick into a separate pile or cup, but adolescent learners are highly attuned to whether their name still has potential to be called, so it is often best to preserve the possibility that anyone may be called on at any time.
Entrance Ticket	This is a brief problem, task, or activity that immediately engages students in the learning target for the day. It enables you to monitor students' readiness to move on and judge their grasp of necessary background knowledge.
	1. For 3–5 minutes at the beginning of a lesson, have students jot down responses or discuss their responses to a simple prompt or question.
	2. Listen in on student conversations or quickly review written responses for a quick assessment.
	3. You might pick out a few typical/unique/thought-provoking responses to spark whole-class discussion.
Thumb-O-Meter	To indicate agreement, readiness for tasks, or comfort with a learning target or concept, students can quickly show their thinking by putting their *thumbs up* to indicate readiness; *thumbs to the side* to indicate that they need some support; or *thumbs down* to indicate discomfort or confusion.

Fostering a Culture of Grappling

"Never help a child with a task at which he feels he can succeed." There are two important messages embedded in this quote by Maria Montessori. The first is that students should have the opportunity to try things and to puzzle through challenges independently or with peers. In other words, they shouldn't always be "taught" how to do things before they try them, and they shouldn't be bailed out at the first sign of struggle, because engaging in a productive struggle is how we learn.

The second is the message about the importance of getting the level of challenge right. Students must be able to see a path to success—they must grapple with something within their reach. This doesn't mean that they won't need scaffolds and support to help get them there, but those must be skillfully employed. Some of the most intricate work of designing this curriculum was finding this sweet spot with the level of challenge. What are the texts and tasks that will give students an opportunity to grapple productively and to see that they can succeed by persevering through something difficult? What scaffolds can we predict students will need to find success?

The close reads that are woven throughout the curriculum (which are explored in great depth in Chapter 3) often involve grappling as students have a first go at reading complex texts. The process is carefully scaffolded so that students have the experience of pushing through challenging material in a way that leads to success, not to frustration. Close reading is also carefully introduced to students at the start of the year, in Module 1, in a way that builds in them a sense of meaningful, collaborative exploration and academic courage.

It is important to note that often lesson arcs of two to three lessons might feature a period of grappling in the first lesson, with students reaching greater clarity over the course of a few days. They won't always push through and reach those "aha" moments during one lesson. This is why it is so important to look out ahead with lessons so you have a feel for these rhythms and can help students stay in the zone of the productive struggle without being tempted to "rescue" them.

Building Academic Courage

A sense of academic courage, which allows grappling and productive struggle to thrive in the classroom, can be fostered in all parts of the school day. For adolescent learners, whose brains light up when they take risks in the presence of their peers, academic risks provide both a physically safe and ultimately productive way to address this drive. The following list provides an overview of strategies you can use to create a class culture in which challenge or struggle is viewed as a way to learn, not as a barrier to learning:

» Build common language in your classroom for "grappling." You don't have to call it grappling, but label it for students and frame it as both an individual skill to build (e.g., "grappling is key to learning, and you can improve through practice") and a group endeavor (e.g., "we all get smarter when we grapple as a group"). Make grappling a class routine with specific strategies (e.g., anchor charts for what to try when we feel stuck).

» Give students tangible successes early in the year by designing tasks you know they can be successful with and supporting them to do the tasks with quality. Give students lots of individual feedback to help them grow, and regularly point out their growth.

» Talk explicitly about the importance of taking on challenges in order to learn. When appropriate, read and discuss with students short pieces of research about having a growth mindset and its impact on learning.

» Use group initiatives to practice grappling with a challenge, tenacity, and problem-solving; discuss application to classroom lessons when debriefing the initiative.

» Engage students in discussions that make the link between character traits and the grapple phase of your lessons (e.g., "What does *perseverance* look like? What are tips for helping yourself keep going when the going is hard?")

» Create meaningful metaphors for instilling a growth mindset (e.g., the mind is a muscle that can get stronger).

» Do a "zones of comfort" activity: Draw concentric circles for the comfort, stretch, and panic zones. Students identify the types of experiences they have that fall into the different zones. Point out that the stretch zone is our learning zone—we learn best when we are a little uncomfortable.

While our curriculum, particularly at the beginning of the school year, goes slow with grappling activities, this is an area that benefits from a holistic approach across the school, and productive struggle is certainly recognized as powerful in disciplines beyond ELA. When leaders and teachers build a culture of grappling throughout the day—from advisory meetings to P.E. to math class—students can build a growth mindset, persevere through challenging material, and take academic risks in an emotionally safe and supportive environment.

Using Questions to Promote—Not Just Assess—Student Learning

One of your best tools for nurturing a culture of grappling and collaborative intellectual exploration in your classroom is questions. Asking open-ended questions, rather than those with "right" answers, gives students a chance to come up with their own ideas, individually or in collaboration with peers, and defend them with evidence. Such questions engage students more deeply in the lesson content, help them make connections, and require them to articulate their learning in their own words. In this way, questions are used to promote learning, not just assess it.

"Every time we ask students, 'What was the name of the town in which the characters in this story lived?' we leave less time for questions like 'Why do you think the characters never left home?'"

Alfie Kohn, "Who's Asking?"
Educational Leadership, September 2015

In our curriculum, each lesson contains suggested questions that are designed to intentionally scaffold student learning, often moving students toward more complex thinking. However, given the reality of life in the classroom, it is often the case that you will need to think on your feet with additional follow-up questions if students seem off track. Developing your own "question-asking muscles" will help you be more strategic about what you ask (and when), while still maintaining the integrity of the lesson. It will also help you prepare for ways to probe for deeper understanding or to encourage students to build off of their peers' responses to questions so that the focus isn't always on you asking a question, students responding, and you evaluating the answer.

Understanding the considerations that went into our development of questions will help you ask additional questions that give you the information you really need from students. It is also important to remember that asking too many questions and following students' lead in too many new directions has a big impact on the pacing of your lessons and can get you off track. The best questions drive at learning targets, stimulate and assess powerful thinking, and ensure that all students are engaged in thinking and supporting their ideas with evidence. Figure 2.2 illustrates strategic questioning strategies along with accompanying examples.

Figure 2.2: Pre-Planning Strategic Questions

Strategy:	Example:
Design questions to provide a clear vision of the learning target(s). Use questions to clarify the meaning and connections between learning targets, to connect prior lessons, establish criteria for success, and track learning along the way.	In Grade 7, Module 1, Unit 1, Lesson 1 students "discover the topic" of the module: The Lost Children of Sudan. The lesson will require them to use evidence to infer the topic, so it's essential that the learning target is unpacked carefully to ensure that all students understand what it means to *infer*. It's also critical, at this early stage in the module, that students understand the purpose of learning targets: to help them identify where they are headed with their learning and take ownership of their progress.

From the lesson:

Direct students' attention to the posted learning target, and select a volunteer to read it aloud:

» "I can use evidence to *infer* the topic of this module from the resources."

Guide students through an intentional Think-Pair-Share:

» "Why do we have learning targets? What is the purpose of learning targets?"

Underline the word *infer* in the learning target. Ensure that students have access to an online or print translation dictionary. Invite students to Turn and Talk with their partner:

» "What does *infer* mean? If you are going to infer the topic, what does that mean?"

Cold-call students using equity sticks to share their responses. With student support, record the meaning of *infer* on the academic word wall.

Strategy:

Scaffold questions from basic to complex. Ask questions that start at the knowledge and comprehension levels and move quickly to reasoning and critical thinking. This helps students practice thinking skills, make connections between ideas, align and evaluate evidence, synthesize information, and apply learning to new situations. These questions are generative, eliciting multiple correct answers.

Example:

In Grade 8, Module 1, Unit 1, Lesson 3 you can see how questions begin with "what happened?" and "what's the gist?" and then progress to a much greater level of sophistication as students are asked to consider characters' points of view and emotional reactions to events in the story. All students are fully engaged in responding to these questions through the Back-to-Back and Face-to-Face protocol.

From the lesson:

Guide students through an intentional Back-to-Back and Face-to-Face protocol on the following questions:

» "What happened? What are the main events? How is the plot unfolding?"

» "What is the gist? What is this chapter mostly about?"

» "In what ways did characters show respect or empathy in this chapter? Did any characters face challenges in showing respect and/or empathy?"

After recording notes, students Think-Pair-Share on the following questions:

» "From what point of view is this novel written? How do you know?"

» "From reading this excerpt, what do you, the reader, know that Mama doesn't know? What effect does this create?"

Strategy:

Ask questions that are text dependent. To check for understanding and comprehension of complex texts, ask questions that are text-dependent rather than drawn from the students' personal opinions or past experiences. This questioning strategy compels students to read carefully and cite evidence, which in turn raises the quality of student thinking. Carefully crafted questions serve as a scaffold to "lift" students to the text and build higher-order thinking skills and new perspectives. (Note: text-dependent questions are explored in greater depth in Chapter 3.)

Example:

In Grade 6, Module 1, Unit 1, Lesson 5, students close read the text "Why Ancient Greek Mythology Is Still Relevant Today. The text-dependent questions in the Close Reading Guide consistently invite and challenge students to dig back into this complex text. The examples that follow focus students on just one short section of the text, "What Did These Myths Do?" and how the section is connected to the larger piece. For each question, the teacher prompts the students to draw specific evidence from the text and defend their answers.

From the lesson:

Focus students on the Key Vocabulary column of their note-catchers, and use the question provided to discuss the meaning of the word *immortal*.

Invite students to reread the section heading and the main idea given in the right-hand column of their note-catchers. Reinforce the connection between the section heading and the main idea of the section. Ask:

» "What are some of the details the author uses to support the main idea of this section?" Refer to the close reading note-catcher provided for sample responses.

Guide students in adding supporting details to their note-catchers. Ask:

» "How does this section support the central idea that myths are still relevant?"

Strategy:

Clarify expectations. Use questions to clarify criteria for success and help students check their own understanding to determine their next steps.

Examples:

In Grade 6, Module 4, Unit 3, Lesson 11 students examine narrative nonfiction texts and record notices and wonderings about the genre of narrative nonfiction. This process prepares students to generate their own narratives about real events for their performance task.

From the lesson:

Inform students that if they need to take notes as they listen to the text, they may document their thoughts on scrap paper, an index card, or a sticky note. Read aloud *Hidden Figures: The True Story of Four Black Women and the Space Race*. At the end of the reading, ask:

» "Which characteristics of narrative nonfiction did you see evidence of in this book?"

» "How does this book represent craftsmanship?"

» "How will what we write for the performance task differ from what we wrote for the Mid-Unit 3 Assessment?"

In Chapter 2A, we explored the steps necessary to prepare for each lesson, which include reading through the entire lesson carefully and preparing for its delivery. This is the best time to make decisions about questions that may need to be added or tweaked to best meet the needs of your students. Keep in mind that any questions you develop should advance the discussion of a text, the understanding of a topic, or the synthesis of the lesson's activities: "If the questions are not causing students to struggle and think, they are probably not worth asking" (Wiliam, 2014, p. 16). Questions should demand that students think deeply and critically, not just that they remember or relate to their own experience.

Engaging Students with Protocols

Protocols are an important feature of our curriculum because they are one of the best ways we know to engage students in discussion, inquiry, critical thinking, and sophisticated communication. A protocol consists of agreed-upon, detailed guidelines for reading, recording, discussing, or reporting that ensure equal participation and accountability in learning. Importantly, protocols allow students to talk to one another, not just to you. As a result, they build independence and responsibility. Protocols in the curriculum range from very quick protocols like Back-to-Back and Face-to-Face to longer lesson-length protocols like Socratic Seminars (see box: Socratic Seminar for a full description).

Speaking and listening protocols are especially useful for scaffolding the learning experience for students who may struggle with reading grade-level texts. These students will likely be able to contribute to conversations and discussions when using an appropriate discussion protocol. The repeated academic and procedural language of protocols also facilitates language acquisition, making them especially productive for ELLs.

Committing to Teaching the Protocols

Since the first edition of our curriculum came out in 2012, we unfortunately have heard from some teachers that they often skip the protocols. They usually do this for one of three reasons:

» *They don't think their students can handle the activity level of the protocol (or they're not sure they can handle the classroom management aspect of the protocol).*

- However... even though this is a real concern, and there's no doubt that classroom management is one of the hardest things about teaching, especially in an active, collaborative classroom full of adolescent learners. The protocols can help students take more ownership of their behavior. Chapter 2C is dedicated to this topic, so keep reading!

» *They don't feel they have time to do the protocol and choose instead a more traditional method for "delivering" the content.*

- However... just because you deliver the content doesn't mean students have learned it. Students need time to *think* and *do* to make the learning stick. Protocols give students a chance to synthesize and communicate knowledge and to practice important skills. Protocols don't always take more time; once you and your students learn the protocols, they should run quite efficiently, and middle school students can begin to take greater levels of responsibility for leading the protocols themselves as the year goes on.

» *They don't place as much value on Speaking and Listening standards (usually because they aren't assessed on high-stakes tests) and skip the protocols, thinking that they are only about speaking and listening.*

- However... protocols are about much more than speaking and listening. They serve as an important scaffold for reading and writing. Discourse is a way for students to make meaning and rehearse their ideas. Adolescent learners in particular deeply need the learning-through-interaction afforded by protocols; if we don't offer it to them in these structured ways, they will find other, often less productive ones.

We urge you not to skip the protocols! They are vital. The most important thing about the protocols in the curriculum is that they deepen learning experiences for students. They give students a chance to play with ideas and to engage in oral rehearsal before writing. They help students synthesize their understanding and learn to have academic conversations with one another. They take the focus off you and let students take charge of their own learning.

Learning the Routines

Key to the success of any protocol is practice. It will take time, especially for students who have never gotten to use a classroom protocol, to get used to their structure and "rules" for participation. Spending a little more time on the front end modeling the procedures and expectations of protocols will go a long way toward their efficient use throughout the year. As you look ahead through a unit, as part of your planning process, be sure to identify which lessons feature the first use of a protocol, and decide *in advance* if there are other parts of the lesson you might trim or if you can allow that lesson to span two days in order to teach the protocol well and relieve pressure for you and your students. Also important for you to take into consideration is that protocols involve many transitions—from independent work to partner work, from partner work to group work, from one part of the room to another. Looking ahead throughout a series of lessons and planning for these transitions will help the protocols run smoothly. Once you've got it and the students have got it, protocols will be a powerful tool for learning in your classroom.

You can find full descriptions of all of the protocols used in the curriculum in the online appendix of protocols, which can be found at http://eled.org/tools. The appendix gives you everything you need to learn the steps of the protocols called for in each lesson and will no doubt inspire you to explore new or different protocols that you might want to use with your students. You can also find a collection of protocol videos on our website at: https://eleducation.org/resources/collections/protocols-in-action-videos. A video of a commonly used text-based protocol—the Jigsaw protocol—is highlighted in Video Spotlight 2.3.

▶▶ **Video Spotlight 2.3**

In this video, teacher Jennifer Dauphinais leads her fifth-grade students from Brennan Rogers Magnet School in New Haven, Connecticut, through a Jigsaw protocol. In a Jigsaw protocol small groups of students become experts in one section of text and hear oral summaries of the others. The protocol allows students to synthesize across texts and gain new understandings from their classmates about the topic as a whole.

https://vimeo.com/84899673

The Purposes of Protocols

The protocols in the curriculum serve a variety of purposes:

» **Reading, writing, and annotating:** Protocols for reading, writing, and annotating hold all students accountable for building background knowledge about a topic and for analyzing what they read by annotating the text with questions, comments, or summary language. Protocols are not text-specific; instead, they provide students with tools to dig deeper into any text. These protocols also allow you to assess which students are struggling with the text and may need further support for comprehension. Finally, they allow students to gather and organize their thoughts before discussion or writing.

» **Building vocabulary:** Protocols for building vocabulary make domain-specific and general academic vocabulary come alive for students through creating meaningful context, connecting new words to previous schema, and repeating shared use of the words. Vocabulary protocols and strategies help students understand that acquiring new words is an active process requiring interaction and application.

» **Collaboration and discussion:** Protocols for collaboration and discussion invite students to value different perspectives and new insights. They make room for listening as well as contributing to discussion: guidelines for timekeeping, turn taking, and focusing help students develop the skills they need for productive discussions. Sentence stems for academic conversation and asking questions, norms for honoring diverse perspectives, and procedures for synthesizing contributions to a discussion hold individuals and groups accountable for pushing their thinking further. Discussion protocols and strategies can be embedded into a daily lesson, or they can be the entire lesson.

» **Sharing and presenting:** Protocols for sharing and presenting focus on fairness and equity. They enable all members of a group to see or hear the work done by individuals or small groups in an efficient way. Timekeeping and turn-taking norms are emphasized to maximize equity of sharing.

» **Critique:** Protocols for peer critique are essential for teaching students how to offer and receive kind, specific, and helpful feedback. They allow students to navigate the tricky social terrain of giving constructive criticism, while keeping them focused on sharing and supporting rigorous content. The Speed-Dating Critique protocol is a great example and is highlighted in Video Spotlight 2.4.

▶▶ Video Spotlight 2.4

In this video, tenth-graders in Monet Cooper's English class at Capital City Public Charter School in Washington, DC, engage in a Speed-Dating Critique protocol. They spend 10 minutes in pairs, offering each other specific feedback on a high-stakes writing assignment, before moving on to another partner for another round of critique.

https://vimeo.com/124633818

Socratic Seminar

Purpose

Socratic Seminars promote thinking, meaning making, and the ability to debate, use evidence, and build on one another's thinking. When well designed and implemented, the seminar provides an active role for every student, engages students in complex thinking about rich content, and teaches students discussion skills.

Materials

» Provocative question for discussion, chosen beforehand

» Associated text(s)

» Anchor chart for protocol norms

Procedure

1. Select a significant piece of text or collection of short texts related to the current focus of study. This may be an excerpt from a book or an article from a magazine, journal, or newspaper. It might also be a poem, short story, or personal memoir. The text needs to be rich with possibilities for diverse points of view.

2. Develop an open-ended, provocative question as the starting point for the seminar discussion. The question should be worded to elicit differing perspectives and complex thinking. Students may also generate questions to discuss.

3. Students prepare for the seminar by reading the chosen piece of text in an active manner that helps them build background knowledge for participation in the discussion. The completion of the pre-seminar task is the student's "ticket" to participate in the seminar. The pre-seminar assignment could easily incorporate work on reading strategies. For example, students might be asked to read the article in advance and to "text code" by underlining important information, putting question marks by segments they wonder about, and exclamation points next to parts that surprise them.

4. Once the seminar begins, all students should be involved and should make sure others in the group are drawn into the discussion.

5. Begin the discussion with the open-ended questions designed to provoke inquiry and diverse perspectives. Inner circle students may choose to move to a different question if the group agrees, or the facilitator may pose follow-up questions.

6. The discussion proceeds until you call time. At that time, the group debriefs their process; if using a fishbowl (see below), the outer circle members give their feedback sheets to the inner group students.

7. Protocol norms: Students...
- Respect other students. (Exhibit open-mindedness and value others' contributions.)
- Are active listeners. (Build on one another's ideas by referring to them.)
- Stay focused on the topic.
- Make specific references to the text. (Use examples from the text to explain their points.)
- Give input. (Ensure participation.)
- Ask questions. (Clarifying questions, and probing questions that push the conversation further and deeper when appropriate.)

Variations

» Combine with the Fishbowl protocol. When it is time for the seminar, students are divided into two groups if there are enough people to warrant using a fishbowl approach. One group forms the inner circle (the "fish") that will be discussing the text. The other group forms the outer circle that will give feedback on content, contributions, and/or group skills. (Note: "Fishbowls" may be used with other instructional practices such as peer critiques, literature circles, or group work. If the number of students in the seminar is small, a fishbowl does not need to be used.) Each person in the outer circle is asked to observe one of the students in the inner circle. Criteria or a rubric for the observations should be developed by/shared with students in advance so observers can track such things as if their peers are making eye contact, referencing the text, or asking probing questions.

» Provide sentence stems or Conversation Cues that allow students to interact positively and thoughtfully with one another: "I'd like to build on that thought..." "Could you tell me more?" "May I finish my thought?"

References

Israel, E. (2002). Examining multiple perspectives in literature. In *Inquiry and the literary text: Constructing discussions in the English Classroom*. Urbana, IL: NCTE.

Figure 2.3: Sample Question Diagram, Fifth Grade

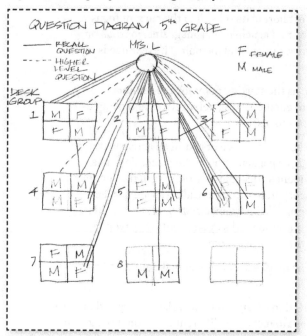

Figure 2.4: Sample Question Diagram, Eighth-Grade ELA

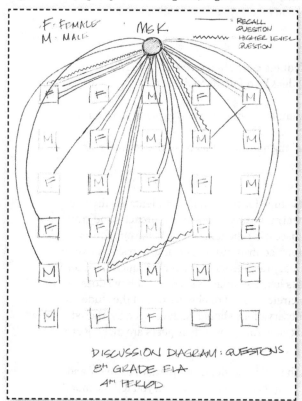

Deepening Student Discourse

There is no better indicator of the quality of learning taking place in a classroom than the quality of student discourse. Over the past few years, Harvard researchers Jal Mehta and Sara Fine have traveled across the United States visiting exemplary classrooms as part of their research for their 2019 book *In Search of Deeper Learning*. They quickly found that regardless of the reputation of the school or teacher, or the stated outcomes of the lesson, what really mattered was *what students were discussing and how they were discussing it*. In the best classrooms, students were taking the lead in offering ideas and analysis of deep topics, were responding to the comments of other students with respect and interest, and were insightful in the questions they asked of one another and of the teacher.

Students *can* learn the skills for powerful discourse. Regardless of grade level and academic background, students will change their behaviors to fit into the culture of a high-level classroom when they are guided and supported to do so. Once students have made this shift and developed these skills, it can spill over into all of their academic and personal life: they learn that they have the courage and ability to speak up with clarity and eloquence.

Modeling Discourse

The first step in students learning the skills of strong discourse is modeling. When you listen carefully to the ideas and questions of students, and unpack and analyze them in front of the class, students learn that their own ideas and those of their peers have value. Formalizing student ideas by naming them by that student (e.g., Kara's hypothesis; Carlos's approach) helps students take pride in themselves as intellectuals and thinkers. When you direct students to ask questions and make responses to one another, rather than keeping the dialogue just between you and the students (e.g., "Brianna, why don't you address that question to Simeon? He has strong opinions about that"), students get in the habit of building student-to-student discussion in class. It may be helpful to think of this as a volleyball match, with ideas bouncing from student to student before going back over the net to you, rather than a ping-pong match, with the discussion passing back and forth between you and individual students. Adolescent learners are deeply oriented toward their peers, both in terms of taking cues about what matters and craving interactions, and this practice helps them exercise that need for the good of the group.

Using Sentence Frames

For students of all ages, sentence frames can be powerful in shifting the quality of conversation. Simple phrases can become the norm in classrooms and elevate the level of conversation, making it more respectful and productive. Sentence frames are a consistent structure used throughout the curriculum, designed to foster discourse and support productive and equitable conversation among students. Supported discourse of this nature is an important part of the process of acquiring literacy skills for all students, and for ELLs it plays a key role in language acquisition.

Additionally, when students build new vocabulary through their reading and their studies, that vocabulary will become a part of the discourse when you model its use and when you celebrate students who include it in their arguments (e.g., "Anthony, I'm impressed that you used the word *theme* in your argument. Can you remind us what that word means in this case?").

Assessing Yourself

It may be difficult for you to judge the level of student discourse during a lesson while you are teaching. Consider enlisting the help of an observer—a fellow teacher, coach, or administrator—who can take notes or record the lesson, not for an evaluation, but for learning. If the observer makes a diagram of who speaks to whom, and what they say, it is likely to surprise you to see this data after the lesson. What kinds of questions were asked? How much conversation was teacher-student versus student-student? Which students spoke a lot or very little, and were patterns of participation correlated with student identity? (e.g, How much did boys speak versus girls? How often did ELLs participate?) These data can be analyzed non-judgmentally to support your efforts to deepen classroom discourse, a powerful tool for student learning. See Figures 2.3 and 2.4 for two sample diagrams.

Co-Constructing Anchor Charts with Students

By recording content, strategies, processes, cues, and guidelines from their learning on anchor charts and posting them in the classroom, teachers are able to help students make their thinking visible. Anchor charts empower students to own their learning because they are a place for students to look to for support when answering questions, contributing to discussions, processing their ideas, and writing. When students know where to look for help independently, they don't always have to ask you. Anchor charts also give students a chance to process their thinking and hear the thinking of others before or during writing, close reading, or other activities that may be challenging for them without such support.

Building Anchor Charts

There are many ways to build anchor charts. In the curriculum, there are some places where you will be cued to create anchor charts in advance of the lesson, others where you will co-create them with students during the lesson, and others where students will create them together in small groups. Sometimes students might work together in small groups to record their ideas on an anchor chart, come back together, present it to the class, and then contribute to one combined class version of the chart. Alternatively, you might work as a whole class to clarify and capture the most important ideas or questions on one anchor chart before students work independently or in small groups.

Generally, anchor charts are living documents that are clarified and added to by you and students. By adding to anchor charts throughout a unit or module or across an entire year, students are able to clarify, update, and expand their growing knowledge. In this way, the charts remain relevant and supportive over time and ensure that all students have access to the same information. There are other times when anchor charts support specific lessons or arcs of lessons and will be created and taken down in short order.

Supporting Students with Anchor Charts

Anchor charts are supportive of students' varied learning needs and play a valuable role in their learning. This is especially true for ELLs and students who may need additional support with perception and information processing. The very nature of anchor charts allows them to be easily customized based on students' needs, and they offer an alternative to providing only auditory information. And, unlike text written on a whiteboard, anchor charts can live on in the classroom long after a lesson has ended.

Characteristics of an Effective
(QUALITIES) Summary (# HIGH QUALITY)

- An introduction to the text stating the title and central idea.
- A brief outline of what the text is about.
- Key supporting details that convey the central idea.
- No opinions or judgements
- Concluding sentence.
- A possible theme (point/message author is trying to teach you)

Visual aids and predictable ways of organizing information make anchor charts supportive of students' learning needs.

We recommend that you add visuals, definitions, or translations to anchor charts to support ELLs' language acquisition and ability to access the information on the chart. Anchor charts will provide them with concrete examples as they try to apply the content, strategy, or process represented on them. You can also manipulate the display of information by using larger font or highlighting certain words or phrases. In addition to customizing the charts themselves, you may also want to provide individual copies to students who may need additional support to help them maintain focus, monitor progress, sketch or take notes about their thinking, and access important information as they work independently.

Chapter 2C:
How Can I Create the Kind of Active and Collaborative Classroom Culture the Curriculum Requires?

Instructional practices like those described in Chapter 2B, which permeate the curriculum, result in classrooms that are active and collaborative, alive with energy and movement. This hum and buzz will be familiar and comfortable for some of you. For others, it may be new and potentially a little unsettling. Classroom management is one of the hardest parts of being a teacher in general—and a teacher of adolescents in particular—and the truth is that our curriculum may require a few changes, depending on your current approach. If you are accustomed to a classroom that is always quiet, where your students sit up straight with their eyes on you for the majority of the time, or one where students work mostly independently, you may need to stretch a little out of your comfort zone.

Learning to teach a new curriculum is a lot for any teacher; learning new classroom management strategies on top of that may feel overwhelming. Rather than thinking of this as "layering on," however, we encourage you to reframe the work of creating an active and collaborative classroom culture as a deepening or enriching of our curriculum. The truth is that all of the work you do to teach your students to read and write and comprehend complex text with this curriculum will be easier for you and more effective for them if you spend some time on the front end cultivating the soil of your classroom culture.

Managing an active classroom full of students doing collaborative work is different from managing a quiet classroom full of students doing independent seat work, and you may need to learn a few new techniques. Those we offer here are really just a start to get you on your way to making the most of this curriculum.

Much of what follows comes from our 2015 book *Management in the Active Classroom*, which describes self-managed classrooms and our approach to twenty-three classroom management practices. These practices cover topics ranging from "Transitions" to "Giving Clear Directions" to "Restorative Practices," and everything in between. The book also includes videos showing students and teachers in action; the full collection of videos can be viewed on our website at: https://eleducation.org/resources/collections/management-in-the-active-classroom-videos.

We start here by describing what we mean by self-management and then move on to highlighting and summarizing some of the classroom management practices described in *Management in the Active Classroom* that will be most supportive when teaching the curriculum.

▶ WHAT IS SELF-MANAGEMENT, AND HOW WILL IT HELP MY MIDDLE SCHOOL STUDENTS BE SUCCESSFUL?

There's a certain instantly recognizable energy present in a high-achieving classroom. You can see it in the faces of the students: lighting up as they make new connections between their background knowledge and their reading, or settling into deep concentration on an entrance ticket. You can hear it in the respectful but warm conversations that occur between student and teacher, and in the way students take control of their classroom routines and procedures with only the gentlest of reminders. You can touch it: the poster of jointly written classroom norms, the materials organized and ready for students when they enter.

A successful classroom is obvious to all our senses. But the steps to take to create that classroom often are not. Ironically, a robust body of research has identified effective classroom practices: we know what works. However, few educational researchers or teacher preparation programs in the United States address effective classroom management (Emmer, Sabornie, Evertson, and Weinstein, 2013).

As a result, teachers can be at a loss, particularly as novice educators, as to what "magic" is needed to keep students engaged, on task, accountable, compassionate, and safe. It can seem to be a kind of "secret sauce," or perhaps something only certain teachers are born with. Teachers who have the magic often have a difficult time explaining what their magic is—and yet they will also tell you that the most brilliant, creative lesson plan in the world will not work without it.

In fact, effective classroom management is not magic, secret, or a lucky gift given to a chosen few. It is this: teachers, with their students, taking full responsibility for developing thoughtful, proactive, foundational management structures that are implemented and reinforced throughout every learning experience. It starts with the belief that students can and will succeed with effective support, and it is one of the most valuable investments of time you can make. The best news of all is that it is something every teacher can learn, practice, and master.

Good classroom management practice comes under many names: "the orderly classroom," "the rigorous classroom," or "the focused classroom." We invite you to think of it as "the self-managed classroom." A self-managed classroom is respectful, active, collaborative, and growth-oriented.

By using the term "self-managed," we don't mean to imply that classrooms will run themselves or that students don't need the authority and support of their teachers—academically and behaviorally. Rather, self-management is an ethos and a belief system that permeates the classroom and says students have the power, within themselves, to make wise choices that best serve them as learners and people and maintain a respectful classroom culture. Self-discipline is the end goal of all management structures. Students and teachers in the self-managed classroom are people who have self-knowledge, self-compassion, and self-control.

As a result, students in a self-managed classroom do not constantly need authority figures to compel them to exhibit correct behavior; ultimately, with guidance and practice, they own and enact that behavior themselves. Students reach this point through the consistent implementation of the formative assessment practices of modeling, practice, and reflection.

Finally, students in a self-managed classroom also understand that a "self" does not stand alone. A healthy sense of self necessarily includes a strong sense of community. Self-managed classrooms know and nurture their place as a learning community unto themselves and alongside other classrooms with their own identities within a broader school community.

A Closer Look at the Self-Managed Classroom

Self-managed classrooms share basic characteristics, no matter the age of the students. These characteristics are rooted strongly in high behavioral and academic expectations, which in turn positively reinforce and support each other.

Figure 2.5 The Self-Managed Classroom

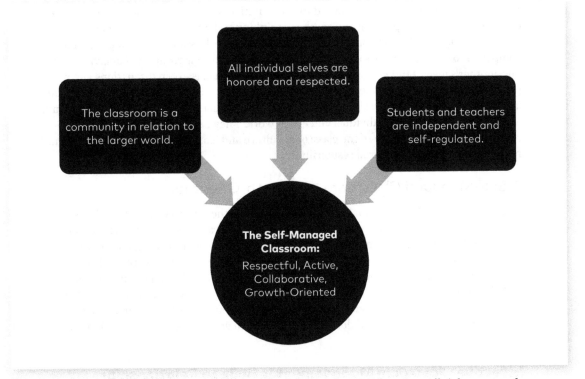

A Self-Managed Classroom Is Respectful.

Respect is the bottom line for all academic and social interactions in the classroom. Teachers explicitly lead and model for students an unwavering disposition of respect in the way they interact with the class and with their colleagues. Students are held to impeccable standards of respect toward one another and toward adults. Norms for respectful communication are set, modeled, and enforced without compromise. Cultural differences in the classroom are honored and respected. Students are not simply directed to "be respectful," however. They discuss respect every day; they hold themselves and one another accountable for respectful behavior. They are considered partners in the learning process, deserving the respect and expectations given to adults: engagement, support, and accountability. As a result, students feel safe and trust one another.

A Self-Managed Classroom Is Active.

In a self-managed classroom, all students contribute to the learning experience and are held accountable for that contribution. Multiple entry points are evident, honoring different learning styles, strengths, comfort levels, and development. Self-managed classrooms help students learn about their own social and academic strengths and contribute to the class in significant and varied ways. Students and teachers shift through multiple configurations of learning (whole class lessons, group work, independent research, guided work) with grace and speed, with the ultimate goal of student independence in mind. Self-managed classrooms are silent and still at times, when that fits the nature of the work. Students can demonstrate alertness when needed, following the speaker with attention and courtesy. At other times, self-managed classrooms are alive with movement and a productive "buzz" of discussion, problem-solving, critique, and creation when the work demands activity and collaboration. Like a real-world workplace, the classroom is often busy with a range of focused and productive independent and group work at the same time.

A Self-Managed Classroom Is Collaborative.

A self-managed classroom is committed to collaborative, social construction of knowledge—a community of learners pushing one another's thinking and building one another's understanding—in whole class, small group, and paired work. Students are impelled and compelled to share their ideas and understanding with different groups and analyze and critique one another's ideas. Students often take leadership roles in classroom discussions and protocols, particularly at the secondary level. Students work together to maintain a classroom climate that is physically and emotionally safe and positive, keep their classroom space neat and organized, and produce high-quality individual and group work. They have individual and collective responsibility for the quality of the classroom culture and learning. It is not just the teacher's responsibility—it is their shared responsibility.

A Self-Managed Classroom Is Growth-Oriented.

In a self-managed classroom, making mistakes is part of the territory. In fact, students and teachers understand that mistakes are not only normal but a necessary sign that learning is occurring. To that end, students demonstrate, analyze, and celebrate academic courage, taking risks to speak up in class, ask questions, pose ideas, and try out new concepts and vocabulary. They are not afraid or embarrassed to show that they care about learning. They understand and discuss the concept of growth mindset—that practice makes you stronger, that engaging in harder work and more challenging problems "grows your brain." They thrive on embedded cycles of practice, feedback, and documented growth in academics, communication, routines, and procedures.

Effective Classroom Management Is Built on Relationships

Every student wants to be known and valued—by their teachers and their peers. The better you know your students, the more effective you can be. It's possible to run a classroom without knowing students particularly well through stern and rigid, or entertaining and clever, teacher-centered lessons. It's even possible to keep students engaged much of the time through ritualized, fast-paced practices that keep eyes on the teacher. But to build a self-managed classroom where students are engaged, self-motivated, and self-disciplined while working actively and collaboratively, fostering good relationships with those students is the foundation of success.

Classroom management often breaks down when a student is struggling academically, socially, emotionally, physically, or any combination of those. If you have built trust with that student, you have a foundation to intervene, subtly or demonstrably, to support and redirect them. It is especially important to be able to cite specific positive attributes of students when working with them—especially when their behavior is challenging—so that there can be a genuine basis for your faith in them to succeed. This doesn't guarantee an easy solution, but without this foundation, there is little to build on to help the student grow.

We believe that great teachers teach from the heart: They have a love of their subject areas, and, beyond this, they believe in and care deeply about their students. They genuinely feel that their students are capable of more ambitious success than their students themselves imagine. Because the purpose of this book and our curriculum is to support great teaching, we join what we know about classroom management to the positive belief in the capacity of students to succeed at high levels—independently and collectively.

Classroom Management for All

One of the greatest challenges for any teacher is finding strategies that work for all students. Just as academic instruction must be differentiated to meet the needs of diverse learners, often classroom management must be differentiated to meet the needs of the diverse young people in our classrooms. One-size-fits-all approaches may work some of the time, but they rarely work all of the time.

Responding to students' varied needs is an essential ingredient in any inclusive approach to classroom management. It starts with relationships: knowing students well, building trust, and listening to and responding to their needs. It also must include *learning* about the individual realities that students bring into the classroom with them. If, for example, you have a new student with an autism spectrum disorder, *learn* about that diagnosis. Read, ask questions, and collaborate with colleagues, specialists, and especially families to identify strategies that will make your classroom just as productive and supportive for that student as it is for other students. Understand the cultural differences among your students (and you) and what that means when building an active and collaborative classroom culture. Ask questions, be open to change, and don't assume that your way is the right way.

The Relationship between Classroom Management and Student Engagement and Motivation

The best management tool is creating engaged and motivated students. When schoolwork is personally meaningful, appropriately challenging, and invites creative and critical thinking, it brings out the best in student behavior. The same group of students who may be considered "behavior problems" or "unfocused" in one classroom may be "model students" in another classroom where the work is compelling. On the flip side, effective classroom management also creates the conditions that allow all students to engage in their academics.

Classroom management is most successful when students are not only academically motivated, but also motivated to be their best selves. This is most effective when students are primarily motivated not by compliance to rules (though compliance is necessary) or by external rewards and tracking systems (though for some situations or students, those may be helpful), but by their aspiration to be good and positive members of a classroom community that they respect and value.

The most powerful engagement and motivation is not created by clever structures. It is created by a sense of belonging to a positive academic community. In our curriculum, students are grounded every day in their habits of character. Based on our three Dimensions of Student Achievement (see Figure 1.2), our habits of character are designed to help students become effective learners and ethical people who contribute to a better world. Working together toward these goals and reflecting on them frequently creates the sense of belonging students need to be most successful academically.

It is easy to see where this approach to classroom management is different. Traditionally, classroom management conceives of students as needing to be guided and controlled for the smooth, orderly operation of a school. Management is something done *to* students. Although we recognize the essential need for adult guidance, the self-managed classroom is created *with* students, promoting self-discipline and self-guidance, and thrives within classroom and school cultures that promote habits of character and intentionally work to help students become their best selves.

Self-Management as an Engine for Equity

When classrooms are genuinely respectful, active, collaborative, and growth oriented, they are also engines for equity. Every student has access to the resources, rigor, and representation they need in order to develop to their full academic and social potential, regardless of race, gender, ethnicity, language, disability, immigration status, family background, family income, or any other group characteristic[3]. This entails a process of ensuring high outcomes for all and removing the predictability of success or failure that correlates with any social or cultural factor.

---

3. Adapted from Aspen Institute, Pursuing Social and Emotional Development Through a Racial Equity Lens, 2018; and National Equity Project, 2017

Such classrooms hold a vision that all students *can* and *want to be* part of a thriving classroom community, and charges adults with setting up the structures and culture that bring all students in.

A **respectful classroom** is an equitable classroom when "respect" as a concept is demystified, when the behaviors that are perceived as respectful by both teachers and students are named, and when both teachers and students attend to the impact of their actions as well as the intent. A **collaborative classroom** is an equitable classroom when the success of the whole depends on the meaningful contribution of each member. An **active classroom** is an equitable classroom when teachers reflect honestly on how their biases shape their instincts about how students should move and speak. A **growth-oriented classroom** is an equitable classroom when teachers and students believe that *all* students have great potential to grow their brains.

In self-managed classrooms, the stakes are higher than just the noise level. This is why an equity stance is so important. If our classrooms are only based on obedience, we build a world of followers and don't give our students essential skills and practice to become strong leaders. We risk reproducing the large-scale inequalities many of us believe education can ameliorate, and we risk denying the students right in front of us the best chance we can give them.

Self-Managed Classrooms in Support of College- and Career-Ready Standards

The way you choose to structure and run your classroom sends a powerful message to students about their capacity and responsibility and helps define the nature of the learning process. When management structures align with the cognitive demand of college- and career-ready standards—demanding individual responsibility and independence, critical thinking, and collaborative work—then students can thrive in a coherent academic culture that promotes real-world skills. In simple terms, the classroom can promote college, career, and civic readiness through responsible self-management, rather than constrain student growth in a classroom that is exclusively teacher-driven and compliance-based.

When you communicate with students in ways that align with the highest aims of college- and career-ready standards, a synergy results that makes the standards not only meaningful and accessible, but also attainable. In this way, both classroom instruction and classroom management can and should be aligned to standards.

Consider these seven descriptors of college- and career-ready students from the introduction to the Common Core English language arts/literacy standards:

» They demonstrate independence.

» They build strong content knowledge.

» They respond to the varying demands of audience, task, purpose, and discipline.

» They comprehend as well as critique.

» They value evidence.

» They use technology and digital media strategically and capably.

» They come to understand other perspectives and cultures.

Our experience has taught us that a self-managed classroom—one that is respectful, active, collaborative, and growth-oriented—is one where this vision of a college- and career-ready student not only lives but thrives.

The section that follows highlights and summarizes some of the classroom management practices described in *Management in the Active Classroom* that are most salient to our curriculum.

▶ WHAT STRUCTURES AND STRATEGIES WILL BE MOST EFFECTIVE IN HELPING ME BUILD AN ACTIVE AND COLLABORATIVE CLASSROOM CULTURE?

At EL Education, we believe that classrooms should be lively and learning-centered, where students feel a sense of independence and responsibility for their learning and are interested and compelled by the work at hand: reading, writing, talking, creating, and contributing. In such an environment, classroom management works because students feel a sense of ownership over their work and behavior.

We aspire for students to be delighted and engaged, not quiet and compliant. Our curriculum both requires and promotes a self-managed learning environment that is *respectful*, *active*, *collaborative*, and *growth-oriented* so that students can create authentic, high-quality work, tackle real-life problems, and take charge of their own learning within a collaborative setting. Taking steps to build a classroom culture of trust, challenge, and joy for students to draw upon is an important foundation as they take on the challenges in the curriculum.

Building and strengthening such a classroom culture happens throughout the year, but it is critical to the start. For students, the first few weeks of school are the first stepping-stones to becoming successful—opening wide the school door and beckoning them to come in and begin.

In this section, we highlight two areas of focus for building a strong foundation:

1. Creating the Conditions for Success:

   - Teacher presence

   - Classroom spaces that teach

   - Building community

2. Structures and Strategies for Building an Active and Collaborative Classroom Culture:

   - Crafting norms together

   - Making expectations clear: problem-solving and consequences

   - Establishing routines through modeling and think-aloud

For more information about these practices, and many others, we encourage you to read our 2014 book *Management in the Active Classroom*, which we wrote specifically to support the kinds of classroom management practices that make our curriculum most effective. You will find videos from the collection that accompanies the book sprinkled throughout this chapter. The full collection can be accessed at: https://eleducation.org/resources/collections/management-in-the-active-classroom-videos

Creating the Conditions for Success

Teacher Presence

Researchers Carol Rodgers and Miriam Raider-Roth (2006) describe a teacher's presence this way: "[We view] teaching as engaging in an authentic relationship with students where teachers know and respond with intelligence and compassion to students and their learning. We define this engagement as 'presence'—a state of alert awareness, receptivity, and connectedness to the mental, emotional, and physical workings of both the individuals and the group in the context of their learning environment" (p. 149).

Your attitude and mindset form the foundation for your presence: knowing and valuing yourself as a teacher, knowing and valuing your students for who they are, acting as your authentic self, and knowing that your ability, like your students', grows with your effort.

Considerations:

» Develop your own mindset by thinking about who you are as a teacher; your strengths, weaknesses, passions, and values; and the things that you want to learn.

» Develop relationships with students that let them know who you are and that you are interested in who they are.

» Check any biases and assumptions you may hold (consciously or unconsciously) about your students, given your background and theirs. Be aware of how students from different backgrounds may have experienced school, interpersonal relationships, and interactions, and commit to making your classroom welcoming for all.

» Get to know your students not just by previous test scores, but also by what they care about and what brings them joy. Know their cultures, backgrounds, and needs, perhaps through an interview with them or their families. Likewise, share what you care about and what brings you joy, along with stories from your culture and background, and challenges you've faced (as appropriate). This helps students respect your authenticity and feel respected in return.

» Attend to language. In Table 2.9, we offer examples of teacher language that conveys a trust in students' ability to think deeply and share about something of importance, and that honors adolescent learners' needs and gifts.

Table 2.9: How Language Conveys Teacher Presence

Language	Example
Language of inquiry *Conveying curiosity and inviting conversations*	"What did you notice about this essay checklist? What do you wonder?"
Language of observation *Describing without judging*	"I see that some of you are using a lot evidence from Chapter 2, and some are leaning more heavily on Chapter 3."
Language of focusing *Inviting students to think about something of note rather than looking to the teacher for answers*	"Where would you assess your progress now according to our rubric? What are your reasons for that assessment?"
Language of choice *Giving options; opportunities and practice for making decisions; inspiring ownership*	"Jonathan, I see you are having a hard time settling in. I'll give you a choice: take a quick stretch and try again, or go get a drink of water and try again."
Language of access *When critical, repeating and rephrasing questions and answers and providing think time to give students greater access to understanding*	"It looks like you and Jade came up with a different answer to this question. What do you notice about the inferences each of you made?" After some think time: "Think about each of your responses. Can you tell me what's the same and what's different?"

Voice: Management in the Active Classroom
from EL Education

Voice

01:19

In the video, "Voice," you can see the power of a teacher's voice to set the tone in the classroom. Calm and measured tones support students to regulate their own voices and behaviors.

https://vimeo.com/123124604

Classroom Spaces that Teach

The physical classroom space sends a potent message to students about what is valued, and in turn how the teacher wants them to behave and learn. The wall space, seating, work areas, and materials not only support instruction, but also support strong habits of scholarship, independence, and responsibility central to the curriculum. If the physical classroom works against these principles (e.g., desks in rows), much time and energy will be spent "fighting" the space rather than teaching and learning.

By contrast, if the space is organized to encourage collaboration, to showcase student work, to meet the physical and learning needs of all students, with resources easily accessible, the form of it will fit the function of the classroom and enhance the learning and teaching that takes place there.

Considerations:

» Create a respectful, personalized space where students feel welcomed, peaceful, and at ease.

» Set up the space you have to prioritize flexibility for various configurations: independent work, group work, and whole class work. Our curriculum uses all of these configurations frequently. If you have a space you don't believe will accommodate the protocols in the curriculum, consider teaching students to use a nearby common space like a hallway, and/ or invite them to problem-solve with you about how to best accomplish the aims of a space-intensive protocol.

» Organize the space so that students can easily access and care for materials. Provide enough room for students to store both their work and their personal belongings. Invite students to help in the arrangement of the classroom by creating labels, sorting books, making charts, or arranging classroom materials.

» Create a growth-oriented space that prioritizes effort and promotes goal-setting and reflection. Make space for charts of classroom norms, academic anchor charts, module guiding questions, and documentation panels that show both students' finished work and their growth through multiple drafts.

» Involve students in discussions about the care of the classroom, and create classroom jobs around that care.

» Set up and use anchor charts, learning targets, and other strategies for setting and reflecting on goals. These are used throughout the curriculum to focus students' attention and engage them in learning. Anchor charts often stay on display throughout a unit or module, so you will need to find a place where they can stay up for the long haul.

▶▶ Video Spotlight 2.6

In the video, "Setting up Your Classroom Environment," you can see how your choices about how to set up your classroom—including multiple configurations for whole group, small group, and independent work—promote learning and self-management.

https://vimeo.com/124453007

Building Community

The desire for love and belonging are basic human needs. Students arrive on the first day with pressing questions: "Where are the bathrooms?" "When is lunch?" "Will my teachers be fair?" "Will people like me?" "Am I safe here?" And, most importantly, "Do I belong here?" Though many of these questions are unspoken, students look to you and to one another for answers. On day one, it is important to take the role of a welcoming host, inviting students in and modeling clearly how members of the community treat one another. But it's also important to quickly address students' basic questions and move them toward a sense of "ownership" of the classroom.

Nothing is more important in fostering students' growth than the degree to which they care about their own work and the success of the classroom community as a whole. And nothing fosters caring more than feeling that one is a valued member of a community. Creating positive relationships with students and families lays the foundation for a self-managed classroom, which in turn lays the foundation for success with the curriculum.

Considerations:

» Use humor and playful interactions to help students to get to know one another and build group identity. Invite participation through noncompetitive games and structured personal sharing. Remember that adolescents are intensely oriented to their peers, so it is your role to offer them lots of opportunities to be social *in service of* building community and learning. Often, playful interaction is viewed as in opposition to serious learning. But experience and research show the opposite: play is a natural way to learn; interaction is mandatory for adolescents to thrive; and both are joyful ways to build the group cohesion that is so necessary for collaborative, deeper learning.

» Take time to get to know students personally as well as academically. Share your personal and academic stories when appropriate. Be aware of differences that may exist between your own background and experiences and that of many of your students, and how those differences shape your interactions. If you find that differences in identity or experience are shaping your interactions in a harmful way, ask your students for their perspectives on your differences and suggestions for next steps; adolescent learners are quite capable of offering them!

» Encourage families to share their excitement and concern about the classroom and curriculum, and integrate these considerations. Invite them into the classroom to convey their excitement and care and to serve as experts on particular topics.

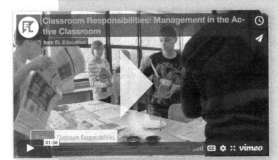

In the video, "Classroom Responsibilities," the principles of self-management allow students to take charge of taking care of their classroom. Students take on leadership roles and even conduct "staff meetings" with their classmates to reflect on quality control.

https://vimeo.com/142645382

Structures and Strategies for Building an Active and Collaborative Classroom Culture

Crafting Norms Together

Rules, constitutions, guidelines, expectations, community commitments—the behaviors we wish students to exhibit have a variety of names. In many classrooms they are called "norms." Norms are the foundation for respectful behavior among students, between students and teachers, and among teachers.

Through a process of co-creating norms, students appreciate immediately that they are not being asked to regurgitate your thoughts, but are genuinely included in the process of governing themselves and their classroom. Because they have authored the guidelines themselves, students understand clearly the intent behind them and are invested in respecting them. The key when creating norms is to generate a positive, thoughtful discussion and to distill student suggestions into a clear and effective list. Norms can then be discussed and used to guide discussions and interactions. In our Grades 6–8 curriculum, you won't be guided through a process of co-creating *classroom* norms, as you might be in a self-contained classroom with younger students; however, you will periodically be guided through a process of creating *discussion* norms before intensive discussion protocols like Socratic Seminars. We believe that devoting time with students to thinking through what they want their interactions to look like and sound like—especially when the success of the lesson depends on the quality of their discussion—is time well spent.

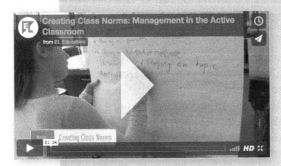

In the video, "Creating Class Norms," students develop class norms and reflect on their use. Classroom norms for communication and respect help students feel safe and focused.

https://vimeo.com/124448656

Considerations:

In Grade 6, Module 1, Unit 1 there is an arc of lessons that serves as a good example of how discussion norms can be built with students. These lessons lead up to a text-based discussion at the end of the unit. To prepare for this discussion, students engage in an abbreviated, modified Socratic Seminar in a "fishbowl." The inner circle (inside the "fishbowl") practices the text-based discussion and the outer circle observes so that the group can begin to develop discussion norms. Students consider the following questions while the teacher records responses on an anchor chart:

» What did the group do well when discussing? What should we be mindful of whenever we participate in group discussions? Why?

» How could the group or you have improved the discussion? Are there any norms we could add to make our collaborative discussions more effective?

In the course of that debrief, students and the teacher are working toward not just naming behaviors, but grounding themselves in a shared sense of what a discussion is *for*, and thus what it means for a group to do well.

The next day, they continue their work building the norms:

» How did either the group or you encourage someone else to clarify when you didn't understand? What questions can you ask when you don't understand what someone is saying?

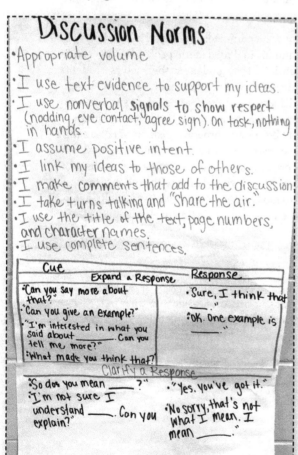

» How did you find out more about the ideas of others? What questions can you ask when you want to find out more?

Before the text-based discussion begins in the third lesson of this arc, the teacher grounds students in the norms and reminds them that effective participation is not just about talking; it is also about listening to others and asking and answering questions in order to be completely clear about what others are saying and to clarify their own points. The norms will offer guidance for students in when and how to do this.

Making Expectations Clear: Problem Solving and Consequences

When you work together with students to create norms for important conversations, as in the previous example, you are not abdicating your authority for classroom management; rather, you are making a promise to uphold what is most important to the students. Perhaps nothing you do carries more weight than how you manage behavior that doesn't align with what you've all agreed matters to you. All your norms, circles, advice, and advisory periods mean nothing if you don't deliver on what you say when it really counts.

Discussion Norms anchor charts like this one, which includes Conversation Cues, support productive student-led conversations.

"Where did we ever get the crazy idea that in order to make children do better, first we have to make them feel worse?"

Jane Nelsen
Positive Discipline

Your approach to problem-solving and consequences should be in service of helping students self-manage within an active, collaborative community. Fair and logical consequences make students feel supported and help strengthen the classroom community. "Fair and logical" does mean "generally predictable" but does not mean "rigidly applied." We know that a trauma-sensitive approach requires that when a student's behavior doesn't match the community's expectation, our first response is to ask "what is happening for this student?" rather than "what does the consequence chart say?" and to let our response flow from what we learn. To take full advantage of our curriculum that teaches *collaboration*, *perseverance*, and *initiative*, students must be able to depend on this level of emotional safety. In the curriculum, students are regularly asked to take risks academically. They need to feel emotionally safe to do so. If community members (students or adults) violate the norms, that must be addressed directly, specifically, and with compassion. Remember that adolescents are exquisitely sensitive to issues of justice and social difference; if the adult community does not abide by the standards of interpersonal conduct to which the students are held, students will be far less likely to view those standards as worthy of their own efforts.

▶▶ **Video Spotlight 2.9**

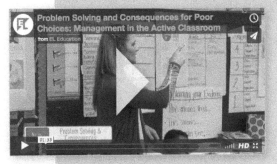

In the video, "Problem Solving and Consequences for Poor Choices," you can see the importance of teacher voice and body language for helping students get themselves back on track after making poor choices. The way you handle poor choices sends a powerful message to students.

https://vimeo.com/124448651

Considerations:

» Carefully choose your words and tone. Students should hear, "You made a bad choice," not "you are a bad person." Deliver consequences firmly and gently, striving to communicate your belief that the student can and will do well with the right supports.

» Use reminders or quick redirections. Rather than a long lecture, give a quick, subtle gesture that is culturally appropriate for all students. Fewer words frequently bring the best results because little attention is taken from the flow of the class.

» Consequences should be:

• **Relevant.** A consequence must be relevant to the deed (e.g., if students write on their desks, then they should clean it up).

• **Respectful.** A consequence is not a punishment; it is feedback from which a student can learn (e.g., rather than assigning detention for writing on a desk, having the student clean the desk communicates that "don't write on desks" isn't an arbitrary guideline, but one that's in place to avoid the need for the extra work of constantly cleaning them). No consequence should be forever, or delivered out of frustration.

- **Realistic.** A consequence must be doable for the student and for you and not overly harsh (e.g., if a student writes on a desk, then they should fix the mistake by cleaning the desk, not cleaning *all* the desks).

» Introduce the concept of consequences and problem-solving through discussions and modeling. Question the idea that all students are familiar or comfortable with a consequences-driven approach to problem-solving. Discuss your approach and rationale with families.

» Discuss the *positive* consequences when students *do* follow the norms: "What happens when you choose to cooperate with your classmates? Why might that be important?"

» When students violate a norm or feelings get hurt, have set guidelines for fixing the mistake that repair the harm done. Use restorative questions (rather than accusations) to find out what happened and what can be done to fix it (e.g., "What were you thinking at the time?" or "Tell me what you think happened").

» Ask a student who has caused harm to think with you about what they need to prevent similar behavior in the future. Be clear about your orientation toward preventing harm (which will limit what solutions you can accept), but also open to hearing what's going on for the student and what changes might make a big difference.

» Look for areas in which you can give students increasing ownership over classroom routines and procedures, so they can put their burgeoning independence to use. Once specific protocols are well-established, students can lead them, and they will feel acutely aware of how their peers are or aren't following agreed-upon norms.

Establishing Routines through Modeling and Think-Aloud

Inviting students to feel welcome in and responsible for the classroom requires taking time to teach and practice daily routines. This is best done through modeling, think-alouds, and guided practice, just as with all new academic routines that are introduced in the curriculum.

Modeling is a way to scaffold learning. It is a participatory strategy that goes beyond just telling students what you expect; it *shows* students what is expected, invites them to reflect, and allows them to practice, leading them to ever more independence. Students who are learning to self-manage require a growth mindset so that they view routines and transitions as skills to practice and improve upon. Modeling is effective to teach start-of-the-year routines (e.g., working with classroom materials, responding to teacher signals for attention, transitions). These routines need to be efficient, practiced, and purposeful. Combine modeling with think-alouds, which show students the internal and external language that supports decision-making and thinking processes.

Considerations:

» Model routines just as you would model academic work. Begin with an exemplar or ideal behavior, deconstruct the parts so students understand, and finally put it back together to practice. Suggested steps for modeling routines:

- Model the routine, including thinking aloud if appropriate.

- Ask the students what they noticed about what you did (e.g., "When you raised your hand, other students did, too").

- Summarize the routine, and have students repeat the steps.

- Call on one or two students to demonstrate.

- Ask again what students notice.

- Have everyone practice until it is one hundred percent correct for all students. Don't settle for less.

» When practicing, consider aspects of teacher presence, such as body language and voice, to convey the message that you know students can succeed.

» With adolescent learners it can be especially supportive and entertaining to ask students to first playfully demonstrate the behavior that *isn't* desired, and then the behavior aligned with community expectations; this helps students feel that they aren't just imitating *you*, but are choosing between two courses of action they've publicly acknowledged as different.

Chapter 2:
Instructional Leadership

We believe that impactful instructional leadership involves cycles of action and reflection. Here we offer questions for reflection, indicators of progress, and resources that will help you support teachers as they *plan and prepare to teach.*

Table 2.10: Chapter 2 Quick Guide for Instructional Leaders: Planning and Preparing to Teach

Questions for Reflection
» What system is in place to ensure that teachers have time to plan and prepare to teach the modules? <ul><li>What structures exist that can support teachers in their daily and long-range planning—lesson, unit, module, and year-long planning?</li><li>What planning paradigm guides teachers in their planning and preparation process?</li><li>How will you and your staff make use of the task cards and digital planning tools? Or do you have a different plan for how to analyze curriculum documents with teachers (e.g., Module Overviews, Curriculum Maps, Assessment Overview and Resources)? How will you engage and support teachers to make instructional decisions based on careful planning?</li><li>What structures exist for classroom teachers to collaborate with support specialists (e.g., reading interventionists, English as a second language teachers)?</li></ul>
» What is your school's vision for what teaching and learning should look like in all classrooms? <ul><li>How do you engage and support teachers to make that vision a reality in their classrooms?</li><li>Are you prepared to make practices that promote student engagement and ownership of learning (e.g., learning targets, protocols) as much of a priority as more traditional literacy-focused practices? How will you support teachers to also make them a priority?</li><li>How does the configuration of classrooms (e.g., desks, work areas, supplies) reflect the vision for teaching and learning?</li><li>What are your expectations regarding classroom management? Are you vocally supportive of the collaborative, active learning in the curriculum? How will you support teachers? How might you need to adjust your expectations for what classrooms will look like and sound like when teachers are teaching the curriculum?</li></ul>

Indicators of Progress

» The district/school consistently provides teachers time, structures, and supports for planning and professional learning.

Not Yet True   *Somewhat True*   *Very True*

» Planning time is protected for teachers, coaches, and specialists to both look out across units and modules and to plan for daily lessons.

Not Yet True   *Somewhat True*   *Very True*

» Teachers report clarity around the school's accountability system for lesson preparation and planning.

Not Yet True   *Somewhat True*   *Very True*

» The master schedule reflects regular collaborative planning time for grade-level and department teams, and all critical support specialists are able to consistently engage.

Not Yet True   *Somewhat True*   *Very True*

» Teachers understand the purpose of all curricular documents and fully leverage them in both their long-term and daily planning.

Not Yet True   *Somewhat True*   *Very True*

» Teachers consistently make instructional decisions that reflect a full understanding of the logic and structure of the curriculum.

Not Yet True   *Somewhat True*   *Very True*

» Teachers, coaches, and specialists begin long-range and daily lesson preparation and planning with the "end in mind." They begin with high-level documents (e.g., Curriculum Plan, Curriculum Map) and aim for a deep understanding of the Four T's within a module, unit, and lesson.

Not Yet True   *Somewhat True*   *Very True*

» Teachers demonstrate a growth mindset with regards to their own professional learning.

Not Yet True   *Somewhat True*   *Very True*

» Coaching and professional learning is in place to help staff learn and master new instructional practices. Staff know when it's okay to make adjustments and when it's not, and they ask for help when they need it.

Not Yet True   *Somewhat True*   *Very True*

» Teachers consistently set up routines that allow students to be responsible in a self-managed classroom.

Not Yet True   *Somewhat True*   *Very True*

» Classrooms are configured in a way that allows students to easily move in and out of small groups.

Not Yet True   *Somewhat True*   *Very True*

» Teachers set clear expectations and enact classroom routines that support students in assuming the responsibility for their learning.

Not Yet True   *Somewhat True*   *Very True*

» Students are clear on classroom expectations and contribute to an engaging and joyful learning experience for themselves and others.

Not Yet True	Somewhat True	Very True

» Staff receive coaching and support for classroom management that elevate respectful, active, collaborative, and growth-oriented classrooms.

Not Yet True	Somewhat True	Very True

» Students consistently self-manage behaviors in transitions.

Not Yet True	Somewhat True	Very True

» Teachers post learning targets, unpack learning targets, and explain how each section of a lesson moves students toward the learning target.

Not Yet True	Somewhat True	Very True

» Teachers consistently use quick checks for understanding.

Not Yet True	Somewhat True	Very True

» Students consistently self-identify goals and clarify how they will be working toward those goals.

Not Yet True	Somewhat True	Very True

Resources and Suggestions

» The curriculum itself, along with a full suite of companion resources and tools, can be found at: Curriculum.ELeducation.org. Resources include:

- Digital/Printable Versions of All Task Cards from Chapter 2A

- Digital Lesson Preparation Tool

» Resources available on the main EL Education website (ELeducation.org):

- Screencasts (overviews and grade-level specific)

- Videos: https://eleducation.org/resources/collections/your-curriculum-companion-6-8-videos

- PD Packs

  ○ Leaders of Their Own Learning

  ○ Collaborative Culture

- Professional Development Opportunities (or email pd@eleducation.org)

» Books by EL Education that deepen understanding of the practices in this chapter:

- *Leaders of Their Own Learning: Transforming Schools through Student-Engaged Assessment*

- *The Leaders of Their Own Learning Companion: New Tools and Tips for Tackling the Common Challenges of Student-Engaged Assessment*

- *Management in the Active Classroom*

» Book: *Total Participation Techniques: Making Every Student an Active Learner*

» Resources on Protocols:

- Classroom Protocols collection at Curriculum.ELeducation.org

- National School Reform Faculty website (nsrfharmony.org)

- School Reform Initiative website (schoolreforminitiative.org)

» Article: "Habits Improve Classroom Discussions" by Paul Bambrick-Santoyo

» Article: "Collaborative Conversations" by Douglas Fisher and Nancy Frey

Chapter 2:
Frequently Asked Questions

Those task cards seem helpful, but when will I ever have time to do them?

Some of the task cards—those that look out across the year and across modules and units—take some significant time to complete. Since you won't need to spend your planning time *designing* your ELA curriculum, we advise that you spend that time carefully analyzing ours so that you can make it the best it can be for your students. That means looking ahead and planning backward from assessments and noticing how lessons build students' skills and knowledge. It means understanding how the Four T's—topic, tasks, targets, and texts—interact with one another at the module, unit, and lesson level. It means reading the texts before using them with your students.

The process will take some time—it has to. We hope that the lesson-level task card will be the one that you learn to move quickly with. Over time, you'll probably find that it takes less and less time or that you have favorite questions that you like digging into and others that you skip. That's okay. The point is for you to feel well prepared, and there's no one right way to achieve that.

I know I'm encouraged to prioritize the integrity of the curriculum over strict fidelity to the way it is written in order to best meet my students' needs. If I have to change something, what do I need to pay most attention to?

The short answer (that we recommend committing to memory and keeping front and center in your conversations with colleagues and in your own planning) is this: texts, protocols, questions, and assessments.

The more complete answer to this question has a few layers. There are a few common adaptations we have seen teachers make within lessons that seem like they may be small and insignificant changes on the surface but actually have a big impact on students. For example, as we discussed earlier in this chapter, teachers are sometimes inclined to skip the protocols. Although this adaptation to the lesson is not necessarily going to impact students' progress toward a particular learning target, it might have a big impact on the quality of discourse in the classroom or on students' growth in habits of character. You may feel that you need to change a protocol because you don't have time to do the protocol that is written into the lesson. This is okay; however, it's important that you swap it out for a different protocol with a similar purpose.

Similarly, we find that sometimes teachers don't ask the questions written in the lesson, but instead ask questions on the fly. Each question in our lessons has been labored over and serves a very specific purpose. We urge you, until you really build your question-asking muscles, to ask questions as they are written. If you need to adapt the questions, we would suggest prioritizing a smaller set and asking fewer high-leverage questions, as written, versus making up new ones. You may need to scaffold student understanding with lower-level questions that build to the questions written in the lesson, or extend beyond the questions in the lesson with higher-level questions, in addition to the questions in the lesson.

As for assessments, they should not be changed at all. This includes all of the learning targets that build to the assessments. If you are a skilled curriculum designer who can backward-design learning experiences from assessments, you may be able to make some changes to the lessons leading up to an assessment that don't change the outcomes for students. But we urge you to be thoughtful about your choices. As you know from the exploration of the Four T's in Chapter 1, if you change a text or a learning target, it can unravel other components of a module. Instead, what we recommend is enhancements: make local connections or incorporate service learning, but maintain the spine of the module as is.

What are the best tips and tricks for managing the pacing of lessons?

Like most things in life, you will get better with experience. In this chapter, we offer many suggestions to help with pacing, and we will acknowledge that many of them include a tension between professional discretion and proven effectiveness. There's no absolute resolution to that tension; you will do the best you can, and get better all the time. Here is the big-picture advice we often give:

» Plan for Module 1 to take a little longer, especially if you haven't taught it before. You will be teaching protocols, students may be encountering a way of teaching and learning that is very new, and you may not yet have a sense of where it matters to spend time and where it doesn't. But don't allow it to take forever. At a certain point (something like eleven or twelve weeks), you may have to decide you are going to condense the last few lessons, administer the assessment, and move on, equipped with what you have learned both about where students are and about the way a module unfolds.

» When condensing lessons in any way, you have to know the mid- and end of unit assessments very well. This will ensure you don't inadvertently skip material students need to know or have access to in order to demonstrate their learning later.

» Ask a trusted observer to watch you teach a lesson and time each section for you. Compare that timing with what was recommended, and reflect (with the observer if possible) on the impact of any changes you made, and what evidence you have for that impact (e.g., student work, observations of student discourse).

» Use a timer yourself, and ask a student to be in charge of it: "Give us three minutes to go over these learning targets, please."

» Use a slide deck to keep yourself and students focused on key questions of the lesson. This will help ensure that you don't skip important parts. Put the learning targets on every slide, so if a section is starting to take longer than planned, you can quickly ask yourself: "Is this necessary for students to make progress toward the target?" If not (and in the absence of a compelling reason related to classroom community), wrap it up and keep moving.

» Figure out what you are going to hold in your hands during the lesson and how it will cue you to the purpose, structure, and hoped-for outcomes. Remember, the lessons are not scripts. You know your students best, including what kinds of instructions, questions, and routines they will respond to best as you all move toward those hoped-for outcomes.

I know learning targets are important, but how can I make them come alive more in my lessons? Sometimes I feel like we're just going through the motions.

One of the best ways to make learning targets come alive is to ensure that you yourself really understand what the intended learning is for the lesson, and that you can describe why that learning is meaningful, for example, why it matters that students can revise their essays focusing on evidence and elaboration. The task cards in Chapter 2A will help; however, even if you are not using those, we recommend analyzing each lesson through the lens of the targets, that is, "how does x section move students toward mastery of this target?" Once you are clear, then you can ensure that students also really know not just what they will *do*, but what they will *learn*.

The lessons in the curriculum will cue you to teach the vocabulary of the learning targets and to engage students in thinking about what the learning targets mean, but it's up to you to *really make sure* they know what they mean and how they will guide the lesson. If students seem puzzled or like they are just going through the motions, take a minute to have them turn and talk, or ask them to restate the learning target in their own words. Every so often, incorporate a question about why it matters that they master the skill named in the target. It's critical that students take ownership of meeting the learning targets and deeply understanding them right from the start.

Also critical is that you come back to the learning target(s) throughout the lesson. Look for opportunities to reference them and to check for understanding frequently. Help students see the learning targets as a steady guide and grounding checkpoint on their progress, not just a routine or a bunch of words on the whiteboard.

What should I do if I check for understanding and it's obvious that my students just aren't getting it? How can I stay on pace with the lesson?

It's important to take both a long-term and short-term view of this question. Having a good, solid sense of the longer-term scope of a series of lessons, units, and modules and how standards are addressed over time is the first step. If your students haven't mastered a standard in one lesson, it doesn't mean that they won't have another opportunity to master it. But you may not realize this if you haven't looked ahead at how standards cycle in and out of lessons. As a result, you may find yourself getting hung up on reteaching materials you didn't realize would come back around in a few days or next week. This can throw off your pacing, and it's one of the reasons we urge you to engage in the planning process described in Chapter 2A. Use those task cards to look ahead and get a feel for the focus and flow over the long term.

How can I encourage students who talk infrequently to contribute more, and students who talk too much to listen more?

One of your first steps should be ensuring that you have established norms in your classroom that help all students feel that they belong and that what they have to say has value. Once that culture has been established, there are specific practices that permeate the curriculum that will give students practice (and confidence) contributing to discussions.

A great way to foster equitable and productive discourse is through protocols. A protocol consists of agreed-upon, detailed guidelines for reading, recording, discussing, or reporting that ensure equal participation and accountability in learning. We use protocols a lot in the curriculum because they get students talking; importantly, protocols allow students to talk to *one another*, not just to you. As a result, they build independence and responsibility. In addition to protocols, the curriculum also features the frequent use of total participation techniques, which give *all* students the opportunity to share their thinking with a partner or the whole class, and Conversation Cues, which promote productive and equitable conversations. These three instructional strategies are powerful ways to allow you to hear from *all students*, not just your "frequent fliers." As you gain comfort with these practices, we hope that you will consider using them even more, beyond where you are cued to do so in the curriculum and in other parts of your day.

My students don't seem that excited about the protocols anymore. Are there any others I can swap in to keep things fresh?

We definitely recommend that you build your own library of favorite protocols. If you find any that we have recommended have gone stale or just aren't working well with your students, you should feel free to swap them out. Before doing this, however, be sure that whichever new protocol you choose will serve the same purpose. You can view and download the full suite of protocols used in our curriculum on our website (http://eled.org/tools). This same set is included in our book *Management in the Active Classroom*. The websites of the National School Reform Faculty and School Reform Initiative also have excellent libraries of protocols available for free download.

You might also consider inviting students to lead protocols once they are so routine as to require refreshing. This injects a nice dose of excitement back into familiar processes, and offers an opportunity for the kind of safe and productive risk-taking that adolescent learners deeply need.

I'm still pretty shaky on classroom management. What do you recommend to help me get up to speed?

We recommend that you read our 2015 book *Management in the Active Classroom* and browse its video collection (https://eleducation.org/resources/collections/management-in-the-active-classroom-videos). Though this book can help any teacher, we wrote it specifically to support teachers using our curriculum, especially those for whom an active, collaborative classroom will require some getting used to. You may also want to observe a colleague in your building who has strong classroom management or ask a trusted colleague to participate in a peer coaching session with you. Classroom management is one of the hardest parts of being a teacher—it takes time and practice to build confidence—but there are techniques and practices you can learn. Set goals for yourself, and make a plan for reaching them.

For additional support with classroom management, consider one of EL Education's professional services institutes on Management in the Active Classroom. Find more information at: https://ELeducation.org/what-we-offer/professional-services.

Chapter 3:
The Mighty Text: Worthy, Compelling, and Complex

Chapter 3A:
What Makes a Text Worthy and Compelling?

We have heard time and again from teachers around the country that one of the greatest gifts our curriculum gives them is a collection of rich, compelling, and worthy texts. And, as they learn to teach these texts in new ways, they learn more about what makes a text high-quality and what makes it worth their time to teach and their students' time to read, analyze, and draw meaning from. One teacher told us that the texts in the curriculum were a "gift that just keeps giving."

As you no doubt already know, pulling any eighth-grade book about plastic pollution off the shelf is not enough. When there are literally hundreds to choose from, how do you know where to begin? For us, the Four T's: topic, tasks, targets, and texts (see Table 1.3 in Chapter 1) were our steady guide. We asked ourselves what opportunities a text provides to teach students about the topic and to be a resource for the *tasks* we are asking them to complete. In turn, these questions were always tied tightly to the standards (*targets*). Will the text allow students to meet the standards? Is it sufficiently complex?

And then, of course, there is the intangible aesthetic element: beauty. Is it beautifully written? Is it compelling? Does it motivate students to read closely and investigate the topic deeply? Is it a good model of the author's craft? Will students not want to put it down and jump back into it eagerly as soon as they get the chance? Does the book's quality give students the energy they need to persevere through challenges?

Because texts are one of the four key pillars that hold up our curriculum, it is important to spend some time understanding why and how we chose the ones we did and, more generally, why text selection is so vitally important to student achievement. What follows is a list of criteria for how we selected the texts for the curriculum:

» We addressed the instructional shifts called for by the college- and career-ready ELA/literacy standards: *building knowledge through content-rich nonfiction; reading, writing, and speaking grounded in evidence from literary and informational text; regular practice with complex text and its academic language.*

» We ensured that texts are "worthy" in terms of the content: they teach important information and concepts, and build students' understanding.

» We ensured that texts are sufficiently complex (in both quantitative and qualitative measures) for the grade level/grade band.

» We paired informational and literary texts and toggled between them to build background knowledge and engagement.

» We identified informational texts, which often serve as the conceptual framework for a module/unit.

» We attended to diversity and inclusion in the texts, ensuring that a range of experiences across lines of difference are represented. Table 3.1 highlights some of the questions we asked ourselves to ensure that the topics and resources in the curriculum and related professional learning offerings reflect the diversity of our student population and contribute to inclusion and equity.

Table 3.1: Questions to Promote Diversity and Inclusion in Topics and Resources

Questions We Asked Ourselves Related to: Author, Character, Content, Illustrator, and Illustration
How are **race and ethnicity** represented and treated in this resource?
How is **self-efficacy** represented and treated in this resource? *
How is **language** represented and treated in this resource? **
How is **country of origin** represented and treated in this resource?
How are world, U.S., and regional **geography** represented and treated in this resource?
How is **gender** represented and treated in this resource?
How is **sexual orientation** represented and treated in this resource?
How is **age** represented and treated in this resource?
How is **family structure** represented and treated in this resource?
How is **physical ability** represented and treated in this resource?
How is **socioeconomic status (SES)** represented and treated in this resource?
How are **majority and minority status** represented and treated in this resource? ***
How is **education** represented and treated in this resource? ***
How is **religion** represented and treated in this resource?
How are **politics** represented and treated in this resource?
To what degree does this resource seem to represent a **normal, typical life** for the characters?
To what degree does this resource acknowledge and celebrate differences?
To what degree does this resource acknowledge and celebrate similarities?
What are the overall **ethics** of using this text in EL Education resources?
* **Self-efficacy:** Does the text respect cultures by showing people helping themselves, as opposed to outsiders intervening to help? (e.g., Is the text about African architects helping to build the African school, or do American architects fly in to build the school?) ** **Language:** Does the text represent diversity of world languages? Is the language compelling, beautiful, and complex? *** **Majority and minority status:** What is the relative power in society of the characters and author? *** **Ethics:** If EL Education uses the text, how will it affect the people represented in the story? How will it affect the author?

» We chose the appropriate type of text needed to address specific Reading standards.

» We sought out shorter texts from reputable sources (e.g., National Archives, Project Gutenberg, Cricket).

» We sought out provocative texts that offer multiple perspectives on issues that matter to middle school students.

» We studied texts closely and aligned them to specific standards or "bundles" of English language arts (ELA) standards that arose authentically from the tasks students were being asked to do.

One of the things you'll notice from this list and from studying the standards themselves is that, often, one book can't do *all* of the work you need a text to do. Most of the time, it is a carefully chosen set of texts that gives students a full and rich opportunity to explore the topic, complete the tasks, and meet the standards (targets).

▶ HOW WILL RICH SETS OF INFORMATIONAL AND LITERARY TEXTS ACCELERATE LITERACY LEARNING FOR MY STUDENTS?

"By asking students to read both informational and literary texts with shared topics and themes, we offer many more opportunities to experience big ideas in profound ways. Informational text suddenly becomes personal in the way that we've always understood literature to be. The elegant interplay—the movement from stories and poems that are personal to information that is convincing—gives students tools for taking a personal stand on challenging, real-world topics."

Dolly Higgins
Teacher, Boise, Idaho

There are a few phrases from the preceding quote that stand out: the opportunity to experience *big ideas in profound ways* and an *elegant interplay* of informational and literary texts. These phrases beautifully state why sets of texts are so powerful. Finding five texts on the Harlem Renaissance, even ones that you feel are strong texts and have taught before, is not the same as looking specifically for an *elegant interplay* among texts that will allow students to experience *big ideas in profound ways*. The former suggests a utilitarian purpose for the texts; the latter suggests something deeper.

One of the three big instructional shifts of the standards is *building knowledge through content-rich nonfiction* (see Chapter 1 for more information). Our curriculum's content-based literacy approach responds to this shift by focusing on building students' literacy skills and their knowledge of the world with a balance of informational and literary texts that are representative of diverse people and cultures around the world.

When and How Do Students Read in the Curriculum?

Students interact with texts in three main ways in the curriculum: There's the text that engages students in the topic and sets the purpose for the module. These texts are on grade level and are engaging and accessible; most anchor texts for the modules fall into this category. Then there are the complex texts, which students will read closely. Lastly, there are additional texts on the topic (i.e., research reading), or of the students' own choice, that ensure that each student experiences a volume of reading at their independent reading level.

We have built rich sets of texts around the topics in the modules that allow students to build the skills and knowledge they need to meet standards and complete meaningful tasks—the Four T's in action. Students build knowledge of the world by reading multiple texts on a topic—ranging from novels to scientific articles to speeches—and the more they read and build knowledge, the more challenging texts they can read, even about new topics, thus building their literacy muscles.

Pairing texts around a compelling topic is a strategic move that improves students' reading comprehension. The well-known "Baseball Study" by Recht and Leslie (1988) showed that middle school students with low reading ability but high knowledge of baseball were able to outperform students with high reading ability but low knowledge of baseball on a test of reading comprehension related to a challenging text about baseball. The authors of this study concluded that knowledge of the topic had a much bigger impact on reading comprehension than did generalized reading ability.

Figure 3.1: The "Baseball Study"

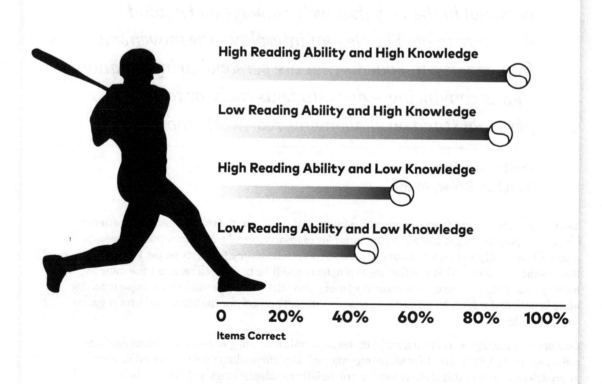

Strategies for Pairing and Sequencing Texts

Within each set of informational and literary texts in the curriculum, there are a variety of ways they are introduced and woven together that help students draw meaningful connections. In the curriculum, you may find the texts sequenced in any one of the following ways[1]:

» **From mystery to understanding.** This sequence starts with a text that is intentionally dense or that presents a partially obscured presentation of the topic. Students are engaged in the "mystery" of figuring things out and will likely generate many questions that they become increasingly eager to answer. The main strategy for solving the mystery is reading other related texts on the same topic. For example, in the first unit of Grade 6, Module 4, students read plenty of texts about space science, but encounter nothing about the crucial contributions of the first black female mathematicians hired by NASA. It isn't until Unit 2 that *Hidden Figures* is introduced as an anchor text. Once students learn about these brilliant women, they are aghast that so many texts simply don't mention their work. Students are fired up to figure out how and why these mathematicians' remarkable accomplishments went unheralded for so long. Over the course of the module, students eventually build a great deal of knowledge about this topic by reading related texts.

» **From literary to informational text and back again (and vice versa).** In this back-and-forth relationship of texts, literary texts with relatable characters and stories help students engage more deeply with the content they read about in informational texts. Similarly, the knowledge gleaned from the informational texts helps students better understand and persevere with complex narratives or story structures in literary texts. The two types of text work together to deepen students' learning about a topic. This strategy also appeals to students with different preferences for the types of reading they enjoy best. In Grade 6, Module 1, for example, students learn about aspects of Greek mythology first through Rick Riordan's novel *The Lightning Thief*, and then through informational text on the relevance of myth in the modern world. They return to narrative texts by reading the actual myths, which, along with their informed perspective about the power of myth, serve as inspiration and grounding for when they write a "revised scene" of *The Lightning Thief*.

» **From personal to universal.** Texts grouped in this way help students develop interest in a universal concern or topic. Starting with narrative helps students understand the personal side of an issue through the people in the book, fictional or real. This builds their motivation to read informational texts that help them explore the issue more broadly. In Grade 6, Module 2, students read the true story of William Kamkwamba in *The Boy Who Harnessed the Wind* (Young Readers' edition) and how he used design thinking to confront the devastating effects of famine in his country, Malawi.

» **From universal to personal.** Conversely, students might begin their journey through a set of texts by starting with a framing document that provides universal concepts or ideas to think about, followed by reading something else that shows how the ideas or concepts affect people. For example, Grade 7 students learn about plastic pollution through informational film, text, articles, and online resources. In Unit 2, they read "Boyan Slat: The Great Pacific Garbage Patch Kid," and learn how one individual approached this massive environmental challenge. Students eventually write an argument essay about which point in the plastic life cycle they believe would be most effective for solving plastic pollution, and develop an action plan they can enact through research, advocacy, or personal commitment.

Finding Just-Right Texts

When designing the curriculum, and for any teacher designing their own curriculum, one of the most important considerations is not whether we are including *enough* informational

---

1. Much of the information in this chapter about text sets and anchor texts is drawn from our 2014 book *Transformational Literacy: Making the Common Core Shift with Work That Matters.*

texts, but whether we are including informational texts that are worth reading. Textbooks are informational texts and are readily available in most schools, but they are not sufficient for meeting college- and career-ready standards; they don't typically represent multiple perspectives on complex subjects or engage students and motivate them to persevere with their reading. "The greatest benefit for students—in terms of their development as readers, their engagement with and ownership of their learning, and their ability to think critically—will result from teachers approaching text selection with a 'beyond the textbook' mentality" (Berger, Woodfin, Plaut, and Dobbertin, 2014, pp. 30–31).

For middle school students in particular, informational texts need to present topics that matter and that respect their intelligence and agency. Many texts in the curriculum were chosen because they appeal to adolescents' developing sense of—and questions about—justice. They tackle such issues as human rights, scientific ethics, and the human impact on the environment. Part of what makes these topics perfect for middle-schoolers is also what makes them sometimes intimidating for teachers: they elicit strong opinions and strong emotions. We believe that not only is it worth the *potential* for impassioned discussions to break out, but that impassioned discussions are part of the point, and how reading comes alive for students. To support teachers in preparing to teach topics that will potentially ignite middle-schoolers' passions, there are three places to look for support:

1. The Support All Students section of the Teaching Notes in each lesson names issues of equity, inclusion, and representation that may be present in the reading or that may come up in discussion for a particular text students will read in that particular lesson.

2. Each Module Overview includes a section called Notes from the Designer here any sensitive topics in the module and the text(s) are described (see Figure 3.2 for an example).

3. Each anchor text in the Grades 6–8 curriculum is accompanied by an Anchor Text Guidance Document, which describes any sensitive issues in the text or the issues students might find challenging with the text, and explains how we have handled those issues in the curriculum. These guidance documents can be found on our website at https://eled.org/tools.

Figure 3.2: Notes from the Designer: Sample Excerpt

Notes from the Designer

The Lightning Thief incorporates many figures from Greek mythology into the plot, including gods, goddesses, and monsters. Be mindful about issues and characterizations that may be sensitive for students or with which some students may connect personally or deeply. Students may be surprised or offended by the relationship depicted between gods and humans. They may also be disturbed by the description of battles between demigods and monsters. Allow time and space for students to reflect on and speak about their reactions.

During lessons, students read excerpts from the anchor text rather than complete chapters to ensure sufficient time for students to think and respond to the text. Invite students who would like to read the rest of the chapter to do so for homework. If there is extended time for language arts, reading the entire chapter might be an option.

In Unit 3, students research a Greek god or goddess in preparation for the end of unit assessment, in which they rewrite a scene of *The Lightning Thief*, inserting a new character

Nested within the search for compelling and worthy texts, of course, is the search for texts that also ensure students have the opportunity to meet the grade-level demands of specific Reading standards. Texts must offer clear and compelling opportunities to learn and practice each standard. The fit between the standard and the text is never forced. Each text lends itself to the type of thinking we want students to do.

Often the standards themselves offer helpful guidance. For example, CCSS RI.6.9 states: *Compare and contrast one author's presentation of events with that of another.* In Grade 6, Module 4, students compare and contrast authors' presentations of the moon landing, so they read two different accounts of the lunar landing from different sources. They read one version in the anchor text *Hidden Figures*, and one called "One Giant Leap for Mankind" written by NASA in 1969. Students compare the presentations of this same event in the two texts in terms of content, author methods, and point of view. Students then use the knowledge they have built to develop their own opinions about the topic.

Determining Text Complexity

It is easy to think—especially for those who are not teachers—that text complexity boils down to a number. If the Lexile® measure says a text is appropriate for eighth grade, then it must be. Right? Well... not necessarily. The Lexile® measure considers only quantitative factors such as word frequency and sentence length, and that's not enough to truly determine how your students will experience a text.

Teachers know that determining text complexity is itself a complex process. What makes a text complex? Three main factors determine a text's complexity: quantitative measures, qualitative measures, and reader and task considerations. The last factor—reader and task considerations—is not an independent measure of complexity, but rather something that must be taken into consideration when determining how to make a text accessible for particular students.

We're not going to delve into all of these factors in any comprehensive way in this book; however, we do want to provide you with some detail on how we assessed texts along qualitative measures because we think this will be the most transferable for you in your own efforts to select appropriate texts for your students beyond our curriculum.

Qualitative Measures of Complexity

Once a text has been assessed for complexity using quantitative measures (e.g., Flesch-Kincaid, Lexile®), which is easily determined using computer programs or online searches, we use a simple tool called the Four Quadrants of Qualitative Text Complexity (see Table 3.2) to help us determine qualitative complexity. At any given grade level, most texts will be complex in one or more of the following areas: meaning, structure, language features, and knowledge demands[2]. These "Four Quadrants" help us assess the specific ways in which a text is complex. Once we have determined how the text will challenge students, we can focus instruction to offer support in those areas as they read.

Table 3.2: The Four Quadrants of Qualitative Text Complexity

Meaning	Structure
Consider the layers of meaning in the text, as well as the purpose and the complexity of ideas/concepts in the text.	Consider the organization of the text, including factors like text features, genre, and how the ideas or events in the text build on one another to make meaning.
Language features	**Knowledge demands**
Consider factors like vocabulary, sentence structure, figurative language, and variety of English (e.g., dialect) used in the text.	Consider students' background experiences and knowledge with the topic of the text. What "outside" information or experiences will they need to understand the text?

---

2. These four factors are derived from Appendix A of the Common Core State Standards.

Figure 3.3: "The Land of Red Apples"

"The Land of Red Apples" by Zitkala-Sa

RI.6.10

Name: _____ Date: _____

1. There were eight in our party of bronzed children who were going East with the missionaries. Among us were three young braves, two tall girls, and we three little ones, Judéwin, Thowin, and I.

2. We had been very impatient to start on our journey to the Red Apple Country, which, we were told, lay a little beyond the great circular horizon of the Western prairie. Under a sky of rosy apples we dreamt of roaming as freely and happily as we had chased the cloud shadows on the Dakota plains. We had anticipated much pleasure from a ride on the iron horse, but the throngs of staring palefaces disturbed and troubled us.

3. On the train, fair women, with tottering babies on each arm, stopped their haste and scrutinized the children of absent mothers. Large men, with heavy bundles in their hands, halted nearby, and riveted their glassy blue eyes upon us.

4. I sank deep into the corner of my seat, for I resented being watched. Directly in front of me, children who were no larger than I hung themselves upon the backs of their seats, with their bold white faces toward me. Sometimes they took their forefingers out of their mouths and pointed at my moccasined feet. Their mothers, instead of reproving such rude curiosity, looked closely at me, and attracted their children's further notice to my blanket. This embarrassed me, and kept me constantly on the verge of tears.

5. I sat perfectly still, with my eyes downcast, daring only now and then to shoot long glances around me. Chancing to turn to the window at my side, I was quite breathless upon seeing one familiar object. It was the telegraph pole which strode by at short paces, along the edge of a road thickly bordered with wild sunflowers, some poles like these had been planted by white men. Often I had stopped, on my way down the road, to hold my ear against the pole, and, hearing its low moaning, I used to wonder what the paleface had done to hurt it. Now I sat watching for each pole that glided by to be the last one.

6. In this way I had forgotten my uncomfortable surroundings, when I heard one of my comrades call out my name. I saw the missionary standing very near, tossing candies and gums into our midst. This amused us all, and we tried to see who could catch the most of the sweetmeats.

7. Though we rode several days inside of the iron horse, I do not recall a single thing about our luncheons.

8. It was night when we reached the school grounds. The lights from the windows of the large buildings fell upon some of the icicled trees that stood beneath them. We were led toward an open door, where the brightness of the lights within flooded out over the heads of the excited palefaces who blocked the way. My body trembled more from fear than from the snow I trod upon.

9. Entering the house, I stood close against the wall. The strong glaring light in the large whitewashed room dazzled my eyes. The noisy hurrying of hard shoes upon a bare wooden floor increased the whirring in my ears. My only safety seemed to be in keeping next to the wall. As I was wondering in which direction to escape from all this confusion, two warm hands grasped me firmly, and in the same moment I was tossed high in midair. A rosy-cheeked paleface woman caught me in her arms. I was both frightened and insulted by such trifling. I stared into her eyes, wishing her to let me stand on my own feet, but she jumped me up and down with increasing enthusiasm. My mother had never made a plaything of her wee daughter. Remembering this I began to cry aloud.

10. They misunderstood the cause of my tears, and placed me at a white table loaded with food. There our party were united again. As I did not hush my crying, one of the older ones whispered to me, "Wait until you are alone in the night."

11. It was very little I could swallow besides my sobs, that evening.

12. "Oh, I want my mother and my brother Dawée! I want to go to my aunt!" I pleaded; but the ears of the palefaces could not hear me.

13. From the table we were taken along an upward incline of wooden boxes, which I learned afterward to call a stairway. At the top was a quiet hall, dimly lighted. Many narrow beds were in one straight line down the entire length of the wall. In them lay sleeping brown faces, which peeped just out of the coverings. I was tucked into bed with one of the tall girls, because she talked to me in my mother tongue and seemed to soothe me.

14. I had arrived in the wonderful land of rosy skies, but I was not happy, as I had thought I should be. My long travel and the bewildering sights had exhausted me. I fell asleep, heaving deep, tired sobs. My tears were left to dry themselves in streaks, because neither my aunt nor my mother was near to wipe them away.

Source: Zitkala-Sa. *American Indian Stories.* Hayworth Publishing House, 1921. University of Pennsylvania Library. Web. Public domain.

Using the sample text from "The Land of Red Apples" in Figure 3.3, we have analyzed the text in Table 3.3 using the Four Quadrants of Qualitative Text Complexity. With this example, it becomes easier to see how the complexities within a *particular* text emerge by looking closely at these qualitative factors. You will see "The Land of Red Apples" again in Chapter 3C as it is part of the Grade 6 close reading lesson we annotate there.

Table 3.3: Sample Four Quadrants Analysis of a Sample of Text from "The Land of Red Apples"

Meaning: Moderately complex The meaning of the text is mostly straightforward from the perspective of the narrator. However, in the close read, students are asked to look more deeply at the contrasting perspective of the missionary teachers, which is more nuanced.	**Structure: Slightly complex** The structure of this text is narrative sequential, so very accessible to students of this grade level.
Language features: Moderately complex Some of the vocabulary is sophisticated and unfamiliar ("*iron horse*" for train, *scrutinized, missionary, trifling, downcast, reproving*). The context supports building meaning of these words. In addition, students work directly with these terms during the guided close read.	**Knowledge demands: Moderately complex** Students read the text early in the module, so some of the context/information will be new to some students. The close read is designed to help students gain this knowledge. In this way, the text helps build overall knowledge of the topic of American Indian boarding schools and how they affected the students who attended them, and to support the reading of the anchor text.

What about Reader and Task Considerations?

When considering the reader and the task (i.e., the real students sitting in front of you in your classroom) and how to make the text accessible for them, consider what students are being asked to do with the text, as well as the potential needs of specific groups of learners. What is the purpose of the text in this module? What are students being asked to do? How much support is provided in working with this text? What experiences have students had that might make working with this text easier (or more difficult)? In the case of "The Land of Red Apples," this text is written from a child's perspective, which makes the topic of American Indian boarding schools, of which most students will have little previous background knowledge, more accessible.

Once a text has been chosen, "Reader and Task" is the area over which we, as designers, and you, as teachers, have the most control. In our curriculum, challenges that emerge when we analyze a text using the Four Quadrants of Qualitative Text Complexity are always addressed by the instruction and tasks we plan. Considerations about what may make a particular text challenging for certain groups, such as English language learners (ELLs) or students whose life experiences make the content or context of a text unfamiliar, are addressed either within the design of the task itself or in the Teaching Notes that accompany the lesson.

▷ Students deserve to read beautifully written and worthy texts. If it is literature, let it be great literature. If it is informational text, let it teach students new words and new ideas in sophisticated ways. Let it, always, be worth their time and effort to read.

Why All The Fuss Over Text Complexity?

The end goal is for students to be prepared to read and learn from college-level texts when they leave high school. Therefore, the work of K–12 educators is to build students' knowledge and guide them up the ladder of complexity so that they are ready for the demands of college and career when they graduate. Texts that are at the right level of complexity—taking into account both quantitative and qualitative measures as well as reader and task considerations—are key to ensuring that students are able to meet the standards that will prepare them for life after high school.

Common Core Reading anchor standard R10 outlines this ladder of complexity explicitly. But for each grade level, Reading standards 1–9 also offer signals about the complexity of the text needed to support the kind of thinking required by the standards. For example, CCSS RI.6 requires students to assess how point of view or purpose shapes the content and style of a text. There are nuances in this standard across Grades 6–8 that have implications for text selection. In Grade 6 students must determine an author's point of view or purpose in a text and explain how it is conveyed in the text. In Grade 7, they must dig further to analyze how the author distinguishes their point of view from those of others. And by Grade 8, they must analyze how the author acknowledges and responds to conflicting evidence or viewpoints. This standard comes to life in Grade 7, Module 4, when students use the text *Trash Vortex* to analyze how the author's viewpoint differs from those of others. The choice of text is important here because the author's point of view is explicitly positioned as distinct from others. The text (or text set) must give students the opportunity to meet the standard.

The considerations for text complexity and meeting standards are important. Equally important for us are the more nuanced considerations that come from looking at the quality of the texts. Students deserve to read beautifully written and worthy texts. If it is literature, let it be great literature. If it is informational text, let it teach students new words and new ideas in sophisticated ways. Let it, always, be worth their time and effort to read.

▶ HOW WILL THE ANCHOR TEXTS IN THE MODULES MAXIMIZE MY STUDENTS' OPPORTUNITIES TO MEET STANDARDS?

In our curriculum, the anchor text is the centerpiece of students' reading. This text is one that all students will read in order to build content knowledge and literacy skills. "In the universe of all the rich resources students will read in a given unit, the anchor text is like the sun: All the other articles, poems, maps, charts, and other forms of text circle around this one text" (Berger, Woodfin, Plaut, and Dobbertin, 2014, p. 38). Although no single text is perfect, the following criteria and related questions helped our curriculum designers focus on the work a text needs to do and what additional texts might be necessary to fill in the gaps.

» **Content.** To what extent will this text help students learn something important and enduring about the big ideas of an academic discipline? How can the text help to build students' knowledge about the world? In a literary text, what understandings about the human experience can students draw from it? To what extent does this text provide sufficient information, so students can successfully respond to an evidence-based writing task?

» *Example* (Grade 8): *Farewell to Manzanar* by Jeanne Wakatsuki Houston and James D. Houston. This memoir, told through the eyes of Jeanne Wakatsuki Houston, chronicles the experiences of her and her family at the Japanese American internment camp Manzanar. Through close examination of this text and of other supplemental texts that provide context about the impact of internment, students deepen their understanding of this dark time in history and of the lessons that can be learned from it.

» **Interest.** Is the text compelling for students? Will students love digging into this text? Why? Is the text developmentally appropriate—does it treat the issues that matter to middle school students with respect? Is it high-interest in terms of content or format? Is it particularly beautifully written or a striking example of a less commonly read genre?

» *Example* (Grade 8): *Summer of the Mariposas* by Guadalupe Garcia McCall draws on Latin American folklore to explore the way culture and family shapes identity. Students in the midst of the major shifts of adolescence build on these explorations to develop their ability to analyze narratives and, most importantly, create their own stories.

» **Complexity.** Is the text appropriate in terms of qualitative and quantitative measures of complexity? What makes this text challenging? Based on qualitative measures, in what ways will the concepts, structure, language, and meaning give students something worth grappling with? Based on quantitative measures, is this text sufficiently demanding in terms of syntax and academic vocabulary? Does this text provide sufficient complexity to ensure that students have to work hard to build their literacy muscles as they work through it? How will this text be paired with others of greater or lesser complexity?

» *Example* (Grade 6): The Young Readers' edition of *Hidden Figures* has a high Lexile® measure for Grade 6 (1120). To account for the challenges with this text, Module 4 is designed so that the entirety of Unit 1 is building students' background knowledge of the "Space Race." By the time *Hidden Figures* is introduced in Unit 2, not only do students have the vocabulary and historical and scientific content knowledge they need to help them access the text, they are also hooked by the fact that none of the other texts they have read so far have mentioned these important women in America's history. Their engagement in this injustice motivates them to persevere with this challenging and worthy text.

» **Reading standards.** Does the text offer opportunities to teach grade-level standards at a specific grade level of rigor? If the Reading standard requires students to infer, is the text sufficiently rich to require such inferring, or are the ideas all right on the surface? If the Reading standard requires students to interpret information presented visually, orally, or quantitatively, does the text include the types of diagrams and charts that would make this work possible? Usually, a complex text will provide opportunities to address many of the Reading standards at once. But some texts provide a particularly elegant fit for addressing a given standard at a given grade level.

» *Example* (Grade 7): In the first half of Module 2, Unit 1, students examine the wide variety of text features and structures incorporated in each chapter of *Patient Zero*, as well as how major sections contribute to the whole text and the development of ideas. The text, *Patient Zero*, is filled with text features that support students to meet CCSS RI.7.5: *Analyze the structure an author uses to organize a text, including how the major sections contribute to the whole and to the development of the ideas.* Students practice determining the meanings of words and phrases, especially technical terms associated with epidemiology.

» **Writing standards.** Does this text offer specific information that students can synthesize in their own written arguments, informative writing, or narrative writing? Can this text—or sections of this text—serve not only as a source for students to build knowledge, but also as an example of author's craft that students can emulate in their own writing?

» *Example* (Grade 8): Among the questions students investigate in Module 2 are: Where does our food come from? How do we analyze arguments about how food should be grown and processed? What factors influence our access to healthy food? Michael Pollan's text, *The Omnivore's Dilemma*, is one source of evidence for students as they build background knowledge about food choices. By Unit 3, students also analyze this text to better understand the author's meaning and what he intends for his readers to understand. Pollan's book serves as a model as students prepare to write their own argument essays about a choice their community can make to eat in healthy and sustainable ways. Students plan and draft argument essays to defend their claim (CCSS W.8.1).

▶ USING TEXT TO BUILD VOCABULARY

Texts of all kinds play an important role in building students' vocabulary, which is one of the highest-leverage instructional moves we can make in our effort to accelerate literacy learning and excellence for all students. Word-learning strategies transfer across content and context, and word knowledge is critical for reading comprehension. Simply put, students need to know a lot of words! They particularly need to learn academic vocabulary (or "Tier 2 words" such as *community* and *relate*) that they will encounter across contexts and content. (See box: Three Tiers of Vocabulary for more information about the vocabulary tiers.)

Three Tiers of Vocabulary

Tier One: Basic Vocabulary

» Words found in everyday speech

Tier Two: Academic Vocabulary

» High-frequency words that are found in academic texts across a variety of domains

Tier Three: Domain-Specific Vocabulary

» Low-frequency words specific to a particular field of study and often found in informational texts about that subject

Why Is Academic Vocabulary So Important?[3]

It is simple to recognize the importance of teaching discipline-related vocabulary within a particular topic of study. For example, if you and your students are studying the importance of protecting a watershed, you know that students need to know and be able to use science words such as *habitat*. But what is less clear and more central to building students' literacy skills is the need to address the academic vocabulary found in watershed-related texts. Consider the following short passage from the website of the nonprofit Center for Watershed Protection:

> *During the land development process, forests are cleared, soils are compacted, natural drainage patterns are altered, and impervious surfaces, such as roads, buildings, and parking lots, are created. These changes increase the amount of polluted runoff that reaches our local waterways. As a result, stream banks begin to erode, critical in-stream habitats are washed away or filled in with sediment, downstream flooding increases, and water becomes too polluted to support sensitive fish and bugs or recreational activities. (Center for Watershed Protection, n.d.)*

To fully comprehend this passage, students must know the contextualized meaning of words like *development, process, altered,* and *sensitive* (certainly the author of this passage does not mean to suggest the fish are reacting emotionally). These words are likely to appear again and again in different texts and across several disciplines. Knowing these "academic" vocabulary words will strongly support students as they continue to read all kinds of text. Therefore, college- and career-ready standards emphasize the teaching of Tier 2 (academic) vocabulary in addition to Tier 3 (domain-specific) vocabulary.

Vocabulary learning can be indirect—the result of reading closely, using morphology, using context clues, and writing about and discussing complex texts—or it can be explicitly taught. Both are valuable in terms of addressing students' vocabulary development needs (and both are built into the design of our curriculum).

Our curriculum takes every opportunity to emphasize vocabulary; it is taught in every lesson, any time students work with text. From unpacking learning targets, to working with domain-specific and academic word walls, to close reads, students learn strategies to explore the meanings of words they read and put them to use in their writing. What follows are some highlights of our approach to teaching vocabulary throughout the curriculum:

» Lessons often begin with teachers guiding students through a process of reading (or hearing read aloud) the learning targets, and then "unpacking" them. Typically this focuses on academic vocabulary related to the standards (e.g., *determine* the main idea; *build on* one anther's ideas). The targets themselves serve as text and often signal how students will work with text in the lesson.

» Students keep vocabulary logs in which they record words introduced in the learning targets or lesson. Students often work collaboratively to discern the meanings of words from context before looking up the definition. Students also note academic and domain-specific vocabulary words in their logs.

» Frequently, lessons include prompts for teachers to explicitly call students' attention to vocabulary before or during their work with the text. What follows are some questions teachers can ask themselves that influence when to explicitly teach vocabulary:

- What words are critical to students' understanding of the texts?

- What words are students likely not to know?

- Which words should I teach students before reading (be cautious here—don't rob students of the opportunity to practice learning words from context)?

- Which words can students learn by inferring from context?

---

3. This section is informed by our 2014 book *Transformational Literacy: Making the Common Core Shift with Work that Matters.*

- Which words present the opportunity to teach word parts (prefixes, root words, suffixes)?

- Which words can just be mentioned, and which should students store through a strategy for long-term use?

- Which words can I use to help students develop webs of word meaning (e.g., teaching the word *altered* provides the opportunity to teach *alternate* and *altercation*)?

» Students and teachers together build word walls of academic vocabulary (Tier 2) and domain-specific vocabulary connected to the content of the modules (Tier 3). They return to these word walls over and over as students read more texts and build knowledge.

» Vocabulary is always a strong component of close reading. The process walks students deep into text and brings their attention to the meanings of words and to questions about how individual words may affect the meaning of an entire text. (Close reading is the focus of Chapters 3B and 3C.)

» Lessons prompt teachers to help students define words that they encounter in text based on context when possible, and to use word roots and affixes; these word-learning strategies focused on morphology become a habit for students as they progress through the year. Such practices develop a habit of mind of being "word detectives" and applying what one already knows when encountering new words.

» Writing, speaking, and listening tasks require and support students to use the vocabulary they learn based on their reading and discussions. Students engage with and apply new vocabulary in a variety of ways, which helps the meanings of words stick.

» Scaffolds for ELLs frequently help students connect new words they are learning from text, or from instruction, to words in their home language (e.g., "How would you say this word in your home language?"; "What word would you use to describe this in your home language?").

▶ HOW WILL THE CURRICULUM ENSURE THAT MY STUDENTS EXPERIENCE A VOLUME OF READING WITH A VARIETY OF TEXT TYPES?

College- and career-ready standards challenge students to read complex texts to build content knowledge, literacy skills, and academic vocabulary. At all grade levels, our content-based curriculum includes one or more anchor texts as well as complex texts that all students read with support from teachers and peers. It is important that all students have access to and support with reading text at the appropriate level of complexity for their grade level.

But they also need to read a volume of texts—in other words, students need to read both complex text and *a lot* of text! Before focusing on complex texts in Chapters 3B and 3C, here we will focus briefly on other kinds of reading students do in the curriculum to give them the volume of reading they need at their independent reading level, which may be on, above, or below grade level. Table 3.4 summarizes the types of text found throughout the curriculum that support a volume of reading, and the purpose of each.

Table 3.4: Types of Texts throughout the Curriculum that Support a Volume of Reading

Types of Texts	Purpose
Anchor text on module topic	To hook students into the topic and (in the case of an informational anchor text) to build knowledge on the topic. The anchor text is at the appropriate level for the grade. It is not usually a complex text so that it is accessible to as many students as possible with minimal support.
Complex texts on module topic	To allow students to learn and practice comprehension strategies with texts with rich content, diverse structures, and increasingly sophisticated vocabulary and syntax. Complex texts also build knowledge on the module topic.
Additional texts on module topic	To build reading comprehension skills and knowledge on the module topic. These texts are included in the module materials and are part of the lessons.
Research texts (for independent reading) on the module topic	To build fluency, knowledge, and engagement using texts on the module topic at a variety of reading levels. These texts are not included with the materials; they are listed on the Grades 6–8 Recommended Texts and Other Resources list.

To give students the amount of reading practice necessary, they need reading opportunities that are varied in purpose and type of text. Ensuring that students are given ample opportunity to read a variety of materials in a variety of ways increases their motivation—you will have a better chance to tap into students' interests and give them enough practice for reading proficiency to develop.

Reading development does not occur in a linear fashion, and students' reading proficiency occurs at different rates. Students need opportunities to be challenged while reading, as well as to read texts that provide for easy, fluent reading (National Governors Association Center for Best Practices, Council of Chief State School Officers, 2010). These experiences can occur when students read a range of texts within a given topic of study. They also may occur during independent reading when students have more choice over what they read.

Reading to Systematically Build Knowledge

Engaging students in reading a variety of texts on the module topic helps to build their knowledge of that topic and the world, as well as crucial academic vocabulary that they can carry with them to another text in the same or a different domain. This focus builds the knowledge and skills students need to read increasingly complex texts—this is content-based literacy in action.

You may recall from Chapter 1 our desire to turn on the "curiosity motors" in students by systematically building their interest in compelling topics. As they are guided through experiences with texts through carefully scaffolded close reading and captivating sets of texts that engage their hearts and minds, they go deeper and deeper into these topics and become engaged with more and more texts. They view text as a way to learn more, to build knowledge, and to feed their curiosity.

Our content-based curriculum is designed to build this interest in systematic ways. Students generally read the anchor text early in the module to begin building content knowledge and vocabulary, and also to hook them into the topic and spark their interest for inquiry. In some modules, however, students may not begin the anchor text right away, instead building knowledge first through other kinds of texts, including complex texts. The order depends on when a text will offer students the best opportunity to build knowledge and understanding from it. No matter what, throughout a module, students will read a variety of texts to answer a guiding question and build expertise on the topic. Grappling with a variety of text types and sources pushes students to expand their vocabularies and their repertoire of text structures, as well as their understanding of a topic.

▷ No matter what, throughout a module, students will read a variety of texts to answer a guiding question and build expertise on the topic. Grappling with a variety of text types and sources pushes students to expand their vocabularies and their repertoire of text structures, as well as their understanding of a topic.

Throughout a module, students read in order to gather and record the information most relevant to their inquiry. For example, in Grade 6, Module 1, students gather evidence of how Percy's character changes over the course of *The Lightning Thief* in order to engage in an academic discussion about it. At all grade levels, students learn to organize the information they gather using various tools such as note-catchers and graphic organizers, which often focus them on analyzing texts through a specific lens. Gathering evidence in this way prepares them to talk and write about their ideas. (For more on the relationship between reading and writing in the curriculum, see Chapter 4).

A page from Trash Vortex, *the anchor text for Grade 7, Module 4. Informational texts like these that are visually stimulating help turn on students' "curiosity motors." Reprinted with permission.*

Independent Reading

Research Reading

Independent reading is an opportunity for students to enlarge their world and find joy in learning new things. In the curriculum, independent reading time is referred to as research reading and is designed specifically for students to read additional texts on the module topic in order to build content knowledge and develop vocabulary. The Grades 6–8 Recommended Text and Other Resources list provides a range of options on the module topic so that students can find texts that will be of interest to them at their independent reading level.

Research skills are important for success in a technological society; they are also an excellent opportunity to engage students in reading a variety of resources. Research on a topic develops students' knowledge about words, which increases reading proficiency. "Every concept—simple or complex, concrete or abstract—is learned in terms of its similarities, differences, and relationships with other concepts with which we are familiar" (Adams, 2011, p. 8).

When students are engaged in research reading in the curriculum, they are reading many texts about the module topic. This volume of reading builds background knowledge, word knowledge, and confidence in reading.

Reading for Pleasure

According to Clark and Rumbold (2006), "Reading for pleasure refers to reading that we do of our own free will, anticipating the satisfaction that we will get from the act of reading. It also refers to reading that, having begun at someone else's request, we continue because we are interested in it" (p. 6). College- and career-ready standards have brought a great deal of focus to the cognitive aspects of reading: word recognition and comprehension of complex texts. It is important for us to keep in mind, however, that even if students can read, it does not mean they will choose to do so, and adolescent readers in particular need us to acknowledge and honor their agency. Allowing students choice over what they read during independent reading time helps them discover what they want to read, as well as uncover new knowledge and connect with their world.

Independent reading is an opportunity for students to enlarge their world and find relevance. This of course must include additional texts on the topic of study (i.e., research reading). We also must encourage students to choose books on topics of their personal interest, which are likely to bridge a vast range of complexity. Allowing students to choose texts for independent reading helps them discover what they want to read, as well as to uncover new knowledge and connect with their world. Teachers and library media specialists can play a vital role in fostering a rich reading life for all students.

Chapter 3B:
How Will the Curriculum Support My Students to Read Complex Texts?

Regular practice with complex text and its academic language is a big—and important—instructional shift of college- and career-ready ELA standards. We want to acknowledge from the outset, however, that reading complex text through close reading is not a universally loved practice. Many teachers complain that it is tedious or boring for their students. Others feel that it is rigid and doesn't account for students' individual needs, that by the time students get to middle school, the variance in their reading levels is so extreme as to make a classwide, focused exploration of a single complex text foolhardy if not impossible.

We hear you, and we agree that close reading can be all of those things, but it doesn't have to be and certainly shouldn't be! Close reading should be about helping students read texts that are stimulating and exciting because they are challenging and sometimes mysterious (think about the lobster text in Chapter 1, Figure 1.1) and because the texts contain information that students really want to understand. It *should* be about building students' skill to read with greater independence. Often students need help unlocking complex text because it is too complex for them to read on their own.

The purpose of close reading is not to march students through a tedious set of steps, but to hand over the keys so that they can unlock the texts on their own. Close reading is as much about supporting students to make meaning of a *particular* complex text as it is about fostering the habits of mind they will need for approaching and making meaning of new texts, on their own. That is the ultimate goal.

▶ WHY IS CLOSE READING SO IMPORTANT FOR MY STUDENTS?

Giving students the opportunity and the strategies to tackle complex text builds their independent reading skills and their belief in themselves as readers. And, importantly, it gives them access to not just *our* curriculum, but any curriculum. It is difficult to build knowledge of the world—whether in first grade, twelfth grade, or college—if the ability to read and make meaning from text is a barrier.

Becoming a capable and confident reader opens many doors for students. A special educator supporting teachers using our curriculum in Cabell County, West Virginia, summed up the power of giving students the tools they need to read complex text: "They would go to their general ed. classroom, and they started participating and raising their hands. I had students actually say, 'I feel like a real fifth-grader. I'm doing grade-level work.'"

Whether students are listening to complex text read aloud or learning strategies to read complex texts on their own, we're committed to close reading because it's an effective practice that accelerates skill- and knowledge-building, and develops the habits of mind they need to read complex text independently. As we emphasized in Chapter 3A, we certainly don't want close reading to be the only kind of reading students experience. We make plenty of time for research reading so that they can dig into a variety of engaging texts on their own on the topic being studied in the modules (e.g., the design process in Grade 6 or food chains in Grade 8).

Students need time for devouring books like *Wonder* or *Children of Blood and Bone*, but we also need to carve out space for students to push into new territory and build up their reading muscles. If *Children of Blood and Bone* is the eighth-grade equivalent of a leisurely stroll through the park, let's be sure to vary the workout with occasional vigorous hikes with more challenging texts, such as *The Omnivore's Dilemma*. Just like a varied physical workout is good for the body, a varied reading workout is good for the mind.

▷ Just like a varied physical workout is good for the body, a varied reading workout is good for the mind.

Although students don't read (or hear read aloud) complex texts every day in our curriculum, they do it frequently enough that they are able to develop a rhythm of close, attentive reading, get the regular practice they need, and internalize close reading strategies. A close reading lesson, which typically happens once or twice per module, will often pair a complex text with other kinds of texts; for example, students may toggle back and forth between close reading of a complex informational text and independent reading of a related literary text that helps them make greater meaning of the complex text.

Close Reading Is an Equity Issue

Students should experience a "staircase of complexity" in the texts they read Grades K–12 so that they are prepared for college- and career-level reading by the time they leave high school. If we deny students the opportunity to learn the skills they need to read complex texts, they'll never catch up. They'll stay behind, caught in a vicious cycle. In the pages that follow, we hope you'll see that, yes, they can do it, and yes, you can help them.

We often hear a concern from teachers that the close reading of complex texts is too difficult for their students. Many find themselves "rescuing" students who struggle. This is a natural instinct, but keeping in mind our commitment to equity and excellence for all students, as well as the value of productive struggle, we encourage you to let the practice take hold and give your students a chance to surprise you. A good close read is designed so that productive struggle and success are interwoven. Thoughtfully scaffolded questions, strategic rereading, and lots of oral processing with partners and the full class, can and should give students an "I can do this!" experience.

The first key to success with close reading, for teachers, is to check in with yourself about your mindset. Do you harbor doubts that all your students can read complex texts? Do you find the prospect intimidating? Do you worry that close reading will take the joy out of reading for your students?

These are all legitimate questions, and we take them seriously. We are committed to making close reading collaborative, purposeful, and engaging for students and to helping you feel empowered with this critical literacy practice.

And, by showing you how we made decisions about the texts students read in our curriculum in Chapter 3A, we hope we have counteracted your fears that close reading means *boring* reading. Rest assured that we don't ask students to read dry texts about nothing just for the sake of reading complex texts. We chose the texts we did because they help students explore compelling topics and characters, which motivates them to persevere when the going gets tough. All students deserve this opportunity, not just those who already have strong reading skills.

▶ WHAT EXACTLY *IS* CLOSE READING?

Close reading is a process of careful, analytical reading. It involves repeated reading, text-based discussion, and (often) written analysis of complex text. At all levels—whether with our youngest readers in the primary grades or all the way into high school and beyond—the purposes remain the same: to gain a deeper understanding and appreciation of the specific text, to build world knowledge, to learn academic vocabulary, to build analytical reading skills, and to foster perseverance and passion for deep reading of worthy texts. The close reading you'll find in our curriculum helps students build these skills through collaborative, meaningful interaction with rich and compelling texts that help instill a spirit of courageous exploration. Peek into a classroom in Detroit to see what we mean. Video Spotlight 3.1 features students in Detroit who approach their close reading with curiosity, collaboration, and joy.

What *Isn't* Close Reading?

It's important to note at the outset that close reading isn't only one thing—it's not a protocol to be followed exactly every time students read complex texts. Sometimes students will need to reread (or hear read aloud) an entire text three times to unpack all of the layers of meaning. Other times, one time through the whole text is enough, with short passages chosen for further rereading. It is really the text and the task that dictate the approach in a particular close read—not every text needs the same treatment. To further demystify close reading, Table 3.5 summarizes what close reading is and what it isn't.

Table 3.5: What Close Reading Is and What It Isn't

What Close Reading Is	What Close Reading Isn't
A way to level the playing field by making complex text accessible to all students through carefully planned instruction	An unfair practice that forces struggling readers to read text they can't possibly understand
Exciting and enlightening, as students unlock the mystery of complex and often beautiful stories and poems, as well as rich informational text	Boring, dry, and dull
Crucial in a time when so much information is available through text and reading complex text is a prerequisite for success in college and careers	Unnecessary
A way to introduce developmentally appropriate strategies that support students in developing the kind of deep understanding of text that may have previously been available only to older students and excellent readers	A watered-down version of high school reading for younger students
A way to help students do the cognitive work of college- and career-ready standards that focus on deep comprehension (e.g., Reading: Literary Text and Reading: Informational Text standards)	A way to teach comprehension strategies (e.g., asking questions or drawing inferences)
A way to *build* understanding by guiding students on a coherent journey through a text and monitoring their understanding as they go	A way to *check* understanding with a "quiz" or set of comprehension questions
Confidence building	Confidence destroying

▸ HOW ARE CLOSE READS DESIGNED TO HELP MY STUDENTS BUILD DEEP UNDERSTANDING AND LITERACY SKILLS?

As we have done in other parts of this book, we want to spend some time "looking under the hood" at what goes into the design of the close reads in the curriculum. Understanding the important decisions that go into creating these lessons will help you teach close reads with greater nimbleness and authority. As we stated in Chapter 1, we hope that teaching our curriculum will be its own form of professional learning for you. Learning the ins and outs of these practices may positively impact the way you and your students approach reading across all subjects.

Three main ingredients contribute to the design of close reads in our curriculum:

1. The first ingredient is the *text*. In addition to offering students an important opportunity to build their knowledge, each text selected for a close read in our curriculum has been carefully chosen so that it is at the right level of complexity for students. The close reads were designed to support students in navigating the complexities of a text, which we identified using the Four Quadrants of Qualitative Text Complexity analysis (see Table 3.2). Not every text is complex in the same ways. Once the specific complexities of a text are identified, close reads can be designed to address *some of* those specific complexities with students. The challenge for curriculum designers is to first identify how a particular text is complex, and then to determine which of those complexities to focus on, given the larger purpose of the module.

2. The second ingredient is the *purpose*. Why are students reading this text closely, given the larger context of the module? How will understanding this text help them understand the module topic more deeply?

3. The third ingredient is the *process* by which students read the text. "Rather than reading to merely learn 'about' the text, students must be able to read texts analytically, gathering information for a particular purpose and synthesizing it to create deeper understanding" (Berger, Woodfin, Plaut, and Dobbertin, 2014, p. 180). Along the way, students should be interacting with the text and one another to help deepen their understanding.

Close reading as an instructional strategy for tackling complex text will represent a shift in reading instruction for many teachers (see Table 3.6).

Table 3.6: What's In and What's Out for Teaching Complex Texts

In	Out
Regular encounters with complex texts	Leveled texts (only)
Texts worthy of close attention	Reading any old text
Mostly text-dependent questions	Mostly text-to-self questions
Mainly evidence-based analysis	Mainly opinion-based analysis
Accent on academic vocabulary	Accent on literary terminology
Emphasis on reading and rereading	Emphasis on pre-reading
Reading strategies (as a means)	Reading strategies (as an end)

In the video, "Close Reading," teacher Pamela Hornbuckle and her fifth-graders at Maybury Elementary School in Detroit Public Schools Community District engage in a close read. Students work collaboratively—and with great enthusiasm—through a process of careful, analytic reading that involves repeated reading, text-based discussing, and written analysis of a complex text.

https://vimeo.com/386910186

The Planning behind Close Reading Sessions

Close reads are like an iceberg; what the student experiences above the waterline is built on careful planning below the waterline. And, just like an iceberg, the planning and foundational work is actually much larger than the close read itself. Before students begin reading a complex text, there are many decisions to make. As curriculum designers, the following steps were a part of our planning process:

Step 1: Evaluate the Context

» Determine the purpose for reading. What will students understand or do with the information they acquire?

» Look ahead. Where is this heading? Why do students need this information?

» What is the assessment? How will students write about what they read? What is the performance task?

» Choose compelling texts and be able to explain why a particular text was chosen.

• What makes it worth reading?

Step 2: Analyze the Text

» What excerpts are particularly critical (in terms of the content students need to learn or make sense of)? Of those, which will need to be read slowly, deeply, more than once, and with support? (See Table 3.3 in Chapter 3A for an example of an analysis from "The Land of Red Apples.")

» Specifically, what challenges will students need to overcome in terms of the text's meaning, requisite background knowledge, structure, and language?

» Attend to syntax and vocabulary. Determine what vocabulary students might be able to learn in context and what words will need to be defined for them.

» Should students first hear a particularly critical or difficult passage read aloud? (If so, students need to follow along.) Or can students first have a go on their own and then, if needed, hear the text read aloud after?

Step 3: Prepare Questions, Engagement Strategies, and Scaffolding

» Which text-dependent questions will lead students through the text to the big ideas? The questions are really the heart of the lesson. See the "Lifting Students to Greater Understanding of the Text through a Carefully Crafted Series of Text-Dependent Questions" section later in Chapter 3B for more on text-dependent questions.

» How will students engage with the questions, the text, and one another during each close read? See the "Engaging Students in Discourse about the Text" section later in Chapter 3B for more on engagement strategies.

» Are there students who will need a differentiated approach? What scaffolds can be put in place that will lift them to the text and not take away their opportunity to read and make meaning independently? See the "Supporting English Language Learners and Others Who May Need Additional Scaffolding" section later in Chapter 3B for more on scaffolding and differentiated instruction.

What Happens during a Close Read?

In our curriculum, we include Close Reading Guides that walk you through the close reading of a particular complex text from beginning to end. These guides are backward-designed from a clear understanding of what knowledge and skills students should build as a result of reading the text and of the challenges the text presents. The primary goal of close reading is deep understanding of the text (or a particular part of the text) and how it relates to the module topic as a whole. Remember, we don't ask students to read closely just for the sake of reading closely; we do it to give them access to knowledge. We also want to build, over time, the habits and mindsets students need to be able to tackle complex texts independently.

Close reads include certain elements that are the same, no matter the text:

» Setting purpose for the close read

» Giving students an initial sense of the text through a "first read" or read-aloud

» Lifting students to greater understanding of the text through a carefully crafted series of text-dependent questions

» Working with vocabulary in context during close reading

» Engaging students in discourse about the text

» Supporting English language learners and others who may need additional scaffolding

» Synthesizing understanding of the text

Let's take a closer look at each of these elements of close reads.

Setting Purpose for the Close Read

It is important for students to know why they are going to read a complex text before they begin reading it. One common misconception about close reading is that it is merely close reading for the sake of close reading (which implies that the purpose is only to develop a reading skill, such as annotating a text). Yet that is far from the case. Setting a greater purpose for students will engage their curiosity and their motivation. In our content-based curriculum, doing the hard work of reading complex text is in service of building knowledge of the world. Students also learn skills (e.g., annotating) and habits of mind (e.g., rereading), but comprehension and knowledge-building is paramount.

With their curiosity motors in high gear, we want students to be ready and willing to dig into the text. Connecting it to their desire to learn about the world is key. Think back to how the teacher introduced the lobster text (Figure 1.1) to her students in Chapter 1: "This is a great scientific paper by one of the world experts on lobsters. It has important information that will inform our study of Boston Harbor. But almost no one in the world has read it, and few people can understand it. Even your parents may not be able to understand it. Some of the teachers here may not understand it. At least not right away. But together, we can make sense of it." This teacher made an extremely complex text something these students suddenly couldn't live without reading.

In the Grade 6 close read that we unpack in Chapter 3C, students begin their close read of "The Land of Red Apples," with an understanding that they will be analyzing the point of view of the narrator, a girl arriving at an American Indian boarding school. Students have previously read the point of view of a white person in favor of the boarding schools, and now they will read a first person account of a student. Understanding the purpose of their reading—to analyze the narrator's point of view, which is a shift from what they have read previously—sets students up to read critically and with engagement.

Giving Students an Initial Sense of the Text through a "First Read"

The first read of a complex text is almost always a read-aloud, even with older students. When you read aloud, fluently, with expression, and all the way through, you give students a sense of the whole piece and allow all students equitable access to a text some may otherwise struggle with. Despite its simplicity, the first read of a complex text is challenging for many teachers. It may require some unlearning of the way you have always done things. In the past, read-alouds have often involved frequent pauses to ask students questions about the text, to think aloud about the text, or to explain things to students: "Why do you think she said that? What do you think will happen next? How does this idea connect to what we learned yesterday? So in this part of the text, the author is really saying such-and-such." During the first read, we want you to resist this urge and to keep reading the whole piece.

There will be plenty of time for students to answer questions about the text. But the first read is not that time. It is important for students to hear the text read fluently and with expression. Hearing the text read as the author intended it to be read helps students enjoy the text, connect to its message, and get a sense of the flow and meaning of the whole piece. It's totally fine if students don't understand everything; we wouldn't expect them to. Think about the first time you read a dense poem, a contract, or an explanation of new science discoveries in a magazine or newspaper. You get something, but you know you'll need to keep digging in. The same is true with close reading. After the first read, subsequent close reading sessions devote time to helping students drill down into certain words, sentences, and paragraphs to make sense of the deeper meaning of the piece.

Lifting Students to Greater Understanding of the Text through a Carefully Crafted Series of Text-Dependent Questions

Strong text-dependent questions are the foundation of close reading—they take students on a journey through the text and build their understanding as they go. The questions ground the purpose of the reading for you and your students, they are the basis of class discussion and inquiry, and they shape how the text will be used in the lesson, including what parts of the text will be unpacked, individually and together, and to what depth. Unlike questions we often instinctively ask (because they were asked of us as students), this carefully crafted set of text-dependent questions is not designed to assess students' understanding of text. Instead, the questions draw attention to key ideas in the text and model strategies for unlocking meaning in complex text. The questions act as a scaffold to lift students to greater understanding of the text.

Any worthy complex text, by nature, invites many rich questions. When reading closely, it is important to ensure that the questions serve the larger purpose. When creating the text-dependent questions in close reads in our curriculum, we ruthlessly prioritized; we sought not to distract students (or teachers) with questions that would send them on tangents. Instead, we identified where it is crucial to slow down and take more time with a sentence; what concepts, themes, and issues are most important; and what vocabulary and language learning is best served by the piece.

It is important to help students move through the text in a logical sequence. The series of questions should help students build a holistic understanding of the text, rather than creating a fragmented experience (another reason it is important that students read/hear all of the text first, keeping in mind that sometimes the lesson focuses students on just selected passages, not an entire text.) The best questions span a range of complexity, including concrete questions of recall and basic understanding, as well as questions that require critical thinking: inference, analysis, application, and transference to new contexts. In practice, the questions are generally not planned in a simple sequence of increasing complexity; instead, purpose and understanding shape the order of questions used for discussion or written prompts. The challenges of making meaning within the text itself, rather than the specific standards to "cover," drive the sequence of questions, though typically a strong sequence of text-dependent questions will inherently hit many of the Reading standards.

▷ Unlike questions we often instinctively ask (because they were asked of us as students), this carefully crafted set of text-dependent questions is not designed to assess students' understanding of text. Instead, the questions draw attention to key ideas in the text and model strategies for unlocking meaning in complex text. The questions act as a scaffold to lift students to greater understanding of the text.

Questions as a Tool for Analysis of Text

As the name suggests, text-dependent questions must drive students back to the text, requiring them to read, and often reread, the specific text closely to answer them. Although questions must require analysis of the text and compel students to focus sharply on the language of the text itself, students may inevitably connect the text to their own experience, background knowledge, and other texts they have read. Indeed, this is how readers integrate new texts into what they already know to expand their schema for understanding the world.

Text-dependent questions should require students to look sharply and analytically at the text itself—not just the general ideas in the text, but the specific structure, language, and meaning of the text and the decisions that the author made to use particular words, phrases, and images. The questions can require students to make connections to broader themes, current issues, and even personal experiences but are always strongly grounded in the text itself. One simple test for whether a question is text-dependent: would students need the text in hand, and eyes on the text, to answer it? If not, the question may be "about" the text but not "dependent on" the text. Typical text-dependent questions ask students to perform one or more tasks, which are highlighted with examples in Table 3.7.

Table 3.7: What Is the Work Text-Dependent Questions Ask Students to Do?

Task	Example
Paraphrase to convey basic understanding.	Students Turn and Talk with a partner: how would you put this sentence in your own words?
Analyze paragraphs sentence by sentence and analyze sentences word by word to determine the role played by individual paragraphs, sentences, phrases, or words.	Students underline a particular word repeated in a paragraph and consider why the author chose to repeat it, and how the paragraph would change if the author had instead chosen synonyms for that word instead of repetition.
Probe each argument in an opinion/argument text, each idea in informational text, and each key detail in literary text, and observe how these build to a whole.	Students engage in a QuickWrite about the big ideas in a story.
Note and assess patterns and structures in a text and what they mean; to illuminate these patterns, close reads often incorporate anchor charts.	Students record cause and effect as they read an article about climate change.
Question why authors choose to begin and end when they do.	Students engage in a Think-Pair-Share protocol to consider how a narrative would change if a story ended one paragraph earlier. What would be lost? What would be gained?
Consider what the text leaves uncertain or unstated.	Students discuss possible evidence-based reasons for the author's choice.

Working with Vocabulary in Context during Close Reads

As we have emphasized, teaching vocabulary extends far beyond close reads; we take every opportunity to build students' vocabulary banks (see Chapter 3A for a fuller description of the various ways vocabulary is taught). Specifically during close reads, we focus on key vocabulary, often toggling between instances when we need to define a word for students, if it can't be figured out in context, and instances when we ask students to grapple with the meaning, based on context, morphology, or past learning. This toggling also supports the pacing requirements of the curriculum. In the annotated lesson in Chapter 3C, you will see examples of this dance back and forth between helping students figure out vocabulary on their own and providing definitions when necessary.

Vocabulary is often the subject of text-dependent questions. Exploring the meanings of words is one way to help students be evidence-based readers—by understanding the meaning of a word and how it affects the meaning of a piece overall or by exploring an author's choice to use a particular word, students are pushed to comprehend a text based on what the text actually says. In a progression of text-dependent questions, vocabulary is often a low-stakes place to start, to warm students up to looking closely at the text before they move on to syntax and structure and toward the big questions of the themes and central ideas of a text.

Engaging Students in Discourse about the Text

Text-dependent questions are not necessarily answered by students putting pencil to paper in order to independently answer each question or by teachers asking the class and calling on students ready to answer. Close reads are designed so that students engage in some kind of discourse about the questions. When students talk through their ideas, they are more likely to understand them. Often, brief protocols are used as the structure for that discourse so that all students have the opportunity to speak. The following brief protocols are used commonly during close reads in the curriculum:

» Think-Pair-Share: This protocol promotes productive and equitable conversations in which all students are given the time and space to think, share, and consider the ideas of others. It ensures that all students simultaneously engage with the same text or topic, while promoting synthesis and the social construction of knowledge.

» Back-to-Back and Face-to-Face: This protocol provides a method for sharing information and gaining multiple perspectives on a topic through partner interaction. It can be used for reviewing and sharing academic material, as a personal "ice breaker," or as a means of engaging in critical thinking about a topic of debate.

Brief protocols like these promote greater engagement from students. They are also highly supportive for ELLs or for those who might struggle with complex text. Close reading is by design highly scaffolded and supportive, as students move slowly and deliberately through text. And the use of brief discussion protocols gives them plenty of opportunities to talk about the text with their peers, which helps students to solidify their understanding of vocabulary, syntax, and meaning and to articulate their ideas.

Note that more in-depth protocols, such as Socratic Seminars, may be used to bring students deeper and deeper into a text; however, these protocols are not frequently used during close reads. This is because protocols are designed so that teachers can use them with *any* text. And because close reads are *text-specific*, asking students to look closely at words and sentences in the text itself, protocols may be a useful early step but overall have more limited use. (Note: More in-depth protocols will be explored in Chapter 4 when we explore the read-think-talk-write cycle.)

In addition to brief protocols and total participation techniques, there are myriad other ways to increase students' engagement with complex text. Many of these are suggested in the Close Reading Guides. Others you may choose to add based on the needs of your students.

» Movement: Circulating to analyze text excerpts or images, standing in groups to chart their analysis of the text

» Drama or role-play: Acting out events or ideas in a text in small groups or as a class

» Physical manipulation of text: Manipulating excerpts of the text (e.g., mystery quotes, sorting evidence into more or less relevant)

» Sketching: Making a quick drawing to show a key idea in the text or communicate ideas

» Annotating text: Writing in the margins or placing a sticky note with a note or visual to answer a question or explain the gist of a section of text

» Text-coding: Using symbols to indicate reactions to the text (e.g., a question mark for questions, a check mark for connections)

» Color-coding: Using various colors to indicate different aspects of a text's structure (e.g., highlighting key details in yellow or painting the focus statement in a model essay green, as in the Painted Essay® format used throughout the curriculum)

Close reading will be a challenge for many students. It is rigorous cognitive work. There are a few things about the design of the close reads in our Grades 6–8 curriculum that will help make these important literacy-building experiences effective and engaging for all of your students:

» Students are reading compelling and worthy texts that they will *want* to dig into.

» Close reads are typically between 20–35 minutes and they only happen once or twice per module.

» Students are not just reading independently. They are talking to one another, writing, and maybe even drawing—they are actively interacting with the text and, often, with one another, while reading.

» The questions and activities in close reads represent a line of inquiry that leads students to an understanding of the text most would not have come to on their own. Close reading offers *all* students access to the kind of experiences those of us who love to read often take for granted. For readers who have been labelled "struggling," and who have been offered only simplified texts for years, this may be the first time they know the excitement and satisfaction of unlocking the deeper meaning and beauty of the words on a page.

▷ Close reading offers *all* students access to the kind of experiences those of us who love to read often take for granted. For readers who've been labelled "struggling," and who have been offered only simplified texts for years, this may be the first time they know the excitement and satisfaction of unlocking the deeper meaning and beauty of the words on a page.

Supporting English Language Learners and Others Who May Need Additional Scaffolding

Although close reads can seem intimidating to students because of the complexity of the text, they are designed to be deeply supportive of ELLs and students who may struggle with reading. Because students are walked carefully through text, slowly and deliberately parsing words and unpacking layers of meaning, they learn essential reading strategies and have opportunities to build knowledge of the world.

Though the texts are challenging, the process of close reading, which happens regularly in the curriculum, gives students who may need additional support with reading new skills and strategies for tackling complex text. For ELLs in particular, this practice reflects the fact that students learning a new language deserve—and need—access to challenging texts and sophisticated ideas.

Planning Appropriate Scaffolds

Like everything you do in the classroom, close reads will require planning and forethought to meet the needs of your diverse group of learners. Because these lessons are designed to challenge students with complex texts, it is important that all students read the *same* challenging text. With that in mind, scaffolding strategies can then be applied to lift all students to the text, though we offer a word of caution when applying them: It is important not to *over-scaffold* the reading experience for students. Too much front-loading will take away their opportunity to figure things out on their own.

The curriculum already offers you many specific scaffolds, which you can find in the Support All Students section of the Teaching Notes for each lesson and the Teacher's Guide for English Language Learners. Taking the time to read and understand the lesson well ahead of time so that you can see how scaffolds are intentionally woven into the close read will help you avoid too much frontloading. Among the suggested scaffolds, you will find some that should happen before the lesson and some that should happen during the lesson. The list of options in Table 3.8 can help you understand the types of supports you'll find in close reads, as well as additional strategies you might consider to meet your particular students' needs. Chapter 5A explores these scaffolds in much greater detail, and Chapter 5C is devoted to supporting ELLs.

Table 3.8: Scaffolding Options for Close Reads

	Scaffolding Options
Lesson calls for reading chunks of the text independently	» For students who might get overwhelmed by seeing the whole text on a page, format the text into "bite-sized" pieces (e.g., one paragraph at a time on index cards or one page as a separate handout). » Have students read with a buddy. » Have small groups read with you or another teacher (or via technology). » Provide structured overviews for some sections of text. » Predetermine importance for selections of text, and highlight those. » Reformat texts to include more embedded definitions or even picture cues. » Provide the text to students in a clear format, either on a handout or displayed clearly via technology.
Lesson calls for answering questions	» Start with concrete text-dependent questions before moving to the abstract. » Tackle small sections at a time. » Once students have tried the task, provide additional modeling for those who need it. » Provide sentence stems or frames. » Use a highlighter to emphasize key ideas/details in the text. » Modify graphic organizers to include picture cues or additional step-by-step directions. » Post directions and anchor charts. » Provide "hint cards" that give students more support with text-dependent questions (students access these only when they get stuck). » Indicate where students may find key information in the text or on an anchor chart by marking with sticky notes or highlights. » Give options for responding to questions with discussion before writing. » Use the lesson's Work Time for guided work with the teacher.
Lesson calls for writing	» Modify graphic organizers to include visual cues or additional step-by-step directions. » Provide sentence starters and sentence frames. » Use discussion, including Conversation Cues, to help students orally rehearse their answers before responding in writing. » Model writing using a similar prompt or a different section of the text. » Use the lesson's Work Time for small group guided work with the teacher. » Use the lesson's Work Time for conferring with individual students.
Lesson calls for collaborative work	» Review norms for collaboration in advance and after group work. » Have small groups work with a teacher.

	» Form heterogeneous pairs (strategic partnerships). » Monitor specific students more strategically (e.g., seat them closer to a teacher). » Provide (and model) structured roles for group members.
Other literacy or intervention time	» Offer additional practice with Speaking and Listening standards (e.g., oral reading, speaking with expression) and grammar rules. » Offer additional writing practice. » Pre-read with students the text used in the lesson. » Have students read additional (easier) texts on the same topic. » Have students reread texts used in lessons. » Provide additional quality read-alouds, including via technology. » Pre-teach critical vocabulary. » Engage students in word study (e.g., structural analysis of specific words from the text).
Homework	» Provide students with read-alouds via technology (e.g., audiobooks). » Provide visual cues or additional directions. » Provide sentence starters or sentence frames. » Provide video or slides of class examples on a website. » Modify expectations of quantity.

Synthesizing Understanding of the Text

As a bookend to setting purpose at the start of the close read, students also need an opportunity to synthesize their understanding of the text once they are done. A culminating task gives students a chance to step back to think about what they understand about the text.

In the Grade 6 close read example we unpack in Chapter 3C, the culminating task is directly related to the purpose of the close read, which is to analyze the narrator's point of view in "The Land of Red Apples": *How does [the final sentence of the close read] capture the central idea of Zitkala-Sa's point of view toward her new life at the [American Indian boarding] school?* Throughout the close read, students have engaged in discussion and have recorded notes on their note-catcher in order to build their understanding of the narrator's point of view. Importantly, they have also considered how her point of view differs from those around her. For example:

» What is the narrator's point of view toward the journey she and the seven other Yankton children are about to take? How do you know?

» How does Zitkala-Sa's choice to include this detail about the missionaries handing out candy impact the reader's understanding of the text?

» Why are the words *excited* and *trembled more from fear* important in this section? How do they help us see the difference in point of view between the white people at the school and Zitkala-Sa?

» What does this description of Zitkala-Sa being picked up and tossed into the air show us about her point of view toward coming to the school?

Synthesizing their understanding of a text at the conclusion of a close read is a form of debrief that not only builds students' understanding of the module topic, but also builds their capacity to track and take ownership of their learning. And, connecting the synthesis to the purpose for reading set out at the beginning of the close read deepens students' motivation to dig into challenging texts.

Chapter 3C:
What Does Close Reading Look Like in Action?

Lessons that include close reads feature Close Reading Guides, which are found in the Teacher Supporting Materials for the lesson. Each guide walks you and your students through a complex text. Close reads typically take 20–35 minutes of a 45-minute lesson. Lessons that include close reads will look like typical lessons in your Teacher Guide, but when it's time for the close reading, you will be directed to the Teacher Supporting Materials for the Close Reading Guide.

Here in Chapter 3C, we unpack and annotate a close read of a complex text. We will start by orienting you to the entire 45-minute lesson and then zoom in on the Close Reading Guide. Throughout, we will draw your attention to instructional strategies that are described previously in this chapter or in previous chapters, especially Chapter 2B.

▶ Sample Lesson

Grade 6, Module 3, Unit 1, Lesson 4

Lesson Title: Close Read: Analyze Point of View and Unfamiliar Words: "The Land of Red Apples"

Examining a Close Read for "The Land of Red Apples"

Let's look "under the hood" and examine a Grade 6 close read. This close read supports students in deeply understanding point of view. Before diving deeply into the module anchor text, *Two Roads*, students examine supplementary texts carefully selected to develop their understanding of the historical context of American Indian boarding schools, the topic of Module 3. In Unit 1, Lesson 3, students analyze a speech by Captain Pratt, the founder of Carlisle Indian boarding school. In the following lesson, which is annotated on the pages that follow, students engage in close read of "The Land of Red Apples" a first-person account of this school by Zitkala-Sa, a member of the Yankton tribe. These reading experiences allow students to examine and reflect on multiple perspectives. Students also use these texts to practice explaining how an author's point of view is conveyed and what impact connotative and figurative language has on meaning.

Figure 3.4: Close Reading Lesson Agenda

Agenda

1. **Opening**

    A. Engage the Learner – RI.6.2 (5 minutes)

2. **Work Time**

    A. Analyze Point of View: "The Land of Red Apples" – SL.6.1d (15 minutes)

    B. Close Read: "The Land of Red Apples" – RI.6.6, L.6.5 (20 minutes)

3. **Closing and Assessment**

    A. Analyze Point of View: "The Land of Red Apples" – RI.6.6 (5 minutes)

4. **Homework**

    A. Analyze Language and Point of View: Students complete Homework: Analyze Language and Point of View: "Iron Routine."

How Is the Close Reading Integrated within the Lesson?

Close reads are embedded within lessons. The agenda for the lesson in Figure 3.4 shows where the close read we are using as an example fits within this particular lesson. We'll start with the full lesson. As you review the lesson, notice how the close read of "The Land of Red Apples" integrates with other parts of the lesson to support students in exploring point of view and deepen their understanding of the text and the concepts that underlie the module. As you orient to this lesson, which includes a close read, it may help you to go back to Chapter 2B and refresh your memory regarding some of the high-leverage instructional practices used in the curriculum to empower students to own their own learning (Table 2.5 in Chapter 2B offers a useful summary). You will see many of those practices in the lesson that follows.

Note: We have excluded the prefatory material for this lesson, such as the Teaching Notes and materials list; instead, we start with the Opening section and go through the Closing and Assessment section. Immediately following the main lesson is the annotated Close Reading Guide. The two-page complex text, "The Land of Red Apples," can be found in Figure 3.3 in Chapter 3A for your reference.

- ☑ Print or online dictionary (one per pair)
- ☑ Homework: Analyze Language and Point of View: "Iron Routine" (one per student; see Homework Resources)

Opening

A. Engage the Learner – RI.6.2 (5 minutes)

- Repeated routine: Follow the same routine as previous lessons to distribute and review the **Entrance Ticket: Unit 1, Lesson 4** or the optional **Entrance Ticket: Unit 1, Lesson 4 ▲**. Refer to the **Entrance Ticket: Unit 1, Lesson 4 (example for teacher reference)** for possible responses. Students will need their copies of **Captain Pratt speech excerpt** and **Analyze Point of View: Captain Pratt note-catcher**. Refer to **Analyze Point of View: Captain Pratt note-catcher (example for teacher reference)**.

- Repeated routine: Follow the same routine as the previous lessons to review learning targets and the purpose of the lesson, reminding students of any learning targets that are similar to or the same as previous lessons. Invite students to choose a habit of character focus for themselves for this lesson.

Work Time

A. Analyze Point of View: "The Land of Red Apples" – SL.6.1d (15 minutes)

- Remind students that the anchor text is historical fiction. In this lesson and the next, students will continue to read supplemental informative texts to build background on this historical topic to better understand the novel.

- Distribute the **Analyze Point of View: "The Land of Red Apples" note-catcher**.

- Cold-call students to read the directions, column headings, and questions aloud. Clarify that students will listen to a chapter from Zitkala-Sa's memoir. After the reading, students will record their responses in the middle column.

- Direct students' attention to the **Point of View anchor chart**, specifically the notes related to informational texts. Inform students that the text they will be reading is a person's recollection of events that happened to her; therefore, even though the text may read as a narrative, the text is informational.

- Read aloud **"The Land of Red Apples" by Zitkala-Sa**.

- Direct students to complete the Listen column of the note-catcher.

- Explain that they will complete the Read column later in the lesson.

- Repeated routine: Invite students to reflect on their progress toward the relevant learning target.

Activating Schema: *The teacher activates students' background knowledge by connecting similar learning targets from previous lessons to today's learning targets.*

Support All Students: *The black triangle signals to the teacher that an alternate entrance ticket is available in the Teacher's Guide for English Language Learners for students who need greater support with this task.*

Unpacking learning targets with habits of character and the characteristics of middle school learners in mind: *Based on what they know of the lesson so far from the learning targets, students consider the habit of character that will make the most sense for them to focus on during the lesson.*

Setting Purpose: *The teacher situates the complex text within the module topic and connects it to the anchor text. As a pair, one text is historical fiction and other supplemental texts are informative texts that will help build background knowledge on the topic.*

Total Participation Techniques: *The teacher uses a total participation technique—Cold Call—to engage all students.*

Co-constructing Anchor Charts: *The teacher refers to the Point of View anchor chart to preview how the point of view of today's text will inform their experience of it. Anchor charts make students' thinking permanent and public and promote an evidence-based classroom culture.*

Read-Aloud of Complex Text: *The teacher reads the text aloud as students follow along. This ensures that all students have access to the text and models fluent reading. Even with students who are able to decode, read-aloud is used strategically throughout the curriculum to promote comprehension.*

Checking for Understanding: *The teacher chooses a checking-for-understanding technique to allow students to self-assess progress toward the learning target.*

Note: Lessons are for example only. They may look different from actual curriculum materials.

Work Time

B. Close Read: "The Land of Red Apples" – RI.6.6, L.6.5 (20 minutes)

- Focus students on the **Close Readers Do These Things anchor chart** and remind them that digging into the text deeper can help them understand it better.
- Move students into predetermined pairs. Distribute "The Land of Red Apples" by Zitkala-Sa.
- Use **Close Reading Guide: "The Land of Red Apples"** to set the purpose of the close read and to guide students through a close read of this excerpt. Refer to the guide for how to integrate the following:
  - **Close Read: "The Land of Red Apples" note-catcher**
  - **Print or online dictionary**
- Refer to **Close Read: "The Land of Red Apples" note-catcher (example for teacher reference)** as necessary.
- Repeated routine: Invite students to reflect on their progress toward the relevant learning target.

Closing and Assessment

A. Analyze Point of View: "The Land of Red Apples" – RI.6.6 (5 minutes)

- Refocus students on Analyze Point of View: "The Land of Red Apples" note-catcher. Ask students to complete the Read column of the note-catcher.
- Collect the note-catcher as students leave the class.
- Repeated routine: Invite students to reflect on their habit of character focus for this lesson.

Homework

A. Analyze Language and Point of View

- Students complete **Homework: Analyze Language and Point of View: "Iron Routine."**

Promoting positive mindsets: The teacher reviews the Close Readers Do These Things anchor chart with students to prepare them for a positive and productive reading experience.

Strategic Grouping: The teacher may pair students for the close read in whatever way will be most supportive (e.g., with other students at a similar level of English proficiency).

The Close Reading Guide: The guide is anchored in the lesson here: Look for instructions in all close reading lessons that direct you to the guide, which can be found in the Supporting Materials for the lesson. (Note: You will find annotations of the Close Reading Guide immediately following this lesson.)

Checking for Understanding: The teacher chooses a checking-for-understanding technique to allow students to self-assess progress toward the learning target.

Checking for Understanding: Students are invited to complete their note-catchers and turn them in as a formative assessment at the conclusion of the lesson.

Repeated Routine: Here and elsewhere in the lesson, teachers are invited to use their judgment as to the best total participation technique, protocol, or other method to engage students in conversation or reflection.

Chapter 3

EL Education Curriculum **67**

Note: Lessons are for example only.
They may look different from actual curriculum materials.

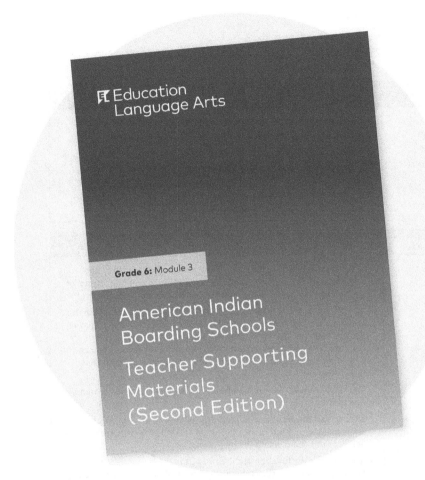

Grade 6: Module 3

American Indian Boarding Schools

Teacher Supporting Materials (Second Edition)

The Close Reading Guide

For each close read, there is a Close Reading Guide (found in the Teacher Supporting Materials for the lesson) that will support students to navigate the complexity of the text in order to form a deep and lasting understanding of both the text and the skills needed to read it. Remember that one of the main purposes of close reading is to help students deeply understand a text so that they can learn about the world. Like all texts in our content-based curriculum, "The Land of Red Apples" was chosen to help students learn about the topic of the module, which in this case is American Indian boarding schools.

In this close read, students analyze the text for how it shows the point of view of Zitkala-Sa, the narrator, as a young child when she first leaves home to go to the American Indian boarding school. Students have already listened to the text read aloud. This lesson provides a second reading as a read-aloud in class. In a series of cycles of read-think-talk-write, students dig into chunks of text, discuss with a partner, and record their responses to text-dependent questions on their note-catchers. For each part of the text, they focus on key vocabulary. As a bookend to the stated purpose of the close read at the start of the lesson, the culminating task asks students: *How does the final sentence of the text captures the central idea of Zitkala-Sa's point of view toward her new life at the school?*

What follows is the Close Reading Guide for "The Land of Red Apples." This close read has been annotated to highlight some of the questions and strategies to actively engage students in deeply understanding the text. Note: The two-page complex text, "The Land of Red Apples," can be found in Figure 3.3 in Chapter 3A for your reference.

Excerpt of Text	Questions and Directions
Complete these tasks before reading.	• Distribute the Close Read: "The Land of Red Apples" note-catcher. • Explain that we are about to read the text we just listened to. • Remind students that when we read, we are able to take time to reread and notice ideas and language that we may not have noticed from listening. • Explain that we will be thinking about point of view and language to help convey point of view today when we read.

Excerpt of Text	Questions and Directions
Read paragraphs 1 and 2.	• Read the text aloud as students read along silently. Pause to define **missionaries** in the first sentence (a person who is sent by a church or religious group to a foreign country to teach, convert, heal, or serve). • Working in partners, direct students to discuss, and then record in their note-catchers, their responses to this question: "What is the narrator's point of view toward the journey she and the seven other Yankton children are about to take? How do you know?" (She is looking forward to it—"impatient to start," "dreamt of roaming as freely," "anticipated much pleasure") • Say: "Underline the words **iron horse**. What is she referring to here?" (the train). • Explain that this term was commonly used during this time period, and it marked the shift in transportation and industry from reliance on horses to the steam engine. • Ask: "What is the function of the word **but** in the last sentence?" (It lets the reader know that she is about to contrast what she thought the trip would be like with what it actually is like.)

Setting Purpose: *The teacher reminds students of the purpose of the close read, which is to analyze how the narrator's point of view is conveyed through language.*

Chunking the Text: *Students focus on one part of this complex text at a time.*

Structures for Collaboration: *Students discuss answers to questions with their partner before recording their responses. Cycles of read-think-talk-write are highly supportive of students learning English, who benefit from oral processing and the social construction of knowledge, and, in general, of the varied learning styles represented in classrooms.*

62

Note: Lessons are for example only.
They may look different from actual curriculum materials.

Pacing: The lesson features a balance of telling students the meanings of words and having them determine the meanings of words independently. This keeps things moving forward at a productive pace.

Vocabulary in Context: *Students consider how key vocabulary (e.g., scrutinized, riveted) conveys the author's point of view.*

Excerpt of Text	Questions and Directions
Read paragraph 3.	• Read the text aloud as students read along silently. • Ask: "What do you think the word **scrutinized** means?" (loo[k] closely; inspected) • If students seem uncertain about the word, show them how to use the sentences around it to figure out what it means. For example, the men and women on the train are both stopping, and the men "riveted their glassy blue eyes" on them—so **scrutinized** may have something to do with looking at them or staring at them. • Say: "Let's check that in a dictionary and see if we were right." • Students check the word in a dictionary. If using a print dictionary, be sure to explain that words are listed in alphabetical order. • Direct students to record this definition on their note-catcher. • Working in partners, direct students to discuss, and then record in their note-catchers, their responses to these questions: • Ask: "So now that we know that 'scrutinized' means 'staring,' how are the connotations between those two words different?" (Scrutinized has a more negative connotation than staring; it implies the looking is critical and judgmental in nature, not just observing or watching in an approving or neutral fashion.) • Ask: "How does Zitkala-Sa's use of **scrutinized** help to convey her point of view toward her experience on the train?" (The use of this word suggests that Zitkala-Sa understands that she is being judged in a disapproving fashion by the white people on the train, and she feels very different from those people.) • Ask: "What other words in the paragraph have connotations that also convey that point of view?" ("**stopped**," "**halted**," and "**riveted**")

Note: Lessons are for example only.
They may look different from actual curriculum materials.

Chapter 3

Excerpt of Text	Questions and Directions
Read paragraph 4.	• Read the text aloud as students read along silently.
	• Working in partners, direct students to discuss, and then record in their note-catchers, their responses to this question: "At the start of the paragraph, she says she 'sank deep into the corner of my seat.' Another way she could have said this is 'I sat down in my seat.' How are the connotations between those two versions different and how does the connotation of the way she chose to write it help to convey her point of view?" (**"Sank deep"** and **"corner"** imply that she is trying to be small and unnoticed because she feels judged by the white people because she is different from them. If she had just said she sat down, it wouldn't help to convey exactly how she was feeling at this moment.)
	• Use a total participation technique to ask: "What other evidence do we see in this paragraph of Zitkala-Sa's point of view that she feels judged by and very different from the white people on the train?" (The white children point at her feet, their mothers point out the blanket she is wearing; she tells us she is embarrassed and almost crying.)

Total Participation Techniques:
The teacher is invited to use a total participation technique (e.g., Turn and Talk, Cold Call) to engage all students in collaborative discussions and, depending on the technique chosen, to invite students to share with the group. Teachers should choose a technique that will best support pacing and students' needs.

Excerpt of Text	Questions and Directions
Read paragraph 5.	• Read the text aloud as students read along silently.
	• Point out that telegraph poles are like telephone poles or electric poles today. Ask students to underline the words
	• "Now I sat watching for each pole that glided by to be the last one."
	• Ask: "What does this sentence convey about how Zitkala-Sa was feeling at this moment?" (This sentence makes clear how different her current experience is from her previous life. Before she saw the poles outside her mother's yard, and now she's watching each one pass her as she moves far away from that old life.)

Text-Dependent Questions:
Questions are designed to enhance students' understanding of the text in ways that align with the learning target by pointing them back to the text in strategic locations.

64

Note: Lessons are for example only.
They may look different from actual curriculum materials.

Excerpt of Text	Questions and Directions
Read paragraph 6.	• Read the text aloud as students read along silently. • Ask: "Here Zitkala-Sa gives readers a bit of insight into the p[oint of] view of the people who are taking them to the school. What a[re the] missionaries doing?" (Giving candy to Zitkala-Sa and the others.) • Ask: "What does this show you about their point of view toward taking the children to the new school?" (They seem to be trying to do something kind for the children.) • Working in partners, direct students to discuss, and then record in their note-catchers, their responses to this question: "How does Zitkala-Sa's choice to include this detail impact our understanding of the text? (It shows how very different the points of view were toward the school—the missionaries who thought they were doing something good, and the children who were entering a foreign and frightening culture.)

Student Discourse: Students have frequent opportunities to converse with peers about their understanding of the text. Here they work together to find evidence of the point of view of the missionaries and consider what this adds to their understanding of the text. Student discourse is especially supportive of multilingual learners.

Excerpt of Text	Questions and Directions
Read paragraphs 7 and 8.	Read the text aloud as students read along silently. Have students continue to work in pairs to discuss, then an[swer the] following questions on their note-catcher. Ask: "Why are the words '**excited**' and '**trembled more fr**[om]' important in this section? How do they help us see the diff[erence] of view between the white people at the school and Zitkala[-Sa?] school staff are pleased that the American Indian children have arrived; in contrast, Zitkala-Sa is very frightened by this strange new world.) As time permits, remind students that they already have read about General Pratt's point of view toward the schools' "civilizing Indians" being a good and positive thing—here they are seeing a student's very different experience of that sentiment.

Activating Schema: The teacher activates students' background knowledge, and deepens their understanding of point of view, by reminding them that they have already read about a very different point of view of American Indian boarding schools.

EL Education Curriculum **65**

Note: Lessons are for example only.
They may look different from actual curriculum materials.

Excerpt of Text	Questions and Directions
Read paragraphs 9 and 10.	• Read the text aloud as students read along silently.
	• Say: "It looks like the word 'insulted' is important here, because it seems to describe Zitkala-Sa's feelings during this encounter. Let's look it up in a dictionary to see precisely what it means." (treated with deep disrespect or rudeness)
	• Ask: "What does this description of Zitkala-Sa being picked up and tossed into the air show us about her point of view toward coming to the school?" (She is frightened and confused. She is also offended—her personal boundaries have been violated.)
	• "What words does she use to help you see that?" (**escape, frightened, insulted**)
	• Have students continue to work in pairs to discuss, then answer the following questions on their note-catcher.
	• Ask: "Look at the phrase '**increasing enthusiasm**.' What does this phrase show us about the woman's point of view toward this moment?" (She seems to be energetically welcoming Zitkala-Sa, not realizing how it is affecting Zitkala-Sa.)

Text-dependent questions *are designed to support the four aspects of qualitative text complexity:*

Meaning (the purpose and complexity of ideas in the text): *"It looks like the word 'insulted' is important here, because it seems to describe Zitkala-Sa's feelings during this encounter. Let's look it up in a dictionary to see precisely what it means."*

Structure (the organization of the text and text structure): *Paragraphs 9 and 10 are joined together here to deepen students' understanding of the juxtaposition of two different points of view.*

Language features (vocabulary, figurative language, and dialect): *"Look at the phrase 'increasing enthusiasm.' What does this phrase show us about the woman's point of view toward this moment?"*

Knowledge demands (background knowledge this text presumes readers will possess): *The juxtaposed points of view in the two paragraphs are by now familiar to students and reinforced with this text.*

Excerpt of Text	Questions and Directions
...raphs	• Read the text aloud as students read along silently.
	• Ask: "Underline the phrases '**very little I could swallow besides my sobs**' and the '**ears of the palefaces could not hear**.' Are these phrases used literally or figuratively?" (figuratively)
	• Have students continue to work in pairs to discuss, then answer the following questions on their note-catcher.
	• Ask: "What do each of these phrases mean within the context of the text?" (The first means she was so upset that she was unable to eat and could only cry instead; the second means that the adults at the school neither understood or seemed to care that Zitkala-Sa was upset.)
	• Ask: "How does Zitkala-Sa's use of figurative language in these two short paragraphs help to convey a key idea of the text?" (They highlight the difference in point of view between Zitkala-Sa and the white people toward the school and the disconnect between how each experiences the events. The adults at the school misunderstood the cause of her tears and gave her food; she pleads to go home but the "ears of the palefaces could not hear me.")

Meaning: *The teacher asks students to consider how figurative language helps convey key differences in point of view in the text. This supports students in meeting CCSS RL 6.4: Determine the meaning of words and phrases as they are used in a text, including figurative and connotative meanings; analyze the impact of a specific word choice on meaning and tone.*

Note: Lessons are for example only.
They may look different from actual curriculum materials.

Culminating Task

Excerpt of Text	Questions and Directions
Read paragraphs 13 and 14.	• Direct them to the Culminating Task short response question on the Close Read note-catcher. • Look at the last sentence, **"My tears were left to dry themselves in streaks, because neither my aunt nor my mother was near to wipe them away**." How does this sentence capture the central idea of Zitkala-Sa's point of view toward her new life at the school? (Her point of view toward it is that she is entering a strange and frightening world and that she is isolated and alone in it.)

Source: Zitkala-Sa. *American Indian Stories*. Hayworth Publishing House, 1921. University of Pennsylvania Library. Web. Pub

Culminating Task: *Synthesizing their understanding of a text at the conclusion of a close read is a form of debrief that not only builds students' understanding of the module topic, but also builds their capacity to track and take ownership of their learning.*

Chapter 3

EL Education Curriculum   **67**

Note: Lessons are for example only.
They may look different from actual curriculum materials.

Where Does This Close Reading Go Next?

In the next lessons, students continue to develop their ability to examine author's point of view by reading the Meriam Report. Students compare the point of view of the author of the Meriam Report to the points of view of General Pratt and Zitkala-Sa. Throughout the rest of this half of the unit, students examine photographs of the scenarios described in the report. They practice integrating the information from the text excerpts with information from the photos to develop a more cohesive understanding of the module topic as a whole. For the Mid-Unit 1 Assessment, students examine a different section of the same narrative from Zitkala-Sa, and answer questions about vocabulary and figurative language in the text and about Zitkala-Sa's point of view and how it is conveyed in the text. Students also integrate ideas from the text with their interpretations of two related photographs.

Chapter 3

Chapter 3:
Instructional Leadership

We believe that impactful instructional leadership involves cycles of action and reflection. Here we offer questions for reflection, indicators of progress, and resources that will help you support teachers as they *engage students with complex text*.

Table 3.9: Chapter 3 Quick Guide for Instructional Leaders: Engaging Students with Complex Text

Questions for Reflection
» What support do teachers need to create print-rich environments in their classrooms where students are experiencing a volume of reading?   • Are additional resources needed? How can you ensure that teachers have what they need?
» Have you created time and support for teachers to read, discuss, and analyze the texts they use with students? What tools can you provide to help them structure this important work?   • What systems and structures are in place to help teachers analyze and prepare to teach the close reads in the curriculum?
» What do your teachers know about complex text: what it is, why it matters, how to help all students access it through close reading?   • Do your teachers have a solid understanding of the research behind the learning opportunity gap and understand the critical role that both content-based literacy and close reading of complex text play in students' literacy development? Are you confident in articulating the idea of reading strategies as a means, rather than as an end in themselves?   • Do teachers understand and see the value in all students doing regular work with complex text? How can you help them debunk any misconceptions they may still have about close reading?

Indicators of Progress
» Professional learning time is devoted to helping teachers read and analyze texts. They practice doing Four Quadrants of Qualitative Text Complexity analyses and consider the challenges a text may pose for particular students.   *Not Yet True*   *Somewhat True*   *Very True*

» Practice reading and analyzing the texts leads teachers to consider the additional scaffolding that may be necessary to help all students succeed.		
Not Yet True	*Somewhat True*	*Very True*
» School and classroom libraries are filled with books—complex texts and texts at students' independent reading levels—that help students explore module topics.		
Not Yet True	*Somewhat True*	*Very True*
» Teachers help students approach complex texts with a spirit of courageous exploration.		
Not Yet True	*Somewhat True*	*Very True*
» Teachers never express to students that a text will be too hard for them or swap in an easier text in an effort to "protect" students from challenge. Instead, teachers use scaffolding techniques to "lift" students to complex texts.		
Not Yet True	*Somewhat True*	*Very True*
» Teachers approach teaching close reading as a skill that they can practice and hone.		
Not Yet True	*Somewhat True*	*Very True*
» Teachers consistently and adeptly use questioning to deepen or support students' understanding of the text or task.		
Not Yet True	*Somewhat True*	*Very True*
» Structures are in place for school leaders and/or peers to observe close reads and offer feedback that helps everyone improve.		
Not Yet True	*Somewhat True*	*Very True*

Resources and Suggestions

» The curriculum itself, along with a full suite of companion resources and tools, can be found at: Curriculum.ELeducation.org. Resources include:

- Topic and Text Selection Rationale for Grades 6–8

- Anchor Text Guidance for Grades 6–8

- Text Analyses for Grades 6–8

» Resources available on the main EL Education website (ELeducation.org):

- Videos: https://eleducation.org/resources/collections/your-curriculum-companion-6-8-videos

» Common Core State Standards: Appendix A

» Website: Achieve the Core (achievethecore.org) offers numerous resources:

- Understanding Text-Dependent Questions

- Qualitative Complexity Resources

- Reading between the Lines: What the ACT Reveals about College Readiness in Reading

» Website: Fisher & Frey Literacy for Life (fisherandfrey.com)

» Website: Shanahan on Literacy (shanahanonliteracy.com)

Chapter 3:
Frequently Asked Questions

I want to give my students more time for independent reading. Where can I fit that in?

Early in each module, at every grade level, 20–30 minutes of a lesson will be devoted to launching independent research reading. During this lesson students will set up their independent reading journals and choose a book on the module topic for research reading. Beyond this lesson when the routine is set up, students don't have time during lessons to actually do their independent reading, though they do share their progress during lessons. Should you or your colleagues wish to offer students in-school time for research reading or other choice reading, this is likely a school-level question that may require scheduling changes. The lessons in our Grades 6–8 curriculum are designed to be 45 minutes long; in many schools, an ELA period will be 60 or even 90 minutes, and portions of that could fruitfully be used for additional time for independent reading or other literacy needs.

I understand that close reading is a highly scaffolded process, but I still think it's going to be too hard for my students. How can I modify those experiences for students who need it?

It is critical that all students have access to the same complex texts; our stance on this is grounded in our commitment to equity for all students. If we deny some students the opportunity to read the same complex texts as their peers, because we fear they can't do it, they will never catch up. The key is to scaffold the experience for students so that they can access the text. Chapter 5A offers many scaffolding strategies (as well as more information about why this point is so important to us). Also, get in the habit of carefully reviewing the Support All Students section of the Teaching Notes for each lesson, which will provide you with specific, targeted suggestions for scaffolding in that lesson. Consult the Teacher's Guide for English Language Learners as well. This resource contains a wealth of scaffolded student-facing materials that can be used with any students, not just ELLs.

My students are getting bored reading the same thing over and over during close reading sessions. Can we skip some of the rereading?

Close reading has been designed to include *purposeful* rereading. Students won't be asked to reread just for the sake of rereading. Be sure to explain the purpose of each rereading to your students so that they understand why they are doing it. And, use the strategies for active engagement included in the close read so that the work is collaborative (and more fun). Be sure that in your tone and body language, you convey your own sense of curiosity about the text and your sense of excitement that each time you dig in, you notice more. Rereading is a crucially important strategy for comprehending complex text and should become a lifelong habit. If started as a standard practice in younger grades, most students will comfortably and purposefully reread for meaning. Try to make multiple readings an expectation—part of the culture of your school—starting with the first grades you serve. If you haven't yet viewed the Close Reading video in Video Spotlight 3.1, you should do that now (https://vimeo.com/386910186). The video is a window into what close reading can and should look like—the curiosity and joy factor for both teacher and students is high.

What if I'm not comfortable reading aloud?

It is crucial for students to hear you regularly model fluent reading. If you are not yet a fluent reader yourself or find some texts in the curriculum particularly challenging, you are not alone. Consider finding audio recordings of the texts to listen to, as a scaffold for yourself. But challenge yourself to read aloud in front of your students, so you can pause and ask questions. If it is hard for you, this is another opportunity to model growth mindset for your students: our ability grows with our effort. Use audio recordings with your students as well, so they can hear a variety of fluent readers. Many of the anchor texts in the Grades 6–8 curriculum have readily available audiobooks (e.g., *A Long Walk to Water*).

I can't seem to keep pace with the close reading guides. Do you have any tips for pacing so that I don't get behind?

The questions in a close reading session are scaffolded to follow a line of inquiry. The questions support students in making connections between the words and ideas in the text. Often these connections are clearer if the questions move at a crisp pace. Understanding is built throughout the process, so don't worry if student understanding isn't crystal clear at every step. The culminating task will help you assess whether you need to return to key sections or concepts. Try to avoid stopping to answer too many questions, engaging in long discussions, or offering too much explanation during a close reading session. Let student understanding ride on the wave of the carefully constructed set of questions, and check for understanding by evaluating the culminating task.

The close reading guides are very detailed. Am I allowed to modify them based on students' needs? Are there certain things that are important not to change?

Before making any changes, it is crucial to understand the big picture and purpose of the close reading sessions, including what the unit's writing or speaking task entails. Given that purpose, consider what your students already "get" and omit steps or questions that feel redundant (e.g., my students already showed me they know what *scrutinize* means, so I can skip that question). If you decide to omit a step or a question, do it to support pacing, not because you are concerned that your students can't do the cognitive work. Be sure to maintain the synthesis or culminating task as a check of students' understanding; this will help you know if anything you have omitted has impacted students' ability to achieve the goals of the close reading sequence. Depending on your students' needs, you may also choose to add in more movement or swap out protocols or total participation techniques as long as they achieve the same purpose.

Chapter 4:
Reading for and Writing with Evidence: Deeper Learning in Literacy

Chapter 4A:
How Does Evidence-Based Reading, Writing, Thinking, and Talking about Text Deepen Student Learning?

A focus on evidence is one of the key instructional shifts of college- and career-ready English language arts (ELA) standards. This shift brings together the paired practices of reading for and writing with evidence. Students need to be able to use evidence in their writing, but they also need to have enough evidence, through reading, that they have something to say when it's time to write. A focus on evidence is not new in classrooms, but it has taken on a certain urgency in schools across the country.

There's much to celebrate in this instructional shift. Learning to read for and write with evidence will better prepare students for college and careers, where unsupported views matter less than well-reasoned arguments based on evidence. And, importantly, a focus on evidence supports equity and excellence for all students. As noted in Chapter 1, the goal of college readiness for all students is relatively new in the United States. In the past, students from households with background knowledge that most aligns with what is taught in school (and how) were privileged with many advantages in school, particularly when considering the common practice of writing personal narratives and persuasive essays.

All students bring valuable assets with them to school. Yet many carry significant additional advantages with them, based on what they have had the opportunity to learn at home (e.g., advantages in *word* knowledge through discourse and print at home that matches what schools often expect; and advantages in *world* knowledge through access to people, places, events that match what schools often presume). This disparity is often called the "learning opportunity gap," since it has nothing to do with students' intelligence or abilities, but rather with what they have access to outside of the schoolhouse doors.

Importantly, a focus on reading for and writing with evidence allows us to level the playing field to some degree. With text as *the* source all students are working from, rather than experience or previously built schema, all students have a chance to build new knowledge together. Everyone is grounded in the text and can make a contribution. For example, in Grade 6, Module 2, students consider the guiding question: "How can design thinking help solve a critical problem?" This question leaves room for students' own prior knowledge and opinions about what problems matter most in our world, but through the text *The Boy Who Harnessed the Wind*, students are first grounded in a specific instance from which they can learn what makes a problem "critical," and how the framework of design thinking has been previously applied. This positions them to consider other problems, and evaluate possible solutions.

The focus on writing with evidence represents a similarly significant shift in writing instruction. In the past, as part of the "personal engagement" paradigm for literacy, schools of education have promoted the idea that if we simply got students writing about what interested them and reading "high-interest literature," they would "catch" good writing skills. In an article in the *Atlantic*, education professor Steve Graham says, "Research tells us some students catch quite a bit, but not everything. And some kids don't catch much at all." The kids who do "catch quite a bit" tend to be from groups that the education system has historically served well. So this paradigm for literacy not only fails to disrupt educational inequity, it exacerbates it.

In order to counteract the effects of systemic opportunity gaps in our society and help students achieve at high levels, we must do everything we can to ensure that all students have equal access to the learning opportunities they need and deserve. Our curriculum is designed to challenge and support students in equal measure. They all deserve the challenge of higher-order reading, writing, and thinking, and they all deserve the scaffolds and supports necessary for success.

▶ WHAT DO THE READING AND WRITING STANDARDS REQUIRE OF MY STUDENTS?

The Reading Standards

The Common Core includes Reading standards for literature (RL), informational text (RI), and foundational skills (RF). In this chapter, we focus on the ten RL and RI anchor standards, which are designed to promote deep comprehension, a grasp of key ideas and details, an appreciation of structure and author's craft, and an ability to integrate knowledge and ideas—and all of this with appropriately complex texts.

These ten anchor standards for reading focus on students' ability to read carefully and grasp information, arguments, ideas, and details based on evidence in the text. The "anchor standards" articulate the intent of each standard by describing what students should know and be able to do as readers by the time they finish high school. Sitting beneath the anchor standards are the grade-level standards, which go into much greater detail about the skills and understandings students must demonstrate at each grade level. Guidance for teachers on how to scaffold students toward the ultimate goal of college and career readiness is embedded in the very specific language of the grade-level standards themselves.

Using two anchor standards as an example, CCSS R.1 and RI.9, Table 4.1 shows how the skill of reading for evidence becomes increasingly sophisticated as students get older. For example, R.1

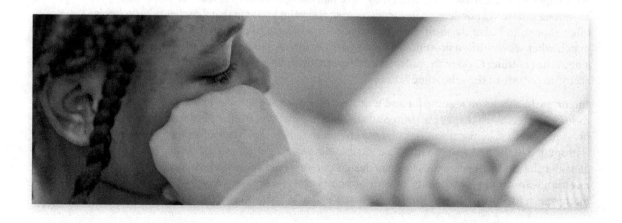

requires that all students in Grades 6–8 cite textual evidence and make logical inferences; however, as they get older, the standards change in small but significant ways. In Grade 7, students must cite several pieces of textual evidence. In Grade 8, they must cite the textual evidence that most *strongly* supports their analysis, which is a key stepping-stone to college- and career-readiness. Similarly, by Grade 8, RI.9 requires deeper analysis from students than the Grade 6 standard. At each grade level, the standard deepens and requires more sophisticated analysis.

Table 4.1: Reading Anchor Standards R.1 and RI.9 across Multiple Grade Levels

Anchor Standard CCSS R.1: *Read closely to determine what the text says explicitly and to make logical inferences from it; cite specific textual evidence when writing or speaking to support conclusions drawn from the text.*		
Grade 6	**Grade 7**	**Grade 8**
Cite textual evidence to support analysis of what the text says explicitly as well as inferences drawn from the text.	Cite several pieces of textual evidence to support analysis of what the text says explicitly as well as inferences drawn from the text.	Cite the textual evidence that most strongly supports an analysis of what the text says explicitly as well as inferences drawn from the text.
Anchor Standard CCSS RI.9: *Analyze how two or more texts address similar themes or topics in order to build knowledge or to compare the approaches the authors take.*		
Grade 6	**Grade 7**	**Grade 8**
Compare and contrast one author's presentation of events with that of another (e.g., a memoir written by and a biography on the same person).	Analyze how two or more authors writing about the same topic shape their presentations of key information by emphasizing different evidence or advancing different interpretations of facts.	Analyze a case in which two or more texts provide conflicting information on the same topic, and identify where the texts disagree on matters of fact or interpretation.

The Writing Standards

There are ten Common Core anchor standards for writing. There are three official "types" of writing, two of which have a heavy focus on writing with evidence: CCSS W.1 (argument writing) and CCSS W.2 (informative/explanatory writing). For CCSS W.3 (narrative writing), the third type of writing emphasized in the standards, writing with evidence is not particularly germane, except in the case of writing historical fiction, when students will need to draw on details and evidence from text to create historically accurate characters or scenes. CCSS W.7 (research) and CCSS W.9 (which focuses on drawing evidence from multiple texts to support analysis and research) also heavily emphasize writing with evidence. In our curriculum, even the narrative stories and poems students write are based on knowledge they have built on the module topic. For example, in Grade 8, Module 1, students read *Summer of the Mariposas*, which includes a modernized depiction of "La Llorona" from Latin American folklore. They analyze the techniques the author used for including this figure, and then create their own narrative featuring a modernized "monster" from Latin American folkloric tradition.

CCSS W.1 focuses on writing arguments with evidence. Table 4.2 shows how students are expected to do this with increasing sophistication as they progress through the grades. For example, as students move into Grades 7 and 8, they must begin to acknowledge alternate claims (Grade 7) and then acknowledge and distinguish the claim(s) from alternate or opposing claims (Grade 8). The writing tasks in our curriculum reflect the step-up in sophistication of standard W.1.

Table 4.2 Writing Anchor Standard 1 across Multiple Grade Levels

Anchor Standard CCSS W.1: *Write arguments to support claims in an analysis of substantive topics or texts using valid reasoning and relevant and sufficient evidence.*		
Grade 6	**Grade 7**	**Grade 8**
Write arguments to support claims with clear reasons and relevant evidence.	Write arguments to support claims with clear reasons and relevant evidence.	Write arguments to support claims with clear reasons and relevant evidence
» Introduce claim(s) and organize the reasons and evidence clearly.	» Introduce claim(s), acknowledge alternate or opposing claims, and organize the reasons and evidence logically.	» Introduce claim(s), acknowledge and distinguish the claim(s) from alternate or opposing claims, and organize the reasons and evidence logically.
» Support claim(s) with clear reasons and relevant evidence, using credible sources and demonstrating an understanding of the topic or text.	» Support claim(s) with logical reasoning and relevant evidence, using accurate, credible sources and demonstrating an understanding of the topic or text.	» Support claim(s) with logical reasoning and relevant evidence, using accurate, credible sources and demonstrating an understanding of the topic or text.
» Use words, phrases, and clauses to clarify the relationships among claim(s) and reasons.	» Use words, phrases, and clauses to create cohesion and clarify the relationships among claim(s), reasons, and evidence.	» Use words, phrases, and clauses to create cohesion and clarify the relationships among claim(s), counterclaims, reasons, and evidence.
» Establish and maintain a formal style.	» Establish and maintain a formal style.	» Establish and maintain a formal style.
» Provide a concluding statement or section that follows from the argument presented.	» Provide a concluding statement or section that follows from and supports the argument presented.	» Provide a concluding statement or section that follows from and supports the argument presented.

CCSS W.2 (*Write informative/explanatory texts to examine and convey complex ideas and information clearly and accurately through the effective selection, organization, and analysis of content*) encompasses quite a broad range of evidence-based writing: to inform, to explain, and often to share research findings. In the modules, many of the shorter pieces of writing students do align to CCSS W.2 (e.g., entrance or exit tickets, reflections, summaries of text, explanation of research). Students also write to inform or explain in more extended writing pieces, such as scaffolded tasks or formal unit assessments. One of the keys to meeting college- and career-ready standards is that students write regularly, for multiple purposes and audiences.

CCSS W.7 focuses on research: (*Conduct short as well as more sustained research projects based on focused questions, demonstrating understanding of the subject under investigation*). In many ways, research is the nexus of reading and writing, and is therefore a strong example of both the read-think-talk-write cycle and the more big-picture Writing for Understanding framework, both of which will be explored in depth later in Chapter 4A. Students closely read and analyze texts to identify the information and evidence they need to answer a research question. They often do some form of shared research as a class, and then do a related research project with increasing independence.

In our curriculum, students learn skills and gain practice in all of these forms of writing. What follows are a few examples:

» In Grade 6, Module 4, students learn about the long-unrecognized contributions to space science made by "hidden figures" like NASA mathematicians Dorothy Vaughn, Katherine Johnson, and Mary Jackson. Students then conduct independent research into another "hidden figure" of their choosing, to locate particularly remarkable accomplishments worthy of being shared. These individual stories are compiled into an anthology-style picture book geared toward an elementary-age audience.

» In Grade 7, Module 2, students read to develop background knowledge about epidemics in many forms: historical and current, medical and social. While students learn about the scientific investigation and medical intervention in these outbreaks, they also focus on the social and cultural responses to develop a model of how best to respond to challenging circumstances. Students then research and develop a podcast about an epidemic that concerns them or their community, sharing the dynamic podcast complete with sound effects and music with others beyond the classroom.

» In Grade 8, Module 2, students research plastic pollution using informational film, text, articles, and online resources. Students use this research to write an argument essay about which point in the plastic life cycle is most effective for solving plastic pollution. Then, students develop an action plan they can enact through further research, advocacy, or personal commitment, and create a documentary film clip that conveys their research-based argument, action plan solution, and conclusions about plastic pollution.

The Special Place of Argument

Of the three types of writing represented in the Common Core standards—argument writing (CCSS W.1), informative/explanatory writing (CCSS W.2), and narrative writing (CCSS W.3)—the standards reserve a special place for argument writing because of its critical importance in college, careers, and civic life.

At its best, the world of college and work is a culture in which individuals influence attitudes, beliefs, and practices by making cogent, evidence-based arguments for change. "Theorist and critic Neil Postman (1997) calls argument the soul of an education because argument forces a writer to evaluate the strengths and weaknesses of multiple perspectives. When teachers ask students to consider two or more perspectives on a topic or issue, something far beyond surface knowledge is required: students must think critically and deeply, assess the validity of their own thinking, and anticipate counterclaims in opposition to their own assertions" (National Governors Association Center for Best Practices, Council of Chief State School Officers, 2010, appendix A, p. 24).

Our curriculum reflects this focus on argument writing, which demands that students use evidence to support their claims and prove the validity of their position. In Grades K–5, the standards refer to argument as "opinion," since the authors of the Common Core view it as a more teacher- and student-friendly term. Beginning in Grade 6, the standards refer to "argument," and this has led to some confusion in the field. However, the underlying emphasis is the same: a focus on evidence-based reasoning. In kindergarten, that begins as the seed of stating one's preference; by Grade 8, students support claims with clear reasons and relevant evidence.

Later in this chapter, you will learn more about Writing for Understanding and the read-think-talk-write cycle, two related frameworks that allow students time to find, evaluate, and communicate evidence in support of their arguments/opinions and claims.

How Does Our Curriculum Address these Standards?

Overall, this focus on evidence has the potential to be quite positive for students. However, like many changes born from the best intentions, the devil is in the details. Many curricula have implemented this instructional shift by mistakenly doing away with personal narratives and poetry, and teachers and students have felt this loss acutely. Still others have narrowly focused on teaching students to identify evidence in sentences and paragraphs and state it back through simple writing tasks that may not be connected to any larger purpose beyond practicing this discrete skill. In the first scenario, students would not even be able to master the standards, as narrative writing is a valued part of the standards. And in the second scenario, while students could technically master the standards, there are ways to deepen the experience for them, and that's what we are after with our curriculum.

Our focus is on the deeper challenge of students gathering evidence on a compelling topic over several weeks (weaving in stories and poems to text sets whenever possible), analyzing and synthesizing it, and then presenting it, often in writing, to answer a compelling question or serve a meaningful purpose. Our modules are designed strategically to scaffold this work:

» Unit 1 tends to emphasize *building background knowledge* about the topic, which usually means an emphasis on the close and careful reading of complex text that anchors students' learning about the topic. Students also often write with evidence. Equally important during Unit 1 is hooking students into the topic with an engaging anchor text, which sometimes, but not always, also builds background knowledge.

» Unit 2 can play out in a number of ways. Students are always *going deeper on the topic*. This often includes more extended reading and research as students widen their reading to a greater variety of informational and literary texts and "write to learn" about the module topic. Again, since reading and writing are so interrelated, students typically write with evidence as well.

» Unit 3 is unique in that it almost always includes *extended writing* of the performance task, in which students complete a high-quality, scaffolded writing task and engage in a feedback and critique process to strengthen their writing (note, however, that performance tasks sometimes focus more on speaking than writing). In Grades 6–8, students are learning about topics that matter deeply to them, and Unit 3 often aims to give them an outlet for taking action, for example: telling untold stories of American Indian boarding schools (Grade 6, Module 3) and the "hidden figures" of space science (Grade 6, Module 4); publicizing the power of individual and collective actions to combat plastic pollution (Grade 7, Module 4) or increasing access to healthy food (Grade 8, Module 2).

Along the way, students use various tools and protocols to help them make sense of evidence and use it to support their claims. What follows are some of the key curricular and instructional features of our content-based literacy curriculum that build students' capacity to read for and write with evidence.

Evidence-Based Curricular Structures

» Modules focus on building students' content knowledge, related to a compelling aspect of typical science and/or social studies standards for that grade level. Students read and reread and engage in multiple experiences with that topic.

» Lessons are sequenced to ensure that students deeply understand the content before they begin formal writing about it. Students prepare to write about the topics and content they have studied deeply through reading, discussion, and other activities that scaffold toward effective writing.

» Throughout the curriculum, students do both "on-demand" writing tasks to show what they can do independently (e.g., assessments) and more scaffolded writing tasks to show what they can do with support (e.g., performance task).

» The majority of writing tasks requires students to write from sources.

» Writing tasks at each grade level become increasingly complex over the course of the year.

Evidence-Based Instructional Strategies

» Often students will engage with a protocol, which offers detailed guidelines for reading, recording, discussing, or reporting that engages all students and gives them a chance to process evidence and talk about its importance (see box: Infer the Topic for a sample evidence-based protocol).

» Students read to research, learn more about topics, and answer compelling questions. They sort, sift, and weigh both evidence and the credibility of its sources, rather than simply "report" on a topic. Students use graphic organizers and note-catchers to help gather information and plan their writing. They are exposed to a variety of tools—such as sketching, text-coding, marking evidence with sticky notes, and completing structured note-catchers—and are empowered to analyze which tools work best for them.

» Many lessons make use of class anchor charts, which are a way to collaboratively collect evidence, make inferences, and synthesize thinking. Anchor charts make the thinking permanent and public. These charts then serve as a critical scaffold for students' writing. Students can use the anchor chart for ideas or as a source of evidence that the class has gathered that they can then use in their writing.

» In almost every lesson that involves working with text, the teacher questioning emphasizes evidence, with questions like: "How do you know?" "What evidence did you see in the text that supports your claim?" "What in the text helps us define/explain/understand ___?" "Where do you see ___ in the text?"

» Students write in multiple modes: They support arguments with evidence, use evidence to explain their ideas, and write or tell narratives informed or inspired by prior learning.

Part B: In the space below, design a note-catcher to capture research notes. (W.7.7, W.7.8)

Be sure to include space to quote or paraphrase the evidence to answer the question, to cite the source, to explain why you think the source is credible, and to record questions raised by reading the text.

Website I found

cite	quote	explain	record
www.litcharts.com	"Nya filled the container all the way to the top, then placed the heavy gourd on her head & began walking home.	I think this source is credible because it meets all the criteria	There are no questions

Students learn to use note-catchers and graphic organizers as tools to help them gather information and plan their writing. In this case, which is part of an assessment, students must design their own note-catcher to capture their research notes.

Infer the Topic Protocol

Purpose: This protocol offers students a chance to work together to uncover the heart of a larger concept before they begin to study a new topic. Students also get a chance to experience the ways an inference can change as they take in new information. The protocol allows students to draw on their own background knowledge and work in a fun, collaborative environment with new information from a variety of peers to uncover meaning.

Materials

» Images and/or artifacts related to the topic of study

» Optional: recording form for each student to write down inferences

Procedure

1. Locate images and/or artifacts with and without key words/quotes related to the concept. The goal is for students to infer what is happening in the image. Images can range from concrete to abstract.

2. Have students select an image and record their inference about the new topic of study.

3. Students mingle about the room and stop when prompted, facing a partner.

4. In 1 minute or less, students view one another's images, discuss, and record a new inference about the upcoming topic of study.

5. Students mingle about the room again, this time with the partner they were just sharing with. When prompted, partners stop, facing another set of partners.

6. All four students share their images/artifacts and inferences, discuss further, and make a new inference about what the new topic of study could be.

7. Students gather as a whole group, each displaying their image for all to see. The teacher invites a few to share their images/artifacts and their inferences about the upcoming topic.

8. After a few have shared, the teacher reveals the topic of study as well as the guiding questions and big ideas.

Variations

» Vary partner instructions or adapt numbers of partners or rounds.

» To monitor understanding and support students struggling to infer the images'/artifacts' meaning, teachers can circulate and give these students a "ticket" in the form of a colored card or sticky note. At an opportune time, call a meeting of an invitational group for anyone with tickets or anyone who is struggling.

▶ HOW CAN I BUILD A CULTURE OF EVIDENCE IN MY CLASSROOM?

There is much to be gained from building a culture of evidence in your classroom that permeates all parts of your instruction, and that students can internalize and carry with them beyond your classroom. This consistency will further develop your middle school students' college- and career-ready habits so that they can think critically and independently and write for a variety of audiences, purposes, and disciplines.

What follows are some instructional techniques and classroom practices—often built into the curriculum, but needing your attention to come alive—that help build a culture of evidence:

» Ask students to reference specific page numbers, paragraphs, and exact phrases in text to support their points. Hold yourself to this same standard.

» Use Conversation Cues to probe for more information from students in ways that invite, challenge, and support them to cite evidence (e.g., "Why do you think that?" "What, in the [sentence/text], makes you think so?"). Conversation Cues are described in detail in Chapter 5C, in particular in Table 5.3.

» Give students specific, positive feedback when they cite evidence (e.g., "I noticed that Alma told us what page number she got her quote from. Great work, Alma.").

» Get students in the habit of coming to discussions prepared, with notes, annotated text, note-catchers, or sticky notes that mark and organize key evidence.

» Emphasize how useful it is to reread a text to identify or analyze key details.

» Connect the idea of citing evidence to the more concrete skill of using context clues to determine unfamiliar words.

» Build students' academic vocabulary related to citing evidence.

» Have students sort evidence (e.g., before/after, stronger/weaker).

» Ask questions that favor textual evidence rather than background knowledge.

» Teach students to use sentence frames, such as "I hear you saying X, but the text says Y" or "I think you are saying X; here is another example to support… " Also teach them to use the same kinds of sentence frames in their writing (e.g., "According to the text, X… "). Create class anchor charts with sentence frames so that students have a "lifeline" if they get stuck. (See box: Sample Sentence Frames to Support Collaboration and Discussion for examples. Note: These sample sentence frames are different from Conversation Cues, which are detailed in Chapter 5C. Each has a similar purpose: to support collaboration and discussion).

Sample Sentence Frames to Support Collaboration and Discussion

Agreement

» "I agree with _____ because _____."

» "I like what _____ said because _____."

» "I agree with _____; but on the other hand, _____."

Disagreement

» "I disagree with _____ because _____."

» "I'm not sure I agree with what _____ said because _____."

» "I can see that _____; however, I disagree with (or can't see) _____."

Clarification

» "Could you please repeat that for me?"

» Paraphrase what you heard, and ask, "Could you explain a bit more, please?"

» "I'm not sure I understood you when you said _____. Could you say more about that?"

» "What's your evidence?"

» "How does that support our work/learning target _____?"

Confirmation

» "I think _____."

» "I believe _____."

Confusion

» "I don't understand _____."

» "I am confused about _____."

Extension

» "I was thinking about what _____ said, and I was wondering: what if _____?"

» "This makes me think _____."

» "I want to know more about _____."

» "Now I am wondering _____."

» "Can you tell me more about _____?"

Review

» "I want to go back to what _____ said."

▶ WHAT STRUCTURES WILL HELP MY STUDENTS READ, THINK, AND TALK ABOUT TEXT?

Ultimately, our goal for students, as they learn about the world through the compelling topics in the curriculum, is first that they deeply understand and then that they effectively communicate what they know. There are many layers to this work, which are addressed systematically in our curriculum.

▷ Ultimately, our goal for students, as they learn about the world through the compelling topics in the curriculum, is first that they deeply understand and then that they effectively communicate what they know.

Writing for Understanding

We designed the curriculum with the principles of Writing for Understanding at its core. This approach (see Table 4.3), developed by the Vermont Writing Collaborative, is based on the premise that students need to deeply understand the topic they are writing about to use writing structures and tools effectively. After examining Table 4.3, you may recognize certain parallels between the Writing for Understanding approach described here and the basic flow of the units that make up each module of our curriculum. We start with a focus on building background knowledge about a compelling topic, move on to extended reading and research, and finally end with students communicating what they know, most often through writing. This structure allows students to gain the deep understanding they need to write purposefully and effectively.

Table 4.3: Writing for Understanding

Enduring Understanding/Big Idea What understanding about the content will this writing show? What understanding about the craft of writing should it show?	
Essential focusing question	What question will I (as a teacher) pose so that students can see how to approach this work in a specific, appropriate, manageable way?
Building working knowledge	How will students gain the content knowledge they need to be able to work with this?
Processing the knowledge	How will students select from and analyze the knowledge through the lens of the essential focusing question, and then capture it in notes so that they can use the ideas in their writing?
Structure	How will students know how to construct this piece of writing so that their thinking is clear, both to them as writers and to the readers of their work?
Writing process	How will students use the writing process (draft, confer, revise) so that their final writing is clearly focused, organized, and developed to show understanding of the Big Idea?

Source: Adapted with permission from Writing for Understanding: Using Backward Design to Help All Students Write Effectively *by The Vermont Writing Collaborative.*

The Read-Think-Talk-Write Cycle

While the Writing for Understanding approach guides our overall curriculum design, when we talk about daily lessons we often use the organizing principle of the read-think-talk-write cycle. It may be helpful to think of this cycle, which lives dynamically in many of the lessons in our curriculum, as a microcosm of Writing for Understanding in action. Cycles of read-think-talk-write give students an opportunity to synthesize evidence, play with ideas, develop arguments, and "rehearse" various forms of communication during lessons (or sequences of lessons). This process allows students to cycle in and out fluidly—in no set order—from text, to think-time, to discussion, to writing tasks. It is highly supportive of students learning English, who benefit from oral processing and the social construction of knowledge, and, in general, of the varied learning styles represented in classrooms.

Figure 4.1: Reading, Thinking, Talking, and Writing about Worthy Text

The video in Video Spotlight 4.1 will help you visualize the read-think-talk-write cycle in action. Though the video features first- and fourth-graders, the principles are still the same and we think it's worthwhile viewing, especially if this instructional approach is new for you.

Note: A lesson featuring the read-think-talk-write cycle is annotated in Chapter 4B.

▶▶ Video Spotlight 4.1

In this video from Detroit Public Schools Community District, first-grade Teacher Tawana Jordan and fourth-grade teacher Kaitlyn Billops engage students in the read-think-talk-write cycle. This dynamic cycle gives students an opportunity to synthesize evidence, play with ideas, develop arguments, and "rehearse" various forms of communication during lessons, and supports them to demonstrate a deep knowledge and understanding of the topic in writing. This approach integrates reading, speaking and listening, and writing, and results in the production of high-quality, evidence-based writing.

https://vimeo.com/348852048

Read about It: Let the Text Do the Teaching

Letting the text do the teaching may sound simple, but in reality it can be quite difficult. As teachers, we often have an instinct to preview for students what they are about to read, or to engage in a think-aloud with them to support them as they read (common in a traditional Readers' Workshop). Sometimes, after students have read a text, we will lead a whole class discussion about it, asking questions that fish for details about the information in the text, in effect summarizing its contents. In each of these cases, it is not the text that's doing the teaching; it's primarily the teacher.

Our approach is different. We position the text as the "expert" in the room. We structure lessons so that students are active readers, annotating as they go, using note-catchers to organize information and ideas, engaging in discussion protocols, and completing short writing tasks that bring them back into the text over and over.

This approach takes practice for teachers because, for many of us, it goes against our instincts to guide students toward the answers they are looking for or to help them when the going is tough. But, harkening back to Chapter 2B, where we discussed the benefits of grappling and productive challenge, students build their literacy muscles when they are given opportunities to figure things out on their own. In the curriculum, lessons scaffold this process for students as they learn strategies to find answers and evidence directly from the text. Key to this practice is that students are reading worthy texts that give them plenty to dig into (see Chapter 3A).

Think about It: Set a Purpose for Reading and Provide Time for Students to Think about the Text

Students need time and a focal point to comprehend what they read. Often what focuses students is a question, which is followed by a structure that gives them time to think about their response and ultimately to talk and write about it. These structures are often simple, like brief protocols or total participation techniques (e.g., Think-Pair-Share), and sometimes the structures are more complex (e.g., a Socratic Seminar). In either case, they are designed so that *all* students are thinking and talking, not just those who are already most inclined to do so. During close reads, for example, text-dependent questions, which cannot be answered without reading and referencing a specific text, direct students back to portions of the text for a particular purpose. As the Close Reading Guide in Chapter 3C shows, each time the teacher asks a question, students nearly always work together in pairs to grapple with the question and discuss their responses.

▷ ## Rarely do we recommend that teachers ask a question and call on volunteers to answer it.

Questions that are prepared before the lesson will ensure that they point students back to the text in a way that builds their understanding of the text and their literacy skills, which is why you will find questions written right into the lessons in the curriculum. Asking deep questions—higher-order thinking questions on Bloom's taxonomy—that ask students to think about the text in ways that deepen their understanding is difficult to do on the fly. If you do find yourself needing to ask different questions from what you find in the lesson, it's important to keep in mind the purpose of each question, and plan in advance whenever possible. It's also a good idea to plan follow-up questions in case students get stuck with a question or move in an unproductive direction. Developing good questions takes practice. As you gain familiarity with the curriculum, the way that questions are asked, and the structures in place for students to think and talk about them, you will likely feel more confident with this practice. (See Figure 2.2 in Chapter 2 for further guidance).

One important feature of the questions in our curriculum is the way in which they are asked. Rarely do we recommend that teachers ask a question and call on volunteers to answer it. Instead, we usually suggest a total participation technique or a brief protocol so that *every* student can think about their answer and then talk to a peer about it, which deepens and extends students' thinking. Or we suggest a short writing task, such as a particular kind of annotation, a note-catcher, or an exit ticket, that gives students a chance to think and write independently. Brief writing like this may or may not be followed by a time for sharing with peers.

It's also important that questions be asked in an inviting tone that says, "Let's dig in together." The way you ask the question should set a tone of curiosity (i.e., "I can't wait to figure this out!") versus a tone of compliance (i.e., "I have to answer this question.").

Talk about It: Help Students Deepen Their Understanding of Text through Discourse

If you have read this book from the beginning, you have by now probably caught on to how important student discourse is in our curriculum. We subscribe to the idea that "learning floats on a sea of talk" (Barnes, 1976). At every grade level, in every lesson, we have built in structures that promote productive and equitable conversation among students. For example:

» Pairs: strategically assigned pairs to make partner talk both efficient and effective. This partner talk may sometimes serve as oral rehearsal prior to writing or for partners to give each other kind, specific, and helpful feedback on their drafts. Pairings might be grounded in what you know about students' content knowledge, or language ability, or style of interacting. These pairs should be varied, not static, so students have a wide range of interactions and language models. With strategically varied partners, students can experience being both "the support" and "the supported" when working with their partners.

» Triads: similar to conversation partners, but in groups of three, triads add more variety of perspective, voice, and language to peer conversations.

» Expert groups: a small group of students assigned to research and become "expert" in one aspect of the topic (e.g., in Grade 7, Module 4, the class investigates "What can be done about plastic pollution?" First, they research where and how plastic pollutes as a whole group. Then in small groups, students zero in on where in the plastic cycle they believe intervention is most needed: how plastic is made, how it's used, or how it's disposed of.)

» Protocols: routines that offer a structure and a set of steps to help students talk to one another and dig deeper into text or ideas. Protocols allow students to talk to *one another*, not just to you.

» Total participation techniques: Rather than just calling on those students who may have their hands raised, these techniques (e.g., Turn and Talk) hold all students accountable.

Talking to one another about what they are reading gives students a chance for "oral rehearsal" of their ideas. It also allows students to hear the ideas of their peers, build off of them, and clarify their own misconceptions. Opportunities for student discourse are especially important for English language learners (ELLs) who can thrive on interaction with a wide range of peers. Before writing about text, students think about and talk to one another about such things as what the text is about, what evidence from the text supports their opinions and claims, the meaning and purpose of academic structures, author's craft, and the organization of ideas. This process gives ELLs a structure for simultaneously trying out their ideas and the language they need to express those ideas, learning about and clarifying the ideas of their peers, and deepening their understanding before writing. Furthermore, this oral rehearsal provides ELLs with the time they need to formulate what they want to say and communicate their thoughts, and then reformulate their speech if they notice a need for it.

Strategic grouping can also help you support ELLs in specific ways. For example, a home language group might be a good place for ELLs to work through big ideas and get oral rehearsal before writing, whereas a heterogeneous grouping of ELLs with native speakers or more proficient ELLs might be a better way for them to fine-tune their ideas and the language used to express them.

Many lessons and sequences of lessons in the curriculum are designed to bring students through a read-think-talk-write cycle. Often, students engage in conversations with one another using a specific protocol with predictable steps and rules. Protocols are a great way for all students to hear from others and add to or change their own developing ideas. Because students follow set "rules" for discussion during protocols, everyone has an equal opportunity to talk, listen, and respond. The process helps students develop their growth mindset, learning and contributing to the learning of others, and not getting "stuck" believing that their ideas or answers are the only correct ones. "By following rules for talking (rather than rules that ban talking) students learn to listen first to understand and then speak to be understood; to use evidence from the text to support their opinions or inferences; and to respond with appropriate focus, tone, and equity of participation" (Berger, Woodfin, Plaut, and Dobbertin, p. 101). This social construction of knowledge helps students stay nimble and flexible with their thinking. (See box: Back-to-Back and Face-to-Face Protocol for an example.)

Also, not inconsequentially, engaging in productive and equitable conversation with peers is one way that adolescents' natural inclination to be social and talkative can help them master Speaking and Listening standards, such as anchor standard CCSS SL.1: *Prepare for and participate effectively in a range of conversations and collaborations with diverse partners, building on others' ideas and expressing their own clearly and persuasively.* Throughout the curriculum, Speaking and Listening Checklists (see Figure 4.2 for an example) are used to scaffold students' speaking and listening skills. Speaking and listening are critical scaffolds for reading and writing. But they are also crucial literacy skills in their own right.

Figure 4.2: Sample Grade 6 Speaking and Listening Checklist

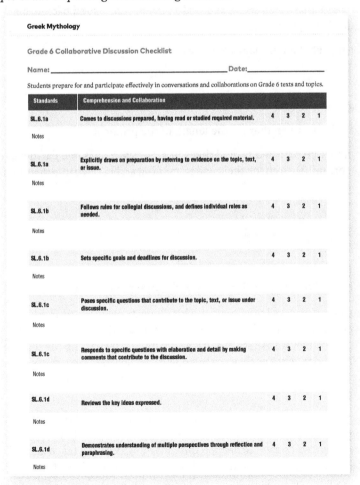

Greek Mythology

Grade 6 Collaborative Discussion Checklist

Name: _____ Date: _____

Students prepare for and participate effectively in conversations and collaborations on Grade 6 texts and topics.

Standards	Comprehension and Collaboration				
SL.6.1a	Comes to discussions prepared, having read or studied required material.	4	3	2	1
Notes					
SL.6.1a	Explicitly draws on preparation by referring to evidence on the topic, text, or issue.	4	3	2	1
Notes					
SL.6.1b	Follows rules for collegial discussions, and defines individual roles as needed.	4	3	2	1
Notes					
SL.6.1b	Sets specific goals and deadlines for discussion.	4	3	2	1
Notes					
SL.6.1c	Poses specific questions that contribute to the topic, text, or issue under discussion.	4	3	2	1
Notes					
SL.6.1c	Responds to specific questions with elaboration and detail by making comments that contribute to the discussion.	4	3	2	1
Notes					
SL.6.1d	Reviews the key ideas expressed.	4	3	2	1
Notes					
SL.6.1d	Demonstrates understanding of multiple perspectives through reflection and paraphrasing.	4	3	2	1
Notes					

(Note: Checklist is for example only. It is incomplete and may look different from actual curriculum materials.)

Back-to-Back and Face-to-Face Protocol

Purpose: This protocol provides a method for sharing information and gaining multiple perspectives on a topic through partner interaction. It can be used for reviewing and sharing academic material, as a personal "ice breaker," or as a means of engaging in critical thinking about a topic of debate.

Materials:

» Questions to be asked between student partners, prepared in advance

Procedure:

1. Have students find partners and stand back-to-back with them, being respectful of space.

2. Have students wait for the question, opinion, etc., that they will be asked to share with their partner.

3. Have students think about what they want to share and how they might best express themselves.

4. When you say, "Face-to-Face," have students turn, face their partners, and decide who will share first if you have not indicated that a certain person should go first.

5. Have students listen carefully when their partners are speaking and to be sure to make eye contact with them.

6. When given the signal, students should find a new partner, stand back-to-back, and wait for the new question, opinion, etc.

7. This may be repeated for as many rounds as needed/appropriate.

Variations:

» Partners may be assigned.

» Partners may also stay together for the length of the protocol.

» The protocol may be repeated several times in a row with the same partners, to give students multiple opportunities to check their understanding and receive information from their partners.

Write about It: Writing to Learn and Learning to Write

The final component to discuss in the read-think-talk-write cycle is writing; however, writing doesn't happen only at the end of the learning process. Instead, writing is an integral part of the learning process. When we ask students to annotate text by writing the gist in the margin, to complete a graphic organizer as they are reading or discussing a text, or to write short paragraphs in response to a prompt, writing is a way for them to crystallize their thinking. They are "writing to learn."

Writing is also a way for students to communicate their learning, and they must learn to do so effectively. In the curriculum, students read, think, and talk as a way to prepare themselves to write. And the writing itself serves to deepen their learning. Writing takes many forms in the curriculum, from writing gist statements on sticky notes, to note-taking, to collaborative, highly scaffolded writing and everything in between. These examples and more will be explored in the section that follows, which describes writing structures in the curriculum.

▶ WHAT ARE ALL THE WAYS MY STUDENTS WILL WRITE IN THE CURRICULUM?

Students do a great deal of writing in the curriculum, even though there isn't a standard "writing time" or "Writers' Workshop." Instead, the read-think-talk-write cycle calls for a deep and fluid integration of writing with reading, thinking, and talking. The full range of the kinds of writing students do in the curriculum is explored in the pages that follow.

Writing Structures in the Curriculum

» **Independent writing:** After reading and discussing texts, students are often required to independently capture their thinking or demonstrate their understanding about what they have read by writing about the text. This writing may take the form of notes on a graphic organizer or note-catcher, for example, or writing short answers to questions on an exit ticket, or writing a paragraph. Depending on their learning needs, sentence frames may be used to scaffold the writing. The Teacher's Guide for English Language Learners is a powerful resource for scaffolding writing.

» **Writing assessments:** In each module, one of the six formal on-demand assessments addresses one of the writing types held in the standards: CCSS W.1 (opinion), W.2 (informative/explanatory), or W.3 (narrative). This is a moment for students to show what they can do on their own as writers, although assessments are often supported with graphic organizers as a part of the assessment itself. (For more on assessments of all kinds, see Chapter 6.)

» **Scaffolded high-quality writing:** For performance tasks that involve writing, and for some other writing tasks, students begin to spend more time on scaffolded high-quality writing tasks, the elements of writing (e.g., focus statements, conclusions, linking words, character development, narrative techniques), and the writing process. (For more information, see the following Scaffolded High-Quality Writing section.)

Independent writing and writing assessments allow you to assess individual students' progress toward mastery of standards, while more scaffolded writing tasks that lead to high-quality work help students build formal writing skills and a sense of purpose, audience, and impact for their writing.

The combination of individual independent writing tasks and scaffolded high-quality writing tasks allows you to get a holistic picture of student progress toward standards. Providing opportunities for both kinds of writing also supports students to develop confidence as writers, building their skills but also their *belief* that they can succeed through clear expectations, a structured process, frequent feedback, and multiple opportunities to revise. Scaffolded high-quality writing allows students to take real pride in their work and to see that they can do more than they may have thought possible.

Scaffolded High-Quality Writing Tasks

The writing process in Grades 6–8, as in K–5, is built on the principles of Writing for Understanding—reading to build knowledge is a big part of how students get ready to write. In Grades 6–8, the writing process includes building content knowledge, planning, revising, editing, and rewriting or trying a new approach. Students participate in multiple rounds of peer critiques, using peer feedback to revise and edit their writing. (Much more on how models, critique, and descriptive feedback help students improve their work can be found in Chapter 4C.)

Defining High-Quality Work

You may recall that high-quality student work is one of EL Education's three Dimensions of Student Achievement (along with mastery of knowledge and skills and character), first described in Chapter 1 (see Figure 1.2). As a result, opportunities for students to produce high-quality writing appear consistently throughout the year at every grade level. Our definition of *high quality* is further broken down into the following aspects:

Complexity

» Complex work is rigorous; it aligns with or exceeds the expectations defined by grade-level standards and includes higher-order thinking by challenging students to apply, analyze, evaluate, and create during daily instruction and throughout longer projects.

» Complex work often connects to the big concepts that undergird or unite disciplines.

» Complex work prioritizes transfer of understanding to new contexts.

» Complex work prioritizes consideration of multiple perspectives.

» Complex work may incorporate students' application of higher-order literacy skills through the use of complex text and evidence-based writing and speaking.

Craftsmanship

» Well-crafted work is done with care and precision. Craftsmanship requires attention to accuracy, detail, and beauty.

» In every discipline and domain, well-crafted work should be beautiful work in conception and execution. In short tasks or early drafts of work, craftsmanship may be present primarily in thoughtful ideas, but not in polished presentation; for long-term projects, craftsmanship requires perseverance to refine work in conception, conventions, and presentation, typically through multiple drafts or rehearsals with critique from others.

Authenticity

» Authentic work demonstrates the original thinking of students—authentic personal voice and ideas—rather than simply showing that students can follow directions or fill in the blanks.

» Authentic work often uses real work formats and standards from the professional world rather than artificial school formats (e.g., students create a book review for a local newspaper instead of a book report for the teacher).

» Authentic work often connects academic standards with real-world issues, controversies, and local people and places.

» Authenticity gives purpose to work; the work matters to students and ideally to a larger community as well. When possible, it is created for and shared with an audience beyond the classroom.

When it is time to write about their content knowledge, our curriculum follows an instructional sequence called the Rule of Three, developed by the Vermont Writing Collaborative (see Figure 4.3).

» **First, students analyze a model,** a teacher-written piece designed to help students understand how to effectively communicate their thinking about the content.

» **Second, students write a practice piece,** similar to the model, with direct instruction and support.

» **Third, students write an independent piece,** similar to both the model and the practice piece, but done independently.

The basic idea of the Rule of Three is that students benefit greatly from gradual instructional steps to independence. Within one topic of the curriculum, students work through three similar instructional sequences. The first is highly guided, close work with a model essay that is very similar in structure and thinking to the essay students will write at the end. Next, students work in partners, with teacher guidance, to plan and write an essay similar to both the model and the final essay. Finally, using the knowledge built over the course of the module and the skills and structures they practiced, students are well prepared to write an independent essay[1].

Figure 4.3: The Rule of Three

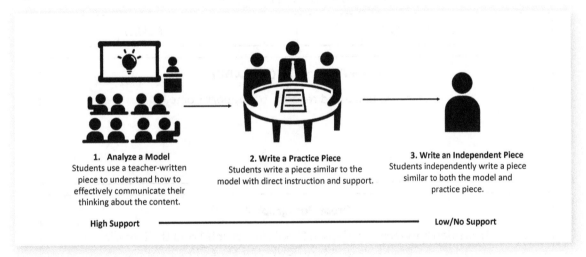

1. Analyze a Model
Students use a teacher-written piece to understand how to effectively communicate their thinking about the content.

2. Write a Practice Piece
Students write a piece similar to the model with direct instruction and support.

3. Write an Independent Piece
Students independently write a piece similar to both the model and practice piece.

High Support ———————————————————— Low/No Support

Part of the process of analyzing the model writing and the practice and independent writing, involves the Painted Essay® structure developed by Diana Leddy at the Vermont Writing Collaborative (see Figure 4.4). The Painted Essay® is a flexible tool for helping students understand and visualize the relationship among purpose, organization, and elaboration of evidence in expository writing. During Painted Essay® writing lessons, students analyze the model essay for content (e.g., "What is this essay about?" "What is the author trying to communicate about the topic?"). They then analyze that same model essay for structure, using watercolors to literally paint the components of a strong essay that they find in the model (e.g., red for the introduction, green for the focus statement, yellow for Proof Paragraph 1, blue for Proof Paragraph 2, and green for the conclusion). They then work with their own arguments and evidence to complete their practice essay using the template in Figure 4.4 before writing their formal essay.

As students write essays, teachers provide critical scaffolding, instructing students on elements of writing (e.g., focus statements, conclusions, linking words, character development, narrative techniques). This scaffolding begins with careful analysis of the specific parts of the model, using the Painted Essay® structure to determine the function and purpose of each part of an opinion or informative essay and determining the content and structural features that make it successful. Students also have the opportunity to practice saying parts orally before writing them.

---

1. From the *Writing for Understanding Workbook* by the Vermont Writing Collaborative

Figure 4.4: Painted Essay® Template

Painted Essay® Template

Name: _____ **Date:** _____

The Painted Essay®

A tool for teaching basic essay form

Introduction (RED)
Catches readers' attention and gives some background information

FOCUS STATEMENT (GREEN)	
Point 1 (YELLOW)	Point 2 (BLUE)

Proof Paragraph 1 (YELLOW)
Gives evidence and reasons to support Point 1

Proof Paragraph 2
Transition between the ideas in Proof Paragraph 1 and the ideas in Proof Paragraph 2 (BLUE and YELLOW).
Gives evidence and reasons to support Point 2 (BLUE)

Conclusion (GREEN)
What?
So what?

For classroom reproduction only
©Diana Leddy and The Vermont Writing Collaborative
The Painted Essay® is a registered trademark. Permission is granted for classroom use only. For more information about the Painted Essay and other teacher created tools for teaching writing, visit www.vermontwritingcollaborative.org.

Chapter 4

Using the Painted Essay® Flexibly

The Painted Essay® is a structure for expository writing. It helps the writer make their thinking clear to the reader. At its most basic level, the Painted Essay® is a four-paragraph essay: introduction (with thesis/focus statement that states the main point of the essay); two body paragraphs ("proof paragraphs"), which support/develop the thesis; and conclusion (which restates and reflects a bit on the thesis). The colors of each of these parts are useful to both teachers and students because they capture how the major parts of the essay are related.

The basic Painted Essay® structure is a flexible tool. As such, it can be used to capture a whole range of types and levels of thinking, at a wide range of grade levels. For example, a fifth-grader might use the four-paragraph Painted Essay® to write a literary analysis in which they compare and contrast characters' responses to events in *Esperanza Rising* ("In the dark of night, each responds differently to this crisis. Esperanza seems unable to do anything, while Miguel jumps straight to action"). An eighth-grader might use the four-paragraph Painted Essay® to inform readers about factors that influence access to healthy food ("CSAs have an influence on our access to healthy food. They have many advantages. Two of the most important are the high quality of the food itself, and the positive impact on the use of fossil fuels"). Same structure—but very different writing.

At the same time, while the structure of the Painted Essay® is useful at all grade levels at this most basic four-paragraph level (right up through high school, in fact), it is also helpful to recognize that it is really a schematic for clear thinking and expression. This is most likely to happen if we give students ample opportunity to work with the Painted Essay® flexibly within the curriculum.

How can we use the Painted Essay® to help students grow as writers?

Offering a variety of structures for communicating different kinds of thinking

The four-paragraph format can be easily adapted to offer students a logical structure for communicating different types of thinking. For example, the body paragraphs in the essay can be used to convey

» cause/effect,

» problem/solution,

» change: before/after, and

» comparison: same/different.

Tweaking the structure itself

The Painted Essay® structure can and should be tweaked, as a structure, so that students are more able to internalize it as a schematic, not as a formula. This might include

» adding a narrative lead or other type of "hook" to the introduction,

» adding additional evidence paragraphs (yellow, blue, or both), or

» adding an additional structural paragraph (what makes a character change, in a literary analysis; counterclaim paragraph in an argument, etc).

In fact, effectively flexing the structure to meet the needs of a particular writing task is one sign of student mastery. The colors are an instructional tool, designed to teach the basic components of expository writing. The colors give teachers and students a tool for describing these components and understanding their relationship to one another. *They should never be used prescriptively*. What follows are some ways that teachers can consider flexing the Painted Essay® structure.

The Painted Essay® structure can work with more complex ideas. This might include

» using a more complex text as the basis for writing,

» asking a more complex question about the text, or

» asking a question that requires a more precise thesis statement.

The Painted Essay® structure can incorporate more analysis within evidence paragraphs:

» explaining/analyzing evidence to greater depth.

The Painted Essay® structure can incorporate deeper thinking in a conclusion:

» drawing a conclusion about a theme for a literary analysis.

The Painted Essay® structure can incorporate more precise language and/or varied syntax:

» incorporating use of direct quotes in more selective ways (partial phrases, ellipses, etc.),

» using a greater variety of transitions (such as *however, in contrast*, etc.), and

» using sentences with variety of dependent and independent clauses, etc

As you plan to use the Painted Essay®, keep in mind that it is designed to grow and flex with the needs of the writers in your classroom.

★ Before You Assign Writing Tasks: Test-Drive Them Yourself

You know your students best, and only you can identify what might trip them up as they embark on any given writing task. It is crucial to test-drive major writing tasks before you assign them. This will give you a chance to be metacognitive about the task, noticing the kinds of thinking and writing students will need to do to succeed. This knowledge will not only help you support students as they write, but it will inform your instruction throughout the module as students learn about and gather evidence they will need down the road. You can then more effectively plan backward to scaffold student success. Knowing where students need to be at the end of a module will add urgency to lessons in which they are gathering, organizing, and synthesizing evidence.

Discovering and overcoming the same obstacles that students are likely to encounter is an opportunity to revise the task or plan for additional scaffolding throughout the learning process. As you write your own response to the writing task, ask yourself:

» To what extent is the task clear, doable within the time frame, and connected to the big ideas of the module?

» Does the task require me to use evidence from the research/reading?

» What content knowledge do I need to successfully complete this task?

» What writing skills do I need to successfully complete this task?

Writing Supports for English Language Learners

One of the most effective supports for ELLs completing writing tasks of all kinds is talking about their ideas before writing. The read-think-talk-write cycle is inherently supportive, since it affords students rich interaction and opportunities to orally rehearse their ideas. For example, the process of identifying and synthesizing evidence from text by engaging in a Fishbowl conversation protocol gives ELLs a structure for trying out their ideas, learning about the ideas of their peers, and deepening their understanding before they are faced with what can feel like an intimidating task when learning an additional language: writing. Many of the structures that support student discourse used throughout the curriculum at all grade levels support this cognitive process.

For example, when students write their argument essays about American Indian boarding schools in Grade 6, Module 3, Unit 3, they might discuss reasons why the character Cal in the anchor text *Two Roads* stays home while his father, "Pop," travels to Washington. A multilingual learner can test and revise their language and content ideas simultaneously:

» "The best way Cal supports Pop is stay Challagi."

» To which a peer might respond with an informative language model: "Yeah, you mean 'stay *at* Challagi'? Yeah, I agree."

» The multilingual learner may then process the model language: "Yeah, stay at Challagi. Because it supports Pop."

In this way, these conversations are crucial to language development for multilingual learners.

The read-think-talk-write cycle is a good example of how the curriculum was designed from the outset to be supportive of students' varied levels of language. We have designed lessons to predict and proactively plan for the kinds of instruction that will be most effective for students learning English, which includes learning to become more effective writers in English. The features "baked into" the lessons are geared toward ELLs who have been classified in the intermediate language proficiency range by standardized assessments. The Teacher's Guides for English Language Learners for each module also contain lesson-by-lesson suggestions for offering lighter or heavier support. What follows are supports and considerations in place for ELLs, some of which are part of lessons and some that are offered in the Guide. (Each of these practices is explored in much greater detail in Chapter 5C.):

» **Language Dives:** This practice not only supports students as readers, but it also supports them as writers and speakers. As they analyze sentence-level "models" to learn the language structures that show up in the complex texts they are reading, they can apply them to their own speaking and writing. For example, in Grade 7, Module 2, students read *Patient Zero* by Marilee Peters, featuring true stories about people who contributed to advancements in treatment and medicine. They read about Mary Mallon, who was kept in seclusion on a remote island by the New York Health Department because they thought she was the cause of an outbreak of typhoid fever. In the Language Dive, students play with one key sentence in four chunks: "Over the next three years/ Mary Mallon spent her time writing letters,/ protesting that her civil rights had been ignored,/ and pleading for help to get her released from quarantine." They work to figure out why the third phrase begins with an *-ing* word used as an adjective, how that adds to their understanding of the text and the module topic, and how they can use this construction in their own writing.

» **Additional scaffolds:** Throughout the curriculum, you will find recommendations in the Teacher's Guide for English Language Learners for additional support with writing leading up to assessments and performance tasks. For example, students might be encouraged to use sentence frames from previous Language Dives as "checkpoints" around which the remainder of an essay can be built.

» **Models:** Reading and analyzing a model of writing that is similar to the writing they are doing helps ELLs not only build knowledge (since they always first analyze the model for its content), but also understand expectations for structure and syntax. It is common to find Language Dives throughout the curriculum that use key sentences from the model for further analysis.

» **Error correction:** Teachers are often the primary source for pointing out errors in student writing; however, structures in our curriculum, such as the read-think-talk-write cycle and peer critique, also help students give one another feedback on errors. In either case, the goal is for students to move to independent error correction. Error correction can be bucketed as follows: global (interferes with overall meaning), pervasive (common), stigmatizing (disturbs more proficient speakers), and student-identified (errors students notice themselves) (Ferris and Hedgecock, 2013). Even as we want students to move to independent error correction, it's important to be thoughtful about which errors to correct, and how frequently. This isn't a settled point in second-language acquisition research, and considerations vary according to whether the errors are in spoken or written language, but there is general agreement that it is supportive to students when we alert them to errors that impede communication.

When thinking about error correction in particular, it is important to understand—and help students understand—that in different parts of the country, people may speak different varieties of English, which are rule-governed and legitimate forms of communication. Those can and should be honored as one mode of communication that students have access to. But teachers should also talk with students about the language they use in specific pieces of writing: "How you write *this piece* has to be in classroom, or academic, English because we are learning the kind of writing that is often expected for college and career." Some of the texts selected for the curriculum lend themselves beautifully to precisely these conversations. In Grade 6, Module 3, students are invited to explore the language of one character in the book who uses a different variety of English, and to think of his choices as strategic, rather than the result of any deficit. Students then explore how they vary their own language strategically, according to where they are, and this opens an opportunity to talk as a class about how and why the language of the classroom, and of classroom writing in particular, may be different. In Grade 7, Module 3, the use of dialect in the works of the Harlem Renaissance is explored as a tool for both artistic expression and social commentary. In these and other instances, students are invited to view the command of multiple varieties of English as a skill to be developed and used strategically, reflecting and instilling an asset-based view of language variation. This benefits all students, not just ELLs.

It is important to remember that ELLs in your classroom may be learning the academic norms of U.S. classrooms, in addition to academic English and the varieties used in more casual conversation. When it comes to academic norms of the writing process in particular, we offer the following considerations:

» **Considerations regarding peer feedback:** Giving and receiving peer feedback is a common practice in our curriculum. This practice may be unfamiliar to students of any background. It may seem particularly odd to those who've recently come from a cultural context in which the expertise or authority of teachers is deeply revered, and students aren't accustomed to turning to peers for academic input. If it is new, acknowledge that, and offer opportunities to process the experiences by asking questions like, "What are some of the thoughts and feelings you experienced when you tried this for the first time?"

» **Considerations regarding attribution and citation:** Depending on their academic and cultural background, some ELLs may have learned different norms for using another person's words as part of their own writing. In many classrooms in China, for example, students are asked to learn and memorize important pieces of writing and insert them, without citation, in their own writing as a way to develop initial levels of competency. When they come to school in America, these students may be surprised that this practice, valid and adaptive in one context, is referred to as "plagiarism" and given the moral judgement of dishonesty in another. Our curriculum includes lots of emphasis on citations, and it will be important for you to be clear with all students not just *that* citations are important, but *why*, in the context of U.S norms for academic writing.

In instances like these, or anytime you detect a difference between the assumptions you have about writing and those of your students, it is a good opportunity to model or nurture an asset-based outlook. This may mean thinking and talking with your students about how these different ways of doing things don't have objectively different worth or value; they are what's called for by the contexts in which they arise. The fact that our context—the context in which you are using this curriculum—includes peer critique and in-text citations doesn't make those things better or worse, it simply makes them useful skills for U.S. classrooms.

Chapter 4

Chapter 4B:
What Does the Read-Think-Talk-Write Cycle Look Like in Action?

The read-think-talk-write cycle is a central feature of our curriculum. It is a part of nearly every lesson, but it isn't a step-by step process that looks the same from lesson to lesson. It may be useful to think of the cycle as more of a philosophy than an instructional practice. The main tenet of this philosophy is that when students interact with text in dynamic and collaborative ways, they comprehend the text more deeply and can communicate their learning from the text more effectively.

What this looks like in practice varies. There are myriad lessons we could have chosen to highlight for you here. The one we chose from Grade 8, Module 3, features the Think-Pair-Share protocol used throughout a lesson in which students read the obituary of a Holocaust upstander, take evidence-based notes, and prepare to write a text reflection.

Throughout, we will use annotations to draw your attention to instructional strategies that are described previously in this chapter or in previous chapters, especially Chapter 2B.

▶ Sample Lesson

Grade 8, Module 3, Unit 3, Lesson 3

Lesson Title: Voices of Upstanders: Marek Edelman

The Read-Think-Talk-Write Cycle in Action

Let's look "under the hood" at a lesson that features the read-think-talk-write cycle in action. In the first half of Module 3, Unit 3, students read informational accounts of upstanders during the Holocaust in order to learn more about how and why many people took action against Hitler and the Nazis during the Holocaust. Students write reflections about how these individuals took action and what makes them upstanders. Students also participate in mini lessons on and practice with how to use punctuation such as commas, ellipses, and dashes. In this lesson, students read the obituary of Marek Edelman and engage in multiple rounds of the Think-Pair-Share protocol as they unpack the text and gather evidence about his life as an upstander. Students record notes on note-catchers and use a class anchor chart to support them in writing a text reflection. This lesson also features a Language Dive.

Opening

A. Engage the Learner – L.8.2a (5 minutes)

- Repeated routine: As students arrive, invite them to complete **Entrance Ticket: Unit 3, Lesson 3**.

- Using a preferred classroom routine, collect or review the answers to **Homework: Practice Punctuation and Verb Voice and Mood** from Lesson 2. Refer to the **Homework: Practice Punctuation and Verb Voice and Mood (answers for teacher reference)**.

- Repeated routine: Follow the same routine as the previous lessons to review learning targets and the purpose of the lesson, reminding students of any learning targets that are similar or the same as in previous lessons.

Work Time

A. Read "Marek Edelman Obituary" Excerpt, and Identify Central Idea – RI.8.2 (15 minutes)

- Review the appropriate learning target relevant to the work to be completed in this section of the lesson:

  "I can determine a central idea and analyze its development in 'Marek Edelman Obituary' Excerpt."

- Distribute and display **"Marek Edelman Obituary" Excerpt**. Read the text aloud, stopping as needed to check comprehension. As students Think-Pair-Share, highlight or underline key details in the displayed text, and instruct students to track the central idea of the text using the **Track Central Idea: Voices of Upstanders note-catcher**. Refer to **Track Central Idea note-catcher: Voices of Upstanders (example for teacher reference)** for the answers.

- With students' support, record the meanings of *ill-fated* (destined to fail or have bad luck), *uprising* (a rebellion, or act of resistance), and *corralled* (gathered together) on the **academic word wall**. Write synonyms or sketch a visual above the key terms to scaffold students' understanding. Invite students to record each word in their **vocabulary logs**, and encourage them to record the definitions in both English and their home languages.

- Think-Pair-Share, and remind students of the habits of an ethical person, particularly empathy, as they discuss the character of Marek Edelman:

  "What did Marek Edelman do?" (He lead the Warsaw uprising.)

  "The resisters knew they couldn't win the fight against the Nazis. Why did they still rebel?" (They wanted to choose how they would die instead of letting the Nazis take them to a camp.)

  "How does Marek's empathy for his people influence his rebellion?" (He understood that many felt hopeless, so he decided to fight on their behalf.)

  "How did Marek get people to follow him?" (He got a job as a hospital messenger and recruited people.)

EL Education Cu

Framing Purpose: *In the Opening of the lesson, all three of the lesson's learning targets are unpacked with students. At the start of Work Time A, the teacher focuses students on the first learning target to frame the purpose for their reading of Marek Edelman's obituary.*

Support all Students: *The text is displayed, distributed, and read aloud to support varied learning styles.*

Read-Think-Talk-Write in Action: *Because an obituary is likely an uncommon format for most students, the teacher pauses reading periodically to give pairs time to mark up their text (think), discuss what they heard and its relationship to the learning target (talk), and record notes on their note-catchers (write).*

Academic Vocabulary: *Key vocabulary is added to the academic word wall.*

Support All Students: *The teacher writes synonyms or sketches visuals of academic vocabulary on the academic word wall to scaffold understanding.*

Home Language Honored in Tandem with English: *When students record words in their vocabulary logs, they are encouraged to record them both in English and their home language.*

Think-Pair-Share Protocol: *This lesson features repeated use of the same protocol. When students become accustomed to the rhythms of protocols, the protocols are more efficacious—students take more ownership of their learning and talk to one another about their questions and ideas rather than just to the teacher.*

Habits of Character: *Students are reminded of the habits of ethical people, both as they learn about Marek Edelman's heroic life, and as they endeavor to make sense of this tragic time in history.*

Chapter 4

Note: Lessons are for example only.
They may look different from actual curriculum materials.

"As you read about Marek's plan of resistance, why do you think it was important for the resisters to choose how they died?" (They wanted to have some kind of power over their fate.)

"What additional habits of character did Marek Edelman exhibit in his actions as an upstander? Explain any habits of character connected to his life experiences and use evidence from the text to support your thinking." (Answers will vary, but may include that he showed empathy when he fought on behalf of those who could not.)

- Ask students to Think-Pair-Share about central idea by asking the following questions:

  "What do you think is the central idea of the text?"

  "What evidence in the text supports the central idea you determined?"

- As students share, record responses on the displayed Track Central Idea: Voices of Upstanders note-catcher. Instruct students to follow along and record these notes in their note-catcher.

- Repeated routine: Invite students to reflect on their progress toward the relevant learning targets.

Work Time

B. Write a Text Reflection – RI.8.1 (15 minutes)

- Review the appropriate learning target relevant to the work to be completed in this section of the lesson:

  "I can write a text reflection about 'Marek Edelman Obituary' Excerpt."

- Display the **Characteristics of Upstanders anchor chart**.

- Think-Pair-Share:

  "What examples of these characteristics did Marek Edelman demonstrate?" (Compassion, leadership.)

- As students share, record their responses in the third column of the anchor chart.

- Explain to students that they will write another text reflection that explains how Marek Edelman was a Holocaust upstander. Remind them that, in the second half of this unit, they will write a narrative interview about an imagined Holocaust upstander based on the upstanders they read about in this unit.

- Display **Criteria for an Effective Text Reflection anchor chart**. Ask a volunteer to read the criteria aloud for the class to review.

- Display and distribute **Text Reflection: "Marek Edelman Obituary" Excerpt.** Read directions aloud.

- Instruct students to begin writing their text reflections independently using the Criteria for an Effective Text Reflection anchor chart to guide them.

- Circulate to support students as they write to ensure they are on task.

Support All Students: *Since Marek Edelman's obituary contains wide-ranging information about his life, the Teaching Notes for this lesson cue teachers to highlight specific portions of the obituary that are related to his role as an upstander for those students who need additional support.*

Checking for Understanding: *Students self-assess their progress toward the learning target. Likely, the rich opportunities for reading, thinking, talking, and writing (note-taking) in this lesson support almost all students to meet the target. And even if not, students at least are coming to see that they will regularly have opportunities for interaction as they work to comprehend and analyze text.*

Synthesizing Learning: *Students' note-catchers serve as a form of evidence as they begin to independently craft their text reflections.*

Co-constructing Anchor Charts: *The Criteria for a Text Reflection anchor chart serves as an important tool for students as they work independently on their text reflections.*

Note: Lessons are for example only.
They may look different from actual curriculum materials.

- Remind students to use key details from "Marek Edelman Obituary" Excerpt to determine how Marek Edelman was a Holocaust upstander. Refer to **Text Reflection: "Marek Edelman Obituary" Excerpt (for teacher reference)** as necessary.

- Repeated routine: Invite students to reflect on their progress toward the relevant learning targets.

Closing and Assessment

A. Language Dive: "Marek Edelman Obituary" Excerpt, Paragraph 10 – L.8.2a (10 minutes)

- Review the appropriate learning target relevant to the work to be completed in this section of the lesson:

  "I can use commas, dashes, and ellipses to indicate a pause, break, or omission."

- Display the **Questions We Can Ask during a Language Dive anchor chart**. Ensure students understand how to use these questions, pointing out that the questions underlined on the anchor chart are questions that students should always ask when they dive into a sentence.

- Refer to the **Questions We Can Ask during a Language Dive anchor chart (example for teacher reference)** as necessary.

- Reread paragraph 10 of "Marek Edelman Obituary" Excerpt.

- Focus students on the sentence below:

  - He joined the anti-communist Workers' Defence Committee after 1976 and would defend the record of Catholic Polish partisans when scholars accused Poles of conniving in the murder of Jews, yet with equal vigour he spoke out against a memorial to displaced Germans.

- Use the **Language Dive Guide: "Marek Edelman Obituary" Excerpt, Paragraph 10 (for teacher reference)** and the **Language Dive: "Marek Edelman Obituary" Excerpt, Paragraph 10 Sentence Chunk Chart** to guide students through a Language Dive conversation about the sentence. Distribute and display the **Language Dive: "Marek Edelman Obituary" Excerpt, Paragraph 10 note-catcher**, and the **Language Dive: "Marek Edelman Obituary" Excerpt, Paragraph 10 sentence chunk strips**. Refer to the **Language Dive: "Marek Edelman Obituary" Excerpt, Paragraph 10 note-catcher (for teacher reference)** as necessary.

- Repeated routine: Invite students to reflect on their progress toward the relevant learning targets.

Homework

A. Punctuation and Verb Voice and Mood

- Students complete **Homework: Punctuation and Verb Voice and Mood: Text Reflection** to answer selected response questions on punctuation and verb voice and mood.

Language Dive: This lesson features a Language Dive. Some Language Dives are specifically tailored for ELLs and some are designed for the whole class. Each Language Dive conversation adopts a "Deconstruct, Reconstruct, Practice" routine as a necessary part of building language, building literacy, and building habits of mind. First students work with chunks of the sentence (i.e., its essential phrases) and discuss each one. Then, they work collaboratively to put the sentence back together chunk by chunk. Finally, they practice using one or more of the language structures in the sentence.

Checking for Understanding: Students have another opportunity to self-assess their progress on the learning target. As a "repeated routine," teachers are invited to choose a checking-for-understanding technique best suited to the needs of their students and to the moment. Some techniques are quick and verbal. Some are written and may take a few minutes. Others may involve movement.

Chapter 4

Note: Lessons are for example only.
They may look different from actual curriculum materials.

Chapter 4C:
How Can Models, Critique, and Descriptive Feedback Strengthen Student Writing within and beyond the Curriculum?

In our curriculum, we use models and descriptive feedback (often in the form of peer critique) to not only strengthen students' writing, but also to help them develop habits of character and resiliency as learners. When students analyze models, they continue to build knowledge as readers; as writers, they develop a clear understanding of the characteristics of quality writing in various formats and for diverse purposes. Understanding these characteristics gives them a path to success. And descriptive feedback, often given through peer critique that is focused and specific, can have a powerful impact on student learning: students who are taught to identify and correct their own errors are more likely to make long-term gains (Beach and Friedrich, 2006).

EL Education has written extensively on the use of models, critique, and descriptive feedback to support students to create high-quality work, including high-quality writing. Our book *Leaders of Their Own Learning: Transforming Schools through Student-Engaged Assessment* (Berger, Rugen, and Woodfin, 2014) includes a chapter on these practices that has greatly informed how we approach the writing process in our curriculum. Rather than reinventing the wheel, we have excerpted parts of the "Models, Critique, and Descriptive Feedback" chapter of *Leaders of Their Own Learning* for you here. We hope these excerpts will give you greater insight into how to approach these practices when teaching our curriculum and also generate excitement for how you might use the practices during other parts of your students' day, beyond the curriculum[2].

It is important to note that we have excerpted portions of this chapter for you here because we feel that using models, critique, and descriptive feedback to help students improve the quality of their work can be a game-changer for students. Not everything in this chapter, however, is germane to our curriculum. But because we know that you may teach other things in addition to our curriculum, we have included examples we think will prove useful. We want to keep encouraging you to see the curriculum and this book as a form of professional learning. Rather

---

2. Full, formal group critique lessons, in which students and teachers use models to define the qualities of high-quality work in a specific genre, thus helping students build understanding of content and setting a standard for high-quality work, are not emphasized in our curriculum. However, these lessons are still a potentially powerful practice for your students and will be explored in this chapter as a "beyond the curriculum" extension.

than thinking "this doesn't apply to the curriculum," think: "How can I bring this practice to my students during other parts of their day beyond the curriculum? How might these practices serve my students as mathematicians, athletes, or artists? What can I learn from this? How can it help me grow as a teacher?"

If you are just getting your sea legs with the curriculum, you may wish to wait to read Chapter 4C until you are feeling comfortable and confident. That's perfectly fine. Come back to it when you're ready to fine-tune these practices.

▶ HOW CAN I USE MODELS, CRITIQUE, AND DESCRIPTIVE FEEDBACK AS TOOLS FOR IMPROVEMENT?

It is a challenge to think of a skilled profession that does not rely on models, critique, and descriptive feedback to improve performance. Imagine fields such as medicine, journalism, or software development without clear models and continual critique and revision. Professionals in these fields know what a high-quality product looks like—whether it's a Pulitzer Prize–winning article or a software application with record-breaking sales—and these models provide them with a reference point for productive critique and feedback that will enable them to improve their own work. Professional dancers have watched thousands of dance performances and have them etched in their minds. Professional basketball players have watched thousands of games. They have a clear picture of where they want to go, and they need continual critique from coaches and colleagues to get there.

Picture a ballet troupe without someone continually adjusting posture and position, or a basketball team never critiquing strategies during halftime or analyzing their play on video. These ongoing feedback practices, which help us improve, are essential in nearly every field. Despite its prevalence in the world, this kind of on-the-job, on-the-spot feedback, based on strong models, is still strangely absent from many schools and classrooms. To be sure, grades and test scores abound, and occasionally students get assignments returned with comments, but these "results" are often thin and too distant from the moment of learning or effort to be useful.

In this era of of rigorous college- and career-ready standards, students need models of work that meets standards, and they need structured opportunities for critique and descriptive feedback so that they, too can produce work that meets the standards. Students and teachers alike will benefit from seeing—sometimes even holding in their hands—examples of what they are aiming for. See box: Defining Models, Critique, and Descriptive Feedback in the Curriculum and Beyond for brief definitions. Much more detail, including examples and videos, is provided in the pages that follow.

Chapter 4

Defining Models, Critique, and Descriptive Feedback in the Curriculum and Beyond

Models. Models bring standards to life. They are exemplars of work used to build a vision of quality within a genre. Models are generally strong in important dimensions, which are discussed with students before they create their own work based on the model.

> » **In the curriculum.** Models are provided for you in the curriculum. These models are always based on content students know and set expectations for quality work; however, they don't "give away" the thinking we want students to do in their own work. For example, if students need to write about a character in a story, the model will be about a different character in the same story.

> » **In lessons beyond the curriculum.** Models can be drawn from current or prior student work or the professional world, or they can be created by the teacher.

Critique lessons. In a critique lesson, students look at models together to develop criteria for quality work in a genre. The cognitive work they do to generate those criteria (by discovering and naming features that demonstrate quality) leads them to new learning and understandings about content. Critique lessons are standards-driven, with clear objectives, and are designed to support the learning of all students, not primarily to improve the work of one (as would a one-on-one peer critique).

> » **In the curriculum.** We don't typically include full critique lessons in the curriculum, but students do "unpack" models and "non-models," looking for attributes that make them high-quality work (or not).

> » **In lessons beyond the curriculum.** A full critique lesson, with clear objectives, is a powerful lever to kick off students' own efforts to create high-quality work and build understanding of content. Models, which serve as the reference point to generate criteria for quality work, are at the heart of critique lessons.

Descriptive feedback. Descriptive feedback may take place in the form of a teacher conferring with an individual student, written comments from the teacher, or a peer critique session. The constructive, precise comments that make up descriptive feedback specifically address a particular piece of work by a single student and are articulated in a way to raise the quality of the work toward the gold standard of the model. Feedback should lift up both positive aspects of the work as well as areas to grow and should always be kind, specific, and helpful.

> » **In the curriculum.** Descriptive feedback often takes the form of peer critique. As opposed to a critique lesson, which is designed to help all students take aim at high-quality work, a peer critique is designed for students to help each other improve their own individual work. (For a specific example of how the curriculum prepares students for peer critique, see Figure 4.10, which is an excerpt from a Grade 7 lesson.)

> » **In lessons beyond the curriculum.** In addition to providing opportunities for students to give and receive peer feedback, honing your own skills at providing students with descriptive feedback will be an additional tool in your toolbox for helping students complete high-quality work.

What Makes These Practices So Effective?

Models, critique, and descriptive feedback are critical to helping students become leaders of their own learning. The practices help students meet standards by giving them the tools they need to answer the question that may paralyze them when they get their work back for revision: "Now what?" Often, students simply copy edit for conventions based on teacher corrections—grammar, spelling, and punctuation—and don't actually revise the work.

Instead, picture a student participating in a group critique lesson of a strong historical essay, chosen by their teacher as a model. The teacher has decided to focus only on the introductory paragraphs; each student reads and text-codes the model for those paragraphs. The class then generates a list of the qualities that stand out as effective (e.g., thesis is clearly stated). Those qualities are discussed and written on chart paper in the front of the room.

When the student's teacher returns the first draft of their essay the next day, the student also receives a copy of the list of qualities that make for a good introduction to an essay that they and their classmates generated. The student must now revise the introduction to match those qualities. The student looks over their own paper and the need for revision is clear, as is the substance of what they need to add and change. Critique, descriptive feedback, and the use of models are all practices designed to give students a vision of quality so that they know what they are aiming for.

Making Standards Real and Tangible

Standards do not create a picture of what students are aiming for. They are typically dry, technical descriptions. When a Common Core standard, for example, requires students to "produce clear and coherent writing in which the development, organization, and style are appropriate to task, purpose, and audience" or "use words, phrases, and clauses to create cohesion and clarify the relationships among claim(s), reasons, and evidence," what does that mean? What does that look like?

Examining models and generating the criteria for success gives students a roadmap for meeting standards. They know what they are aiming for and how to get there. In addition to CCSS Writing standard W.5—*develop and strengthen writing as needed by planning, revising, editing, rewriting, or trying a new approach*—which speaks directly to the benefits of models, critique, and descriptive feedback, other connections to the standards include the following:

» Both the mathematics and literacy standards explicitly demand that students become independent learners who can "critique the reasoning of others."

» The need for students to evaluate the validity and quality of reasoning and craftsmanship permeates the standards. The strategies described in this chapter build students' skills to do so in a sophisticated way.

» Quality critique and descriptive feedback require students to point to evidence to support their claims, a key to meeting the standards.

Starting with learning targets puts standards in concrete terms that students understand. Models then bring those learning targets to life and help students and teachers build a shared understanding of what success looks like.

Building a Mindset of Continuous Improvement

Critique and descriptive feedback help students understand that all work, learning, and performance can be improved. We can tell students that their potential to learn is great, but they won't believe it, especially in areas in which they don't feel confident, until they actually see themselves improve. There is nothing that does this more effectively than when students work through multiple drafts, rehearsals, or practices and end up creating work or performing at a level that is beyond what they thought possible. Participating in critique, developing the criteria for high-quality work, and giving, receiving, and using feedback promotes a growth mindset and teaches students the value of effort and revision. Figure 4.5 is a great example of the power of habits of character (e.g., *work to become effective learners*) and a mindset of continuous improvement.

Figure 4.5: Natalie's Grasshopper: Multiple Drafts

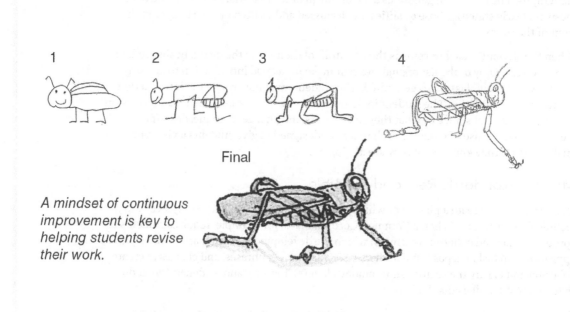

A mindset of continuous improvement is key to helping students revise their work.

Instilling Responsibility and Ownership of Learning

Critique and descriptive feedback emphasize skills of critical analysis and self-assessment and ask students to make important decisions about their work and learning. Because the path to meeting learning targets is clearly defined by a shared vision of what quality looks like, students can work independently and build skills confidently.

▶ HOW CAN I DEVELOP A POSITIVE CLASSROOM CULTURE THAT WILL ALLOW CRITIQUE AND DESCRIPTIVE FEEDBACK TO FLOURISH?

To be effective, critique and descriptive feedback require deliberate and sustained attention to emotional safety and depend on skills of collaboration. These practices help a classroom become a learning community dedicated to getting better together. An essential starting point for critique and descriptive feedback in any classroom is ensuring that the guidelines *be kind, be specific,* and *be helpful* are the backbone of every class. Formal and informal feedback and critique flow from these. Safety and encouragement, as well as structure and clear learning targets, will set students up for success.

Just about everyone has a feedback nightmare, a time when they felt hurt or judged by someone's feedback or criticism. Some students are particularly vulnerable, especially if they have not experienced much school success and have received many messages of negative criticism (both implicit and explicit). School and classroom guidelines must be carefully built and reinforced, but individual feedback also must be tailored and shaped with the particular student in mind. There is not a template or cookie-cutter approach that will work for every student.

"The conversations about habits of character have really impacted students. They focus more on their own learning than on 'getting it done.' Students work from the idea that although this is good, I can make it better and better. As they become more adept at giving and receiving feedback, they can become more critical of the feedback itself. They also become able to self-assess, which is a critical component of being college- and career-ready."

Tammi Bauschka
Literacy Program Specialist, Tucson, Arizona

This kind of safety can be hard to monitor. You must be vigilant and firm, especially when building a classroom culture with a new group. Very young students often don't realize that their comments may be perceived as mean. They can be candid even when it's hurtful to others and need to learn how to word things carefully. Sometimes older students may intentionally, but subtly, undermine a peer's work, such as complimenting work with a sarcastic tone or facial expression. It is imperative that you stop the critique the moment problems happen, deal firmly with unkind or untruthful comments or tone, and reestablish norms. Eventually, students will trust and reinforce the norms themselves. The curriculum's consistent emphasis on habits of character, particularly *work to become ethical people* and *work to become effective learners*, will both create the conditions for and reinforce these efforts. (Note: For more information on habits of character in the curriculum, see Chapter 6C.)

Establishing norms for critique is intimately tied to the work of building an active and collaborative culture described in Chapter 2C. If you haven't read that chapter yet, it's worth reading it before embarking on using models, critique, and descriptive feedback with your students. The Snapshot that follows offers a window into one teacher's work to build this kind of culture in his classroom.

> ### 📷 Snapshot: Building Culture through a Challenging, Accessible Task
>
> "To build habits that establish a culture in which quality is the norm, I begin with a basic but demanding task that each student can accomplish, yet all can improve: the challenge of drawing freehand a straight line," says Steven Levy, former EL Education school coach and former teacher at Bowman Elementary School in Lexington, Massachusetts. "I introduce standards of quality that guide our work throughout the year." Students develop the language, norms, and skills of describing quality through group critique as they analyze lines.
>
> In this task, which Levy has guided many students and adults through, he asks everyone to draw a straight line freehand. He then uses the work to demonstrate how to generate criteria for feedback and critique; revision; planning ahead; taking care of resources; and above all the norms of a safe, collaborative, and constructive classroom. "Practicing these drawings is a particularly effective way to begin the year because everyone has equal access to the assignment. No one can do it perfectly, so everyone is challenged," he says.

"When students have learned this process of producing quality work, they are ready to apply it to more complex tasks. We now go through the same process to develop standards for writing, for presentations, and for major projects. We do not follow the exact steps in the line exercises for everything we do. Sometimes I give more explicit instruction or direction at the beginning. At other times, depending on the effectiveness of the students' work, I recommend additional critique sessions or more practice of discrete skills between drafts. The steps are simply tools and processes designed to help students take more responsibility in producing quality work."

▶ HOW CAN THE USE OF MODELS IMPROVE MY STUDENTS' WORK?

Here, and throughout this chapter, we will consider the ways in which this practice is used within our curriculum and then offer guidance for those of you who may feel ready to extend the practice beyond the curriculum.

Using Models in the Curriculum

Models should show students where they are headed. They don't need to be perfect, but they must be good models of features that are connected to learning targets. Within the set of interrelated practices—models, critique, and descriptive feedback—models are the linchpin. They set the standard and the expectation from which critique and descriptive feedback flow.

In the curriculum, models are generally provided. Often a model of strong work helps ground students in a vision of what excellent work on a particular task would look like. Sometimes, students also may analyze a model of weak work before beginning their own work. The models in the curriculum will be similar, but not exactly the same, as the work students will do independently.

Any time we ask students to analyze models, it is important to first give them time to think about the content and then ask them to analyze the craft. For example, if students are analyzing a Nikki Grimes poem, as they do in Grade 7, Module 3, we wouldn't first ask them "What rhetorical devices did Grimes use?" Instead, we would bring them into the text by asking: "What was Grimes trying to say? Why is it important?" Then we can move students to "How did Grimes craft her poem to have the most impact on her readers?" First we want students to read as readers, and *then* to read as writers.

It is important that the model not give too much away in terms of the kinds of thinking we want students to do, but it should be familiar to them so that they can connect to it easily. For example, in Grade 6, Module 4, students analyze a model argument essay in preparation for writing their own. They analyze each paragraph and consider the work being done by that portion of the essay so that they can approach their own writing with an enhanced sense of organization and overall readiness for writing (see Figures 4.6 and 4.7 for an excerpt of the model essay and excerpt of the lesson that accompanies it).

Figure 4.6: Grade 6 Excerpt of Hidden Figures Model Argument Essay
Figure 4.7: Analyzing a Model: Excerpt of a Grade 6 Lesson

Remarkable Accomplishments in Space Science

Model Argument Essay: "Dorothy"

Name: _____ Date: _____

Focus Question: Why are Dorothy Vaughan's accomplishments remarkable?

When recalling America's race to put an astronaut on the moon, history often overlooks Dorothy Vaughan. She, along with the other women of the segregated West Area Computing Unit, worked on projects that made airplanes faster and more stable, which helped the United States during World War II. Then she was promoted to supervisor of the West Computers. She led the women whose work would make space travel possible. As a brilliant mathematician and one of the first black women to work for NASA as a "computer," Dorothy's accomplishments deserve to be remembered. Her accomplishments were remarkable because they led to major advancements in air travel and because they took place despite tremendous obstacles.

Dorothy's skills and hard work were very important in helping change the face of air travel. When Dorothy first started working at Langley, the laboratory was doing extensive research in aerodynamics. Langley was trying to help the United States military by developing airplanes that were stronger, faster, and more stable than any planes in other countries (52). Dorothy was inspired by this work. She took an engineering physics course, participated in training, and did much independent studying and homework (51). She thought all day about what made planes fly (51). Her calculations

340

Grade 6: Module 4: Unit 3: Lesson 1

Work Time

A. Analyze a Model Argument Essay – W.6.1 (15 minutes)

- Review the learning target relevant to the work to be completed in this section of the lesson:

  "I can analyze the structure of a model argument essay by applying my knowledge of the Painted Essay®."

- Set the purpose for the activity by explaining that students will prepare to write their own argument essays by carefully analyzing an exemplar argument essay.

- Divide the class in half. Distribute the **red, green, yellow, and blue index cards** to one half of the class. Give each student only one colored index card. Remind students that these are the colors used to indicate the key components in the Painted Essay® structure.

- Distribute the **Model Argument Essay: Introduction Chunks** to the other half of the class. Give each student only one chunk of the introduction paragraph.

- Explain that students are about to participate in the Meet My Match activity that focuses on more deeply understanding the introduction of an argument essay. Remind students that they have previously participated in the activity when analyzing the model literary argument essay in Module 3.

- Explain or display the **Meet My Match Instructions**. Answer clarifying questions.

- Direct students' attention to the **Work to Become Ethical People anchor chart**.

- Ask:

  "What would it look like to behave with integrity during this activity?" (only asking yes or no questions; only responding by saying yes or no; trying my best even if the task is challenging)

- Invite students to begin the activity. Display the **Painted Essay® template** as a reference for students. Refer to the **Painted Model Argument Essay (example for teacher reference)** for correct matches.

- After 4 minutes have passed, instruct students to remain standing with their partners.

- Display only the introduction paragraph of the Painted Model Argument Essay (example for teacher reference). Be sure to hide the rest of the painted essay.

- Read the first paragraph, stopping at "... space travel possible."

- Turn and Talk:

  "This red section of the introduction paragraph contains background information. Why is background information important to an argument essay?" (The background information is the context the reader needs to know in order to understand the foundation of the argument.)

- Think-Pair-Share:

  "In your own words, explain the context provided in the introduction paragraph." (The introduction sets the historical time period by referencing the Space Race, World War II, and rampant segregation. The introduction also provides some key background information about Dorothy Vaughan.)

Using Models beyond the Curriculum

Models are provided for you in the curriculum, but if you aren't teaching the curriculum every period of the day and wish to use this practice in those lessons, you'll need to gather your own models. Learning how to recognize and select powerful, generative models is important, and it takes practice. The more compelling the models are, the more powerful students' analysis will be. Ideally, you will begin building an archive of good work models that you gather and store for specific purposes. When you need to teach the format or genre of a research paper, for example, you have a file of research papers by former or other students to draw from.

You might also choose to create exemplary models yourself or find models from the professional world to set a high and authentic bar, especially for older students. If models of current student work are used, it is important to choose samples that represent different approaches to the same assignment, or different strong features, so there is little duplication in what is viewed and discussed. There should be a specific reason for each piece chosen. If the class is going to spend valuable, whole-class time considering a piece, there should be a clear reason and a connection to learning targets.

Using Weak Work as a Non-Example

Although it is most important to have exemplary models, it can also be useful to have examples of pieces that are poorly done in different ways, particularly in those areas in which you feel your students may struggle. For example, to help students remember to be less repetitive with sentence structure in a composition, it can be powerful to have them critique an anonymous student composition that is fraught with repetitive language. The image of this weak work will stay with them and can be discussed regularly to remind the group to be careful to avoid its pitfalls.

When using weak work, there are some cautions. First, the work must be anonymous. Students should never be able to recognize it as the work of a current or former student. Second, the work must be treated respectfully. Modeling mean-spirited critique will promote an unkind classroom climate. We also do not recommend choosing work that is in another variety of English; you might do so to explore with the class what the differences are, and when one might strategically employ them, but not to position such writing as "weak." Lastly, not all weak work is a good choice. Ideally, the work is compelling in its flaws. For example, if it is very strong in some areas but confusing in others, it can invite wonder and analysis. The best weak work is not an example of a student who wasn't trying, but rather a student who was putting in effort and created something interesting to consider, but had confusions that resulted in problems that are likely to crop up for many students.

▶ HOW CAN I BUILD STANDARDS-BASED CRITIQUE LESSONS AROUND MODELS?

In the curriculum, we do not build entire lessons around models. Typically, the models (or non-models) are analyzed with students as one part of a lesson. However, designing standards-based critique lessons is a powerful practice that gives students a deep understanding of what quality looks like in a particular genre. The section that follows on critique lessons should be considered a "beyond the curriculum" practice—it will be well worth your time to read and practice when you are ready, willing, and able.

Conducting Standards-Based Critique Lessons, beyond the Curriculum

In a critique lesson, students look at models together to develop criteria for quality work in a genre. The cognitive work they do to generate that criteria (by discovering and naming features that demonstrate quality) leads them to new learning and understandings about content. A critique becomes more than a simple exercise in closely examining student work when it leads students to new learning, application of knowledge and skills, and meeting standards. It then becomes a standards-driven critique lesson.

Defining the Purpose for Each Critique Lesson

Critique lessons can have a variety of specific purposes: setting standards of quality and developing criteria for work, supporting focused revision, or fine-tuning final presentations, products, or performances. It is important to make the particular focus of the critique clear from the outset. Frame the critique with learning targets so that you can keep track of guiding the inquiry to address them. Clarity about learning targets should not prevent the critique from producing unplanned discoveries, clarifications, and new ideas or directions, and it is important to celebrate and identify these.

Teacher-facilitated critique lessons that include looking together at models can be used to address learning in a variety of disciplines. The lesson could focus on the following:

- » Content (e.g., simple machines, a historical timeline)
- » Concepts (e.g., recurring themes in history, binary numbers)
- » Skills (e.g., keyboarding, interpreting a bar chart, factoring equations)
- » Product formats or genres (e.g., business letter, political map, watercolor portrait)
- » Habits of character (e.g., group collaboration during fieldwork excursions, participation during literature circles, hallway behavior)

In this video, "A Group Critique Lesson," watch as EL Education's Ron Berger leads a group critique lesson with students from the Presumpscot School in Portland, Maine. The third-graders use a piece of student writing as a model from which to identify criteria for a quality story.

https://vimeo.com/44053703

Mastering the Language of a Critique Lesson[3]

Though the video in Video Spotlight 4.2 shows a critique lesson with third-graders, we have included it here because of its overall usefulness as a model lesson. The general flow of the lesson—looking together at a model of student writing and then co-creating with students a list of criteria for what makes it strong writing—is one that teachers of any grade level can follow.

One of the hardest things for any teacher to master when first conducting critique lessons is mastering the kind of language that Ron Berger uses in the video to draw students out as they discuss the model; for middle school teachers, it is also key to adapt that language for adolescent learners. A good critique lesson is empowering for middle school students: it amplifies students' voices and unique perspectives and honors their membership in a community of creative experts. You don't want to spoon-feed your own critique to your students. You want to get them involved. A lesson that engages every student in looking deeply at the model and sharing their insights will ratchet up students' ownership of the lesson and their commitment to using their learning to improve their own work.

The respectful and strategic teacher-student dialogue of a critique lesson, like we see in the video, is critical to its success. For example, when students critique a model, you can slightly reword student comments to make them more clear and useful. When a student offers a grain of something important, build on it yourself (e.g., "Jalen, what I hear you saying is that the opening grabs you—has a good hook—is that right? That is an important observation! I'll write that on our anchor chart."). If students notice that Anton has used an especially efficient strategy in a math problem, label that "Anton's approach." Forever afterward, the suggestion to "try Anton's approach" will make Anton beam with pride, and it will be a shorthand way for other students to easily remember the strategy. Also, if students have missed something important in the work that you wish they would address, bring it up yourself as a question, and prompt them to name it (e.g., "Did any of you notice what Madison did here in this part... ?").

Table 4.4 shows sample sentence stems for various purposes during a critique. The table is in no way complete; you can add to it with your own favorite phrasing that will work best for you and your students.

---

3. The majority of this section on Mastering the Language of a Critique Lesson is pulled from our 2020 book *The Leaders of Their Own Learning Companion: New Tools and Tips for Tackling the Common Challenges of Student-Engaged Assessment.*

Table 4.4: Sentence Stems for Encouraging Engaging Critique Lessons

Purpose	Sample Sentence Stems
To restate a student's comment using more precise language or vocabulary	» Destiny, what I hear you saying is that... » Chris, am I correct in saying that you are suggesting... » Karina, there is a scientific word for exactly what you are describing, it is... » Terrific, Aidan! In English grammar we call that a...
To engage a particular student or make a student feel proud	» Sergio, what do you think about what she did in this section... » Wow, I was so impressed with the improvement by... » We saw this same good idea from Jalen last week... » We could call this the "Kristina Strategy"... » Brianne, your eye is so sharp! Can you say more about...
To ensure a point is made that students haven't yet made themselves	» Your comments made me think of.... » Great! Another feature we could name is... » I love these observations! I want to add... » There is one more thing we all need to consider...

The best way to build understanding and ownership with students is to ask them questions that invite them to examine the model like real investigators. A lesson that ignites curiosity and students' "need to know" engages students because they understand that in order to do their own work, they need to understand how the model represents quality, and in what ways. Model-dependent questions—questions that push students to identify the exact words or numbers or features of the model that show an answer to the question—are key. It's also important that all students feel accountable to probing the model and answering the questions. By summarizing the strategies that students notice on an anchor chart along the way, you also create a helpful resource for students to refer back to as they do their own work.

Determining the Right Timing for a Critique Lesson in a Sequence of Curriculum

Depending on the goals and learning targets, critique lessons can be useful at a variety of times in a curriculum or long-term study:

» **Introductory teacher-facilitated lessons using previously collected models:** to set a high standard for quality and to construct with students a framework of criteria for what constitutes good work in that domain or product format.

» **In process, during the creation of work:** to support focused revision, clarify and tune student efforts to apply criteria for quality, refocus student concentration and momentum, and introduce new concepts or next steps.

» **Just before final exhibition of work:** to fine-tune the quality of the presentation, display, or performance for an audience. Often final details and touches make a major difference in quality.

» **After completion of an assignment:** to reflect on quality and learning and to set goals.

Depending also on the assignment or project being created, each of these points in the sequence of study suggests a different focus and style of critique lesson. Ideally a form of critique will be used at all points in the process.

Opportunities to Conduct Critique Lessons in the Curriculum

» You might choose to add a critique lesson during Unit 3 if you are noticing that students need more scaffolding with a specific aspect of the performance task.

» When students are creating visual products or short written pieces (e.g., graphic panels in Grade 8, Module 3; infographics in Grade 8, Module 2; visual displays in Grade 7, Module 3), you might conduct a gallery critique so that students can identify techniques and strategies that they can use in their own work (see the section that follows for more information on gallery critiques).

As you become more familiar with the patterns of students' work in the curriculum, you can inject critique lessons at strategic points to scaffold toward clearer understanding of the expectations and more consistent high quality.

Two Types of Critique Lessons

Gallery Critique

In a gallery critique, all students post work for everyone to view closely. A gallery critique works best when the goal is to identify and capture only positive features in the selected work that can help everyone improve. Only a small set of the posted work may be cited. With work from the whole class, there is obviously going to be a lot of work with problems; this is not the time to try to point them all out. The point of a gallery critique is to find effective ideas and strategies in strong examples that students can borrow to improve their own work. To keep a session grounded in that purpose, choose prompts for reflection and discussion that emphasize that spirit. For example:

» What is really working about this? (with prompts to refer back to criteria for quality)

» What strengths does your work have in common with this work?

» What did the creator of this work do that you want to try?

If the work is visual, it can be posted for viewing in a gallery style. If the work is written, it may be posted on a wall or copied and distributed. For written work, short pieces or a portion of a larger piece (e.g., the introduction to an essay, a poem) work best.

Clearly there are advantages to sharing every student's work, such as building accountability, excitement, shared commitment, and a realistic sense of how one's work compares with others. However, it is important to create safety for students whose initial performance on the assignment was weak. A protocol for a gallery critique might look something like this:

» **Introduction:** Explain the steps of the protocol and the learning targets. Remind students of the norms of giving feedback: be kind, be specific, and be helpful (see Table 4.5 for kind, specific, and helpful sentence stems).

» **Step 1: Post the work (5 minutes):** Each student tapes their first draft to the wall.

» **Step 2: Silent gallery walk (10 minutes):** Students view all of the drafts in a silent walk and take notes identifying strong examples of a predetermined focus (e.g., descriptive language, use of evidence, elegant problem-solving, experiment design).

» **Step 3: What did you notice? (5 minutes):** Lead a discussion in which students are not allowed to make judgments or give opinions; they can comment only on things they noticed and identified.

» **Step 4: What is working? (15 minutes):** Lead the class in a discussion of which aspects of the posted drafts grabbed their attention or impressed them. Each time students choose an example, they need to articulate exactly what they found compelling, citing evidence from the work itself. If they're not sure, draw them out until they can point to evidence in the work and name something specific. You should also point to examples you are impressed with and explain why. Chart the insights and codify specific strategies that students can use to improve their drafts.

Table 4.5: Kind, Specific, and Helpful Sentence Stems[4]

Criteria	What does this mean?	What does it look like?	What does it sound like?
BE KIND	Always treat others with dignity and respect.	Listening carefully	» "I like the way you have… because it meets these criteria." » "I can see you worked hard to… " » "I wonder… " » "This really helps me understand… "
BE SPECIFIC	Focus on particular strengths and weaknesses.	Identifying the parts that you think were done well using the criteria Identifying the parts that you think could be improved using the criteria	» "This part meets these criteria by… " » "I notice… " » "Remember when we learned about… ? You could apply that here." » "Have you thought about adding/ revising… in order to… ?" » I can't see evidence of this criterion in your work. Where do you think you could revise to show evidence of this criterion?"
BE HELPFUL	Positively contribute to the individual or the group.	Helping a peer identify where he or she can improve	» "Perhaps you could revise this… in order to improve… " » "If this were my work, I would… " » "As a first step, I suggest… " » "What would happen if… "

---

4. This table is from our 2020 book *The Leaders of Their Own Learning Companion: New Tools and Tips for Tackling the Common Challenges of Student-Engaged Assessment*

In-Depth Critique

A single piece of work (or set of related pieces) is used to uncover strengths or to highlight common areas in need of revision or gaps in knowledge that need to be addressed (e.g., use of evidence, descriptive language, topic development). Unlike a gallery critique, wherein the focus is exclusively on positive aspects in the collection of work, an in-depth critique analyzes a particular piece to determine which aspects are working and which are not. The goal is to recognize and name particular features that are effective or ineffective so that the class can learn from them. The critique lesson video featuring third-graders from Presumpscot School in Maine, referenced earlier in this chapter, is an example of an in-depth critique.

Your Role during a Critique Lesson

Teachers must take an active role in facilitation throughout a critique lesson. This process works best when it looks organic (emerging entirely from student ideas) but is in fact skillfully shaped. Choose students strategically for comments, govern the flow of discussion and contribute enthusiasm, interject compelling comments to build interest and make key points, and reframe student observations when necessary to make them clear to the group and connected to the learning targets. Remember that this kind of critique is a lesson, with clear learning targets—don't hesitate to take charge of the flow to ensure that the session is productive.

Be a Strong Guardian of Critique Norms

Your most important role is to foster and sustain a critique culture that is emotionally safe for students and productive for learning. The critique rules, or norms, must be explicit and tracked vigilantly during the lesson to ensure that all students feel protected from ridicule (even subtle sarcasm or facial expressions) and that comments are specific and instructive. The critique rules should require participants to be kind, specific, and helpful in their comments. In the curriculum, students are taught, and given many opportunities to practice, how to give kind, specific, and helpful feedback (see Figure 4.10 for an example).

In addition to guarding against any hurtful comments, this also means guarding against vague comments (e.g., "I like it," "It's good"). Students should point to specific features (e.g., "I think the title is well chosen," "Including the graph makes it much clearer to me") and stay connected to the goals for the critique lesson. Their comments should relate to the group effort to build understanding. Here are additional guidelines that can help to build a positive climate:

» It should always be clear that it is the work itself, not the author of the work, that is the subject of the critique.

» Use "I" statements (e.g., "I don't understand your first sentence" rather than "It doesn't make sense").

» Begin comments, if possible, with a positive feature in the work before moving on to perceived weaknesses (e.g., "I think the eyes in your portrait are very powerful, but I think adding eyebrows would give it more feeling").

» Separate genuine questions from "suggestions masquerading as questions." For example, if an illustration wasn't present where you might have expected one, you might ask "Why did you choose to leave out the illustration on this draft?" However, if you already know you think it would be improved with an illustration, be direct: "This would be more impactful for me with an illustration."

These norms are especially important when students are sharing their work with their classmates, but they apply even when the work is from outside of the class. Explicitly teaching and using critique rules will strengthen students' critique skills as well as their ability to hear and use descriptive feedback.

Distill, Shape, and Record the Insights from the Critique

Many of the insights that you hope students will come to may arise from student comments, but you may need to pause to highlight insights you know will be high-leverage, and collaborate with the class to put ideas in language that will be clear and accessible for all students. Later they may even be codified for the class in the form of criteria or next steps. It is helpful to return to these insights during the critique, explicitly attributing them to the original student ("Tamika's theory" or "Jonathan's observation"), even though you and other students may have since deepened the original comment. If particular key insights don't arise, you shouldn't hesitate to seed them as questions or discovery challenges in viewing the work ("Did anyone notice... ," "Can you see an example of... ") or simply add them directly. See Table 4.4 for suggested sentence stems.

Focus on Naming the Specific Qualities and Strategies that Students Can Take Away with Them

It is not useful for students to leave the session with the idea that "Aliya is a good writer" or "The book review we read was great," but rather, "Aliya used eight strategies that made her piece good, and now I know them and can use them." Naming the effective qualities and strategies must be explicit, openly discussed and negotiated, and must result in terms that students understand—in their language.

The more concrete the naming of features, the better. Charting the names of features and hanging them on the wall for reference helps. Vague insights put on a chart, such as "Use 'voice,'" are less helpful, particularly to weaker writers, than specific suggestions, such as "Include dialogue," "Use verbs other than 'said,'" "Use punctuation marks other than periods." Again, it may be useful to rephrase student ideas (with their permission) into words that you feel will be clear and helpful, and to add to the list if students have omitted important qualities or strategies.

The process of naming qualities and strategies can also be a step in creating a rubric or a criteria list of what constitutes quality for this genre or skill, or it can refer to an existing rubric that the class uses, supporting that rubric with specific strategies. In the curriculum, the criteria for writing are held in writing rubrics that name specific qualities of high-quality writing in the genre (see Figure 4.8 for an example).

Figure 4.8: Sample Excerpt of Grade 8 Informative/Explanatory Writing Rubric

Grade 8 Informative/Explanatory Writing Rubric

Write informative/explanatory texts to examine a topic and convey ideas, concepts, and information through the selection, organization, and analysis of relevant content.

Reading Comprehension

	4 - Advanced	3 - Proficient	2 - Developing	1 - Beginning
R.8.1 W.8.9	Demonstrates a deep understanding of ideas (both stated and inferred) by developing an insightful focus supported by well-chosen textual evidence	Demonstrates a clear understanding of ideas (both stated and inferred) by developing an accurate focus, adequately supported by textual evidence	Demonstrates a limited understanding of ideas, developing an accurate focus weakly supported by textual evidence	Does not demonstrate understanding or shows a misunderstanding of ideas, offering a focus unsupported by textual evidence

Organization/Purpose¹

	4 - Advanced	3 - Proficient	2 - Developing	1 - Beginning
W.8.2a	Focus is effectively communicated and strongly maintained	Focus is clear and consistently maintained	Focus is somewhat unclear and/or insufficiently maintained	Focus is confusing or ambiguous
W.8.2a	Introduces a topic clearly and concisely, previewing what is to follow	**Introduces a topic clearly, previewing what is to follow**	Introduces a topic clearly	Introduction is confusing, missing, or off-topic
W.8.2f	Concluding statement or section synthesizes the information or explanation presented and offers relevant insights or reflection	**Concluding statement or section follows from and supports the information or explanation presented**	Concluding statement or section follows from the information or explanation presented	Conclusion is confusing, missing, or off-topic
W.8.2a	Organizes complex ideas, concepts, and information to make important connections and distinctions	**Organizes ideas, concepts, and information into broader categories**	Uneven progression of ideas from beginning to end; inconsistent or unclear connections between and among ideas	Ideas have an unclear progression or seem to be randomly ordered; frequent extraneous ideas may be evident
W.8.2c	Well-chosen transitions create cohesion and clarify the relationships among ideas and concepts	**Uses appropriate and varied transitions to create cohesion and clarify the relationships among ideas and concepts**	Uses appropriate transitions to clarify the relationships among ideas and concepts	Few or no transitions used
W.8.2a	Formatting, graphics, or multimedia used are well chosen to enhance comprehension	**Includes formatting (e.g., headings), graphics, and multimedia when useful to aiding comprehension**	Formatting, graphics, or multimedia used do not significantly aid comprehension	Formatting, graphics, or multimedia used are poorly chosen, distracting, or interfere with comprehension

¹ W.8.4 is reflected in all descriptors.

(Note: Rubric is for example only. It is incomplete and may look different from actual curriculum materials.)

Teach the Vocabulary So Students Can Talk Precisely about Their Work

Vocabulary is the foundation of effective critique. To use a metaphor, if critique is like surgery, carefully cutting into a piece of work to determine what is working well and what is not, then the surgical tools are the words we use to dissect the piece. If a student can use only simple terms to describe a piece (e.g., "It's good. I like it."), it's like attempting surgery with a butter knife. Students need sharp precision in their language to be effective surgeons (e.g., "I think the narrator's voice sounds too much like a kid our age and not like someone their character's age" or "Since you are writing a cause and effect essay, you may need to use more words that show causation"). The need for precision gives students an authentic reason and immediate application for learning new vocabulary and putting it to use. Critique lessons, peer feedback, and analyzing models together are all good opportunities for students to practice using precise academic and domain-specific vocabulary.

▶ NOW THAT THEY KNOW WHAT THEY ARE AIMING FOR, WHAT'S THE BEST WAY FOR MY STUDENTS TO GET INDIVIDUAL FEEDBACK ON THEIR WORK?

Teachers give students feedback all the time. The question is, how much of this feedback is actually used by students to improve their learning? Figure 4.9 is a continuum of how a student might hear and use feedback.

Figure 4.9: Continuum of How Students Hear Feedback

Doesn't see it as feedback for him/herself. Blames other. "That teacher is mean."

⬇

Hears feedback, but ignores. Does what he/she wants to do anyway.

⬇

Hears feedback, would like to revise, but doesn't know how.

⬇

Receives feedback, revises, but does not meet the goal.

⬇

Receives feedback, revises, successfully meets the goal.

⬇

Receives feedback, revises, successfully meets goal, and can help others reach goal.

Source: Leaders of Their Own Learning: Transforming Schools through Student-Engaged Assessment. Copyright 2014 by John Wiley & Sons, Inc. All rights reserved.

Often the students most readily able to meet the final two points on the continuum in Figure 4.9 are already the most capable, skilled, and successful. "Students can't hear something that's beyond their comprehension; nor can they hear something if they are not listening or are feeling like it would be useless to listen. Because students' feelings of control and self-efficacy are involved, even well-intentioned feedback can be very destructive ('See? I knew I was stupid!'). The research on feedback shows its Jekyll-and-Hyde character. Not all studies about feedback show positive effects. The nature of the feedback and the context in which it is given matter a great deal" (Brookhart, 2008, p. 2).

In this section, we propose that you think more analytically and strategically about the nature of the feedback you provide to students and that students provide to one another through peer critique. Descriptive feedback is distinguished by these features:

» The focus is on supporting the growth of an individual student or small group, improving a particular piece of work, performance, skill, or disposition.

» Feedback is focused on the work and is connected to clear criteria that students understand.

» It is typically an exchange between teacher and student, or student and student, and (unlike a critique lesson) it is not a public learning experience for the class.

» It is nested in a long-term relationship (e.g., teacher-student, student-student, coach-player, supervisor-worker). Maintaining a constructive relationship must be an implicit focus in all feedback conversations, whether spoken or written.

» Individuals are sensitive when receiving personal feedback. It is much more likely that strategic, positive comments will result in improvements than will criticism.

» Feedback ideally flows from strong knowledge of the student—knowing the student's strengths and weaknesses, knowing where they are in their growth and what they need to spark the next step of growth.

It is most productive for students when descriptive feedback is connected to clear learning targets and helpful models, and when students have learned the language and norms of critique. In essence, when students are treated as partners in assessment from the outset, they will be in a much stronger position to make use of teacher and peer feedback.

Attending to How Feedback is Given[5]

The good news is that like every other important instructional practice, feedback can be fine-tuned and improved through careful attention to its delivery and content. This is true for both teacher and peer feedback. Importantly, as students become more proficient giving and receiving feedback, they become more independent learners.

The Tone of Feedback

How words are used matters a great deal in giving effective feedback. Feedback should be understandable and user-friendly. Similar to learning targets, feedback should be framed in language students can readily understand.

» Effective tone:

- Be positive. In particular, research has indicated that the framing of critical feedback really matters to students from historically underserved groups. Researchers Cohen, Steele, and Ross (2012) call this "wise feedback," and it entails the invocation of high standards, and an assurance that the student can meet those standards. In an interview with educator Larry Ferlazzo (2015), Zaretta Hammond offers language for giving such "wise feedback":

  ○ State your confidence in the student's ability to master this concept, process, or skill. ("I know you are a very capable student.")

  ○ Point out explicitly what the student got right and where they went wrong. ("Here is where things got off track... ")

  ○ Name specific actions the student needs to take (e.g., review the steps, learn the procedure). ("How would you fix that? Here's where I'd like you to go back and review," or "When you get to this part, rethink this move here...")

  ○ Re-affirm your belief in the student's capacity and effort to reach the target. ("You've got this.")

- Be constructive when critical; this means making suggestions, rather than pronouncements or mandates.

  ○ Acknowledge subjectivity. Adolescent students already know that what you are sharing is your opinion rather than an objective fact, and if you act like you don't know it, they may dismiss you entirely. So don't adopt a mantle of truth, but do stay grounded in the criteria for the assignment. Use evidence as you describe what you see in their work relative to the criteria, and invite them to do so as well.

» Ineffective tone:

- Finding fault

- Describing what is wrong but offering no suggestions

- Punishing or denigrating students for poor work

The Content of Feedback

Along with tone, the content of feedback is just as important. Assessment expert and author Grant Wiggins tells a useful story: "A student came up to [a teacher] at year's end and said, 'Miss Jones, you kept writing this same word on my English papers all year, and I still don't know what it means.' 'What's the word?' she asked. 'Vag-oo,' he said. (The word was *vague*!)" (Wiggins, 2012, p. 11). The following criteria for effective feedback will support students:

---

5. Based on the work of Susan Brookhart and Connie Moss (Brookhart, 2008; Moss and Brookhart, 2009).

» **Focusing on the work.** Feedback can be focused on the work or task, on the process of learning, or on the way a students self-regulate and use their thought processes to accomplish a task. It should not be focused on the student personally, and personal comments should be avoided. Feedback should always be connected to the goals for learning and be actionable, offering specific ideas for what to do next and how to improve. (For example, in Grade 8, Module 3, when students are creating graphic panels: "I feel like you might have too much information in this one panel. I wonder if dividing it into two or more panels would help you make your point more powerfully?" will be more productive and actionable than: "This looks too cluttered.")

» **Comparing work to clear criteria.** Effective feedback compares student work or performance with criteria and with past performance, benchmarks, and personal goals. Norm-referenced feedback, which compares a student's performance with that of other students, is generally not useful. It doesn't help a student improve and often damages the motivation of unsuccessful students. (For example, you might tell a student, "You met the goal you set for yourself!" versus "This is the strongest work in the class!")

» **Helping students make progress.** The function or purpose of feedback is to describe how the student has done in order to identify ways and provide information about how to improve. Evaluating or judging performance does not help students improve. (For example, providing specific feedback tied to established criteria will help a student revise a draft, as opposed to stating that the work is simply "good" or "bad" or grading work in a draft stage, which tends to shut down motivation to revise.)

"If only using 'descriptive' vs. 'evaluative' feedback were simply a matter of wordsmithing! We could all learn how to write descriptive feedback just as we learned to write descriptive paragraphs in elementary school. Unfortunately, part of the issue is how the student understands the comment. Students filter what they hear through their own past experiences, good and bad" (Brookhart, 2008, p. 24). This brings us back to the importance of fostering a strong collaborative culture and building relationships with students. There are many strategies and techniques, but unfortunately no shortcuts.

Preparing Students to Be Effective at Giving Feedback through Peer Critique

One of the most common structures for feedback and critique in classrooms is the use of peer critique. Often, teachers will ask their students to "find your writing critique partners and give them advice on their first draft" or something similar. In most cases, this practice is largely unproductive. Strategic, effective, specific feedback is a difficult enough practice for adults. For most students, it is impossible without guidance. Most of us have probably had the experience of listening in to these peer feedback conversations among our students and finding the following common challenges:

» Students who can give only general comments

» A confusing mix of copyediting (suggestions for spelling, grammar, and punctuation) with content or language suggestions. (Note: Helping students distinguish between these two types of feedback supports them in better understanding college- and career-ready Language standards about conventions and grammar and Writing standards about student thinking.)

» Students who are reluctant to call attention to aspects of peers' work that need improvement

» Students who finish their comments quickly and then engage in off-task discussions

Peer feedback can be effective when the conditions are right, when students are practiced in giving targeted feedback, and when they have clarity on the specific dimension of the work they are analyzing. Once students have learned the process of giving specific feedback effectively in these formal protocols, there is a positive phenomenon that can develop in which students begin giving one another informal critique, appropriately and respectfully, throughout the day.

The accompanying videos provide a window into how teachers and schools can harness the power of peer critique. Video Spotlight 4.3 looks at the impact of a whole-school culture of critique and revision on the quality of student work. Video Spotlight 4.4 looks at a specific protocol—Praise, Question, Suggestion—that supports giving and receiving quality feedback.

▶▶ Video Spotlight 4.3

In this video, "Peer Critique: Creating a Culture of Revision," students at Two Rivers Public Charter School, a pre-K–8 school in Washington, DC, learn to critique one anothers' work, starting at three years old. Throughout the school, the critique protocol is done as a whole class, in small groups, and in pairs. A strong culture of critique and revision is the norm.

This video was produced by Edutopia.

https://www.youtube.com/watch?v=M8FKJPpvreY

▶▶ Video Spotlight 4.4

In "Praise, Question, Suggestion," eighth-graders in Rich Richardson's class at the Expeditionary Learning Middle School in Syracuse, New York, offer feedback to their peers in preparation for revising their writing. This protocol helps students see the strengths of their work and consider questions and suggestions that will lead to revision and improvement.

https://vimeo.com/84899365

Peer Critique in the Curriculum

In the curriculum, peer critique is an integral part of scaffolding students' high-quality work, which is grounded in CCSS W.5: *Develop and strengthen writing as needed by planning, revising, editing, rewriting, or trying a new approach.* Students learn the academic vocabulary associated with peer critique, such as what "feedback" means and what it means to "improve" one's writing. They also learn the criteria for feedback: it must be kind, specific, and helpful.

Often, the teacher will model giving a student feedback and then students give one another feedback, usually based on a specific criterion from the writing rubric. Students then debrief how well they gave and received feedback, which is connected to their habits of character (e.g., using *compassion* when giving feedback; using *strengths* to help others grow). Throughout the curriculum, students use anchor charts (e.g., Criteria for Effective Text Reflection anchor chart, Criteria for an Effective Literary Summary anchor chart, Work to Contribute to a Better World anchor chart), which offer them an easy reference point for what high-quality work looks and sounds like. This groundwork is emphasized heavily the first time students engage in peer critique and then is reinforced throughout the year. Figure 4.10 shows an excerpt from a Grade 7 lesson in Module 2 that highlights these points.

Figure 4.10: Peer Critique Excerpt from Grade 7, Module 2 in which students are tuning their podcast scripts

Epidemics

Work Time

B. Tuning Protocol: Content – SL.7.4 (20 minutes)

- Review the appropriate learning target relevant to the work to be completed in this section of the lesson:

    "I can offer kind, specific and helpful feedback to my peers."

- Explain that they will now share their script with another triad to get feedback on the content. Allow several minutes for triads to determine who will read the narrative lead. (See Teaching Notes for suggestions on dividing the narrative lead.) Other sections will be read by the person who wrote the section.

- Move students into groups with their own podcast triad and another podcast triad, and invite them to label their groups A and B.

- Distribute **sticky notes**.

- Focus students on the **Work to Contribute to a Better World anchor chart**, specifically: "I use my strengths to help others grow." Remind students that as they work to critique the other triad's work, they will need to use their strengths.

- Tell students they are going to provide the other triad with kind, specific, and helpful feedback against the first three criterion on the Presentation Checklist.

- Direct students' attention to the **Peer Critique anchor chart**, and remind them of what peer critique looks and sounds like.

- Display and distribute **Directions for Tuning Protocol**, and read them aloud for the group. Invite students to ask questions to ensure that they understand the protocol. Remind them of the Tuning protocol they participated in during Unit 2.

- Tell students that for this Tuning protocol and the one in the next lesson, those students giving feedback can play the role of producers, who are responsible for giving feedback on the podcast and making sure it is the best it can possibly be. Students giving feedback should focus on the first three rows of the Presentation checklist, putting themselves in the roles of listeners and telling the presenting group whether their content is clear and engaging. Explain that in the next lesson, they will have a chance to revise their scripts in response to this feedback and prepare for a Tuning protocol based on how they present the content, focusing on the last four items of the Presentation checklist.

- Invite students to retrieve their podcast scripts and Presentation checklists, and instruct students to begin the Tuning protocol.

- Circulate to support students as they work to give feedback to one another. Emphasize that students are not to make revisions yet, as they will be doing this in the next lesson.

- Repeated routine: invite students to reflect on their progress toward the relevant learning target.

Unit 3: Lesson 9

296

▶ PUTTING STUDENTS ON THE PATH TO SUCCESS

Using models to show students what's possible can be magical. Despite the transformational power of these practices, teachers and school leaders must take care (and time) to develop the habits and skills students need to make the most of them. Nurturing a growth mindset is an essential foundation. Students must believe in their own power to improve their work; adolescent learners in particular are looking for confirmation of their newfound sense of agency. With this belief in place, the use of models, critique, and descriptive feedback will give them the skills they need to make improvements that genuinely matter to them.

With time and practice, you will experience the power of these practices both within and beyond the curriculum. Analyzing models of high-quality work and critiquing the work of peers won't be special events; they will be a key part of teaching students content and skills and engaging them in thinking critically about their progress toward quality work.

Chapter 4:
Instructional Leadership

We believe that impactful instructional leadership involves cycles of action and reflection. Here we offer questions for reflection, indicators of progress, and resources for *deeper learning in literacy*.

Table 4.6: Chapter 4 Quick Guide for Instructional Leaders: Planning for Deeper Learning in Literacy

Questions for Reflection
» How does this chapter connect to, extend, and challenge current paradigms and practices for teaching reading and writing? • What is your staff's understanding of the relationship between reading and writing? • Can you and your staff articulate the progression of the Reading and Writing standards and how they build toward college and career readiness? What additional professional learning may be necessary to reinforce the standards' emphasis on evidence? • How do teachers describe the connection between Writing for Understanding and the read-think-talk-write cycle? Is it clear that reading, thinking, and talking about text provide the fodder necessary for students' writing and that writing is another way for students to make meaning of what they read?
» How willing and comfortable are your teachers in helping students engage in rich conversation? • Do they understand the importance of student discourse? • What work have teachers done to lay the groundwork for active and collaborative classrooms where student talk can be productive and lead to new learning? • To what extent are teachers ready to talk less so that students can talk more? Do they view learning from texts and peer conversations as equally worthy?

Chapter 4

» How do teachers set expectations for high-quality student work?

- Do they need more support to use models, critique, and descriptive feedback effectively?

- What schoolwide structures can you put in place to support these practices schoolwide, beyond the curriculum?

- What is the culture of feedback in your building? In what ways do you, or could you, model giving feedback to staff that is kind, specific, and helpful? In what ways might you support staff in doing the same with one another?

Indicators of Progress

» Teachers are talking about the relationship between reading and writing, reflecting their understanding of them as connected subjects, rather than two separate subjects.

Not Yet True   *Somewhat True*   *Very True*

» Writing instruction is well integrated with reading, in lessons within and beyond the curriculum.

Not Yet True   *Somewhat True*   *Very True*

» Teachers are using the curriculum's Recommended Texts and Other Resources to help students engage with a volume of reading on the module topic.

Not Yet True   *Somewhat True*   *Very True*

» Classrooms buzz with student talk. Students have opportunities to think and talk about text before and while writing.

Not Yet True   *Somewhat True*   *Very True*

» Teachers are making time to scaffold high-quality work, using the Unit-at-a-Glance chart for every unit as a resource (but particularly Unit 3 for the performance task).

Not Yet True   *Somewhat True*   *Very True*

» Students give and receive feedback, based on models and clear criteria that help them improve their work. They can persevere through multiple drafts to create high-quality work.

Not Yet True   *Somewhat True*   *Very True*

» A schoolwide culture of feedback helps all staff see their own teaching practice as something that they can refine and improve.

Not Yet True   *Somewhat True*   *Very True*

Resources and Suggestions

» Resources available on the main EL Education website (ELeducation.org):

- Videos: https://eleducation.org/resources/collections/your-curriculum-companion-6-8-videos

- PD Pack: Leaders of Their Own Learning

» Common Core State Standards, Appendix A

» EL Education books that deepen understanding of the practices in this chapter:

- *Transformational Literacy: Making the Common Core Shift with Work That Matters*

- *Leaders of Their Own Learning: Transforming Schools through Student-Engaged Assessment*

- *The Leaders of Their Own Learning Companion: New Tools and Tips for Tackling the Common Challenges of Student-Engaged Assessment*

» Book: *Writing for Understanding: Using Backward Design to Help All Students Write Effectively* by the Vermont Writing Collaborative

» Website: Models of Excellence: The Center for High-Quality Student Work (modelsofexcellence.ELeducation.org)

» Website: Vermont Writing Collaborative (vermontwritingcollaborative.org)

» Website: Fisher & Frey Literacy for Life (fisherandfrey.com)

» Article: "Writing Undergoing Renaissance in Curricula" by Diana Leddy

» Article: "Habits Improve Classroom Discussions" by Paul Bambrick-Santoyo

» Article: "Collaborative Conversations" by Douglas Fisher and Nancy Frey

» Resources on Protocols:

- Classroom Protocols (Curriculum.ELeducation.org)

- National School Reform Faculty website (nsrfharmony.org)

- School Reform Initiative website (schoolreforminitiative.org)

Chapter 4:
Frequently Asked Questions

The shift toward reading for and writing with evidence feels important, but I miss all the stories and poems I used to read with my students and those that they would write. Is there time to bring in more stories and poems when teaching this curriculum?

Many literacy educators love fiction, and some of us may worry that the push on "evidence" has drowned out some of the sheer joy of reveling in a beautiful story or an elegantly crafted poem. In terms of our curriculum, it may reassure you to look at the grade-level Curriculum Map to see all the wonderful literature that does live in the curriculum (from *The Lightning Thief* in Grade 6 to the poetry of the Harlem Renaissance in Grade 7 to *Summer of the Mariposas* in Grade 8). One of the key ways that we enrich our content-based curriculum is by pairing literary and informational text (see Chapter 3A for more information) so that students are able to make connections to characters and communities through great literature as they learn about the world.

Where can I find more evidence-based protocols to use in my classroom?

There are many great resources for additional protocols. Once you get accustomed to how protocols work and the purposes they serve, you may wish to swap in new ones or bring them into other parts of your school day. You can find all of the protocols used throughout our curriculum on our website (http://eled.org/tools) or in our book *Management in the Active Classroom*. If you want to branch out and find totally new protocols, there are two websites worth checking out: The National School Reform Faculty (www.nsrfharmony.org) and the School Reform Initiative (www.schoolreforminitiative.org).

It's been really hard for me to "let the text do the teaching." I still find myself wanting to explain things to my students. What do you suggest?

If talking to your students about the texts they are reading, before giving them a chance to make meaning, is a habit you have been in as a teacher, one of the best ways to get into a new habit is to follow the lessons as they are written. The lessons are designed so that you talk less and students talk more so that they can learn from the text and each other. Spend some time intentionally following the lessons as written (i.e., with fidelity), and reflect on the results for you and your students.

I know it's important to give my students a chance to talk with one another about what they are reading and thinking, but they really struggle with partner and small group work. How can I make that time more productive for them?

The structures in the curriculum are designed to foster student collaboration and discourse (e.g., protocols, total participation techniques, triads) and recur over and over. The curriculum starts slow with these structures, offering guidance for introducing them and gradually building independence as time goes on. However, you know your students best. Just like anything you do in the classroom, these structures may require additional modeling, practice, feedback, and revision. Don't be afraid to take a pause, reinforce instructions or expectations, and start over if students struggle to work together independently.

Our school has used a Readers' and Writers' Workshop structure for many years. I understand that the EL Education curriculum uses the Writing for Understanding approach instead. What does this mean for me?

Many of us at EL Education also were trained in Readers' and Writers' Workshop, and there is much to value in that approach: students have tremendous choice about what they read and myriad opportunities to express their voice as they write about passion topics. However, the challenge with the typical workshop approach is that students, as readers, often may not be "reading for evidence" and building knowledge on one topic, with teacher support, over time. Similarly, as writers, students may get stuck "writing about what they know" (e.g., my favorite sport, outer space) rather than building new knowledge and then writing to communicate that knowledge. Particularly given the emphasis on building world knowledge and tackling complex text, students need more shared experiences (so they can talk with others about the text) and scaffolded experiences (so they can process their reading and apply their new understanding in their writing).

Note that students do still have some choice in their reading when they choose research reading texts. And students do still write narratives, albeit about a topic they have all been studying together (e.g., In Grade 7, Module 1 students create their own stories about a "lost child of Sudan" and the lessons revealed through their journeys). You can certainly add more free writing time if your schedule permits. But the emphasis on reading the same text and writing about the same topic is a shift toward equity; students don't have to rely on existing background knowledge or experiences, as they are all grounded in the same texts and content.

I'm interested in using models of high-quality work throughout the school day with my students, but it will probably take me at least a year to build up my own collection of high-quality work. Do you have any suggestions about where I can find strong models in the meantime?

Talking to your colleagues is a good first step. It's possible that there are others on staff who have strong examples of work that meets specific criteria. EL Education has a free online library of student work from all grade levels and content areas called Models of Excellence: The Center for High-Quality Student Work (modelsofexcellence.ELeducation.org). Work from this site can be downloaded and displayed or printed as models for your students. Ultimately, if you will be teaching the same curricula over multiple years, you will be better served by gathering your own models, but this is a good place to start. Also, the Models of Excellence website welcomes submissions of student work from teachers. If you have models that would benefit other teachers and students, please consider submitting them to the site for consideration.

How can I help my students develop a growth mindset about their work, especially their writing? So many of them feel that they just aren't good at it, and they have a hard time revising their work.

Using models and developing criteria for high-quality work with your students can be a powerful way to help them see that work isn't either *good* or *bad*, but, instead, that it meets criteria (or doesn't) in specific ways. Not every piece of work will meet all criteria equally well. When students see that there are specific ways for work to be improved, they suddenly have a path to success. Though the curriculum provides rubrics for quality writing, it may be useful to spend some additional time helping students set goals related to the rubrics that help them put the criteria in their own words. This can help them more easily see ways to improve their work. It will also be important for you to monitor the language you use when you give students feedback. It's important that they hear messages that emphasize their effort, such as "I like how you kept at this and used your feedback buddy's suggestion here," versus messages that make them feel that they did either a bad or good job, such as "needs work." The latter doesn't give them any information about how to revise their work now or in the future.

How can I help my middle school students give one another more meaningful feedback?

Just like high-quality student work can serve as a model that helps students improve their own work, models of peer feedback, followed by feedback and revision of the process, will help students improve their ability to give meaningful feedback. Adolescent learners' sensitivity to social interaction adds a layer of complexity; students in these grades are especially attuned to how feedback lands, and they need criteria, practice, and support to do it well. Often a Fishbowl protocol is a useful place to start. With two volunteers giving peer feedback in the middle, students around the outside can observe their process and then provide feedback about its quality (e.g., "I like how Isabel gave a specific comment about maybe choosing a different transition phrase between paragraphs," "Carmen's comment 'I really liked it' won't give Micah a good idea of how to improve. Maybe next time she could use the checklist to point out the things Micah did well and say if anything is missing from the checklist in his paragraph"). For another example of a protocol that helps students give kind, specific, and helpful feedback, see the video "Praise, Question, Suggestion" (vimeo.com/84899365), which is highlighted in Video Spotlight 4.4.

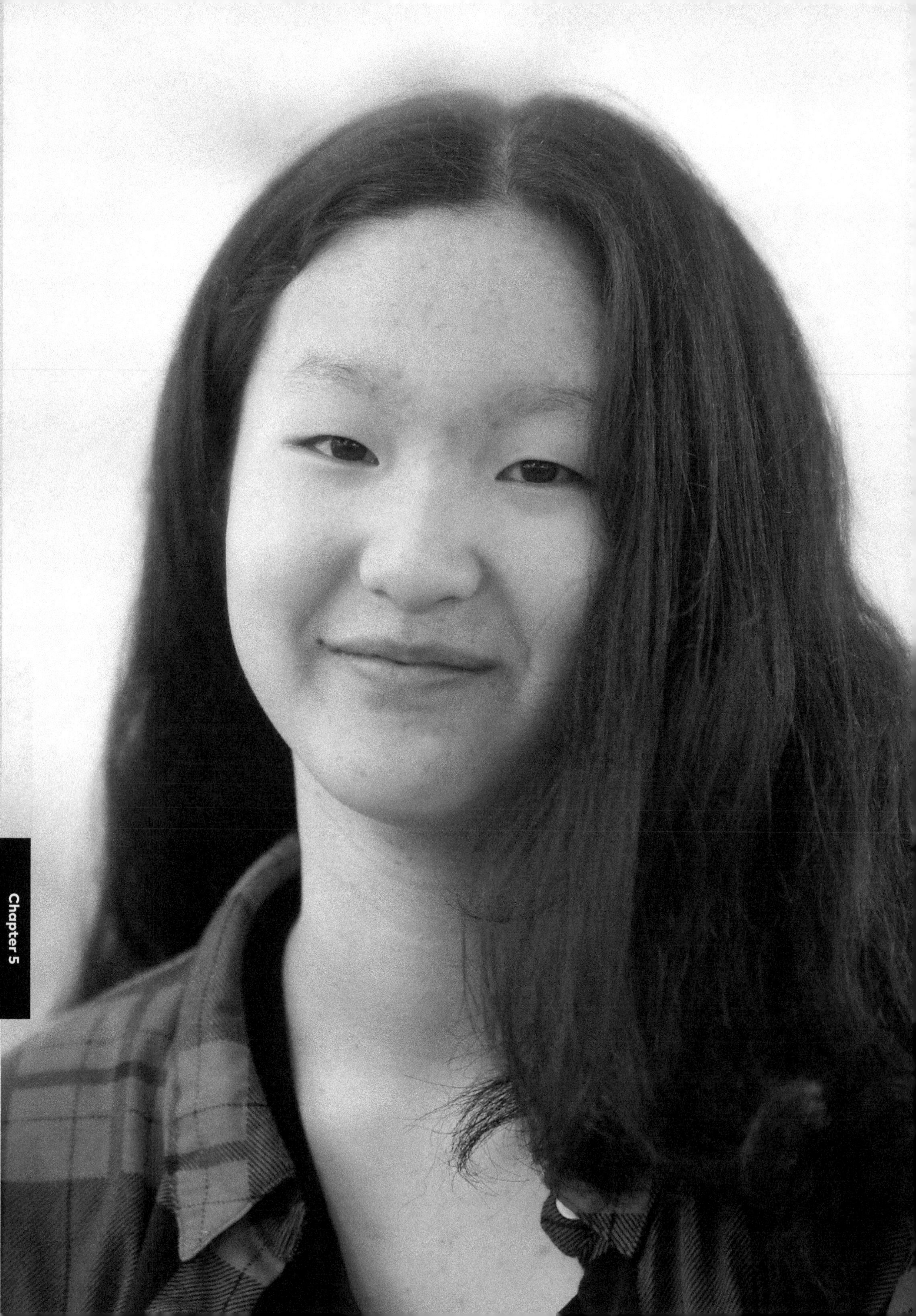

Chapter 5:
Supporting All Students

Chapter 5A:
Supporting Students to Meet Grade-Level Expectations

This curriculum was designed for *all* of your students. As a central part of our mission, EL Education is focused on equity and ensuring that all students have the opportunity to learn and master rigorous content that prepares them for the future. This means that all students must be held to the same high expectations and given the support they need to meet them. It also means that students who need additional challenges must be given meaningful opportunities for extensions.

Much of our curriculum is inherently supportive of students' varied learning needs. From highly scaffolded close reading lessons to discussion protocols that give students "oral rehearsal" before writing, to extensions that build new skills and offer students engaging and empowering challenges, all students have a real chance to succeed. That said, some students or groups of students may need additional scaffolds and supports, either within the flow of daily English language arts (ELA) lessons or during additional intervention time. Still others may need additional challenges and opportunities in order to keep them engaged and enriched. In this chapter, we take a close look at how the curriculum supports students with a variety of learning needs. Chapter 5C focuses specifically on supporting English language learners (ELLs).

▶ HOW CAN I SUPPORT VARIED LEARNING NEEDS IN A HETEROGENEOUS CLASSROOM (AND WHY IS THAT SO IMPORTANT)?

Students excel in diverse and inclusive settings. Our curriculum is designed for heterogeneous classrooms with students of all ability levels. We take the educational and philosophical position that heterogeneous classrooms are the best, most equitable learning environments for most students. Too often, students—particularly those who have been most impacted by learning opportunity gaps and systemic inequities throughout our social institutions—are sidelined into classes that do not challenge them, surrounded by peers who may need support to meet grade-level expectations. Once there, it is difficult for those students to successfully access grade-level content and meet grade-level benchmarks. We believe that strategic scaffolding within heterogeneous classrooms and, when necessary, additional intervention time, is the best way to help all students stay on pace for college- and career-readiness and achieve their full potential.

Students who already excel in school—those labeled "advanced learners" or "gifted and talented" in many settings—also benefit from heterogeneous classrooms. These students typically conform well to the systems and structures of the school environment. They meet expectations for homework completion and perform well on assessments. However, those students who are successful at "doing school" can be risk-averse in their academic thinking and their approach to work completion (in order to get good grades), and often conform to standard academic perspectives. Schools also have a less-recognized talent pool: students who may not be top performers on assessments, but who are savvy and sophisticated thinkers with fresh and compelling ideas and perspectives. When students labeled as advanced learners based on assessment scores are separated from other students, they miss out on the opportunity to hear and learn from peers who challenge their assumptions and provide new perspectives and ways of thinking. Just because a student may struggle to read doesn't mean they struggle to think. Our curriculum is designed to give students plenty of time to talk to and learn from one another, making heterogeneous classrooms that much more important.

How Do the Principles of Universal Design for Learning Support All Students within a Heterogeneous Classroom[1]?

Students learn from one another—and learn to respect one another—when they learn together in the same classroom. At the same time, students sometimes have needs that require various types of differentiation (e.g., scaffolding, specialized instructional approaches). Our curriculum is based on an inclusive model and provides supports and resources for differentiation based on Universal Design for Learning (UDL). UDL, which was developed by David Rose, Anne Meyer, and their colleagues from the Center for Applied Special Technology, is based on the science of neurodiversity. Instead of focusing on learner deficits as a challenge to overcome, UDL sees learner variability as a strength to be leveraged.

Designing a curriculum based on the UDL framework means that it is designed from the outset to meet the learning needs of all students and give them all an equal chance to succeed. UDL offers flexibility in the ways in which students access and engage with material, and show what they know. This approach to curriculum design helps all students learn, not just those who may have learning disabilities or other learning challenges. This universal approach cuts down on (though doesn't necessarily eliminate) the need to retroactively reteach or otherwise adapt learning experiences for those students who may need additional support.

The UDL framework for learning emerged from a similar concept in architecture. Universal design in architecture means that buildings are designed to accommodate—from the outset— the physical needs of all people. Rather than retrofitting the staircase entry to a building with a wheelchair ramp, for example, architects employing universal design would use landscaping and other design elements to eliminate the need for stairs altogether. An entry without stairs helps people in wheelchairs, but it also helps all people access the building more easily (e.g., those with strollers, luggage). We encounter universal design often in everyday life (e.g., closed captioning, automatic doors). These accommodations, which support people with disabilities, are also useful and supportive for many people and for many reasons.

UDL consists of three broad principles, which are aligned with three networks in the brain that guide learning.

Universal Design for Learning Principle 1: Provide Multiple Means of Representation

Learners differ in the ways in which they perceive and comprehend information that is presented to them. Offering information in more than one format (e.g., text, audio, visual) provides options that will suit the variety of learners in your classroom. There is not one means of representation that will be optimal for all learners.

---

1. This information on Universal Design for Learning comes from The National Center on Universal Design for Learning and Understood.org.

How does this principle show up in the design of our curriculum?

» When teachers introduce a new protocol or activity, in addition to verbalizing the instructions, we also suggest creating a chart with each step and, additionally, selecting a pair of students to model the procedure.

» Lessons will periodically point you to audiobook versions of texts to support students who would benefit from audio as a complement to their reading. Similarly, the Teaching Notes of lessons will also guide you to read certain texts or portions of text aloud.

» Texts are sometimes paired with films or documentaries. For example, in Grade 7, Module 1, the text *A Long Walk to Water* is paired with the documentary *God Grew Tired of Us*; in Grade 6, Module 1, the text *The Lightning Thief* is paired with the feature film *Percy Jackson and the Olympians: The Lightning Thief*.

» Protocols such as Gallery Walks or Infer the Topic, which require students to explore a series of related artifacts, feature a range of types of artifacts for students to explore (e.g., text, photographs, video, drawings).

Universal Design for Learning Principle 2: Provide Multiple Means of Action and Expression

Learners differ in the ways in which they navigate a learning environment and express what they know. Some may be able to express themselves well in written text but not speech, and vice versa. Students will benefit from being offered more than one way to interact with classroom materials and show what they have learned (e.g., taking a test, giving an oral presentation). A variety of means of action and expression will best serve the diversity of learners in any classroom.

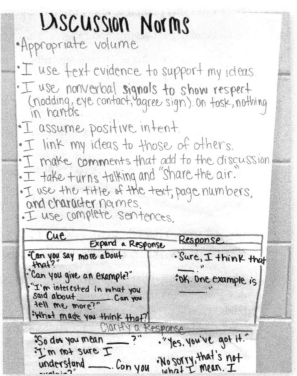

Anchor charts are used frequently to provide visual reminders of everything from norms to procedures to criteria for high-quality work. Here a class has created an anchor chart that combines their co-created discussion norms with select Conversation Cues (see Chapter 5C for more on Conversation Cues).

How does this principle show up in the design of our curriculum?

» Protocols are a common way that we incorporate movement into the lessons in our curriculum, and we encourage you to swap in more movement-oriented protocols (if they serve the same purpose as the protocols identified in the lessons) when your students could benefit from more or different kinds of movement.

» Students are offered choices in the way they present information. For example, in the Grade 8, Module 2 performance task, students have the choice to present their argument in the form of a podcast rather than a presentation; in the Grade 6, Module 2 performance task (which is a solution symposium), students have the option to create a physical model for their display that guests can touch and hold, rather than more standard two-dimensional visuals.

» Other, more nuanced kinds of kinesthetic activities are equally supportive of students' varying needs. For example, a lesson's Teaching Notes may suggest that instead of simply filling in a note-catcher, students may complete the cells of the note-catcher on separate cards or sticky notes and paste them into the correct location on the note-catcher.

Universal Design for Learning Principle 3: Provide Multiple Means of Engagement

Affect represents a crucial element to learning, and students differ markedly in the ways in which they can be engaged or motivated to learn. Some learners are highly engaged by spontaneity and novelty, for example, while others are disengaged, even frightened, by those aspects, preferring strict routine. It is important, whenever possible, to offer students choices and to help them see how their academic work is relevant to their lives. Because students will be motivated and engaged by different things, it is essential to provide multiple means of engagement.

How does this principle show up in the design of our curriculum?

» Ongoing goal-setting and reflection after each assessment

» Frequent collaboration on everything from brief protocols to extended performance tasks

» Students often have a choice in how they read texts. In order to build empowerment and engagement in learning, students may be given choices that include the following: another fluent reader (including students or an audiobook) reads aloud to the whole class, small groups, triads, or pairs; individuals read silently; or a combination of any of these.

Building the curriculum based on the principles of UDL is only one piece of the puzzle of supporting all students to succeed. What's most important is that you build on the foundation of the curriculum's design with instructional decisions that best meet the ever-changing needs of your students. We will explore additional scaffolds later in this chapter.

How Does the EL Education Tier I Core Curriculum Support All Students within a Heterogeneous Classroom?

The EL Education Language Arts Curriculum is a Tier I core curriculum, meaning that it is designed for an inclusive general education classroom. Designed based on the principles of UDL, it challenges and engages all students, and includes support for students to meet grade-level standards and extensions for students ready for more challenge. To understand what the curriculum is and isn't designed to do, it may help to reground in the three tiers of Response to Intervention (RTI) used in many schools and systems:

» **Tier I – Core/Primary-level instruction:** High-quality instructional practices that meet the needs of most students within the regular classroom setting. This level includes ongoing assessment, differentiated learning activities, accommodations to ensure all students access to the curriculum, and problem solving to address behavioral challenges. Tier 1 is often referred to as "core" instruction.

» **Tier II/Secondary-level interventions:** Evidence-based practices that usually take place in small groups for specific periods of time beyond core instruction time outside of the regular classroom. These interventions are focused on addressing students' learning and behavioral challenges that did not respond to the primary interventions. Tier II interventions may be used, for example, to extend instruction on vocabulary or phonemic awareness or to make time for a higher volume of independent reading. (Note: We detail this level of intervention in the second half of Chapter 5A.)

» **Tier III/Tertiary-level interventions:** The most intensive interventions are individualized for students who do not respond to secondary interventions. Students who do not progress at Tier II are then considered for an evaluation of memory, intellectual processing, speech, sensory-motor, or other disorders that may qualify them for special education services. The information collected during the Tiers I and II interventions is used to assist in making decisions regarding special education services in Tier III.

Figure 5.1 shows a variety of instructional approaches and interventions that correspond to these three tiers. At the base of the triangle is the core classroom where most students' needs will be met through scaffolds and extensions in response to ongoing formative assessment by teachers.

As you move to the top of the triangle, students with greater needs may receive additional interventions, and at the very top, some students—very few—may need an alternative program.

Figure 5.1: Instructional Approaches and Interventions

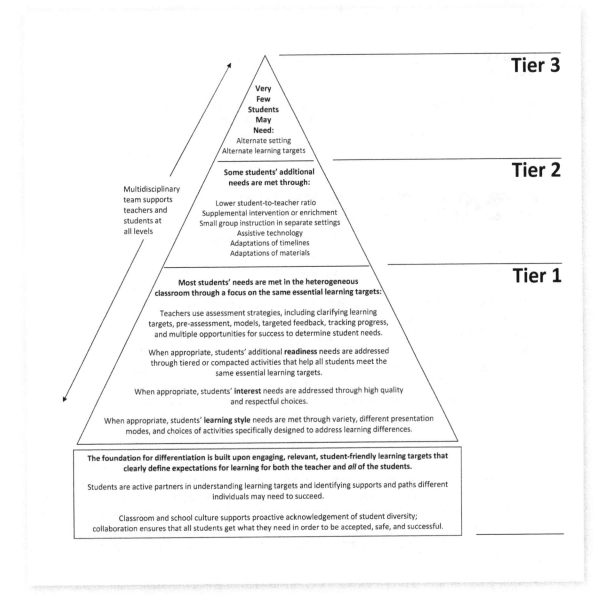

★ **How Is Response to Intervention (RTI) related to the Multi-Tier System of Support (MTSS)?**

The Multi-Tier System of Support (MTSS) is a similar framework to RTI that many schools and districts use to screen students, provide multiple tiers of instruction and support, and collect data to inform instruction. Both frameworks have student support as their primary goal; what differentiates MTSS from RTI is that MTSS is more comprehensive, encompassing the instructional supports of RTI, as well as social and emotional supports for students, including behavior intervention plans, and professional learning for teachers. RTI nests within the MTSS framework, and both are useful for thinking about how best to support students (for more information about MTSS go to u.org/MTSS).

Chapter 5

We have designed the curriculum to be as supportive of the variety of learning needs in your classroom as possible. That said, there will always be students who can benefit from different kinds of support, some of which are built into the lessons and some of which are not. For the remainder of Chapter 5A we explore flexible grouping, differentiation, and scaffolding that you can employ during lessons, as well as interventions that may need to happen beyond ELA lessons.

How Will Flexible Grouping Support My Students and Promote Their Growth?

Within a heterogeneous classroom, flexible grouping is essential. Flexible grouping is a strategy for creating groups that are, by definition, temporary. Students are grouped for specific purposes—perhaps for a day, perhaps for a week or more—and then regrouped based on new needs or assessment data. Once grouped, teachers can more effectively differentiate instruction and student materials (see box: What is Differentiation?).

★ What Is Differentiation?

According to Merriam-Webster's dictionary, to *differentiate* means "to make (someone or something) different in some way"; and "to see or state the difference or differences between two or more things." Both definitions strongly apply in an effective classroom. In differentiated classrooms, teachers are able to recognize and describe the differences among the learners in front of them and apply that knowledge to instruction. Recognizing the neurodiversity of their students, teachers select different instructional approaches and paths depending on the varying needs of the individual students in the classroom. This approach allows each student to work toward the same high standards regardless of learning needs. Differentiation is necessary because every classroom is full of different learners—some may have disabilities and special learning needs, some may advance quickly through their studies and need additional challenges, some may be learning English, and some may be a few or all of those at once.[2]

The needs that determine groups may be learning needs or, sometimes, social-emotional needs. We consider flexible grouping an important practice because not all students progress at the same pace in all skill areas (the same student may be above grade level as a reader, for example, and below grade level as a writer), and because students don't necessarily progress on pace with peers. Students should be continuously assessed, and groups should be created dynamically based on instructional needs. Keeping students in static groups can inhibit their growth and, often, their confidence.

Flexible grouping makes the protocols, which are used throughout the curriculum, more effective. Most protocols simply won't work if students are grouped by ability level, unless there is a very specific supportive purpose for doing so (see following paragraph). In most cases, protocols require a diversity of skill and confidence levels because students need to be able to talk to one another and make meaning of text and content. If all students in a group need support, it will be difficult for them to make progress. Similarly, if all students in a group are advanced readers, for example, they will miss out on the good thinking of their peers who may be able to offer opposing views and challenge their thinking in healthy ways. All students get valuable insights and learning from their peers, more than they can get from the text alone. When protocols enable students to engage in deep dialogue with their peers, students develop stronger speaking and listening skills, are able to understand the text more deeply with the support of their peers, and can more easily make meaning of what they are reading.

---

2. This definition is adapted from our 2016 book *Learning That Lasts: Challenging, Engaging, and Empowering Students with Deeper Instruction*.

Flexible grouping is used throughout the curriculum—suggestions are provided in the Teaching Notes of lessons. Typically students will be strategically paired for partner work, with at least one strong reader per pair. ELLs may be strategically paired, or grouped, at times with students who are more proficient at a specific aspect of English language use (e.g., academic writing, informal conversation), and at other times with students close to their own English proficiency level or by home language, depending on the purpose of the collaborative work. In a partnership where one student is more proficient with oral language, for example, that student may get practice with the skills of initiating discussions and asking good questions, while their partner benefits from hearing a peer's proficient speech and can experiment with adopting what they hear in their own spoken and written language. Much more detail on supporting ELLs follows in Chapter 5C.

How Do Differentiation and Scaffolding Promote Equity in a Heterogeneous Classroom?

We know from experience that there are two big temptations for teachers when they are faced with students who are struggling to make progress. The first temptation is to change the learning targets (i.e., standards). And the second is to change the texts. Teachers are tempted to make these changes out of love; no one wants to see their students frustrated or stuck. However, these changes can have a tragic, unintended consequence: if we change the learning targets (which are tied to standards) and the texts (which are selected to help students engage in the topic and meet those standards), then students who are behind will never catch up to their grade-level peers.

Instead, what we hope will become a guiding light for teachers using our curriculum is the moral imperative to lift *all* students to the same learning targets and complex texts through differentiated instruction and strategic scaffolding *during* lessons and, in some cases, additional interventions, so that they are college- and career-ready when they graduate from high school. Teachers often wrestle with two difficult truths that coexist in the classroom: the fact that all students deserve the same chance to succeed, and the reality that it's not always easy to provide the same opportunities equally in classrooms with twenty-five or more unique sets of needs facing them every day.

We understand this reality—all of us who have been involved with the creation of the curriculum and this book are either current or former teachers. We have tried to provide as many tools as possible through the design of the curriculum and its supportive resources, along with the material in this book, to lighten the load, and for the remainder of this chapter we will explore those supports.

Supporting All Students to Meet the Same Learning Targets

Learning targets—goals for lessons, derived from standards and written in student-friendly language beginning with the stem "I can"—empower students to identify where they are headed with their learning and track their progress in any given lesson or arc of lessons.[3] One of the principles of differentiation is that teachers should differentiate the *process* of learning but not the *content*. Differentiating the learning process includes all of the varied instructional strategies, activities, tools, and resources that help students meet required standards—knowledge, skills, concepts, and habits—that teachers want all students to learn. This means that learning targets remain consistent for all students (with the possible exception of students working toward an IEP-based diploma that calls for curriculum modifications, or for those participating in other alternative pathways).

It may help to imagine us behind the scenes scaffolding the learning targets without actually changing them. Based on learning targets, we create suggested scaffolds and student-facing materials (found in each lesson's Teaching Notes and the Teacher's Guide for English Language Learners) like those in the following examples:

---

3. Learning targets are explored in depth in Chapter 2B.

» **Learning target:** *I can infer the topic of this module from the resources.*

- **All students** will explore the anchor text and materials related to the module topic and take notes on a note-catcher. Based on UDL, the materials students explore are varied—audio, visual, text, etc.

- **Most students** will meet be supported in meeting this learning target by using a blank note-catcher with no scaffolding (look ahead to Figure 5.3 for an example).

- **Some students** will be supported in meeting this learning target by using a scaffolded note-catcher with prompts and questions (look ahead to Figure 5.4 for an example).

  ○ **A scaffolded learning target** might look like this: [*Using a scaffolded note-catcher with prompts and questions to guide my exploration,*] *I can infer the topic of this module from the resources.*

- **Some students** who need additional challenge are invited to go on an inferring hunt through the first paragraph of each chapter of the book and asked to infer what the chapter will be about using evidence from the text to support their analysis.

  ○ **A learning target with an extension** might look like this: [*Using the blank note-catcher and sticky notes for additional chapter-by-chapter inferences*] *I can infer the topic of this module from the resources.*

The bracketing in the preceding examples represents teacher decision making and implementation of differentiated activities and tasks. *We don't include scaffolded learning targets like these in the curriculum*; we are only showing them here to demonstrate how learning targets, and associated tasks, can be scaffolded without changing the expectations for students or limiting their opportunities to meet standards.

Our curriculum includes scaffolded materials to support all students to meet the same learning targets. You can find these in the Teacher's Guide for English Language Learners: scaffolded note-catchers, exit tickets, and other materials that will support students, *not just ELLs*, who may benefit from scaffolding that enables them do their strongest thinking without getting tripped up by language production. We encourage you to use these differentiated resources with any and all students who would benefit.

Note, too, that the students receiving the challenge-level extension in the example above are not given *additional* work to complete but are provided with *more complex* work that invites them to stretch. By ensuring that all students are productively challenged, teachers maximize learning for everyone. (Much more on supporting students who need additional challenge is provided in Chapter 5B.)

Providing scaffolds for students to meet the same learning targets as their peers allows every student to participate in the learning environment in the classroom and, importantly, to meet standards. Remember, just because a student struggles to read doesn't mean they struggle to think. They shouldn't be disengaged from the opportunity to contribute to rich conversations about important academic content because of lowered expectations. They should have the opportunity to meet the same expectations with a different pathway if necessary. A different set of expectations is likely to leave them unchallenged, disengaged, and unempowered.

Supporting All Students to Read the Same Challenging Texts

As we explored in Chapter 1B, the Four T's of our curriculum—topic, tasks, targets, and texts—have been carefully knit together to create cohesive and meaningful learning experiences for students. The texts in our curriculum engage students in the topic and build their content knowledge; they also provide students with opportunities to master standards (targets) (e.g., when working on CCSS RI.5 related to text structure, the text must feature a structure that's worthy of analysis). This accrued skill and knowledge allows students to complete the tasks.

Because of the intricate way in which the Four T's interact with one another throughout each module, it is critical that teachers not switch the texts, even for students who may struggle to read them. If any one text is removed, the design of the module will unravel.

In addition to being critical to the design of the curriculum and the way that students build knowledge of module content, supporting all students to read the same challenging texts is also a critical equity issue. *All* students deserve equal access to the same grade-level texts. If we provide students who are not making meaning from a grade-level text a text that is at a lower level, instead of supporting them to read the grade-level text, they will be denied access to the skills and knowledge available through the curriculum. If this continues to happen, they will get caught in a vicious cycle where they will have less and less opportunity for rigorous and meaningful learning to prepare them for the future.

If students can learn to read and understand complex texts independently, they are far more likely to succeed in college and career. A 2006 American College Testing Service study, Reading between the Lines, states, "The clearest differentiator in [college performance] was students' ability to answer questions associated with complex texts. . . . These findings held for male and female students, students from all racial/ethnic groups, and students from families with widely varying incomes" (2006, p. 2). "Although K–12 text difficulty has decreased over the years, college-level texts have not. Succeeding with complex texts is, in many ways, an equalizer with the potential to make college and workplace success a reality for many more students" (Berger, Woodfin, Plaut, and Dobbertin, p. 181).

The solution is to differentiate reading experiences for students so they all have access to the same challenging and compelling texts. We explore specific differentiation strategies in the pages that follow.

► WHAT ARE THE BEST WAYS TO DIFFERENTIATE AND SCAFFOLD WHEN TEACHING LESSONS?

It may be easy to assume when teaching a curriculum like ours, which is built out to the minute and designed for an entire school year, that there isn't much room for teacher discretion. This is far from the truth. As we stated in Chapter 1, this is a *thinking teacher's curriculum*. Some of the most important work you can do as you prepare to teach each module, unit, and especially each lesson, is to consider the unique needs of your students so that you can plan how to scaffold and differentiate appropriately. The Teaching Notes for each lesson, along with the Teacher's Guide for English Language Learners (which is a useful tool for supporting *all* of your students, not just ELLs) are key resources to guide your work. Table 5.1 highlights some of the key do's and don'ts for supporting students' needs.

Table 5.1: The Do's and Don'ts of Supporting Students' Needs

For Students Who Need Additional Support...	
DO	**DON'T**
Chunk the text to make the amount of challenging text more manageable.	Change the text to a less challenging text.
Sparingly pre-teach vocabulary if student(s) are unlikely to figure out the meaning in context.	Pre-teach too much of the vocabulary if student(s) can grapple with it productively and figure out the meaning in context.
Provide sentence frames for conversation.	Allow students to be silent or passive.
Let students dictate text to you if they are working toward mastery of a Reading standard.	Let students dictate text to you if they are working toward mastery of a Writing standard.
Group students strategically.	Allow stronger students to do all or most of the work in a group.
Group flexibly based on assessments of progress.	Create static groups that are not responsive to assessments of progress.

★ What's the difference between scaffolding and accommodations or modifications?

Scaffolding: A scaffold is simply a way to support all students with specific learning needs with additional supports that help them meet learning targets. Scaffolds are distinct from accommodations or modifications.

Accommodation: An accommodation is similar in concept to a scaffold, but is usually a legally mandated instructional requirement. For example, many states give the accommodation of "extra time" for ELLs or students with disabilities on summative tests.

Modification: A modification goes deeper than a scaffold or accommodation and changes the actual content and/or learning standards for students. For example, a student may require an individual education program that mandates modifications to the curriculum, such as an eighth-grade student who needs direct instruction to help them master elementary-level multiplication facts.

Many—but not all—of the scaffolds described in the pages that follow appear in lessons throughout our curriculum; however, every scaffold doesn't appear in every lesson. Part of your decision-making process as you prepare to teach each lesson should be to consider which scaffolds will be most appropriate for which students. If a scaffold isn't already built into a lesson and you have a student or students who would benefit from it, consider how you can integrate it into the lesson.

> *"As a critical thinker, I'm compelled to adjust the lesson to meet the needs of my students... The great thing about the modules is that the lesson plans, student work, and student texts are already prepared, so my planning time is spent planning the differentiated materials for my students."*

Teacher
Rochester, New York

Scaffolding Reading

One of the key tenets of scaffolding reading is "doing more with less." Shorter chunks of text can enable all students to participate to the best of their ability and enable teachers to closely monitor and assess progress. In some ways, the anchor texts in our curriculum are already scaffolded in this way. Students read excerpts of anchor texts during class and are expected to read any remaining text for homework. However, as every teacher knows, not every student will complete reading assigned for homework; therefore, the excerpts that are critical to students' ability to understand the topic, complete tasks, and meet standards are read together during class.

This same principle can apply to texts of any length. If a lesson calls for students to read an entire article, for example, you may choose to have some students read only portions. It is important to choose chunks of text that allow students to stay on pace with the lesson's learning targets. Shorter, more targeted chunks of text are preferable to asking students to read longer texts from which they will struggle to make meaning.

Scaffolding techniques to support students' reading:

» For students who might get overwhelmed by seeing the whole text on a page, format the text into "bite-sized" pieces (e.g., one paragraph at a time on index cards or one page as a separate handout).

» Have students read with a buddy.

» Have small groups read with you or another teacher (or via technology).

» Provide structured overviews for some sections of text.

» Predetermine importance for selections of text, and highlight those for students.

» Reformat texts to include more embedded definitions or even picture cues.

» Provide the text to students in a clear format, either on a handout or displayed clearly via technology.

Scaffolding Questions

One of the most common ways in which questions are scaffolded in our curriculum is by offering students sentence frames or partially completed note-catchers from which they can build their responses. These clues give students a place to start, and, when well designed, don't take away their opportunity to do their own thinking about the concepts in the lesson or practice the skills called for by the standards. Figure 5.2 shows a portion of an entrance ticket from Grade 7, Module 2. The entrance ticket for this lesson without scaffolding simply contains the question and blank lines. The scaffolded entrance ticket shown in the figure, which can be found in the Teacher's Guide for English Language Learners, contains sentence starters and key vocabulary.

Figure 5.2: Scaffolded Entrance Ticket with Sentence Starters and Key Vocabulary

Grade 7: Module 2: Unit 1: Lesson 3

What were some of the habits of character or mindsets that allowed John Graunt to make the discoveries he did? Use evidence from the text to support your response.

John Graunt showed

when he

The author writes,

Remember:

• Narration: tells a story

• Informational/Explanatory: gives information or explains

• Descriptive: describes or tells what something looks or is like

• Comparison: tells how things are the same and different

• Process: tells steps for doing something

• Argument: tells and supports one or more opinions

The video in Video Spotlight 5.1, though not from a lesson in our curriculum, is a great example of not only scaffolding an article and its questions, but also of an effective collaboration between a content-area teacher and an ELL teacher to best support student needs. Science teacher Peter Hill creates two versions of a complex scientific article for his eighth-graders: one is the original article, plus separate questions; the other is an article that he has chunked and interspersed with the questions. Students are able to choose the format that will be most supportive for them (which, not incidentally, is also highly supportive of middle school learners' need to make their own independent decisions).

In "Reading and Thinking Like Scientists," science teacher Peter Hill, from King Middle School in Portland, Maine, carefully guides his eighth-graders through a challenging scientific text on electricity. Working with the school's ELL teacher, Hill scaffolds his lesson, including the materials, to best support his students.

vimeo.com/117019945

Scaffolding techniques to support students in answering questions:

» Tackle small sections at a time.

» Once students have tried the task, provide additional modeling for those who need it.

» Provide sentence stems or frames.

» Highlight key ideas/details in the text.

» Modify graphic organizers to include picture cues or additional step-by-step directions.

» Post directions and anchor charts.

» Provide "hint cards" that give students more support with text-dependent questions (students access these only when they get stuck).

» Indicate where students may find key information in the text or on an anchor chart by marking with sticky notes or highlights.

» Give options for responding to questions with drawing, drama, or discussion before writing.

» During group work, some students may work with the teacher.

Scaffolding Writing

As already discussed in Chapter 4, one of the ways that our curriculum scaffolds writing is by asking students to think and talk as preparation for writing. Cycles of reading, thinking, and talking about text are highly supportive of students' writing, particularly students who may need additional support. This is as true for preparation for shorter writing pieces like note-catchers as it is for more formal writing. A Turn and Talk may be sufficient to support students in filling in a note-catcher, while a more formal protocol like a Socratic Seminar might be most supportive as preparation for an argument essay.

Similar to the common scaffolds used to support students in answering questions, sentence starters and modified graphic organizers are also commonly used to scaffold writing. Figures 5.3 and 5.4 show two note-catchers for the same lesson. In the Teaching Notes for this lesson, teachers will find the following, along with the black triangle symbol: "Note there is a differentiated version of the 'Infer the Topic: I Notice/I Wonder note-catcher' used in Work Time A in the separate Teacher's Guide for English Language Learners." Figure 5.3 doesn't include any scaffolding. Figure 5.4, which is found in the Teacher's Guide for English Language Learners (and can be used to support any student), includes icons for the headings "I Notice" and "I Wonder" and questions to prompt students as they fill in the note-catcher.

Chapter 5

Scaffolding techniques to support students' with their writing:

» Modify graphic organizers to include picture cues or additional step-by-step directions.

» Provide sentence starters and sentence frames.

» Use discussion, including Conversation Cues (see Chapter 2C), to help students orally rehearse their answers before responding in writing.

» Model writing using a similar prompt or a different section of the text.

» During small group work, some students may work with the teacher.

» Some students may need more frequent conferring with the teacher.

Figures 5.3–5.4: Note-Catcher without Scaffolding and Note-Catcher with Scaffolding

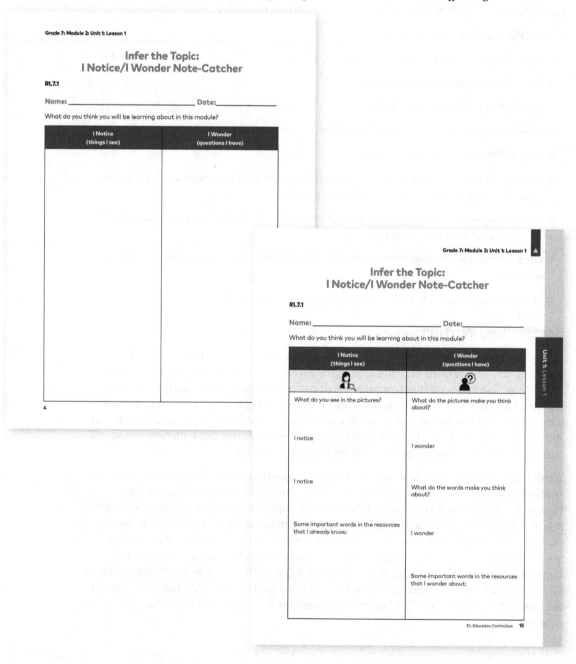

Scaffolding Collaborative Work

We place a high value on collaborative work. However, it's not easy for all students to work with their peers effectively. Just as with academic work, some students will be more positive and productive group members if they have appropriate scaffolding. Chapter 2C is an excellent resource for building a positive classroom culture that will set students up for success with collaborative work. Some students—many, in fact—also will benefit from additional scaffolding to make this work most successful. If you have time, one of the most effective strategies is to model what productive group work looks like and sounds like. Middle school students are especially receptive to playful modeling of what *not* to do in addition to what they should do.

Scaffolding techniques to support students with collaborative group work:

» Review norms for collaboration in advance and after group work.

» Have small groups work with a teacher.

» Form heterogeneous pairs (strategic partnerships).

» Monitor specific students more strategically (e.g., seat them closer to a teacher).

» Provide (and model) structured roles for group members.

Scaffolding Homework

Homework has long been a controversial topic. For a variety of reasons, many of which are beyond a student's control, some students will struggle to complete homework independently at home. For this reason, the most effective scaffold for homework is, arguably, to expect students to complete less of it. Assign targeted and meaningful homework, but don't ask students to practice the same skill over and over—for too many students, this will be a recipe for failure. When homework is assigned, many of the scaffolds already reviewed in this section are just as useful for homework as they are for in-class work.

Scaffolding techniques to support students' with homework:

» Provide students with read-alouds via technology (e.g., audiobooks).

» Provide picture cues or additional directions.

» Provide sentence starters or sentence frames.

» Provide video or slides of class examples on a website.

» Modify expectations of quantity.

▶ WHAT ADDITIONAL INTERVENTIONS MAY BE NEEDED BEYOND LESSONS?

Our curriculum was designed to help teachers build students' capacity to read, think, talk, and write about complex texts. The Grades 6–8 modules fully address college- and career-ready ELA standards: the reading standards for both literary and informational texts; the Writing standards; the Speaking and Listening standards; and the Language standards. However, the 45-minute module lessons alone may not provide enough time for all students to comprehensively practice the skills required to achieve mastery of the ELA standards in the module assessments. To ensure that students receive adequate support and practice, as well as sufficient time to read a "volume of reading," additional interventions may be necessary to support, reinforce, and provide additional practice of the skills learned in the ELA modules.

In this part of Chapter 5A, we focus on helping school leaders, instructional coaches, general education teachers, special education teachers, and intervention teachers think about and plan for strategic ways to use additional support time beyond the typical ELA block. The suggestions here could certainly be applied to all learners, but are targeted particularly for students who aren't yet meeting grade-level expectations during a standard class period.

The activities and examples described here are optional and supplemental and designed to be used during additional time in the school day (e.g., during an intervention period or resource support). These activities are not intended to replace ELA module instruction or to fully address all standards. We offer suggestions that you can adapt to meet the specific needs of your students needing additional support. You will need to use your professional judgment and knowledge of the abilities of your particular students to focus this additional ELA practice and instruction where it is required, and to adapt the activities and examples accordingly.

Depending on your school and system, there are myriad ways that students may be offered additional intervention time. Some students may have support in place through special education services. In some schools, an extended ELA block of 60–90 minutes gives teachers flexibility to offer interventions in the classroom to individual students or small groups. These students may be identified through their assessment data (see Chapter 6 for more information), or they may already be identified through special education, 504, or other programs (see box: A Strengths-Based Approach to Supporting Students with Learning Disabilities for more information). In any case, we recommend, whenever possible, that support, whether provided by regular classroom teachers or specialists, is "pushed in" to the classroom rather than having students pulled out for support. This enables module content to be well understood and supported by all teachers involved and for students to be fully integrated into the life of the classroom.

A Strengths-Based Approach to Supporting Students with Learning Disabilities[4]

"Learning disabilities (LDs) are real. They affect the brain's ability to receive, process, store, respond to, and communicate information. LDs are actually a group of disorders, not a single disorder. Learning disabilities are not the same as intellectual disabilities (formerly known as mental retardation), sensory impairments (vision or hearing) or autism spectrum disorders. People with LDs are of average or above-average intelligence but still struggle to acquire skills that impact their performance in school, at home, in the community, and in the workplace. Learning disabilities are lifelong, and the sooner they are recognized and identified, the sooner steps can be taken to circumvent or overcome the challenges they present." (National Center for Learning Disabilities Editorial Team, n.d.)

Under the Individuals with Disabilities Education Act (IDEA), students with learning disabilities are guaranteed a free, appropriate public education in the least restrictive environment that adequately prepares them for continued education, employment, and independent living. If a student does not qualify for protection under IDEA, they may still qualify for educational protections under Section 504 of the Rehabilitation Act of 1973.

Students with learning disabilities have differing capabilities. Often they show extreme strengths in some domains and struggle with other discrete skills and certain academic content areas. A strengths-based approach that acknowledges the neurodiversity in any group of students leverages the power of students' abilities while focusing on specific scaffolds to ensure that all students can succeed. The more challenging the learner's needs, the more important their strengths, interests, and learning styles become in planning for their learning. We recommend an approach firmly grounded in (a) the legal obligations teachers have to students with disabilities; (b) high, standards-based expectations; and (c) the appropriate level of intervention.

Many students with learning disabilities have either an IEP or a 504 plan in place:

---

4. Adapted from our 2016 book *Learning That Lasts: Challenging, Engaging, and Empowering Students with Deeper Instruction*

» What is an IEP? An "individualized education program" (IEP) is a plan or program developed to ensure that a K–12 student who has a disability identified under the law receives specialized instruction and related services.

» What is a 504 Plan? The 504 plan is developed to ensure that a student who has a disability or medical condition identified under the law—but does not need specialized instruction— receives accommodations that ensure access to the learning environment.

These legally binding documents are the first word on what differentiated supports should be put in place for students with disabilities. They are not abandoned, changed, or overridden by differentiated approaches: in fact, they should determine the primary means by which teachers differentiate for students with learning disabilities. They should be adhered to at all times.

IEPs and 504 plans often look quite different from state to state, district to district, and school to school. Regardless, the plans should be read with two guiding questions in mind:

1. What accommodations, modifications, scaffolds, or supports are required by this plan for my student's success?

2. What strengths of my student are indicated or outlined in this plan?

These two vital pieces of information should form the foundation of all differentiation for students with disabilities.

Remember, however, that although you are legally bound to follow the IEP or 504 plan, the plans do not necessarily mean that you can't put *additional* differentiated scaffolds into place. This is a *thinking teacher's curriculum,* and we encourage you to consider how you can enhance IEP or 504 plans to build on students' assets and potential to meet their specific needs. Unless indicated otherwise on the plan, you can consult and collaborate with leaders and special education teachers to design additional individualized interventions and keep track of your efforts.

For the remainder of Chapter 2A, we describe additional interventions that can be put in place for students who need support beyond the 45-minute module lessons. These interventions are in the following areas:

» Word Study and Vocabulary

» Additional Work with Related Texts

» Fluency

» Grammar, Usage, and Mechanics

» Independent Reading

Word Study and Vocabulary

College- and career-ready standards for Grades 6–8 require students to spell grade-appropriate words correctly, determine or clarify the meanings of unknown words and multiple-meaning words, and acquire and use grade-appropriate academic and domain-specific words. In the lessons in our curriculum, these standards are taught in the context of authentic reading and writing experiences. Research suggests that as much as possible, word recognition instruction should take place in the context of the texts that students are reading, as this supports them in decoding and inferring the meaning of unfamiliar vocabulary. Word analysis skills are key in acquiring core academic vocabulary and ultimately in understanding complex texts that students encounter (Blevins and Lynch, 2001; Hiebert, 2012; Juel and Deffes, 2004).

The 45-minute lessons in our Grades 6–8 curriculum provide contextualized instruction of word analysis skills, particularly during lessons that involve close reading. However, to ensure that all students have the foundational skills necessary to build toward college- and career-readiness, it may be useful for some to have additional support and practice with these skills outside of lessons. This instruction may be presented to the whole class, or it could also take place in small, differentiated groups where students can practice word analysis in the context of the complex texts they are reading in the modules, other independent-level texts, and/or during word study games and activities.

Additional vocabulary and word study is beneficial and interesting to many students; it is particularly helpful to readers who are not meeting grade-level expectations and to multilingual learners, albeit for potentially different reasons. What follows are suggestions for additional vocabulary and word study work that can occur alongside the lessons in Grades 6–8.

Suggestions for Vocabulary and Word Study:

» Incorporate word inventories that can be used to assess students' knowledge of spelling patterns and high-frequency words for grouping and differentiation of instruction.

» Revisit complex texts read during lessons to analyze additional vocabulary words not highlighted in the lesson.

» Conduct Language Dives focused specifically on vocabulary (see Chapter 5C for more information on Language Dives).

» Engage students in Interactive Word Wall or Word Map activities.

» Provide studies of common Greek and Latin roots, as well as prefixes and suffixes and how they affect the meanings of words.

» Include activities that allow students to determine spelling patterns and learn syllabication.

» Give students opportunities to work with words through a variety of learning styles and modalities.

» Allow students to apply newly learned word knowledge and analysis skills to their reading and writing.

» Include ongoing formative assessments to support students in building increasingly sophisticated word analysis skills and progress through the stages of spelling development.

Additional Work with Related Texts

College- and career-ready standards call for a consistent emphasis on increasingly complex texts *for all students* throughout the grades. Instruction with complex text is important for fostering robust reading skills, acquiring academic vocabulary, building content knowledge, and eventually, preparing students for college and career (Hiebert, 2012; Gomez and Zywica, 2008; Liben, 2010). A growing body of research suggests that instruction with increasingly complex texts within the study of a single topic can lead to greater gains in reading rate, vocabulary acquisition, and comprehension (Adams, 2009; O'Connor, Swanson, and Geraghty, 2010; Williams, et al., 2009). Adolescent readers also can benefit from reading less complex texts related to a module topic. As students learn more about a topic, they can read more difficult texts on that topic and, if given support, improve their foundational reading and comprehension skills as well. Such "additional related texts" supplement, but must not replace, work with grade-level complex text, which remains critical. For students needing more support, teachers should take a "both/and" approach, not an "either/or" approach.

Key strategies for teaching students to navigate complex texts successfully, such as close reading, rereading, and defining words from context, are embedded in nearly every lesson in the modules. Still, all students—particularly those who have difficulty reading—can benefit from additional work with related texts that may or may not always be complex. Ideally, this additional work should focus on texts relevant to the topic of study, providing extra practice and support while broadening and deepening knowledge and understanding of the topic.

Choosing a Text for Additional Reading

Choosing a text for additional reading should lead teachers back to unassigned portions of the module texts (or portions that need rereading), or to the Recommended Texts and Other Resources—a list of texts on the module topic that is included with each module. This work should guide students to better understand the meaning, structure, or language of a text, or to acquire additional knowledge and context.

Any text students read during additional literacy time or in an intervention setting should be relevant to the topic in order to provide purpose for the reading and build knowledge on module topic. When choosing a relevant complex text to read in additional literacy time, it is import to consider what students are struggling with in the complex texts they are reading in their ELA lessons and to choose a text that provides opportunities to practice those specific skills. For example:

» Are text features confusing them (structure)?

» Is there a gap in their experiences that makes it hard to understand a key concept (knowledge)?

» Or is there an unusual amount of new academic vocabulary to learn (language)?

For example, if students are struggling with the text features of a text in an ELA lesson, we advise that you choose a relevant text with similar text features and focus the instruction in additional literacy time on helping students become more familiar with those features.

Creating Activities and Differentiating

We recommend planning activities based on meaning, structure, language, and knowledge. Very often, exploring all four areas can boost students' overall understanding and help them develop strategies for reading complex texts. The ideas presented here could be used in a "pull-out" or "push-in" session for a student or a group of students, or even as full-class instruction in an area where most students need remediation or reinforcement. Teachers can further differentiate by:

» Creating different activities (with different areas of emphasis) for individuals or groups of students

» Varying the level of adult guidance provided using specialists, paraprofessionals, or volunteers

» Modifying versions of the same activity to reflect student needs (e.g., adjusting the amount of text, limiting the number of new words, adding sentence stems or "hints")

» Chunking tasks into smaller parts or allowing more time for some students or groups

Focus on Meaning in Texts

"Meaning" activities may focus on an entire text or specific parts of a text, and may target basic understanding or more nuanced understanding of a fiction or informational text. For students who struggle with a complex text used in a lesson, the most useful support may be basic work on literal comprehension before a text is formally introduced in class, or even simply listening to the text being read on an audio recording while following along. For others, work in this area might lead to a more nuanced understanding of a theme or concept.

Activities to help students understand the meaning of related complex texts may include the following:

» Pre-reading or rereading: Students may read part or all of the text silently, whisper read independently or with a partner (the student reads a piece repeated times, in a whisper-level voice), or read aloud into a recording device. Repeated reading is a simple and powerful way to increase comprehension.

» Reading along: Students can read along with a prerecorded version of the text. Try recruiting parents or other students to create a library of texts used in the modules for your classroom. Audio versions of some books can be found at local libraries.

» Comprehension question sheets: Teachers can create sets of comprehension questions tailored to build or extend understanding of a text. Questions may target literal comprehension (for students who need extra time to develop a basic understanding) or higher-level comprehension (for students who need enrichment). They may prompt students to take a deeper look at the whole text or a particular part of the text.

» Cloze procedure: The cloze procedure is a technique in which the teacher reproduces a passage, strategically deleting words and leaving blank spaces for students to fill in. Reading carefully, students insert words that make sense in context to complete and construct meaning from the text. Cloze exercises can focus students when rereading and can be used to develop or assess basic comprehension. More information on constructing this type of activity can be found by searching online using the key words "cloze" and "reading."

» Graphic organizers: Students can complete graphic organizers that scaffold basic understanding. Examples include organizers that prompt students to identify the main characters, setting, problem and solution in a story, or the main idea and details in an informational piece or a single paragraph.

» Summaries: Students can produce written summaries of texts or sections of a text. For students who need additional support, these can be scaffolded using templates or sentence stems, or by having students work together in pairs or small groups.

Focus on Knowledge in the Text

Where possible, students should build background knowledge from the text itself, but sometimes additional information is needed. In these cases, the focus should be on teaching students to find the needed information themselves. It is crucial that any content or concepts needed to understand the text be available to all students.

Activities to help students build a knowledge base around the topic of a text that they are reading may include the following:

» Use audio or visual resources: Students can listen to recordings, watch short videos, learn educational songs, or analyze sets of images to deepen their understanding of a concept or topic. It is important that these resources augment, and not replace, content knowledge built by reading the complex text itself.

» Research: Students can conduct very short, simple research (individually or in groups) related to the text. Research questions should be designed around ideas that are not well covered in the text itself but are important to comprehension. For example, if the text is written in a way that assumes students know the dangers of being lost on a snowy mountaintop, and you live in an area where it never snows, you may want to have students research the hazards of snowy weather. Research like this can be done by individuals or groups using the internet, the library, or other sources and shared with the class.

Focus on Text Structure

Understanding text structures can help students build meaning when reading both literature and informational texts. Structure includes things like text features, organization, sentence structure, and the understanding of genre. The following are suggestions for activities to help students better understand the structure of the text they are working with. These can be done alone or with a group, and are easily adaptable to an interactive whiteboard if such technology is available.

Activities to help students understand the structure of complex texts may include the following:

» Text puzzles: Enlarge and cut apart the text or part of the text and ask students to reassemble the parts so that the text is well organized and makes sense. After they have finished, students can check their work using a copy of the original text. You can create a variety of puzzles and ask students to reassemble a set of paragraphs, sentences within a paragraph, sections of a text, or even complex sentences.

» Connections: To help students develop an awareness of the purpose of text features, prepare a copy of the text in which you have removed selected text features. These could include captions, subheads, or illustrations. Using a glue stick, students replace the missing features— for example, correctly matching a caption with an illustration or a subhead with the correct section of information. Ask students to place paragraphs under the correct subhead or paste transition sentences between paragraphs.

» Color code: Have students use color to show the relationship between parts of a text. This activity can be fairly concrete (e.g., find the word *camouflage* defined in the word box at the bottom of the page. Now find the word *camouflage* in the text. Color them both blue. What does *camouflage* mean in this sentence?); or more abstract (e.g.,This paragraph talks about a problem and solution. Color the problem red and the solution blue).

Focus on Language in the Text

It is important to give students many opportunities to work with specific vocabulary, sentence structures, figurative language, idioms, and other complexities of language in text. Draw language from the text, and choose words, phrases, and sentences that are important to understanding the text. When planning, be sure to reference the specific Language standards for your grade level, since the standards themselves provide very clear guidance about the discrete skills students must master.

Many published resources exist to help students work with the language of texts (i.e., vocabulary, grammar, and sentence structure). The following activities will support students' work with language:

» Create a glossary: Choose three to five academic or domain-specific words from the text, and have students write the definition for a glossary. Scaffold this work by having students work in groups, matching the difficulty of the words to the needs of the students, or focusing on words already introduced in class that still need reinforcement.

» Scavenger hunt: Students underline specific words in the text and copy the sentence in which the word appears. They then generate original sentences using each featured word. This activity could be expanded to include locating the same words in new texts, or "hunting" for different uses of the same word.

» Silly stories: Students work as a group to create a "silly story" that uses all the words on a given list. Words must be used correctly in the piece.

» Word boxes: Students gather words from the text to fit into given categories. These may vary widely based on the purpose of the activity. Example categories include "Words Used to Describe Character Traits" and "Stages of the Water Cycle."

Fluency

Reading fluency is the ability to read accurately, automatically, and with proper phrasing and intonation so that a reader is able to make meaning of a text, whether it is read silently or orally (Kuhn, Schwanenflugel, and Meisinger, 2010). Research shows that the role of fluency is even more important to reading comprehension than once thought (Rasinski, 2004). When students read with automaticity—the ability to recognize and read words without conscious thought—they are able to devote all of their energy to comprehending the meaning as opposed to decoding the words. Fluent readers recognize words automatically and group words quickly to help them gain meaning from what they read. Because fluent readers recognize words and comprehend at the same time, they read aloud effortlessly and with expression. Their reading sounds natural, as if they are speaking.

Students must master the ability to read with proper phrasing and intonation, or prosody (Rasinski, 2006). This means that fluent readers read the words without effort and also attend to syntax, or the structure of sentences and their punctuation. In order to read and comprehend complex texts, students not only have to decode and make meaning of difficult vocabulary, but they must also be able to read more complicated sentence structures. Although being fluent readers alone will not guarantee comprehension, it is another vitally important skill students need in order to become proficient and independent readers of complex texts.

Fluency is not a stage of development at which readers can read all words quickly and easily. Fluency changes depending on certain variables: what readers are reading, their familiarity with the words, and the amount they practice with a text. Even very skilled readers may read in a slow, labored manner when reading texts with many unfamiliar words or topics.

What about Phonics Instruction for Students Who Are Reading Significantly below Grade Level?

There are times when students in middle school may benefit from explicit instruction from a skilled reading specialist in targeted areas (e.g., phonics, phonemic awareness). Phonetic skills are helpful as they relate to decoding words, but as students are exposed to more complex text, the acquisition of academic vocabulary becomes increasingly important to support comprehension skills. When students are able to decode words that are in their active vocabulary, their comprehension skills will increase.

Your school and/or district special educators will need to review available intervention materials and curricula that are age appropriate for middle school students. While EL Education does not offer or take a position on any one particular reading intervention program, we do believe that such programs are helpful for some students at the middle school level and may be an important component of giving all students full access to our curriculum.

Creating a Routine for Fluency Instruction

Historically, there has been a strong focus on building fluent reading skills in the primary grades, with a tendency to shift the majority of our instructional focus to comprehension in the intermediate grades. But despite our best efforts, some upper elementary and secondary students still struggle to make adequate progress toward fluency goals. What can we do to help all learners acquire the skills they need to become highly capable and keen readers?

Good fluency instruction includes read-alouds that model fluent and expressive reading, regular and repeated silent and oral reading of texts in the grade-level band of complexity and at students' independent reading levels, and opportunities for self-assessment as well as teacher and peer feedback (Rasinski, 2006).

Readers who have not yet developed fluency read slowly, word by word. They must focus their attention on figuring out the words, leaving them little attention for understanding the text. Their oral reading is choppy and plodding. Disfluent readers are not likely to make effective and efficient use of silent independent reading time. For these students, independent reading time takes time away from needed reading instruction and support (National Institute for Literacy, 2001). It is important, therefore, for struggling readers to spend significant time working on their fluency. Direct instruction related to fluency is especially important for readers who are struggling.

Creating a Safe Environment for Fluency Practice[5]

If a student is not a fluent reader, they are unlikely to think, "I have a fluency problem." Instead, the student is likely to think, "I can't read" or "I am not smart enough." This likely is not true. Fluency is unrelated to intelligence. However, just telling students who have struggled with reading that they can improve their fluency with practice may not be convincing.

The following activity, designed to demonstrate the effects of practicing fluent reading skills, is best facilitated with an individual student. However, it can also be done in small groups if students are comfortable with one another and the group is led by an adult whom they trust:

1. Make copies of a grade-appropriate short paragraph, and distribute it.

2. Ask the student to read the passage aloud. If working in a small group, try doing this chorally, so each student becomes aware that the passage is difficult to read fluently, but individual voices are not "in the spotlight."

3. Have students follow along silently while you read the passage aloud at least two times.

---

5. Adapted with permission from David Liben, Student Achievement Partners

4. Read the passage chorally at least two more times.

5. Follow this with buddy reading, echo reading, or any similar technique (see the "Practice" section that follows for more ideas).

6. Finally, have the student read the passage aloud again. At this point the reading is likely to be much better.

7. With the student, evaluate, then reflect on what happened. Ask: "Did you get smarter in 20 minutes?" Help the student realize that reading fluently has nothing to do with how smart you are; it has everything to do with practice, just like with basketball layups, fixing cars, or playing an instrument. Point out that, with sufficient practice, they can become a more fluent reader.

Using the MAPP Approach to Fluency Instruction

The four components of the MAPP approach to fluency instruction form an instructional cycle that provides students with the necessary modeling, support, practice, and motivation they need to build their fluency skills (Rasinski, 2006). The components are as follows:

1. Modeling: teacher and peer modeling of fluent reading to help students understand what reading with fluency looks and sounds like

2. Assistance: students reading along with more fluent readers or recordings of fluent readers

3. Practice: students getting to practice reading selected passages aloud to help build their fluency skills

4. Performance: students reading practiced passages aloud to an audience (teacher, peers, or others)

Note: When establishing routines for the MAPP approach, students must feel that they are in a safe learning environment that encourages them to learn from mistakes and celebrate their accomplishments as they practice their reading fluency.

MODELING

Modeling means building in time every day to read aloud to students and model the characteristics that are described on the Fluency Self-Assessment Checklist (see Table 5.2) to help students gain a deeper understanding of what fluent reading is and support their progress in attaining critical reading skills.

During one of the early modules in the year, consider how you can "kick off" students' fluency work by introducing and modeling the characteristics of fluent reading using a fun and thematically related poem or lyrical piece. During this introduction, emphasize with students that the ability to read fluently is not a matter of intelligence. Rather, all students can become fluent readers when provided with opportunities to hear fluent reading; get assistance from adults and peers; and work independently or in groups to practice developing accuracy, appropriate phrasing, and expression. It is also important to help students understand that a reader's fluency can fluctuate—readers may be very fluent when reading texts they love, and even a typically fluent reader may struggle when reading text that is difficult or on a topic with which they are not familiar.

Once you have modeled the characteristics of fluent reading—preferably more than once and with a variety of texts—students can begin to use the Fluency Self-Assessment Checklist as a tool to help them recognize their strengths and set individual goals for areas of relative weakness. Be sure students understand the characteristics clearly and feel safe enough to honestly and accurately self-assess their strengths and gaps. Do not just distribute the Fluency Self-Assessment Checklist without explaining and modeling each of the characteristics. This likely would be ineffective and could have a negative impact on students' self-esteem.

Table 5.2: Fluency Self-Assessment Checklist

Characteristics of Fluent Reading	Advanced	Proficient	Developing	Beginning
I can read all/almost all of the words correctly.				
I can correct myself and reread when what I read was wrong or didn't make sense.				
I can read at a speed that is appropriate for the piece.				
I can read smoothly without many breaks.				
I can read groups of related words and phrases together.				
I can notice and read punctuation. (Examples: Pauses after a comma and period, questions sound like questions, dialogue sounds like someone saying it, exclamations in an excited voice.)				
I can use the appropriate tone to express the author's meaning.				
I can use facial expressions and body language to match the expression in my voice.				
I can use the appropriate volume and change volume naturally as if I am talking to a friend.				

ASSISTANCE

Assistance is when a student reads along with a more fluent reader or recording to help pace and monitor their own fluency. Once students understand the fluent reading characteristics (based on teacher modeling), they can begin to use *assistance* to achieve their fluency goals. Through the multiple sensory experience of reading at the same time as someone else—seeing, hearing, and speaking the text all at once—students make a more solid cognitive connection to the text.

This type of assistance can be offered in various ways:

1. Pair students with another individual to read the same passage aloud simultaneously. Students can partner with teachers, parents, an older student, or a peer.

2. "Evaluate and Emulate":

   a. A student first listens to another fluent reader's audio recording[6] of a piece of text.

   b. Then, the student uses the Fluency Self-Assessment Checklist to evaluate the reader.

   c. The student chooses one area from the checklist that they thought the speaker did exceptionally well and that they want to emulate, or read, in the same way the speaker from the audio recording did.

   d. The student then reads *simultaneously* with the audio recording to repeatedly practice emulating the speaker.

   e. The student may then choose to perform the piece for the class or record (audio/video) the practiced piece for feedback and self-evaluation of their emulation goal (see the "Performance" section that follows for more details).

PRACTICE

Practice means giving students ample opportunity to read passages with the fluency characteristics in mind. Because repetition is critical to this practice, it is important to choose texts that students will enjoy reading multiple times and that give students an opportunity to perform (see the "Performance" section that follows for more details.)

There are many engaging options that give students opportunities to practice mastery of fluent reading skills both independently and with peers. What follows are suggestions for both individual and partner/group work (some activities fit into both categories).

Independent Options (Note that almost all of these options also can and should occasionally be done in pairs.)

» Whisper Reading: A student reads the same piece of text multiple times in a whisper-level voice.

   • This activity can be done in pairs by coupling more fluent and less fluent readers to provide feedback.

   • Focus can vary (e.g., accuracy, expressions).

» Poetry for Multiple Voices: All poetry is written with special attention to language and word choice and is thus great for practice with fluency.

   • A student reads portions of the poem in different "voices" with a focus on appropriate expression and volume.

» Tongue Twisters and Alliteration: A student reads the same piece repeatedly, noting and correcting areas of difficulty with a focus on accuracy and/or rate and flow.

---

6. Audio versions of popular books often can be found at local libraries or ordered through interlibrary loan. Several internet sites also offer free, prerecorded versions of stories read aloud. One such site is Storyline Online (http://www.storylineonline.net/). You can locate other sites by using search terms such as "stories read aloud" or by using the specific title of a piece and "read aloud" (e.g., "To Kill a Mockingbird read aloud").

» Hyperbole and Quotations: To maintain student engagement, select statements and quotes related to topics of student interest or study.

» First-Person Accounts (e.g., interviews, journals, letters, speeches): To maintain student engagement, select statements and quotes related to topics of student interest or study.

- Focus can vary, but these types of resources lend themselves particularly well to practicing phrasing and punctuation and/or expression and volume.

<u>Partner and Small Group Options</u>

» Partner Reading: A student reads the same selection repeatedly with a focus on phrasing and punctuation and/or expression and volume.

- Pair stronger students with students in need of support, having the more fluent student read first and the student developing fluency read the text again, using their peer's modeling as a guide.

- The more fluent student can coach the student in need of support; the student developing fluency can give their peer feedback on what coaching or advice is helpful to them.

- This also can be done with two students of the same ability level regarding fluency, provided that the teacher first models the reading aloud so the students can emulate it.

» Poetry for Multiple Voices: Two or more students read different portions of the poem in different "voices" with a focus on appropriate expression and volume.

- Choose poems that represent a variety of cultural perspectives.

- Poetry for multiple voices can be found at libraries and on the internet.

» "Race for Spelling Patterns": This fast-paced activity helps students recognize spelling patterns with phonograms and supports reading with accuracy.

» Punctuation Pictures: Students are given a statement or question that uses punctuation differently (e.g., "Let's eat, Grandpa" versus "Let's eat Grandpa").

- Students read each sentence aloud with attention to accurate phrasing based on the punctuation to help them determine and discuss with a partner what each sentence actually means and try to create a "mind picture" of each meaning.

- As a possible extension, students can sketch the meaning of each punctuation picture.

» Readers Theater Scripts: Choose scripts that represent a variety of cultural perspectives and, if possible, are thematically related to the content of the module.

- Two or more students work together to practice repeatedly reading various roles/parts of the script with a focus on accuracy, rate and flow, phrasing and punctuation, and/or expression and volume.

- Students may choose to perform the piece or audio/video record the performance (see the "Performance" section that follows for details).

- A variety of Readers Theater scripts can be found online, or students may develop their own scripts.

PERFORMANCE

Performance involves the opportunity to perform practiced pieces aloud in front of an audience. This gives students authentic purpose and motivation to practice their fluent reading skills. Performances can take place in a variety of ways, either whole group, small group, with a partner, or independently. The most suitable passages for performance have a strong "voice," connect to what matters to adolescents, and offer students a medium-stakes opportunity to apply what they know about how to read with accuracy, rate and flow, phrasing and punctuation, and expression and volume.

Some examples of the types of pieces students may consider performing:

» Letters

» Journal entries

» Readers theater

» Poetry/song lyrics

» Speeches/monologues

Performance options can be differentiated by giving students choices:

» What type of piece will be performed? (format, content, and length)

» Who will be the audience? (large or small group, partner)

» How much time is needed to practice before the performance? (Set a schedule/days/amount of time per day.)

» Will the performance be live or audio/video recorded?

» Will students read directly from a script/paper or memorize the piece?

Grammar, Usage, and Mechanics

Research shows that conventions and grammar are best taught within the context of authentic reading and writing tasks (Weaver and Bush, 2008). Students benefit from proactive instruction that uses models of informational texts and literature to teach explicit conventions and grammatical rules that can then be applied in their writing (Weaver, McNally, and Moerman, 2001). Teachers can plan these lessons based on the specific grade-level demands of the standards and on the analysis of student work that's required in the modules.

Students also benefit from instruction later in the writing process that includes targeted mini lessons that support students in revising their work (e.g., you notice common errors and provide targeted teaching or reteaching). As students prepare to publish their work, one option is for teachers to support students in peer editing for these rules in order to reinforce this learning. In this way, students can see the value and practical application of rules of convention and grammar within the context of mentor texts, their own work, and their peers' work.

In the modules, Language standards are mostly addressed during the writing process; however, here we provide examples, guidance, and materials that provide further practice of the "conventions of standard English" and "knowledge of language" standards that are introduced in the Grades 6–8 modules.

Show the Rule[7]

Show the Rule addresses language standards while engaging students in rich literature. The goal of Show the Rule is to support students to immediately practice and apply what they have learned into their own writing. This is not only more engaging, but also provides a more reliable assessment than taking a weekly test, because it provides direct evidence of the students' ability to write about what they have learned. This approach aligns with well-established research that shows that grammar is best taught in the context of students' authentic reading and writing experiences.

Summary of Show the Rule:

» Introduce a specific rule/Language standard through a literary or informational text.

» Students actively listen or look (on overhead or interactive whiteboard) for the rule as it is used in the text.

» As a whole group, students begin to define and form their own examples of the rule.

» Students pick out a picture from a magazine, cut it out, and glue it into their Show the Rule journal. They use this picture to inspire ideas for their own creative writing.

» With the new rule in mind, they write a creative piece using the rule of the week as often as they can throughout the writing piece. This reinforces the newly acquired knowledge and demonstrates the depth of their understanding.

» Students highlight the ways in which they applied the rule in their own writing, either by using a highlighter or by underlining examples.

» Students continue to work on this writing piece all week and self-score using a rubric. They turn it in at the end of the week for the teacher to assess. Students do not formally go back to edit or revise; this is first-draft writing.

There are some similarities between this sequence and the Language Dives that are a feature of the module lessons (see Chapter 5C for more information on Language Dives). Language Dives feature deep, playful looks at chunks of language and fulfill some of the same purposes as Show the Rule. The "Deconstruct, Reconstruct, Practice" process of a Language Dive can

7. Used by permission, Eloise Ginty, Vermont Writing Collaborative. For more information and resources, go to www.vermontwritingcollaborative.org.

extend into students' creative writing when warranted. One difference with Show the Rule is that a teacher has decided that what they are seeing in student work reveals pervasive enough misunderstandings to merit the explicit, upfront teaching of a rule, rather than beginning with a process of discovery as in a Language Dive.

Independent Reading

College- and career-ready standards challenge students to read complex texts in order to build content knowledge, literacy skills, and academic vocabulary. Each of the Grades 6–8 modules includes one or more anchor texts that students work with in class and for homework, with support from teachers and peers. It is important that all students have access to and support with reading text at the appropriate level of complexity for their grade level. However, students also need a "volume of reading," which means they need to read a lot of text (including text beyond the texts central to a module and what they read during school hours or with support). This volume of reading helps students build important world knowledge and acquire additional vocabulary, both of which are critical for reading comprehension.

The curriculum has structures in place to engage students in independent reading, particularly independent research reading on the module topic; however, some students may need additional support to complete their independent reading and to make meaning from it. This is where additional intervention time may become especially important.

Independent Reading Structures

Teachers often are concerned about holding students accountable for independent reading. There are endless ways to track independent reading requirements, but the most successful ways include placing the responsibility on the student. Creating a plan for launching independent reading that includes clear class routines, goal setting, and systems for accountability and student ownership creates a culture of reading in the classroom and the school that will promote students' literacy development.

Each module in the Grades 6–8 curriculum includes a lesson in which independent research reading is launched. There is no one way to launch independent research reading—you will be directed to sample plans on our website (http://eled.org/tools). Once students have selected texts and set up their reading logs, they can record both their research reading and other independent reading. These sample plans are designed to enhance and extend the strong programs many teachers and schools already have in place.

The following process for supporting students to choose texts for independent research reading is suggested in the sample plans:

1. **Book frenzy:** Display various texts for students to peruse. Ideally, these texts would include some of the titles from the list of Recommended Texts and Other Resources with diverse cultures and backgrounds represented. Consider conducting brief teacher book talks on those titles related to the module.

2. Give students time to browse the texts. Make this fun!

3. Encourage students to select a few titles and "test-drive" them. Test-driving involves reading the first few pages of each book to determine which one they would like to continue reading. Help students understand that for the text to be worth continuing, students should be able to read the text with good fluency and understanding. If none of them work, students can repeat this process, but they should not do this more than twice.

4. Consider allowing partner selections, but keep in mind that each student needs their own copy of the text.

5. Once students have chosen their texts, invite them to start reading silently.

6. Circulate to discuss texts with students, being aware of the following:

- With texts that appear "too easy" for a student, understand that:

  ◦ Vocabulary and knowledge can still grow with simple texts.

  ◦ If reading is happening and the student is enjoying it, then that is a success.

  ◦ If the student becomes increasingly interested in the topic, they will likely read more complex texts about it to satisfy a curiosity to know more.

- If a student develops a pattern over a period over time of reading only less challenging texts:

  ◦ Guide the student toward other texts on a topic you know they like or is related to what they are currently reading, rather than telling the student to change texts.

- With texts that appear "too hard" for a student, understand that:

  ◦ A student does not have one reading level, but has many depending on the topic and their knowledge of it.

  ◦ For example: A student may have deep knowledge about baseball and will be able to read more complex texts on this topic. The same student may have less knowledge about boats and will not be able to read texts on this topic that are as complex when first learning about the topic.

- When checking in with students, simply ask the student about their book:

  ◦ If it sounds like they are getting something out of the book, the student should continue reading it.

  ◦ If they cannot easily talk about the book, ask them to read a short section aloud. If the student cannot read with a degree of fluency, support them in finding a new text on the same topic. Only do so if the student cannot read with adequate fluency and they do not seem to be getting anything out of the book.

Conferring with Students during Independent Reading

Conferring one-on-one with students about what they are reading serves both instructional and accountability purposes. A conversation with you about reading will create more accountability for a student than a reading log. Conferring is a rich teaching practice and allows you to build strong relationships with your students as readers and as people. The heart of conferring is simply to ask students, "How's it going?" "What are you learning?" and "What are you figuring out as a reader?"

While students are reading silently in class or during intervention time, circulate to observe and confer. Notice patterns in the types of books students are choosing and in how well they are sustaining engagement with their chosen book. Confer with students to ensure that they are reading books that are on an appropriate reading level and to support them in making meaning of those books. Conferring can include the following:

» Asking a student to read a paragraph or two out loud, noting any miscues (if there are a lot, the book might be too hard for independent reading)

» Asking a student to talk about what is happening in that excerpt, stating simply: "Tell me more!"

» Helping students use "fix-up" strategies when they get confused (e.g., rereading, visualizing, using context clues to determine unknown vocabulary)

» Asking students what they like/don't like about a book and why (push them to cite evidence)

» Suggesting titles that the student might find interesting and appropriate

Recommended Texts

Each module includes a list of Recommended Texts and Other Resources in a broad complexity range for each unit. These books can be used for independent research on a given topic, or students may choose them to read for pleasure during independent reading time at school and at home. They may also be used for small group instruction. Because these book choices have already been identified as aligned to the topic, they are a good starting place for helping students select books to increase their volume of reading, increase their comprehension, and build their academic vocabulary.

Your library is another amazing and often underused asset to promote a volume of reading. There are a number of reading programs across the country that encourage classrooms to build "libraries" for convenient student reading choices. These classroom libraries play a positive role in developing lifelong readers, yet they sometimes have limited choices for students. To support the individuality of each student, encourage students to access the thousands of titles and choices that can be found in the local and school libraries. Contact your school librarian for support in this area, as they are often eager to help.

Chapter 5B:
Supporting Students Who Need Additional Challenges

Students may require additional challenges for a variety of reasons. They may be advanced learners, labeled in many ways in schools (e.g., gifted and talented, accelerated, highly ready). Or, they may be disengaged, in need of different kinds of learning activities to help them live up to their full potential. No matter what the label, it is important to think of these learners in the same respectful way that we think of students who need more support: not as "high" or "low," "better" or "worse," but simply as "students with specific academic needs." All students require and deserve rich, relevant, challenging learning that supports their growth and helps them learn not just more, but more deeply.

"Extending instruction to meet the needs of students who need additional challenges is the mirror image of scaffolding: it allows students who learn quickly and/or who have well-developed background knowledge to move through the instruction in a way that respects their advancement. It is an unfortunate truth that students in need of additional challenge are often overlooked in classroom instruction. Overwhelmed by the practical challenges of their work, teachers rejoice in the presence of students who soak up knowledge, get 'right' answers, and earn 100's and A's, but the same teachers may not know how to challenge these learners. As a result, advanced students are not served well when they are consistently isolated from their peers to work on other materials, relied upon as tutors for other students, asked to 'do more of the same work faster,' or simply left alone" (Berger, Woodfin, and Vilen, 2016, p. 297).

All of the realities described in the preceding paragraph, from our book *Learning That Lasts,* can lead to disengagement. By the time students get to middle school, teachers may be more likely to see disengaged advanced learners than the eager-to-please versions of themselves they were in elementary school.

As we stated in Chapter 5A, our curriculum is designed for heterogeneous classrooms, and we believe strongly that students excel in diverse and inclusive settings. This is as true for students needing additional challenge as it is for students who need support to meet grade-level expectations. And, just as we stated in Chapter 5A, two of the keys to promoting equity in a heterogenous classroom are supporting all students to meet the same learning targets (i.e., standards) and supporting all students to read the same challenging texts. The primary work with students needing additional challenge is to extend their learning—to make it deeper and richer—while keeping them on pace with the curriculum and their classmates so that they don't experience the isolation and lack of clear progress markers that can accompany moving ahead at their own pace.

Chapter 5

Consider the following basic ways to address the needs of advanced learners in the heterogeneous classroom. We draw several of these ideas from the work of Carol Ann Tomlinson (1997).[8]

1. **Remove scaffolds:** This is a very simple way to address learners' more advanced capabilities. If a task has been scaffolded in any way, enact the reverse process and take the scaffolds away. Vocabulary can be left undefined, asking students to use their word study strategies to find their meanings. Concrete text-based questions can be de-emphasized, requiring students to dive into text immediately at more complex levels of understanding. Writing graphic organizers can be used only partially, or even eliminated altogether.

2. **Adjust the degree of difficulty:** "In the Olympics," Tomlinson reminds us, "the most accomplished divers perform dives that have a higher 'degree of difficulty' than those performed by divers whose talents are not as advanced. A greater degree of difficulty calls on more skills—more refined skills—applied at a higher plane of sophistication" (1997). Academic tasks with adjusted degrees of difficulty may require deep insight and broad pattern recognition, require less structure, and sometimes (though not always) may be addressed with more learner independence. Instead of simply analyzing a poem for a theme, for example, an advanced learner might be asked to determine how a theme changes from an author's earlier work to later work. Or, asking students to explain key disciplinary concepts can challenge them in new and deeper ways.

3. **Understand "supported risk":** Advanced learners have often had a very easy time in school. They are used to expending little effort and getting big results. If this has been their experience, making errors is often particularly uncomfortable for them. When genuinely challenged by a task for the first time, advanced learners may react with fear, sadness, annoyance, or confusion: their self-image of success has been challenged as well. They may not have developed the tools of perseverance, good humor, and academic courage to be able to deal successfully with that challenge. "A good teacher of gifted students," says Tomlinson, "understands that dynamic, and thus invites, cajoles, and insists on risk—but in a way that supports success. When a good gymnastics coach asks a talented young gymnast to learn a risky new move, the coach ensures that the young person has the requisite skills, then practices the move in a harness for a time. Then the coach 'spots' for the young athlete. Effective teachers of gifted learners do likewise" (1997).

In our curriculum, there are three primary types of built-in support for students in need of additional challenges, and they are primarily of the "adjust the degree of difficulty" variety from the previous list. In this chapter we explore each of these three types of extensions:

1. The first type is found in the Opportunities to Extend Learning section of the Teaching Notes of every lesson. These extensions are often a content extension (e.g., additional or deeper research) and/or a literacy skill extension that begins to give students additional or deeper practice with the standard(s) covered in the lesson.

2. The second type are extensions to the performance tasks.

3. The final type of extension is found in the Module Overview in a section called Optional: Community, Experts, Fieldwork, Service, and Extensions. These extensions are deeper and longer-range, meant to be applied across the entire module, and meant to deeply engage the entire class, not just a particular group of students.

We begin with the lesson-level extensions; however, we do so against our own better judgement! Generally we recommend starting with a wider view—the module level in this case—because this is how we want you to plan. But for this topic, we have chosen to start with the lesson-level extensions because differentiating well is not easy. If you are new to teaching our curriculum, the lesson-level extensions are likely to feel like an easier place to start. However, if you are ready to

---

8. These three ideas are adapted from our 2016 book *Learning That Lasts: Challenging, Engaging, and Empowering Students with Deeper Instruction*.

do some module-level planning and to think about how to deepen the learning for your entire class, we encourage you to skip ahead to the end of Chapter 5B and then come back here to read about the lesson-level and performance task extensions.

▶ HOW DO I EXTEND LEARNING WITHIN THE DAILY LESSONS OF THE CURRICULUM?

Before we dig into the lesson-level extensions in the curriculum, it's important to pause here briefly on one of the keys to effective differentiation: assessment. If you haven't assessed students' progress, how will you know if they need scaffolds or extensions? Our curriculum provides myriad opportunities to assess student progress: from daily formative self-assessments and in-the-minute quick checks for understanding that happen continuously throughout every lesson, to summative mid- and end of unit assessments. Every note-catcher, entrance ticket, and Thumb-O-Meter can give you vital information about which students need what kind of instructional attention during the lesson. (Chapter 6 is dedicated to helping you make sense of the assessment data you will gather while teaching the curriculum.)

Once you have the information you need to assess student progress, you can employ flexible grouping strategies to ensure that every student receives the scaffolds or extensions that will maximize their learning in the lesson. What follows are descriptions and examples of several typical types of suggestions for extensions that you are likely to encounter in the Opportunities to Extend Learning section of the Teaching Notes of every lesson.

Assigning Different or Additional Research on the Module Topic

Harkening back to the research we discussed on content-based literacy in Chapter 1 (Adams, 2009; Recht and Leslie, 1988), the more one knows about a topic, the more one is able to read and understand about that topic. Assigning students additional research on the module topic will not only build their content knowledge, it will also build critical college- and career-ready literacy skills. It is important that this extension is *on the module topic*, versus asking students to conduct research on a topic of their choice or to engage in a completely independent and unrelated project.

What follows are a few examples of extensions of this type offered in the Opportunities to Extend Learning section of the Teaching Notes:

» Grade 6, Module 1, Unit 1, Lesson 7: A number of figures from Greek myths are introduced in this chapter; encourage students to read the original versions of stories in which these figures are introduced to build background on the topic.

» Grade 6, Module 1, Unit 1, Lesson 8: Given the possible content issues mentioned in Support All Students, one possible idea for extension would be to further examine, unpack, and discuss the ways in which Riordan represents female characters, people of varying physical and cognitive abilities, and social class. Additionally, balance the Western perspective by the inclusion of non-Western influences or by examining similar myths of non-Western cultures—for example, the Ramayana.

» Grade 8, Module 1, Unit 1, Lesson 2: Have students research myths or traditional stories that may be a part of their own culture or another culture they choose to research. Students might reflect on how these stories reflect and impact culture and identity.

Practicing or Deepening Skills Tied Directly to the Lesson's Learning Targets (Standards)

This kind of extension requires looking closely at the precise wording of the standards to consider ways in which students can explore them in deeper, more sustained ways. We have considered how particular standards progress in sophistication from grade level to grade level and have made suggestions that begin to give students practice with some of these skills. We also look at standards that may be incidental in a lesson and consider how students may begin to get practice with that standard before it becomes a focus later in a unit or module.

Our aim with this kind of extension is additional, deeper, and more sophisticated kinds of practice with grade-level standards so that students become more nimble with them. We are not aiming to help students achieve a basic level of mastery on a standard, check it off a list, and move on.

What follows are a few examples of extensions of this type offered in the Opportunities to Extend Learning section of the Teaching Notes:

» Grade 6, Module 1, Unit 2, Lesson 10: Check the Language standards to identify additional goals for a proficient writer to work toward (e.g., utilizing punctuation to set off nonrestrictive/parenthetical elements).

» Grade 7, Module 1, Unit 1, Lesson 1: As students note vocabulary in the text, invite them to elaborate on the figurative and connotative meanings and uses of the words they find (RL.7.4). Provide opportunities for students to create new sentences using the words in their vocabulary logs. (Note: RL.7.4 is not a focus standard of this lesson, but this extension gives students a chance to practice and focus on it well ahead of the lesson where it will be a focus—Lesson 8 and then again in Unit 3).

» Grade 8, Module 1, Unit 1, Lesson 6: Students could rewrite a short excerpt from the perspective of one of the other sisters. (Note: Point of view is a strong focus of this unit.)

Completing Tasks Independently

There are two ways to think about this kind of extension in the curriculum. Each has its own purpose and benefit for students. The first is the most straight-forward, and that is to ask students to complete certain tasks independently. Many of the texts in the curriculum are not necessarily read in their entirety. However, for readers who are able to move quickly through a text while maintaining a high level of comprehension, reading it in its entirely is likely to be enriching and rewarding. Students may also complete independent tasks that mirror the tasks assigned in the lesson, as the final example in the list that follows demonstrates. Especially when there is a new perspective or point of view for students to explore, this can be an especially enriching task, but it is not appropriate for every kind of task.

The other way to think about completing tasks independently is what we typically refer to as "grappling." We want to give students a chance to grapple with concepts, words, and ideas before we explain things through a mini lesson or other instructions. Whenever possible, *all* students should be given a chance to first engage in productive grappling—this is when the best learning happens. For students who need additional challenges, grappling is especially important. Knowing when to release students to more independence and when to provide support requires knowing students well and a positive classroom culture (see Chapter 2C for much more on fostering a culture of grappling).

What follows are a few examples of extensions of this type offered in the Opportunities to Extend Learning section of the Teaching Notes:

» Grade 6, Module 1, Unit 1, Lesson 1: This unit is designed to focus on specific excerpts of the text during class so as to provide time for analysis. To cover the entire text, encourage students to read each chapter in its entirety outside of class time.

» Grade 7, Module 1, Unit 1, Lesson 1: Release more responsibility more quickly to students as they comprehend the tasks or concepts. Select examples:

  • Work Time A: Allow some students to read the chapter independently and record a gist and take notes about setting, character, and plot in their reading notebooks.

  • Closing and Assessment A: Encourage these students to explain point of view, using evidence from the text.

» Grade 7, Module 1, Unit 1, Lesson 1: During Work Time A, observe student interactions, and allow them to grapple. Provide supportive frames and demonstrations only after students have grappled with the task. Observe the areas in which they need additional support.

» Grade 8, Module 1, Unit 2, Lesson 11: Have students write an additional narrative independently to continue to practice the skills that have been scaffolded in this unit.

Engaging Critical Thinking

We all want our students to learn deeply. We want them to feel energized and empowered by what their minds can do and to flexibly apply their knowledge to new situations. We want them to feel equally at home at all levels of the Bloom's Taxonomy pyramid—understanding, applying, analyzing, evaluating, and creating knowledge. This is what makes learning last. Despite knowing that we want this for students, we don't always know how to get there. Many of the module-level extensions that we will discuss further on in this chapter will take aim at the kinds of deeper learning opportunities every teacher wants for their students. However, lesson-level extensions— small instructional moves—can also engage students in critical thinking.

The examples offered here—pulled from lessons in the curriculum—are a starting place for the creativity you can bring to these kinds of extensions. The second bullet on the list is a particularly good example of a suggestion that actually contains multiple possible extensions that can increase the depth and rigor of a task for students who need additional challenge. Webb's Depth of Knowledge, a framework that is easily accessible to any teacher online, offers prompts that will help you push your students' thinking. See Figure 5.5 for sample activities aligned to Webb's Depth of Knowledge. The extension offered in this Grade 6 lesson invites you to consider a number of possible options to engage students in deeper learning.

What follows are a few examples of extensions of this type offered in the Opportunities to Extend Learning section of the Teaching Notes:

» Grade 6, Module 1, Unit 2, Lesson 7: Give students a blank Informative Writing checklist, and challenge them to generate the criteria based on the model essay.

» Grade 6, Module 1, Unit 3, Lesson 9: Some students may not require the level of scaffolding provided in this unit. Prompt students toward deeper levels of understanding and increased rigor by referencing Levels 3 and 4 of Webb's Depth of Knowledge.

» Grade 7, Module 1, Unit 1, Lesson 6: Allow those students who are identifying the gist and other elements quickly the opportunity to develop their own text-dependent questions about the chapter related to the setting, characters, and plot as in Lesson 4. Ask these students to share their questions with the group as a way of generating discussion.

» Grade 8, Module 1, Unit 3, Lesson 7: Gather a number of new texts with effective introductory paragraphs. Invite students to analyze these introductory paragraphs written by professionals to gather more criteria for an effective introductory paragraph.

Figure 5.5: Webb's Depth of Knowledge Activities

Level One: Recall and Reproduction	Level Two: Skills and Concepts	Level Three: Strategic Thinking/Reasoning	Level Four: Extended Thinking
Recall, recognize, or locate basic facts, details, events, or ideas explicit in texts	Make basic inferences or logical predictions from data or texts	Describe how word choice, point of view, or bias may affect the readers' interpretation of a text	Explain how concepts or ideas specifically relate to other content domains or concepts
Describe/explain who, what, where, when, how	Use context to identify the meaning of words/phrases	Apply a concept in a new context	Illustrate how multiple themes (historical, geographic, social) may be interrelated
Apply basic formats for documenting sources	Distinguish: relevant–irrelevant information; fact/opinion	Analyze interrelationships among concepts, issues, problems	Analyze multiple sources of evidence, or multiple works by the same author, or across genres, time periods, themes
Decide which text structure is appropriate to audience and purpose	Generate conjectures or hypotheses based on observations or prior knowledge and experience	Cite evidence and develop a logical argument for conjectures	
Brainstorm ideas, concepts, problems, or perspectives related to a topic or concept		Develop an alternative solution	Evaluate relevancy, accuracy, and completeness of information from multiple sources
			Articulate a new voice, alternate theme, new knowledge or perspective

Source: Derived from Hess' "Cognitive Rigor Matrix": https://www.karin-hess.com/cognitive-rigor-and-dok

Promoting High-Quality Writing

We have all known students who are highly capable writers, but who are not in the habit of revising their writing. Perhaps they don't believe they can really improve it, either because they haven't been provided with a strong model and gotten specific feedback, or because feedback wasn't accompanied by a clear belief in their own capabilities; perhaps the assignment itself didn't activate their intrinsic need to do good work. Whatever the reason, too often students complete a task and turn it in without the attention to detail they will need as they move toward high school, college, and beyond.

Middle school is a critical time to develop good writing habits. Chapter 4C offers an in-depth look at supporting students to do high-quality work. It is a value we hold dear at EL Education. If you have students in your classroom who can use a push to complete their work with quality, we encourage you to read Chapter 4C and/or check out our books *Leaders of Their Own Learning* and *The Leaders of Their Own Learning Companion* for guidance on using models, critique, and descriptive feedback to support your students' growth in this area.

You will also find that the lessons that involve writing tasks in our curriculum offer meaningful and targeted extensions that will further develop the skills and writing habits that many facile writers need to take their work to the next level of quality.

What follows are a few examples of extensions of this type offered in the Opportunities to Extend Learning section of the Teaching Notes:

» Grade 6, Module 1, Unit 1, Lesson 14: Offer a mini lesson on citing text evidence with parenthetical documentation for students who are ready for an advanced writing technique.

» Grade 6, Module 1, Unit 2, Lesson 10: Challenge proficient writers to try more advanced writing techniques like adding direct quotes, pulling in additional sources, or using figurative language and vivid words, especially the vocabulary they have added to their vocabulary logs.

» Grade 7, Module 1, Unit 1, Lesson 9: In Closing and Assessment A, invite students to write a summary of Chapter 6 without analyzing a model and then to revise their first attempt after analyzing the model and generating criteria.

» Grade 7, Module 1, Unit 2, Lesson 7: If students are familiar with the Painted Essay® structure, allow them to paint the model themselves or lead class discussion of the template.

» Grade 8, Module 1, Unit 3, Lesson 7: If students are identifying the parts of the introductory paragraphs and planning them with ease, draw their attention to specific sentences within the paragraphs and ask what the roles of the sentences are and what effect there would be in removing those sentences, as shown in Work Time A.

Encouraging Creative Expression

Harkening back to the principles of UDL, it is important to remember that not all learners will express themselves confidently and capably in the same way. You may have a student whom you would identify as not meeting grade-level expectations as a writer; however, you know them to be an avid reader and sharp thinker. Like a lot of students, they are complex; they need additional challenges to keep them engaged even though they struggle with writing. Extensions that encourage their creative expressions may be the perfect way for them to demonstrate what they know—to synthesize their learning, to creative rich narratives, to summarize dense information. These extensions will not take the place of writing, because it is still critical that they stay on pace with college- and career-ready standards, but adding in these opportunities will enrich their learning and build her confidence.

What follows are a few examples of extensions of this type offered in the Opportunities to Extend Learning section of the Teaching Notes:

» Grade 6, Module 1, Unit 3, Lessons 10–11: Challenge students to learn new presentation programs, such as PowToons or try their hand at the more advanced features of slideshow software of which they are already familiar.

» Grade 8, Module 1, Unit 2, lesson 7: Students may create an artistic expression of one of the monsters they learned about during the whole class share out.

» Grade 8, Module 1, Unit 2, Lesson 7: Students may role-play a potential encounter between one of the monsters and the Garza sisters in *Summer of the Mariposas*.

Promoting Leadership Skills

Promoting leadership among students who need additional challenges is potentially tricky territory in middle school. It's important to understand the social dynamics at play among students before you put any student in a position to teach other students or set themselves up as an "expert." In Chapter 1A we detail how we designed the curriculum with the characteristics of middle school learners in mind, and that, along with Chapter 2C about setting up a positive classroom culture, might be helpful refreshers.

It is worthwhile and rewarding to build leadership skills in students, especially when you sense that they are disengaged; however, it's important to do so with eyes wide open about classroom dynamics and the hyper-sensitivity students this age have to being singled out as better than their peers. You know your students best and should consider how your classroom culture best lends itself to developing leadership skills. For example, rather than considering how some students can be identified to lead a discussion, you may wish to figure out a way for *all* students to lead a discussion in some way.

What follows are a few examples of extensions of this type offered in the Opportunities to Extend Learning section of the Teaching Notes:

» Grade 6, Module 1, Unit 1, Lesson 12: Encourage students to identify the theme in several popular novels and movies. If some students are pre-taught about theme, they could aid in delivering this lesson by preparing visuals (posters, slideshows) in advance that illustrate examples of themes in well-known texts and movies.

» Grade 7, Module 1, Unit 1, Lesson 13: Select student volunteers to participate in a model discussion.

▶ WHAT KIND OF EXTENSIONS CAN I MAKE TO THE PERFORMANCE TASKS?

Every module includes a performance task in Unit 3—an extended, supported writing task or presentation—where students bring together their knowledge of the module topic to celebrate learning. The performance tasks are neither formative nor summative assessments. They are not formative since they come at the end of the module, concluding students' learning about the module topic and the literacy skills they have built over eight or nine weeks. However, they are also not summative because they are heavily scaffolded to help students create high-quality work, and so are not a strong measure of what students can do independently.

We don't recommend analyzing performance tasks with the same lens used to analyze other assessments. Instead, we recommend analyzing performance tasks through the lens of the attributes of high-quality student work (authenticity, complexity, craftsmanship), which we first introduced in Chapter 4. We designed the performance tasks to be opportunities for students to push themselves—and for you to encourage them—to do more than they think they can.

Just as you use the lens of the attributes of high-quality work to analyze students' performance tasks, it makes good sense to use the same lens to plan the extensions you might offer to students who need additional challenge. The definition of high-quality work can help you develop your own unique and creative extensions for your students; it also helped us develop the suggestions that accompany each performance task, found under Options for Students in each Performance Task Overview.

Complexity

Considering the complexity of student work is a chance to engage students in higher-order, critical thinking. The following definition of *complex work* was first introduced in Chapter 4A:

Defining Complex Work:

» Complex work is rigorous; it aligns with or exceeds the expectations defined by grade-level standards and includes higher-order thinking by challenging students to apply, analyze, evaluate, and create during daily instruction and throughout longer projects.

- » Complex work often connects to the big concepts that undergird or unite disciplines.

- » Complex work prioritizes transfer of understanding to new contexts.

- » Complex work prioritizes consideration of multiple perspectives.

- » Complex work may incorporate students' application of higher-order literacy skills through the use of complex text and evidence-based writing and speaking.

We designed the performance tasks and the suggested extensions that accompany them with this definition firmly in mind. However, you may find that you want to use this definition to challenge your students in new or deeper ways, and we encourage you to do so based on their needs and readiness. Extensions in this area should aim to help students become more nimble with the concepts and skills of the module so that they can seamlessly apply them to new contexts. Your students may be ready to consider, for example, how the big concepts of one module connect with a previous module or with work they are doing in a science or social studies class, or to bring in additional perspectives that are not included in the module materials.

Example from the Curriculum

In Grade 8, Module 2, students study food choices. For the performance task, each student creates an infographic, along with a 3-minute oral presentation of the argument they made in their essay. Students share their infographics in a roundtable presentation with an authentic audience of classmates, teachers, families, and community members. One of the extensions suggested for this performance task is:

- » Students could create original artwork for their presentations to accompany their speeches. This could be done as homework or in collaboration with a school visual arts teacher.

This extension has the *potential* to push students around complexity, but it may not without your focus and attention on the definition of *complexity*. To ensure that this work is focused on complexity, versus craftsmanship, it will be important to help students consider how the concepts of the discipline of the module can be represented artistically. Transferring what they understand about the concepts of the module into art is a higher-order application that will enhance and enrich the learning experience for students and engage their minds in new ways.

Craftsmanship

Middle school students will benefit from lots of support, time, and structure to improve their craftsmanship. We define *craftsmanship* as follows:

Defining Craftsmanship:

- » Well-crafted work is done with care and precision. Craftsmanship requires attention to accuracy, detail, and beauty.

- » In every discipline and domain, well-crafted work should be beautiful work in conception and execution. In short tasks or early drafts of work, craftsmanship may be present primarily in thoughtful ideas, but not in polished presentation; for long-term projects, craftsmanship requires perseverance to refine work in conception, conventions, and presentation, typically through multiple drafts or rehearsals with critique from others.

Extensions focused on craftsmanship—including revision and attention to habits of character, such as *perseverance*—will support and stretch students who have a fixed mindset about things they are already "good at." Too often, students who have been labeled "advanced" in school have gotten a message that they don't have to work hard at things in order to do well. Challenging these students with craftsmanship extensions can disrupt that paradigm and teach them the value of learning new skills and working hard, especially for aspects of school that may not come as easily to them. Extensions that require students to do their work with care and precision—to revise based on critique, to polish ideas through discourse, to attend to the beauty of a final draft—are the kind of extensions that you can employ quite flexibly in your classroom. You won't want students to *always* take their work to beautiful final-draft quality, but you can choose to do so with work that will deepen learning for your students and challenge them in new and purposeful ways.

Example from the Curriculum

In Grade 6, Module 3, students create a Voices of American Indian Boarding Schools Audio Museum for their performance task. Students act as witnesses to this time period by organizing an Audio Museum to highlight the experiences and amplify the voices of American Indian boarding school students. One of the extensions suggested for this performance task is:

» Think about other ways to make your recording engaging and meaningful. You might wish to include gentle background music to play while you share your reflection, for example. Check with your teacher to see how you might increase the impact of your recording while still demonstrating respect for the words of your chosen text.

This extension, similar to the previous example in the section on complexity, has great *potential* to challenge students around craftsmanship, but it won't necessarily do so without paying attention to the definition of craftsmanship. Students shouldn't just add their favorite song in the background. Craftsmanship requires care and precision; this means that students need to consider what kind of music they are choosing and why, as well as the quality of the recording. The music must enhance the experience for the audience, not detract from it. This extension asks students to think about how music impacts the tone and mood of their recording so that they can make an appropriate selection. There's more than one way to record music in the background, but one option is for students to learn to use software that allows them to edit their audio recordings, giving them an opportunity to practice perseverance and to work through multiple drafts or versions of their work.

Authenticity

Authenticity in student work has multiple layers and is a versatile lens for thinking about extensions. We define *authenticity* as follows:

Defining Authenticity:

» Authentic work demonstrates the original thinking of students—authentic personal voice and ideas—rather than simply showing that students can follow directions or fill in the blanks.

» Authentic work often uses real work formats and standards from the professional world rather than artificial school formats (e.g., students create a book review for a local newspaper instead of a book report for the teacher).

» Authentic work often connects academic standards with real-world issues, controversies, and local people and places.

» Authenticity gives purpose to work; the work matters to students and ideally to a larger community as well. When possible, it is created for and shared with an audience beyond the classroom.

To be authentic, student work—whether it is a response to a question on an exit ticket or a presentation—must demonstrate students' original thinking. This can be achieved by ensuring that, whenever possible, rather than filling in blanks on a worksheet or answering selected response questions, students are responding to open-ended questions or creating their own original work. Tasks should allow each student's unique voice to shine through. Our curriculum already prioritizes authentic student voice; however, there are myriad ways to offer additional creative extensions. You could consider, for example, asking students to write a new chapter in the voice of the author of *The Boy Who Harnessed the Wind*.

Authentic student work also frequently connects students to the community of the school and the larger world. When students create work for their community, it helps answer the age-old question: "why do we have to do this?" When they know that their work has meaning, they are much more motivated to take on challenges. (The video highlighted in Video Spotlight 5.2 about students in Detroit who build "little libraries" to encourage literacy in their city, is a great example.) The performance tasks in the modules always incorporate some element of authenticity. Still, there is always room to challenge students with additional extensions that add additional authenticity to the performance task.

Example from the Curriculum

For the Grade 6, Module 4 performance task, students create a picture book about hidden figures in space science. Students (working in triads) create and contribute three pages of a class picture book devoted to the stories of hidden figures. Each triad, or crew, is responsible for three pages of content centered on the focus figure of their research. These individual stories are compiled into an anthology-style picture book geared toward an elementary-age audience. One of the extensions suggested for this performance task is:

> » Look for the hidden figures within your school community. Whose efforts at school often go unnoticed? Custodians? Secretaries? Honor them in a public way that highlights their contributions.

An extension like this connects the academic content of the module to students' local community and can lend authenticity to the performance task in any community. This lends authenticity to the work (and helps answer that "why do we have to do this?" question). Of course, an extension like this also has rich potential to push students around complexity as well, transferring what they have learned about the hidden figures of space science to the hidden figures in their own community.

▶ HOW DO I ENGAGE STUDENTS IN DEEPER EXTENSIONS CONNECTED TO THE MODULE TOPIC?

We began Chapter 5B with an exploration of the kinds of lesson-level extensions that are offered throughout every module in the Grades 6–8 curriculum. It makes sense to start there, especially if you are new to our curriculum. Those lesson-level extensions offer important guidance for supporting your students in need of additional challenge day in and day out. The lesson-level extensions are the most responsive to the varying profiles of your students, allowing you to account for change over time, and for relative strengths and needs in different standards so that you can employ flexible grouping to best meet student needs.

As we explored in Chapter 2A, however, it is important to approach your planning with a wide-angle lens, to see the terrain of an entire module and how the units build on one another. This wide-angle lens is useful when thinking about extensions as well.

The module-level extensions offered in the curriculum—found in the Module Overview section called Optional: Community, Experts, Fieldwork, and Extensions—are built on EL Education's commitment to connecting students to the world beyond school. In addition to learning from text- and classroom-based experiences, students use the natural and social environments of their communities as sites for purposeful fieldwork and service connected to their academic work. They collaborate with professional experts and community members with firsthand knowledge of events and issues to ensure accuracy, integrity, and quality in their work.

It is important to keep in mind that the suggestions we offer in the curriculum are necessarily general. The EL Education curriculum is used all over the United States, so we can't, for example, offer site-specific guidance on how best to connect the exhibits at your local museum to our curriculum. It will be up to you to take the germ of an idea and make it come alive for your students with purposeful and meaningful connections between your community and our curriculum.

To get a feel for what it can look like to extend learning from the modules into the community, working with experts and making a difference, explore two compelling stories from schools. The first, shown in Video Spotlight 5.2, features fifth-graders in Detroit who took their learning in Grade 5, Module 1: Stories of Human Rights to heart and found a way to take action and make a difference in their city. The second story is told in the Snapshot. It features seventh-graders in Springfield, Massachusetts, who deepened their understanding of Sudan by connecting with their local community.

▶▶ Video Spotlight 5.2

In this video, schools in Detroit Public Schools Community District join together to support literacy as a civil right in their city, which is declared a book desert. Fifth-graders, along with local artists and activists, built, designed, painted, and stocked four "little libraries" for community organizations that uphold human rights, inspired by the Grade 5 module: Stories of Human Rights.

vimeo.com/352136610

📷 Going into the Community and Inviting the Community into the School to Deepen Students' Learning about Sudan

As a kick-off for reading the anchor text for Grade 7, Module 1[9], *A Long Walk to Water*, teachers at the Springfield Renaissance School in Springfield, Massachusetts, wanted to help their students wrap their minds around the concept of access to water. Students, carrying empty jugs, walked a mile and a half through their city, collected water from a pond, and then worked in groups to carry it back to school. They began their reading, and the module, by comparing their walk to the walk that one of the main characters, Nya, makes twice a day to collect water in her country of Sudan.

Later in the module, to enhance their research as they prepared to write narratives, students interviewed people in their community who had fled violence. Teachers contacted local refugee and immigrant organizations and sent out emails to people with whom they or their colleagues had connections to find community members who would be willing to come to the school to talk to the students. It was not easy for the teachers to locate interview subjects, but they were able to find one person to come to each of the four seventh-grade classes.

To prepare for the interviews, students worked collaboratively to craft their questions. They then invited in a local expert—the leader of a nonprofit called The Performance Project—who did a workshop with students on how to elicit stories from people, and how to tell those stories powerfully.

---

9. This Snapshot is based on the first edition of EL Education Grades 6–8 Language Arts Curriculum—the module topic is the same, but the narratives and research are different than in the second edition.

Experts

Experts are people skilled in a particular field of study, such as the leader of the local nonprofit referenced in the Snapshot from the Springfield Renaissance School. Teachers can use experts to support authentic research, critique student work, model, and provide guidance. EL Education encourages the regular use of experts in the classroom and in the field, not just as "presenters" but as active partners in enriching the quality of student thinking and work. Working with experts makes academic work come alive for students, particularly when students have built enough background knowledge on the topic to engage with experts meaningfully. There are myriad opportunities to invite experts into your classroom throughout the Grades 6–8 curriculum. Whenever possible, joining forces with science or social studies teachers (depending on the module topic) to find relevant experts and prepare students to work with them productively will be beneficial for students.

Consider these suggestions from the Grades 6–8 modules:

» Grade 6, Module 4: Remarkable Accomplishments in Space Science: Invite a local expert in space science (e.g., from a local university, research center, or planetarium) to further educate students and spark interest in the module topic.

» Grade 7, Module 2: Epidemics: The anchor text tells the story of epidemiologists and other medical professionals. Consider contacting local hospitals, universities, or physicians to arrange meetings with those who treat medical epidemics on the front lines. Likewise, as students explore ideas around social contagion, consider arranging meetings with sociologists, psychologists, and other professionals in the field.

» Grade 8, Module 2: Food Choices: The topics within this module relate to food choices. Invite local farmers, CSA [Community Supported Agriculture] workers, farmers-market vendors, grocers, or other food experts to come and share with the class.

Once you are ready to invite experts into your classroom to support your module topic, consider the following guidance (adapted from EL Education's *Core Practices*):

1. Teachers may bring experts from the community into the classroom to collaborate with students on [performance tasks], teach them skills from their field, and critique their work using professional standards.

2. Teachers may reach out to experts who represent multiple perspectives and backgrounds and can expand students' understanding of the knowledge and skills they are seeking to acquire. Experts may be professionals from a particular discipline or community members with firsthand knowledge of the topic being studied.

3. Teachers prepare experts to work collaboratively with students on [performance tasks]. For example, experts may help students critique their work against professional standards.

4. Teachers prepare students to greet experts with courtesy, respect, and background knowledge, with the desire that experts are surprised and delighted by the students' depth of knowledge and preparation.

5. Teachers and students orient experts to the needs of the project and the protocols for class critique.

6. Teachers support students to maintain ongoing relationships with experts. For example, teachers help students take a lead role in communication with experts before (to ensure alignment and focus), during (to keep the collaboration on track), and after (showing appreciation or sharing their work) a visit.

Fieldwork

At EL Education, fieldwork refers to activities—outside the classroom and often off campus—in which students are active investigators, applying the research tools, techniques of inquiry, and standards of presentation used by professionals in the field. Fieldwork is distinct from field trips, during which students are often passive observers. Our curriculum offers many opportunities to incorporate fieldwork as a module-level extension, especially in collaboration with science and social studies teachers. If you teach a 45-minute ELA block, you very well may not have time to consider fieldwork as a viable extension for your students. But if you team-teach and it makes sense for content-area teachers to connect their work with yours (e.g., a history unit on the Holocaust that overlaps with Grade 8, Module 3: Voices of the Holocaust), there are wonderful opportunities for deep and enriching fieldwork.

Consider these suggestions from the Grades 6–8 modules:

» Grade 6, Module 3: Look for local museums or reservations that provide education on Native American culture; contact them to arrange a visit or sign up for an education program.

» Grade 7, Module 3: Consider visiting sites of interest, or the organizations associated with the experts [you have connected with] to meet with artists who have been inspired by the Harlem Renaissance or to see exhibits of Harlem Renaissance works at museums or libraries.

» Grade 8, Module 3: Students might visit local universities and meet with students who are studying this time period [the Holocaust] or professors who teach about it.

Once you are ready to plan and design fieldwork on your module topic, consider the following guidance (adapted from EL Education' *Core Practices*):

1. When planning fieldwork experiences, teachers ensure that they have a clear purpose connected to the curriculum. They prepare note-catchers, procedures, or activities that allow students to be researchers, not spectators.

2. When time and resources allow, teachers schedule fieldwork over an extended period of time with several visits to the same site.

3. Teachers instruct students in procedures and skills for fieldwork before setting out or during the first visit. They create a foundation for all students to be engaged and purposeful.

4. As much as possible, teachers design fieldwork experiences based on the authentic research of professionals in the field (e.g., zoologists, historians, anthropologists).

5. Teachers select data collection tools to suit the purpose of the fieldwork. When data are collected, they are analyzed and used back in the classroom to create a product.

6. Teachers structure fieldwork so that it is safe and productive. Teachers preview sites to shape the field experience effectively and ensure accessibility for all students.

7. Leaders and teachers establish written policies and well-documented safety procedures for conducting fieldwork. These include planning for the logistics of transportation, grouping students, and adult supervision.

8. Teachers prepare students to be ambassadors for their school. Students are courteous, knowledgeable, organized, and helpful during fieldwork experiences.

9. In schools where there are barriers to transporting students off campus, teachers and leaders seek creative options for fieldwork, such as selecting case studies that can be authentically explored through on-campus fieldwork (e.g., bacteria growth in public spaces, invasive species on campus, conducting a schoolwide survey).

Service Learning

Service learning goes beyond charitable acts, such as cleaning up a city park, and extends also to rigorous academic products that provide a service for the community, such as curating a selection of texts on American Indian boarding schools for the local library. The suggestions we offer in the curriculum always strive to help students connect their academic learning to their community through service.

Consider these suggestions from the Grades 6–8 modules:

» Grade 6, Module 1: An area of focus in this module is about how authors develop a character's point of view, and how that character's point of view can change over time. Consider engaging in a service experience in which students interact with others about whom they may have preconceived notions (e.g., people of a different socioeconomic status, age, or ethnicity). Direct students to write about their perception of this group before and after engaging in the service experience. Ask them to pay particular attention to the ways in which their point of view changed as a result of the experience.

» Grade 7, Module 1: There are many initiatives related to *A Long Walk to Water* and the water issues in Sudan and elsewhere. Students can take up the challenge to raise money or awareness for these initiatives, or they can investigate ways to be of service to refugee families more generally.

» Grade 8, Module 4: Challenge students to work with the school librarians to develop book displays or reading lists of texts about Japanese American internment. Refer to the Recommended Texts and Other Resources for suggestions.

Once you are ready to design and plan service-learning opportunities connected to your module topic, consider the following guidance (adapted from EL Education' *Core Practices*):

1. Incorporate service learning into projects and lessons from the outset, not as an afterthought or add-on, but as an integral part of learning.

   a. Connect service learning to habits of character.

   b. Use service as a prime vehicle to teach and take action centered on social justice and to address the challenges and celebrate the assets of living in community.

   c. Research (with students) service opportunities to ensure that service-learning projects provide a real benefit to the community.

2. Design and plan service-learning experiences that go beyond charitable volunteer work to include projects that build important academic skills. These experiences help students see that academic work can be in the service of good for others (e.g., building literacy skills by collaborating with the local refugee center to create a guide to free city services).

Chapter 5C:
Supporting English Language Learners

Students who are learning English as an additional language are referred to by many names in the United States: English as a Second Language (ESL) students, emergent bilinguals, multilingual learners, English language learners (ELLs). By any name, they are a diverse group. Their home languages vary, of course: in the United States, Spanish, Arabic, Chinese,[10] Haitian Creole, and Vietnamese are the home languages most often spoken by ELLs and their families. Many have lived all or most of their lives in the United States; some are more recent arrivals. Their previous experience of school, and the way they are currently served, also vary according to geography and social context.

Of those coming from other countries, their educational backgrounds vary widely. Some will have had many years of high-quality schooling in their home language. Some will come with interrupted educational experiences due to harsh or violent conditions. If they and their families have spent years in a refugee camp, the children may have had sporadic lessons in English, and not have had the opportunity to learn to read or write their home language. There is no generalizing about the lived experience of students from other countries, and it is very important that school administrators and teachers learn as much as possible about the educational experiences students have already had. This will help inform educators as to what types of academic, cultural, and emotional supports will work alongside language supports to ensure that ELLs have full, equal access to learning in alignment with their legal rights.

Though stereotypes persist of students learning English as being "from another country," the vast majority of ELLs are born in the United States. According to a report by the Migration Policy Institute (Zong and Batalova, 2015), Eighty-five percent of pre-K–5 ELL students and sixty-two percent of Grades 6–12 ELL students were U.S.-born in 2013[11]. Some of those students have had the good fortune to be placed in bilingual programs where they develop literacy and academic-level abilities in their first language, while they simultaneously develop their speaking, listening, reading, and writing abilities in English, as an additional language. However, this is not the norm. Most ELLs are taught in English-only programs, and most of their teachers have not had the professional education needed to serve these students effectively. The Council of the Great City Schools (CGCS) reports that only twenty-four percent of elementary school teachers, eleven percent of middle school teachers, and nine percent of high school teachers had the required ESL or bilingual education requirements needed to work with ELLs.

ELLs vary widely in their English proficiency. In most schools, those who are just beginning to learn English are in the minority, and those students who are beginners may quickly move to

---

10. This term incorporates several languages, such as Cantonese, Mandarin, and others.
11. From the Council of Great City Schools, ELL Survey report, 2019

intermediate levels, with proper support. In fact, the majority of ELLs have abilities in the middle ranges as measured by English language proficiency tests (which vary by state, but which can be compared). About sixty percent of the multilingual learner population nationwide is considered "Long Term English Learners" (LTELs), and more than thirty percent of multilingual learners in forty-nine of the nation's largest public school systems are LTELs.

LTELs are defined as those students who have been enrolled in U.S. schools for six years or longer, and who have not made sufficient academic progress due to gaps and deficiencies in the rigor of their education (Olsen, 2010). The language profiles of LTELs can vary widely. They may have great facility in spoken English that they can use with their peers and their teacher but may struggle with academic reading and writing. Those who are literate in their native language may read English relatively easily but struggle with speaking and writing. As with any student, it is critical to know where students' strengths are and where they need more assistance.

At EL Education, we are particularly concerned with the group of intermediate proficiency-level students who, after learning spoken English to a level sufficient for communication, still struggle with academic uses of English, especially in reading and writing. There are several causes for this alarming situation, but most are related to students not receiving the kinds of educational and linguistic supports they need.

It is for these reasons that our curriculum embeds the necessary supports for intermediate ELLs into every module, every unit, and every lesson, while also offering options for "deeper" and "lighter" support for students who are newer to or more experienced using English. In particular, we include high-leverage approaches to supporting ELLs throughout the curriculum, such as Language Dives and Conversation Cues, that we believe will make the difference for ELLs, and especially LTELs. These approaches are introduced in Video Spotlight 5.3. These, along with several other approaches, are discussed in great detail in the remainder of Chapter 5B.

▶▶ Video Spotlight 5.3

In this video, professor of bilingual and ESL education Rebecca Blum-Martinez guides us through four high-leverage approaches to supporting ELLs in the curriculum (Language Dives, Conversation Cues, Levels of Support, and Diversity and Inclusion)—seen in action across grades and disciplines at Lead Academy in Greenville, South Carolina.

https://vimeo.com/305147716

★ A Note about Terms

ELL/Multilingual: To describe the academic English language learning process and the student learning academic English, EL Education currently opts for the widely used, dominant terms *English Language Learner* and *English Language Learning* (ELL). Our primary rationale for the use of these terms is familiarity and clarity for our users who have grown accustomed to using them over time. At the same time, our organization is committed to equity, and we want our language to reflect and operationalize that commitment. With that in mind, we also embrace the term *Multilingual Learners* as a more asset-based reference to the diverse linguistic repertoire these students possess.

Academic English: We use *academic English* to refer to the variety of English that our curriculum and schools in the United States expect students to use in academic contexts in preparation for college and career: everything from written narratives, like the Lost Boy or Girl narratives in Grade 7, to speaking and listening protocols, like the Socratic Seminar about harms and advancements from medical research in Grade 8. Though the Common Core standards refer to "standard English," we avoid this term, since we (along with many linguists) believe that there is not one standard English. Each district, school, or classroom will have its own linguistic style, norms, and conventions that students are supported to understand and expected to master, because those are aligned to what's adaptive in college, career, and community. We also avoid using the phrases "formal English" and "informal English," since these may carry value judgments and also may be inaccurate as formality of language can shift and blur depending on context. We encourage schools and districts to set standards, in collaboration with students, for how students use language in academic contexts.

Home Language: *Home language* refers to languages such as Spanish, Tagalog, Hmong, Arabic, and Somali that students use with their families or communities. Home language may also include code-switching (alternating between two or more languages or varieties of language when communicating) or translanguaging (using a combination of two or more languages to communicate).

Long-Term English Learners (LTELs) are defined as those students who have been enrolled in U.S. schools for six years or longer and who have not made academic progress due to gaps and deficiencies in the rigor of their education (Olsen, 2010).

▶ WHAT ARE THE SPECIFIC NEEDS OF MIDDLE SCHOOL ENGLISH LANGUAGE LEARNERS?

At the middle school level, ELLs share many similarities with peers who speak English fluently. Their bodies are changing, their peers and friends are becoming more important to them, and they are trying out new ways of behaving and dressing in an effort to redefine who they are. However, for ELLs this time may be even more complex. They may already be known as "different" and viewed as "not successful" because of their level of English. This may make them more resistant to English as they seek to identify with their own language and culture, or it may make them ashamed of their language and culture. For this reason, it is critical that teachers and other school personnel be respectful of children's languages and cultures and provide opportunities to incorporate those languages and cultural backgrounds into the curriculum as much as possible.

📷 Snapshot: Meet the Students

Avugwi is a twelve-year-old boy from the Democratic Republic of Congo (DRC) and is in Grade 7. His family speaks Kikongo, and this is the language Avugwi knows best, although he knows a little Swahili, the common language used in his country. Avugwi was six when his family fled the DRC, and he has lived in a refugee camp in Tanzania for five years. Given the conditions in the camp, Avugwi attended an English class sporadically. Once in the United States, Avugwi was placed in an ESL class where he began to learn English and gained some basic literacy skills. He understands more English than he speaks. Because he is friendly, several English-speaking boys have begun to invite him to play soccer during recess, and Avugwi is gaining more spoken English.

Miguel was born in the United States to parents who immigrated from Mexico. Now twelve years old in Grade 7, he speaks Spanish at home and English with his classmates. In elementary school, Miguel was incorrectly assessed as a struggling reader, not as an ELL. ELLs have different needs from struggling readers, so Miguel did not receive the language development support he needed, and as a result, his academic English proficiency is still emerging. Therefore, he needs support to access grade-level language arts content. Miguel is friendly with classmates and teachers and gets excited talking about cars as well as repairing them.

Andrea is eleven years old and in Grade 6. She and her two brothers and three sisters and mother have been in the United States for five years. They are from a Kiché-speaking area in Guatemala. Andrea's mother speaks both her indigenous language and Spanish. Some of Andrea's older siblings can understand Kiché, but most communication in the family is in Spanish. Andrea attended two years of elementary school in Guatemala, so she has basic literacy skills in Spanish. However, given the years she has been in the United States, she prefers to read in English, and is able to speak, read, and write at an intermediate level.

Eric was born and raised in the United States after his parents immigrated from Vietnam. Both of Eric's parents can speak, read, and write English, although they struggle with the more complex language in government documents and legal papers. Now in Grade 8 at age thirteen, Eric speaks some Vietnamese with his grandparents, and he uses translanguaging skills, including common Vietnamese phrases together with English, when speaking with his parents. In school Eric is outgoing and participates in class. However, he still struggles with more complex written English, especially in language arts and social studies.

These four students represent some of the great variation in background, languages, and academic abilities found in ELLs. This great variation makes it difficult to use a single set of strategies to help ELLs learn English (Bunch, Kibler, and Pimentel, 2012). Andrea and Eric are like the majority of ELLs across the country and in many school districts: they are LTELs "stuck" in the middle ranges of English language development, too many of them assigned to remedial programs with little to no access to rich, varied, complex, and compelling material that ultimately would help them become fluent readers and writers. EL Education attempts to disrupt this pattern for this large population of students by seamlessly integrating support into each lesson in the curriculum (see the Module Overviews, the Unit Overviews, and the lessons). At the same time, the curriculum attempts to honor and serve all ELLs, from newcomers and beginners, such as Avugwi and Miguel, to advanced English learners, by providing a range of heavier and lighter supports in the Teacher's Guide for English Language Learners.

What Principles for Supporting Multilingual/English Language Learners Underlie EL Education's Language Arts Curriculum?

Multilingual/English Language Learners Deserve a Rich, Compelling, Challenging Curriculum

We believe that ELLs deserve the same rich, compelling, and challenging curriculum that other students receive. ELLs have developed age-appropriate concepts and understandings about the world—as they have experienced it. They have the same cognitive needs for an enriching and challenging curriculum and learning experiences that any child does. Varying levels of support in using English are built into our curriculum so that ELLs have equitable access to this compelling and challenging curriculum.

Learning English Should Not Be Viewed as a Barrier to Learning

English language learning is not a disability. It is not a barrier. ELLs have at least one language; it is just not English. Lack of English is not perceived as a problem, but rather as an opportunity to add an additional language. When appropriately supported, bi- or multilingualism is an asset, an indicator of intelligence and ability.

Our curriculum encourages teachers to honor and incorporate children's home languages as students learn English. Teachers can learn words and phrases in their students' home languages and publicly acknowledge them, for example, by adding the words and phrases to anchor charts and using them during various classroom routines or inviting students to create two versions of a performance task: one in English and one in a home language to foster and celebrate bilingualism.

All Educators Are Responsible for the Success of Multilingual/English Language Learners

As educators, we all are responsible for educating ELLs. This includes administrators, counselors, assessment specialists, and teachers. At the school level, schedules, materials, and any additional supports need to be in place to support the work with ELLs in classrooms. As educators, how we interact with ELLs and plan for and enact learning opportunities can make a fundamental difference in their educational careers and their lives. Assessment specialists must ensure that the district assessments are fair and unbiased toward ELLs. All educators have the power to make it or break if for ELLs.

Our curriculum integrates high-leverage language development approaches that can assist all learners, but most especially ELLs. Two approaches that can result in the greatest impact are Language Dives and Conversation Cues (these important practices will be detailed later in this chapter). By consistently incorporating these two high-leverage instructional approaches in particular, we hope that all educators will come to understand how to better assist their ELLs on a regular basis.

Second Language Development Reveals Itself in Various Ways

Understanding second language development is important. As demonstrated by the profiles of students in the preceding Snapshot, those who are developing a new language in addition to their home language are often in different places academically. As they embark on learning a new language, ELLs may vary in the speed and accuracy with which they use English. And not all language learning follows a linear path of progression. Often students will seem to regress, reverting to developmental errors they had used previously, then after a few months, jump ahead. In some cases, students may demonstrate understanding through gestures. Some students may learn a short phrase and overextend its use.

Other students, who have more outgoing personalities or whose families encourage them to speak, may attempt to speak regardless of errors. Critical errors should be tracked and addressed, but always with the consideration that language errors are a sign of beneficial risk-taking and growth. It is important to be aware of a student's English level so the student can receive instruction and support that will foster language and academic growth.

A newcomer student may need the support of visuals in order to participate in class activities. However, these initial kinds of supports would not be appropriate or sufficiently challenging for a student who is at a more intermediate stage, and might in fact hinder them from making greater progress. Supports should be gradually modified or removed as a student's proficiency increases. ELLs need to be assisted in ways that will allow them to continuously move to more proficient levels of English. For this reason, we must always combine the appropriate supports with rigor (Wong Fillmore and Fillmore, 2012; Staehr Fenner, 2013; Gibbons, 2010; García and Walqui, 2015).

Productive and Equitable Conversation Spurs Language Learning

Oral language is critical. It is the basis for reading with comprehension and writing fluency. Therefore, for ELLs, it is important to opt for interactions that are more productive and conversations that are more academically based. Before students can write successfully, they must discuss the content they are to write about and the precise language they will need to use to communicate through writing (this is why the dynamic cycle of reading, thinking, talking, and writing about text explored in Chapter 4 is so critical). Conversations should be content-related but also metacognitive. Students should be able to explain why and how they are completing any given task and what they have learned from their work. In Language Dives, for example, students routinely reflect on how the process of analyzing the language structures in one sentence helps them respond to the guiding question of the topic they are studying.

Students need the opportunity to discuss and codify their thought processes in order to rely on them repeatedly, and more heavily, in future tasks. They have to engage in academically productive conversations, guided by the teacher, that call out the language structures that make literary and informational texts complex. In extended, task-based interactions with peers, with teachers present to provide guidance and feedback to support effective communication, ELLs encounter authentic opportunities to grapple with language to achieve specific goals, to self-correct, and to succeed. Indeed, environments where ELLs have multiple opportunities to negotiate the meaning of content are most conducive to second language learning.

Language Dives, a high-leverage instructional approach for engaging students in conversation about how language is used to construct knowledge about content, and Conversation Cues, another high-leverage approach to help teachers and students have and maintain extended interactions around content, will be detailed later in this chapter. Other discussion protocols used throughout the curriculum, such as Think-Pair-Share, can complement these deep, extended conversations. All students, not just ELLs, benefit from reading, thinking, and talking about text as preparation for writing. This practice is central to our curriculum at all grade levels and is highly supporting of language learning for ELLs (see Chapter 4 for more information).

Common Core State Standards + California English Language Development Standards = a Strong Framework for Engagement with Language

College- and career-ready standards provide opportunities for ELLs to interact with challenging, complex, and engaging material. Our curriculum supports students to listen to, talk about, and read and write about literary and informational texts about compelling material.

As described in Chapter 1, our curriculum is built around Common Core standards, and in each lesson specific standards are addressed. State English language development (ELD) standards are a necessary complement to the Common Core because ELD standards help educators gauge language proficiency level and growth as students engage with content.

While states across the country have adopted many different ELD frameworks, our curriculum designers consulted the California English Language Development Standards (CA ELD Standards) to help guide the design of ELL instruction and supports in the curriculum. This framework was selected as a baseline for its balance of specificity with practicality. Of all state standards frameworks, the CA ELD Standards provided us with the most useful framework, offering robust Language standards and proficiency-level descriptors that clearly describe what ELLs should know and be able to do across a variety of contexts and at specific benchmarks. The CA ELD Standards descriptors also draw upon other state and national ELD descriptors.

An important benefit of the CA ELD Standards is that they were developed to connect to the Common Core and to encourage students to engage with rigorous academic content. For example, in Grade 8, Module 3: Voices of the Holocaust, students engage in a Language Dive from a poem written by Magdalena Klein about surviving the Holocaust (Language Dives are a high-leverage instructional practice that we explore in depth in the pages that follow). Curriculum designers were guided by CA ELD Standard I.B.8 to create a Language Dive that prompts students to discuss how a writer uses language resources. CA ELD Standard I.B.8 states: *Analyzing how writers and speakers use vocabulary and other language resources for specific purposes (to explain, persuade, entertain, etc.) depending on modality, text type, purpose, audience, topic, and content area.*

In the Language Dive, which occurs in Unit 2, Lesson 2, students tackle a question that connects with CA ELD Standard I.B.8: "What impact do Magdalena Klein's word choices within the infinitive phrase 'to bear the filth of hatred' have on the tone of this sentence?" This, in turn, connects nicely with several Common Core standards, including RL.8.4: *Determine the meaning of words and phrases as they are used in a text, including figurative and connotative meanings; analyze the impact of specific word choices on meaning and tone, including analogies or allusions to other texts.*

Each lesson in our Grades 6–8 curriculum includes the CA ELD Standards that helped guide the design of the ELL instruction and supports in that lesson. If your district uses a different framework, such as the World-Class Instructional Design and Assessment (WIDA) ELD Standards or other state standards, you may wish to align those standards to the CA ELD Standards for comparison and accountability.

Reading Level Is Not Necessarily Language Level

Some ELLs, like other students who are native English speakers, may face reading challenges. However, it is important to remember that ELLs are faced with a different set of challenges. They must encounter new sounds, new vocabulary, new grammatical structures, and new meanings. For an ELL, decoding may not translate into meaning. Therefore, although phonics practice may assist beginning ELLs with the sounds of English, continuous practice in these skills actually may be counterproductive. In order to grow linguistically, ELLs must have access to rich and complex language as it is used in the different academic subjects. As they come to understand and use this kind of language, their English abilities will grow. Language Dives and productive conversations around these kinds of language uses are critical to academic success for ELLs (Abedi and Liquanti, 2012).

Home Language Should Be Developed and Honored in Tandem with English

All ELLs should have the opportunity to further develop their home language. Some ELLs have had the opportunity to develop literacy in their home language, but many have not. It may be beyond your ability to offer deep support in the home language, but it is important to encourage families to help their children develop literacy and other more complex and academic uses of their home language.

Although you may not speak a child's home language, you can highlight and incorporate the language into the classroom by asking multilingual learners to teach phrases and words to classmates (UNESCO Universal Declaration of Linguistic Rights, 1996; Garcia, 2009; Collier and Thomas, 2004). Throughout the curriculum you will find specific suggestions for when and how you might acknowledge and honor students' home languages.

Diversity Is a Strength to Be Leveraged

Throughout the curriculum, we have included texts and tasks that honor the knowledge, languages, beliefs, and skills that exist in the cultures and backgrounds of our students and their families. For example, in Grade 8, Module 3, students read varying immigrant accounts of victims and survivors of the Holocaust, including Vladek Spiegelman in the central text *Maus I*; Magdalena Klein's poem "Often a Minute"; excerpts from a variety of memoirs; and accounts of upstanders who took action. Students read, think, talk, and write about these texts, working toward creating their own fictional, narrative graphic panel and reflection for their performance task. Honoring students' backgrounds also means asking students and their parents to share their knowledge, languages, beliefs, and skills with their peers and the teacher. In Grade 8, Module 3, teachers can consider inviting family members or community members willing to tell their own upstander stories to the class, or feature a day where students work with community members who are artists or graphic novel specialists. In this way, ELLs can shine, and their classmates can learn from them and their families (Gay, 2000).

⚠ A Caution Regarding Translations

Our curriculum encourages the use of each student's home language because it will benefit the child. However, some cautions are in order regarding extensive translation of the curricular materials themselves.

It may be helpful to use translations of informational texts dealing with science, math, or social science materials if children have had schooling in their home languages, or if their parents are able to help their children understand these texts, and if the translation is performed by a professionally trained translator to ensure accuracy.

But it may not be as helpful to use literary translations, especially when dealing with children's literature, because elements such as meaning, tone, beauty, and cultural nuance may shift or disappear.

And translations of instruction, such as English discourse analysis and writing conventions, may have unintended consequences. The ways in which English expresses meanings can be ambiguous, which can result in translations that shift the meaning or use the home language in stilted, unnatural ways, robbing students of the opportunity to develop rich and expressive home language abilities. Consider, for example, this imperative in English: "Put the books on the table where they belong." In this sentence, it is not clear whether the books are on the table, which is the wrong place, or they are somewhere else and need to be placed on the table. In translating to Mandarin, the translator cannot keep the ambiguity. Thus, these two meanings would be distinctly expressed:

Mandarin	Transliteration	Literal English translation	English translation
把桌子上的书放回原处	bǎ zhuōzi shàng de shū fàng huí yuán chù	take table-top book(s) place back original place	Take the books from the table and put them where they belong.
把书放回原来的桌子上	bǎ shū fàng huí yuánlái de zhuōzi shàng	take book place back original table-top	Take the books (from elsewhere) and place them back on the table where they belong.

The expert translator, unless given guidance by the original writer, would struggle to decide which is the correct translation to convey the ambiguous meaning of the original English sentence.

EL Education supports bilingual curricula that were designed to honor the beauty and literary traditions of all languages. In the meantime, our curriculum, as designed, is not meant to be translated for use in bilingual programs.

When Teaching the Curriculum, What Specific Instructional Strategies Will I Use to Support English Language Learners?

The basic design of EL Education's curriculum is inherently and intentionally supportive of ELLs, incorporating many oral and literacy approaches that support their learning needs. Content-based literacy, for example, which is the foundation of our curriculum, allow ELLs to engage with interesting and cognitively challenging materials as they learn English. Content-based language learning is considered one of the best ways for students to learn a language (Tedick and Wesley, 2015; Walqui and Van Lier, 2010; Bunch et al., 2005).

ELL instruction is seamlessly integrated into each lesson of our curriculum. A special symbol (black triangle) in the lesson indicates instruction that is particularly supportive of intermediate ELLs. The Teacher's Guide for English Language Learners includes language proficiency standards, unit and lesson highlights, and differentiated levels of support for each lesson. To ensure that ELLs of different abilities receive appropriate scaffolding, the curriculum includes specific approaches and strategies at the unit and lesson level, which we detail in the pages that follow. (Note that the ELL instruction and supports embedded in our curriculum are not designed to replace federal- and state-mandated ELL or bilingual instruction. Seek further assistance when attempting to identify how the curriculum may meet federal and state guidelines.)

Language Dives

A Language Dive[12] empowers students to analyze, understand, and use the language of academic sentences, which is critical to college and career, but can often seem opaque to students. During a Language Dive, the teacher and students slow down for 10–20 minutes to have a conversation about the meaning, purpose, and structure of a compelling sentence from a complex text. These structures (or phrases) within the sentences help writers express their purposes for communicating (e.g., if/then), syntactical constructions, collocations, and idiomatic expressions. Students are assisted to figure out why the author chose a particular phrase.

Language Dives are not meant to be grammar lectures, nor do they follow the initiate-response-evaluate pattern typical of many teacher-student interactions. Rather, they are "noticings and wonderings" about the ways in which language is used to convey particular meanings, and students are encouraged to grapple with the meanings, supporting our general philosophy of building perseverance and self-efficacy. Each Language Dive conversation adopts a "Deconstruct, Reconstruct, Practice" routine as a necessary part of building language, building literacy, and building habits of mind:

> » **Deconstruct:** Teachers guide students to deconstruct the sentence by discussing what it means and its purpose in the text by chunking a sentence into essential phrases. For example, in Grade 7, Module 2, students read *Patient Zero* by Marilee Peters, featuring true stories about people who contributed to advancements in treatment and medicine. They read about Mary Mallon, who was kept in seclusion on a remote island by the New York Health Department because they thought she was the cause of an outbreak of typhoid fever. One key sentence from this section of *Patient Zero* is deconstructed into four main chunks:

> Over the next three years

> Mary Mallon spent her time writing letters,

> protesting that her civil rights had been ignored,

> and pleading for help to get her released from quarantine.

---

12. The EL Education Language Dive is based on "Juicy Sentences": Wong Fillmore, L., & Fillmore, C. (2012, January) "What does text complexity mean for English learners and language minority students?" Paper presented at the Understanding Language Conference, Stanford, CA.

In deconstructing this sentence, students might wonder about the third chunk: *protesting that her civil rights had been ignored.* What is the function of this chunk? (to describe Mary's letters). Students might then work to figure out why this adjective phrase begins with an **-ing** word, which is different from many adjective forms. They can pause to consider exactly what Mary may have written in her letters. To build student capacity to independently analyze and ask questions about sentence chunks, the teacher can refer students to the Questions We Can Ask during a Language Dive anchor chart, introduced in Module 3.

» **Reconstruct:** After unpacking the sentence through conversation, students put it back together, chunk by chunk. For example, students could try to break this one sentence into two, check to see if the meaning remains the same, and then speculate as to why and how the author made it into one sentence, including discussing the use of commas. Students talk about how the Language Dive has brought greater meaning to their learning. For example, they might discuss how it added to their understanding of the meaning of the sentence and the guiding question of the unit ("How do people respond to epidemics?"), as well as what the sentence tells them about Mary's habits of character. Students can share the cognitive strategies and habits of character they used to grapple and build ideas.

» **Practice:** Students practice using one or more language structures as they speak about their own lives and write their own sentences. In the preceding example, students can focus on **-ing** adjective phrases as a way to describe a noun using a frame such as "This year, I spent time writing an essay, _____. (explaining that the Lost Children of Sudan overcame many obstacles)." Students also add this adjective structure to their Language Chunk Wall (introduced in Module 2) for future reference. Later, students can use the Language Chunk Wall as support for applying their discussions of these sentences when speaking or writing.

A Language Chunk Wall in a classroom at Lead Academy, Greenville, South Carolina

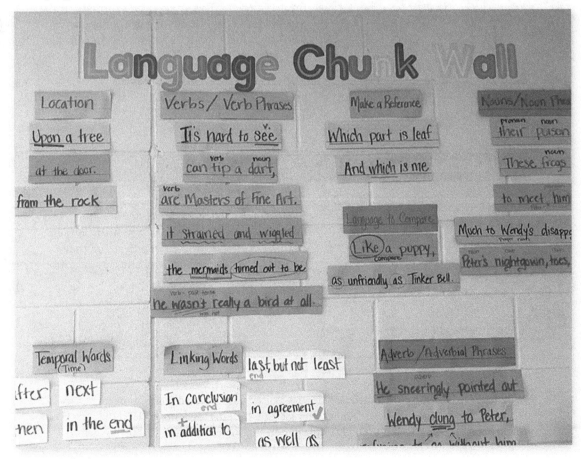

Three related videos bring Language Dives to life. Video Spotlights 5.4 and 5.5 feature Language Dives from Lead Academy in Greenville, South Carolina—one video is a condensed version of a Language Dive and the other shows an entire Language Dive and is nearly 20 minutes long. Video Spotlight 5.6 goes "behind the practice" and interviews the teachers at Lead Academy about their approach to Language Dives and Conversation Cues.

▶▶ Video Spotlight 5.4

In this video, see the rigor and joy of Language Dives in a Grade 4 classroom at Lead Academy in Greenville, South Carolina. Following the engaging "deconstruct, reconstruct, practice" routine, students play with the smallest "chunks" of the sentence, acting them out, rearranging them, or using them to talk about their own lives.

https://vimeo.com/289601263

▶▶ Video Spotlight 5.5

This video is a long version of a small group Language Dive with Stephanie Clayton and third-graders at Lead Academy in Greenville, South Carolina. This small group consists of six ELLs whose native language is Spanish, and two language minority students, all on various academic levels.

https://vimeo.com/271720208

▶▶ Video Spotlight 5.6

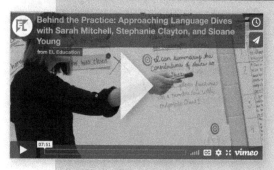

This video features a dive into Language Dives with the instructional coach and two reflective teachers at Lead Academy in Greenville, South Carolina. Sarah, Stephanie, and Sloane describe their approach to Language Dives and Conversation Cues.

https://vimeo.com/289541096

Language Dives help students acquire language through analysis, conversation, and usage, which is almost always more effective than teacher lecture. Helping students understand how the English language works is ultimately important in sharing power and establishing equity.

A consistent Language Dive routine is critical in helping all students learn how to decipher compelling sentences and say and write their own. Proficient writers can use the routine to continue to grow as lifelong learners in the complex task of communication. The routine may hasten overall English language development for ELLs. For this reason, Language Dives are included an average of once a week for all students and twice weekly for ELLs:

» At times, Language Dives are done with the whole class, and all students benefit. ELLs can listen to and interact with native English speakers. Native speakers gain new insight into their native language. These whole-class Language Dives appear as discrete agenda items in about one to three lessons per unit.

» At other times, in the Teacher's Guide for English Language Learners, 5-minute Mini Language Dives are suggested for ELLs. Teachers can guide smaller groups of ELLs while other students are working on independent tasks, or ESL specialists can pull out ELLs for short periods. These Dives are suggested about two to three lessons per unit.

» When helpful, Language Dives can be broken up into shorter sessions. For example, with a focus on deconstructing the sentence on the first day, and reconstructing and practicing it on the second day. Or discussing the first part of a sentence one day, and the latter part on a second day.

In addition to the Language Dives provided in the curriculum, we encourage you to strategically choose sentences and times for additional Language Dives that you design yourself, based on student need. Ideally, the work of Language Dives eventually will go beyond ELA to science, math, history, and social studies texts, offering daily conversation and practice across subjects to meet the language needs of all learners, but particularly of ELLs. Our website includes a resource called How to Design Your Own Language Dive (https://eleducation.org/resources/how-to-design-a-language-dive), and we encourage you to make use of it.

Conversation Cues: Promoting Academically Oriented Conversations

Conversation Cues[13] engage ELLs and their peers in thoughtful and extended, academically oriented conversations. Conversation Cues are questions teachers can ask students to promote productive and equitable conversation, helping to gauge students' thinking. The questions can encourage students to have productive discussions and generate new ideas before they begin writing tasks. Conversation Cues are based on four goals that encourage each student to:

» Goal 1: Talk and be understood (e.g., "I'll give you time to think and sketch or discuss this with a partner," and "Can you say more about that?").

» Goal 2: Listen carefully to one another and seek to understand (e.g., "Who can repeat what your classmate said?").

» Goal 3: Deepen their thinking (e.g., "Can you figure out why the author wrote that phrase?").

» Goal 4: Think with others to expand the conversation (e.g., "Who can explain why your classmate came up with that response?").

See Table 5.3 for the full text of the Conversation Cues.

At all grade levels 6–8 Conversation Cues are introduced one goal at a time across the year. Conversation Cues are designed to slowly build the capacity for all students to engage in rich, collaborative discussions targeted at ELA and ELD standards. This helps to level the playing field and enable all students to participate equitably.

---

13. EL Education Conversation Cues are adapted from Michaels, Sarah and O'Connor, Cathy. *Talk Science Primer*. Cambridge, MA: TERC, 2012. http://inquiryproject.terc.edu/shared/pd/TalkScience_Primer.pdf. Based on Chapin, S., O'Connor, C., and Anderson, N. [2009]. *Classroom Discussions: Using Math Talk to Help Students Learn, Grades K–6*. Second Edition. Sausalito, CA: Math Solutions Publications.

> *"Conversation Cues have been one of the single most important drivers of equity at all grade levels in all subjects... because [they] drive at that core belief that all students have something important to say."*

Sarah Mitchell
Instructional Coach, Greenville, South Carolina

For example, some students who are shy, introspective, or have less knowledge or language ability in some contexts may respond more readily to a Goal 1 Conversation Cue: "I'll give you time to think and write or sketch," while other students may be willing and able to respond to a Goal 4 cue: "How is what Lupe said the same as or different from what Young Bin said?"

Conversation Cues help all students begin to think deeply about the material, to explain their thinking, and to learn to listen to various points of view as they consider the material. Conversation Cues can create a classroom environment that is ideal for language development, as students practice how to communicate clearly.

To expand their independent interactions with their peers, you can encourage students to gradually begin using appropriate Conversation Cues, along with other discussion conventions, themselves. For example, at Conway Elementary School, a K–6 school in Escondido, California, teachers made placemats out of the Conversation Cues to support their students to use them spontaneously and independently.

Table 5.3: Conversation Cues

Conversation Cues	
Cue	**Expected Response**
Goal 1: Help all students talk and be understood (introduced in Module 1, Unit 1).	
Think and Process Language Internally	
"I'll give you time to think and write or sketch." "I'll give you a minute to think and write or sketch." "I'll give you time to discuss this with a partner."	
Elaborate upon or Expand	
"Can you say more about that?" "Can you give an example?"	"Sure. I think that _____." "Okay. One example is _____."
Clarify	
"So, do you mean _____?"	"You've got it." "No, sorry, that's not what I mean. I mean _____."

Conversation Cues	
Cue	**Expected Response**
Goal 2: Help students listen carefully to one another and seek to understand (introduced in Module 1, Unit 3).	
Repeat or Paraphrase	
"Who can repeat what your classmate said?" "Who can tell us what your classmate said in your own words?"	"She said ____." "He was saying that ____."
Goal 3: Help students deepen their thinking (introduced in Module 2, Unit 2).	
Provide Reasoning or Evidence	
"Why do you think that?" "What, in the (sentence/text), makes you think so?"	"Because ____." "If you look at ___, it says ___, which means ___."
Challenge Thinking	
"What if ____ (that word were removed/the main character had done something different/we didn't write an introduction)? I'll give you time to think and discuss with a partner." "Can you figure out why ____ (the author used this phrase/we used that strategy/there's an -*ly* added to that word)? I'll give you time to think and discuss with a partner."	"If we did that, then ____." "I think it's because ____."
Think about Thinking (Metacognition)	
"What strategies/habits helped you succeed? I'll give you time to think and discuss with a partner." "How does our discussion add to your understanding of ____ (previously discussed topic/text/language)? I'll give you time to think and discuss with a partner."	"____ helped me a lot because ____." "I used to think that ____, and now I think that ____."
Goal 4: Help students think with others to expand the conversation (introduced in Module 3, Unit 1).	
Compare	
"How is what ____ said the same as/different from what ____ said?"	"____ said ____. That's different from what ____ said because ____."
Agree, Disagree, and Explain Why	
"Do you agree or disagree with what your classmate said? Why?"	"I agree/disagree because ____." "I think what he said is ____ because ____."
Add on	
"Who can add on to what your classmate said?"	"I think that ____."
Explain	
"Who can explain why your classmate came up with that response?"	"I think what she's saying is ____."

Teachers can use Conversation Cues to support students in conversing with one another. Consider this conversation between a Grade 4 teacher and students discussing the choices authors make when writing sentences. Notice how the teacher uses Conversation Cues (in bold), and how students carry more of the talking and thinking:

» Teacher: **What if** I replace "but" with "and"? "And" is also a conjunction. How would using the word "and" change the meaning? **I'll give you some time to think**. Emma, you want to give it a shot?

» Emma: It is adding on to the, like, the idea of the first (part of the) sentence?

» Teacher: **Can anyone repeat or rephrase** what Emma just said?

» Santiago: It would have the same idea as the first two chunks (of the sentence).

» Teacher: "And" would have the same idea as the first two chunks. Two connecting, same ideas. So how does using the word "but" change that for me? Jazmin?

» Jazmin: "But" would change it.

» Teacher: **Can you say more about that**, Jazmin?

» Jazmin: It would change it because "but" would say there are many things happening, but this is the one.

» Teacher: Right, so **does anyone want to add something** else to that?

» Daniel: "But" is saying this is the main thing happening.

» Teacher: Right, now it's going to the main factor, or a contrast. "But" is something that is going to tell us a contrast. (exchange continues)

Classroom roles begin to shift when teachers use Conversation Cues. Teachers become "facilitator" of the conversation, rather than "driver." They can enjoy getting to know students and their ideas, rather than searching for students to give the "right" answers. ELLs are invited to be a participant in the conversation, expressing their thinking (e.g., "'But' would change it."), deepening their ideas (e.g., "'but' would say there are many things happening, but this is the one."), and refining thinking as a group (e.g., "'But' is saying this is the main thing happening.").

▷ Classroom roles begin to shift when teachers use Conversation Cues. Teachers become "facilitator" of the conversation, rather than "driver." They can enjoy getting to know students and their ideas, rather than searching for students to give the "right" answers.

Offering Differing Levels of Language Support

As we mentioned at the beginning of Chapter 5C, the majority of ELLs nationally (between forty-five and sixty percent) achieve intermediate to high-intermediate levels of English language proficiency, also known as the "Expanding" level in the California ELD Proficiency Level Continuum. Keep in mind, as the name "Proficiency Level Continuum" suggests, that language proficiency shifts depending on content, task, and situation, and proficiency cannot be considered as fixed. However, most students assessed as achieving intermediate proficiency levels get "stuck" there for a few years, and often for their lifetime. These students may be formally classified as "long-term English learners" (LTELs). To help break this pattern, our curriculum targets instruction for LTELs in particular, in large part through Language Dive instruction, to help them reach advanced levels of language proficiency and be reclassified as proficient speakers.

At the same time, in addition to the focus on LTELs, the curriculum honors and supports ELLs at lower and higher proficiency levels. Heavier and lighter levels of support are provided in the Teacher's Guide for English Language Learners for different agenda items within each lesson to support learners at any language proficiency level in accessing content. Examples:

» **For heavier support:** For students who are newer to English, the curriculum provides sentence frames they can use both orally and in writing, as well as suggested word and phrase banks and manipulatives to help them begin to construct their own sentences.

» **For lighter support:** For students who have moved beyond intermediate levels, the curriculum suggests strategic grouping, expanding or condensing sentences, or inviting students with more language proficiency to create sentence frames for students who need heavier support.

Additionally, while heavier support generally targets students at the "Emerging" level of the California ELD Proficiency Level Continuum, and lighter support generally targets students at the "Bridging" level, these supports may, at times, benefit students formally classified at *any* language proficiency level. A relative newcomer at the "Emerging" level may benefit from lighter supports in certain contexts, while a more proficient student at the "Bridging" level may benefit from heavier supports during some tasks. It is essential to observe student ability in various situations and select supports based on need, rather than seeing student ability as fixed at one level.

Knowing each of your students and their level of English is critical in helping you to differentiate supports. Each lesson references relevant descriptors from the California ELD Standards; these, in coordination with your state ELD standards and proficiency continuum, can help you understand where your students are in their development of English and where you need to guide them in their growth. Although the curriculum has built in different levels of support, these may not meet your students' needs specifically at one time or another. For this reason, it may be important to modify these supports and seek further assistance.

Diversity and Inclusion

We encourage teachers to acknowledge, celebrate, and incorporate student knowledge and experiences to promote equity. Throughout the lessons, we have included texts and activities that honor the cultures and backgrounds of our students and their families. Students are asked to reflect on how their own experience connects to the content and are invited to bring language, stories, books, and objects from home to share and discuss.

Students are encouraged to use their home language, when comfortable, to begin negotiating particularly challenging tasks or to bridge their understanding as newcomers. Teachers are invited to get to know students well, and, in turn, share their own national, family, and personal traditions, value systems, myths, and symbols.

The concept of culture is intricate; any given group is not monolithic and should not be stereotyped. Furthermore, each person may identify with several layers of culture—national, community, family, personal—that may shift with situation and time. Therefore, the cultural supports in the curriculum are intended to suggest the infinite possibilities of different student experience, not to essentialize or label any single student or group.

Writing Practice

In the Grades 6-8 curriculum, all students receive ample writing practice throughout each module. In addition to frequent cycles of read-think-talk-write, which is an embedded design feature of the curriculum (see Chapter 4 for more information), there are several additional structures and instructional practices that further support ELLs with writing:

» As students begin to complete more formal extended writing assessments, the curriculum provides writing practice for ELLs that is similar in structure (but not in content) to the assessments. For example, in Grade 7, Module 3, Unit 3: The Legacy of the Harlem Renaissance, students begin by studying Nikki Grimes' poetry in conjunction with the poetry of the Harlem Renaissance, as well as the Golden Shovel method of writing poetry in which one line of text from a Harlem Renaissance poem becomes a part of her poetry. Students study these pairings for structure, language, and theme. They also explore the Golden Shovel approach by writing one or more poems borrowing lines from other Harlem Renaissance poems. For the mid-unit assessment, students examine the structure, figurative language, and themes in Nikki Grimes' "The Sculptor" and its paired poem, Georgia Douglas Johnson's "Calling Dreams." This heavily supported process helps ELLs become familiar with writing expectations.

» Writing scaffolds, such as teacher modeling and sentence and paragraph frames, may be offered for students who need additional support (see Figure 5.4 in Chapter 5A for an example of a scaffolded note-catcher).

» Language Dives support both reading and writing fluency. After students learn to understand language structures through very focused reading at the sentence level, they practice those same structures that will give them greater confidence and skill as writers.

Vocabulary and Phrases in Context

Teachers help students learn and practice vocabulary and phrases within the context of the topic and text they are using. Students learn and practice an unfamiliar word as it is commonly used with other words—in collocation (placed or arranged together). For example, in Grade 6, Module 1, Unit 1: Greek Mythology, students read the learning target: *I can infer the topic of this module from the resources*. They discuss what it means to infer the topic in this sentence and then make and share inferences about the topic from a collection of resources posted around the room. Afterward, students indicate how well they were able to infer. Students get an opportunity to come back to this learning in Module 2 by revisiting the same learning target and comparing different forms of *to infer*: *inference* (noun) and *infer* (verb).

All students use a Word Wall to track and learn selected vocabulary, including *infer*. Students and teachers can also consult collocation and vocabulary references such as the following:

» *Oxford Collocations Dictionary for Students of English*

» https://prowritingaid.com/Free-Online-Collocations-Dictionary.aspx

» http://global.longmandictionaries.com

» http://www.learnersdictionary.com

Language Usage: Celebration and Error Correction

Teachers help students notice effective communication as well as errors in their speech and writing, and students begin to notice their own language usage. They collect and analyze language usage data from multiple sources to adjust instruction.

Teachers and students explicitly and compassionately point out effective communication, especially in alignment to standards, and attend to language errors, as part of the path to establishing equity and building content knowledge. Students can benefit from discussions as to why their communication is effective, or why their communication is inaccurate or incomprehensible, especially during the writing process.

At times, it can be helpful for students to discuss an error that is common to the group. At other times, giving one-on-one, individual feedback may be more respectful. Errors can be identified, logged, and categorized into global, pervasive, stigmatizing, and student-identified errors, and students can practice correcting them over time (Ferris and Hedgcock, 2013). The examples of errors that follow come from the Grade 7 Language Dive sentence discussed previously in this chapter: "Over the next three years Mary Mallon spent her time writing letters, protesting that her civil rights had been ignored, and pleading for help to get her released from quarantine." Here, students use their own words in the Practice section to express how Mary Mallon advocated for her civil rights:

» **Global:** Errors that interfere with overall meaning: "Over the next three years, Mary Mallon spending her time writing letters, protesting her civil rights ignoring, pleading for help to get releasing from quarantine." (Here, a student overgeneralized the participle form [verb + **-ing**].)

» **Pervasive:** Errors that are common. Example: "Over the next three years, Mary Mallon spent her time write letters, protest that her civil rights had been ignored, and plead for help to get her released from quarantine." (Here, a number of students recreated the sentence using a base form [**write**, **protest**, **plead**] instead of the participle [**writing**, **protesting**, **pleading**].)

» **Stigmatizing:** Errors that disturb more proficient speakers. Example: "Over the next three years, Mary Mallon wrote the letters, advocating for the civil rights and pleading for the freedom." (Some students may overgeneralize the article [**the**]. Although more proficient speakers may understand the communication, they may be primarily critical of the learner's language proficiency because of the error.)

» **Student-identified:** Errors that students notice and often correct themselves. Example: "Over the next three years, Mary Mallon wrote letters advocating for his civil rights, and pleading for his freedom." (A student used forms of pronouns that represent the student's current knowledge of how English pronouns work (e.g., *his* to refer to a female), instead of using grammatically correct forms.)

Giving kind, specific, and helpful feedback on successes and errors can help normalize the language learning process and put students "in the know," as well as mitigate the substantial risk students take on as they try out new language. Error correction is ineffective when too much time is spent on less meaningful errors, when the correction is misunderstood, or when students feel targeted. The primary goal is to share power with students by making the rules of language explicit and more accessible to them. By empowering students to identify and correct their own errors, you show them how you care about their language usage and help them communicate their message as intended.

Chapter 5: Supporting All Students

Chapter 5A: Supporting Students to Meet Grade-Level Expectations

Chapter 5B: Supporting Students Who Need Additional Challenges

Chapter 5C: Supporting English Language Learners

▶ Instructional Leadership

Frequently Asked Questions

Chapter 5:
Instructional Leadership

We believe that impactful instructional leadership involves cycles of action and reflection. Here we offer questions for reflection, indicators of progress, and resources for *supporting all students*.

Table 5.4: Chapter 2 Quick Guide for Instructional Leaders: Supporting All Students

Questions for Reflection
How can you foster a professional culture grounded in collaboration and growth mindset?
» What structures are in place to nurture a staff culture of learning and continuous growth? Are staff encouraged to take risks in service of growth and new learning? Do you model being open about taking on new challenges?
» Do your professional learning opportunities and content convey the message that every teacher is a reading teacher? Does every teacher have access to learning opportunities related to literacy?
» How can you create opportunities for all teachers to participate and contribute equitably to problem-solving conversations about literacy outcomes?
» What collaborative structures are in place for ELA, content-area teachers, and support specialists to learn with and from one another (e.g., professional learning communities, peer observations, mentor classrooms)?
» What additional knowledge- or culture-building among staff needs to happen so that all are supportive of the principles of inclusion for ELLs and students who need support to meet grade-level expectations? What can you do to help them feel confident in their abilities to support these students?
» How can you structure data analysis and your communication of student performance in a way that avoids blaming or shaming teachers?
What can you do to build a schoolwide culture that views differences in student learning capacities and neurodiversity not as a problem to be solved, but as an asset to be leveraged?
» What kinds of words and phrases do you and your staff use when talking about students who are struggling and for students who learn quickly or have more exposure to background knowledge at home? Is there any "unlearning" you or your staff need to do in order to support all students to succeed with this curriculum?

» How do teachers support students' academic courage to try hard things and persevere through challenges? How do they create a culture of "we're all in this together and we help one another succeed?"

» What strategies do teachers use to support advanced learners so that they stay on pace with their peers (i.e, encouraged to go deeper with the same content) and don't become isolated with different work?

» What additional knowledge building do staff need around specific terms related to ELLs (e.g., multilingual, academic English, home language)?

What structural changes are you willing and able to make to support the academic needs of all students?

» Have you examined the master schedule and built in additional flex time for literacy interventions and other literacy-related content (e.g., independent reading, extensions)?

» Have you collaborated with special educators to explore and budget for Tier II interventions for students reading significantly below grade level (e.g., students who may still need phonics or phonemic awareness instruction)?

» What systems are in place for support specialists to become knowledgeable about the curriculum—the scheduling requirements, content and instructional strategies—so that they can best support students?

» Do ELA, content-area teachers, and support specialists have adequate time together to plan the most effective literacy supports for students, including scaffolding, interventions, and extensions?

» How can your whole staff get better at the practices designed specifically to support ELLs (e.g., Language Dives, Conversation Cues)?

What support can you offer teachers to effectively differentiate instruction in a heterogeneous classroom?

» What kinds of professional learning can you design that would help staff understand the imperative to scaffold curricular materials to support students to read the same challenging texts and meet the same grade-level learning targets as their peers? What can you do to help staff view the issue through an equity lens (i.e., if students are given easier texts to read and different learning targets to work toward they will never catch up with their grade-level peers)?

» What structures can you put in place for ELA, content-area teachers, and support specialists to review the scaffolds in the Teaching Notes for lessons and the Teacher's Guide for English Language Learners as they prepare to teach? How can they collaborate to develop additional scaffolds to best meet student needs?

» What structures are in place for teachers to plan at the module and lesson level for whole-class and individual extensions that can be put in place to support students who need additional challenges?

» What logistical support can you offer to support teachers to incorporate experts, fieldwork, and service learning into modules?

» How can you support teachers to plan performance task extensions that challenge students to produce high-quality work that demonstrates complexity, craftsmanship, and authenticity?

Have you given teachers the guidance they need for when and how to pull students for small group interventions if necessary?

» Do teachers have the support they need for effectively grouping students and for managing small-group work and independent work effectively?

» What data are teachers using to strategically (and flexibly) group students? Have you provided grouping strategy support to teachers who may need it?

Indicators of Progress

» General education teachers and specialists (e.g., English as a second language teachers, special educators, interventionists) have time to collaborate and plan together to meet the needs of all students.

Not Yet True   *Somewhat True*   *Very True*

» All staff consistently use asset-based language when describing students who need support to meet grade-level expectations, those who need additional challenges, and ELLs.

Not Yet True   *Somewhat True*   *Very True*

» The budget, schedule, and other systems are designed so that students who need support to meet grade-level expectations, those who need additional challenges, and ELLs all have equal access to the curriculum and an equal chance for success.

Not Yet True   *Somewhat True*   *Very True*

» The master schedule includes flex time (e.g., extended ELA block) that can be used for interventions, independent reading, or extensions.

Not Yet True   *Somewhat True*   *Very True*

» Instructional leaders convey the message that all teachers are reading teachers. Professional learning on instructional practices that support success with the curriculum are available to all teachers.

Not Yet True   *Somewhat True*   *Very True*

» All teachers use data collection and analysis strategies that enable them to group students flexibly and differentiate instruction.

Not Yet True   *Somewhat True*   *Very True*

» When teachers are ready to design extensions, instructional leaders provide time and support for teachers to first review curricular materials for the year, the module, and the units (see Chapter 2A for more on unpacking these materials) to see how students are *already* challenged by the curriculum before planning additional extensions.

Not Yet True   *Somewhat True*   *Very True*

» Teachers are encouraged and supported to reach into the community to incorporate experts, fieldwork, and service learning into modules.

Not Yet True   *Somewhat True*   *Very True*

» Best practices for ELLs that are included in the curriculum (e.g., Language Dives, Conversation Cues) are addressed in professional learning and coaching.

Not Yet True   *Somewhat True*   *Very True*

Resources and Suggestions

» Resources available on the main EL Education website (ELeducation.org):

- Videos: https://eleducation.org/resources/collections/your-curriculum-companion-6-8-videos

- PD Pack: Helping All Learners

- Professional Learning Opportunities (or email pd@eleducation.org)

» Resources related to ELLs:

- Research and writing by Lili Wong Fillmore

- Research and writing by Rebecca Blum-Martinez

- California English Language Development Standards (http://www.cde.ca.gov/sp/el/er/documents/eldstndspublication14.pdf)

» Resources related to Universal Design for Learning, RTI, and MTSS:

- The Center for Applied Special Technology (cast.org)

- National Center for Universal Design for Learning (udlcenter.org)

- Understood.org

Chapter 5: Supporting All Students

Chapter 5A: Supporting Students to Meet Grade-Level Expectations

Chapter 5B: Supporting Students Who Need Additional Challenges

Chapter 5C: Supporting English Language Learners

Instructional Leadership

▶ Frequently Asked Questions

Chapter 5:
Frequently Asked Questions

What do I do if the texts are just too hard for some of my students? Can I have them read different texts?

At EL Education, we believe strongly that all students should be supported to read the same challenging texts and work toward the same standards as their grade-level peers. We feel strongly about this because it is an equity issue. If students are denied access to challenging materials or not supported with the tools they need to access those materials, then they are denied access to a rigorous and compelling curriculum. When expectations are lowered, year after year, these students are unlikely to ever catch up. Instead, by differentiating instruction, scaffolding materials, and providing targeted interventions when necessary, students can be lifted to the same high expectations as their peers. Our curriculum is already scaffolded to focus instruction on those portions of the texts that are most critical to students' ability to meet standards, complete tasks, and build knowledge of the module topics.

You may, of course, be required to make adjustments to texts for students with IEPs or 504 plans that call for those specific modifications to the curriculum. ELA and learning specialists should collaborate closely in these cases to determine how best to support students.

I feel overwhelmed by the idea of scaffolding materials for certain students. There's already so much to do! Do you provide scaffolded materials?

Yes! You will see a black triangle in the lessons to denote that there is a differentiated version of note-catchers, exit tickets, and other student-facing materials in the Teachers' Guide for English Language Learners. We can't emphasize enough that the Teacher's Guide for English Language Learners is a treasure trove of resources that will offer support to all of your students who may need additional scaffolding, especially with materials.

Throughout the curriculum, many times some students work independently while teachers work with small groups. What are some strategies for managing a classroom full of students when teachers are busy with small group instruction? How will students stay productive and on task without teacher direction?

We believe strongly that not only can students handle productive academic work when they are working in small groups away from their teachers, but that teaching them strategies to do so should be considered a vital part of their classroom experience. Building their capacity to take ownership of their learning and to work both independently and collaboratively is how they truly engage with and deepen their academic learning and their habits of character. We offer many opportunities, through such instructional practices as protocols and debriefs, for students to have positive interactions that help them learn how to converse with one another, ask and answer questions, and reflect on their learning. These structures build their capacity to "self-manage." (For more on self-management and building an active and collaborative classroom culture, see Chapter 2C.)

If my instructional block exceeds 45 minutes, what's the best way to structure the additional time to best support my students?

It's not uncommon for literacy blocks to be 60 or even 90 minutes. Since our Grades 6–8 lessons are designed for 45 minutes, this extra time can support you in numerous ways. Some teachers will need this additional time to stay on pace—not necessarily every day, but some days. If additional time for pacing isn't needed, we recommend the following:

» Homework reading (e.g., reading the portions of the anchor text that weren't read in class)

» Research reading

» Independent reading

» Differentiated small groups for interventions or extensions

How can I support students reading below grade level (especially those not yet decoding)?

Students who are not decoding have not yet broken the alphabetic code. While holding true to the grade-level expectations of the curriculum, additional work will need to occur outside of the 45-minute instructional period to teach students phonological skills and patterns to improve their ability to decode words. While EL Education does not offer or take a position on any one particular reading intervention program, we do believe that such programs are helpful for some students at the middle school level and may be an important component of giving all students full access to our curriculum. Your school and/or district special educators will need to review available intervention materials and curricula that are age appropriate for middle school students.

I consider much of my class to be advanced learners. Where can I find additional resources to support these students?

In addition to the extensions already offered at the lesson, performance task, and module levels, consider how you can add depth to the quality of questions and discourse in your classroom. Two of EL Education's books, *The Leaders of Their Own Learning Companion* (particularly Chapter 4) and *Learning That Lasts* can support these efforts. *Learning That Lasts* is based on our Deeper Instruction Framework and highlights the kinds of instructional moves that can deepen learning in any lesson. There are also many case studies and examples of experts, fieldwork, and service learning. The Deeper Instruction Framework can be viewed at: https://eleducation.org/resources/indicators-of-deeper-instruction, and the videos that accompany the book can be viewed at: https://eleducation.org/resources/collections/learning-that-lasts-videos. Finally, for advanced learners in search of models for high-quality work, explore: ModelsofExcellence.ELEducation.org.

Does the curriculum help long-term English learners (LTELs)?

Yes, the curriculum targets instruction for LTELs, who represent the majority of ELLs in the country. LTELS are students who have been enrolled in ELL programs in U.S. schools for six years or longer and who have not made academic progress due to gaps and deficiencies in the rigor of their education. Extended practice with the type of interactions introduced in this curriculum for all learners, especially LTELs, is important because students are supported and guided in using grade-level challenging materials that act as rich linguistic input. They are given multiple opportunities to then use this language orally and in writing.

How can I address the needs of students newly learning English?

Although our curriculum will assist all ELLs in gaining academic English abilities, we would offer some additional suggestions for students who are brand new to English. One of the best supports for newcomers in the early days is a functional approach. This involves helping students learn how to use language for particular functions, such as requesting ("Can I go to the bathroom?" "Can you help me, please?" "How do I say... ?"); responding to simple questions ("Yes, I understand." "No, I'm not finished"); and using formulaic language for expressing gratitude, apologizing, clarifying, and advocating. Short lessons with newcomers introducing this kind of language can be helpful so that students can quickly refer to helpful phrases early on.

For newcomers, in general it is important to use consistent phrasing of language and routines every day. For example, if you regularly say, "Everyone find a partner," don't vary it to "Get into pairs" (at least until students have learned "Everyone find a partner"). Visuals and kinesthetics are great ways of building understanding for newcomers. Song, rhyme, and other repetitive language practice can also help—as long as this language represents age-appropriate concepts and thinking. Above all, remember that language learning takes time.

At first, getting the "gist" of what is being talked about will help newcomers link this understanding to what they already know about the world. As time goes on, they will become better able to recognize phrases and common vocabulary and begin to put them to use for their own purposes. With the help of these instructional strategies, newcomers advance to intermediate levels of proficiency, often relatively quickly.

Our school has ESL teachers: how best should we use these specialists?

It is important to establish a close working relationship with ESL teachers and to meet regularly to unpack the curriculum, analyze ELLs' progress, and determine next steps. Specialists can and should preview Module and Unit Overviews for the general curriculum, as well as the Teacher's Guide for English Language Learners, which includes more detailed Unit and Lesson Overviews. Structure time to meet proactively with the specialist to consider how to most strategically apply or enhance the written materials.

What about the other subjects such as math, science, and social studies? How can I help ELLs in those subjects?

Explicit attention to the complex language in the texts—whether ELA, math, science, or social studies—is critical. We recommend that teachers use math, science, and social studies texts to guide students through Language Dives in these subjects. School administrators can support these efforts by ensuring that all teachers learn the "deconstruct, reconstruct, practice" structure of Language Dives so that they can be confident and capable facilitators of this high-leverage practice in their classrooms.

How does EL Education's curriculum address the California English Language Development Standards for English Language Arts for ELLs?

Our curriculum was designed using the California English Language Development (CA ELD) Standards to help guide ELL instruction and supports. This framework was selected for its balance of specificity and practicality. Of all standards frameworks, the CA ELD Standards seem to be the most useful, offering robust Language standards and proficiency-level descriptors that clearly describe what ELLs should know and be able to do across a variety of contexts and at specific benchmarks. An important benefit is that the CA ELD Standards were developed to connect to the Common Core in order to engage students with rigorous academic content. Each lesson in our curriculum includes the CA ELD Standards that helped guide the design of the ELL instruction and support in that lesson. If your district uses a different framework, such as the World-Class Instructional Design and Assessment (WIDA) ELD Standards or other state standards, you may wish to align those standards to the CA ELD Standards for comparison and accountability purposes.

Chapter 5

Chapter 6:
Reflecting on Progress: Helping Students Grow as Learners and People

Chapter 6A:
How Will I Know if My Students Are Making Progress?

Classrooms and schools are *full* of evidence of how students are progressing toward standards, from daily exit tickets to year-end standardized tests and everything in between. There are a variety of ways for teachers, schools, and districts to make sense of this data, but no matter the approach, the goal is the same: to track progress, identify students who may need additional challenge or support, pinpoint areas of instruction in need of improvement, and strategize solutions. Often teachers, led by school leaders, begin the school year by reviewing student data. They look at standardized test scores from the previous year or baseline test scores from the beginning of the year. Then they clump students into differentiated groups based on these scores.

Though this kind of data work has its place in schools, when we talk about using data to inform instruction in our curriculum, this approach is not exactly what we are talking about. Instead, we are focused on offering teachers opportunities throughout the year to look at evidence of student progress—from formative ongoing assessments gathered daily to summative mid- and end of unit assessments.

Evidence of student progress comes from a variety of sources, and all of it can be used to target instruction to best meet students' needs. But so much evidence can sometimes feel overwhelming. How should you collect it, and what should you do with it? How can you help students understand and track their progress so that they can become leaders of their own learning?

In this chapter, we will start out in Chapter 6A exploring the various sources of evidence of student progress in the curriculum. There is potentially a lot to gather, and we'll help you focus on the key evidence and some steps you can take to make sense of it. In Chapter 6B, we will look at how to turn that evidence into systematically collected data that will help you make instructional decisions to best support your students.

And finally, in Chapter 6C we will turn our attention to an outcome for students for which it's difficult to collect data: habits of character. In Chapter 1, we introduced EL Education's Dimensions of Student Achievement. This seminal document (see Figure 1.2 for reference) captures our commitment to a definition of student achievement that goes beyond mastery of knowledge and skills to also include high-quality student work and character. We will explore how the curriculum is designed to help students make progress in this area as well.

Chapter 6

▶ WHAT'S THE DIFFERENCE BETWEEN EVIDENCE AND USABLE DATA?

Students' daily work from the learning activities in our curriculum produces a great deal of direct and indirect evidence. Direct evidence is actual student work that reveals students' knowledge and skills (e.g., end of unit assessments). Indirect evidence is teacher perceptions of student performance (e.g., observation checklists). In the pages that follow, we will show you examples of direct and indirect evidence. Both are critical to assessing student progress.

When it comes to data, we use the term differently than you may be used to: we use it when referring to an organized subset of evidence that is systematically collected so that it can be used for analysis. To be considered data in this case, evidence must meet three criteria:

1. It must be systematically collected (e.g., you collect and score each student's work, versus "I feel like students are starting to get it").

2. It must be organized to aid its analysis (e.g., you create a spreadsheet to record all scores, versus a pile of completed assessments that are not organized in any way).

3. It must be based on a valid and reliable assessment.

Paul Bambrick-Santoyo, the author of *Data Driven Instruction: A Practical Guide to Improve Instruction* (2010), remarks that "if assessments define the ultimate goals, analysis identifies the strategy and tactics to get there." Helping all students meet the standards that form the foundation of assessments means we have to continually analyze student work and create effective action plans to change the outcome of students' learning. Using students' daily work as an important measure of their learning gives you an up-close-and-personal view of what enables a student's success. Using the analogy of watching a swim meet, Bambrick-Santoyo underscores the importance of seeing student learning in action, rather than just perusing their scores.

> *"Imagine a swimmer and her coach. The swimmer is a hard worker in practice, but when she goes to her first competition she finishes in third place. If the coach skips the meet and only reads the results in the newspaper, his advice will probably be that his student should focus on swimming faster. Had the coach actually gone to the pool, however, he would have seen that his swimmer was actually the fastest in the pool, and that her slow time was the result of her being the last racer off the starting blocks"* (p. 41).

The swim meet analogy illuminates an important point about analyzing student work. In this illustration, the coach analyzes the swimmer's performance in one type of race and creates an action plan—focus on the start—to improve her performance. Similarly, in the classroom, teachers frequently focus on one student's work and offer that student feedback in an effort to improve their performance the next time around. Gathering and analyzing the daily work of students in this way is the bread and butter of a teacher's job.

An essential next step is turning this evidence into data, which gives you the opportunity to analyze a collection of student work and organize it into data sets that may suggest bigger shifts in instruction for you, your grade-level team, or specialists who are assisting you with particular students or classes. To illustrate how evidence can become usable data, let's peek into a Grade 7 classroom in the Snapshot that follows.

Teachers collect evidence of English language learners' (ELLs) language proficiency from multiple sources in our curriculum, such as Language Dive conversations, mid- and end of unit assessments, note-catchers, and exit tickets. This evidence helps teachers identify where student language meets standards and where it does not so that they can adjust instruction to support and challenge students. When systematically collected, teachers can turn this evidence into usable data that informs their planning process, looking for opportunities to support students in meeting Language standards by annotating the Curriculum Map, Unit-at-a-Glance tables, and specific lessons.

When Grade 7 teacher Ms. Ocampo taught Module 2, Unit 2, Lessons 12–13, she collected and analyzed her students' Language Dive note-catchers for a sentence from *Patient Zero*: "Over the next three years, Mary Mallon spent her time writing letters, protesting that her civil rights had been ignored, and pleading for help to get her released from quarantine." In the Practice section, her student Miguel had written, "This year, I spent time writing an essay, talk with my classmates about epidemics." Ms. Ocampo noticed that Miguel needed to add **-ing** to **talk** to create an **-ing** adjective phrase in academic English ("talking with my classmates about epidemics"), which corresponds with CCSS L.7.1a, *the function of phrases and clauses*.

In looking at all of her students' work, Ms. Ocampo found that twelve other students had made a similar academic English error. While celebrating that students seemed to understand the function of the adjective phrase, Ms. Ocampo concluded that about fifty percent did not use the correct academic English form. After analyzing the student note-catchers and the most recent module assessment, Ms. Ocampo realized that there were a number of linguistic challenges her students faced. She decided to narrow the focus to CCSS L.7.1a, based on the significant need shown in the note-catcher and the module assessments.

Ms. Ocampo took the following steps to support her students:

» She consulted resources:

- In the Unit-at-Glance table, she found that students would have another opportunity to discuss and practice CCSS L.7.1a in Module 2, Unit 3, Lessons 5–6.

- When skimming the Curriculum Map, she also found that in Module 3, students would have yet another chance to revisit L.7.1a.

- To substantiate her instructional plan, she revisited the California ELD Standard 7.II.2.B.5: *Modifying to add details on a variety of new and familiar and new activities*

» She modified her instruction:

- She planned to extend the time with CCSS L.7.1a in Lessons 5–6 in Module 2, Unit 3, and, consequently, condense Lesson 1.

- After talking with her ESL specialist, she decided to use some of the designated ELD time over the subsequent two weeks for students to attend to the form of the **-ing** adjective phrase.

- The day after students completed the Language Dive note-catcher, she shared the assessment and note-catcher data with students in class and asked them to find and correct the common error.

Finally, Miguel and his classmates created a special CCSS L.7.1 learning target tracker, marking the L.7.1a column in red to indicate an area for growth and to set a goal for Unit 3. Students use "Track Progress" forms following every summative assessment (see Figure 6.1 for an example that Ms. Ocampo's students used in Module 2, Unit 2, Lesson

14). The students took one row of the form shown in Figure 6.1 to show the breakdown of the three sub-parts of L.7.1. They continued to use the tracker throughout the year to monitor their progress along L.7.1a. Tracking their own language ability progress using learning target trackers that focus on Language standards and setting language goals independently and in conversation with their peers is a key to empowering students to take ownership of their growth and learning.

Figure 6.1: Track Progress Form

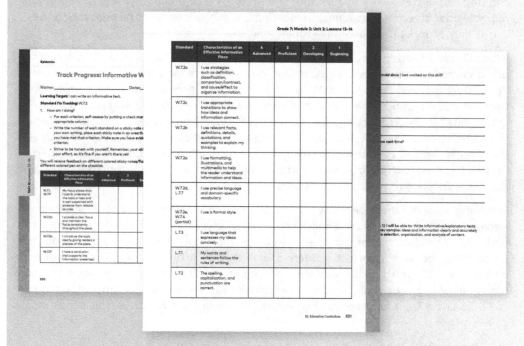

► THERE'S SO MUCH EVIDENCE TO COLLECT: WHAT SHOULD I FOCUS ON?

When you collect evidence of students' thinking, talking, and writing, you are gathering information about what students know and can do. Looking at student work individually or with a teammate can guide minor course corrections for the daily journey of teaching.

As you teach the curriculum, you will gather many sources of evidence. But the reality is that you probably won't have time for a careful analysis of all of it. Of course, you can and should focus on the summative assessments in the curriculum as a key source of evidence for further analysis, but beyond that it is up to you (hopefully in collaboration with your administrators, instructional coaches, and teaching teams) which of the ongoing/formative assessments to focus on more closely. Not every note-catcher, for example, will require analysis; however, those that ask students to demonstrate skills they have struggled with in the past, especially if they will be featured on an upcoming summative assessment, may be worth a closer look. See the box: Test-Drive Summative Assessments before Teaching the Lessons Leading up to Them, which guides you through a process of test-driving the assessments in the curriculum. This process will give you a lot of information about the sources of evidence you might want to pay extra attention to leading up to each assessment.

We will spend some time in this section exploring all of the sources of evidence in the curriculum so that you have a better feel for what to expect. And then in Chapter 6B, we'll explore more about what it means to turn this evidence into systematically collected data that is organized in such a way that aids analysis and is most useful to you.

The summative assessments in the curriculum are designed to assess students' progress toward specific standards. And the ongoing formative assessments that happen in every lesson offer you important evidence of how students are doing leading up to those summative assessments. Therefore, it will be an important part of your planning process to look ahead to the mid-unit and end of unit assessments and take them for a test drive.

> *"When we test-drive, we monitor the decisions we make as readers, writers, and thinkers... Because we are working backwards, we look at and lift the lessons that will guide our students in reaching the end goal. We feel more confident in our work as teachers and our students become more confident in the work that they are doing."*

Veronica Carrejo
Teacher, Denver, Colorado

Doing the assessment yourself will allow you to identify the obstacles your students may encounter when they are given the task. During this step, be sure you know which standards are being assessed and how each question pushes you to demonstrate your knowledge and skills with reference to the specific standard. Connecting the dots among the standards, the assessment, and the flow of lessons leading up to it will guide you as you look for evidence of student progress in ongoing formative assessments.

How do I test-drive?

Many teachers find that following a predictable test-drive routine alongside colleagues is most supportive and beneficial. Key steps:

1. Become a student of the standards:

- For each assessment, identify the standards being assessed.
- Clarify the thinking required by each standard.
- Determine what mastery of each standard looks like.

2. Take a closer look at the assessment:

- Read the assessment prompt.
- Analyze the answer key and/or rubrics.
- Take a look at the assessment texts and other supporting materials (e.g., recording forms, graphic organizers).

3. Have a go! Take the assessment as written. As you do so, ask yourself these key questions:

- What challenges do I anticipate students might face?
- What content knowledge did I need to successfully complete this task?
- What skills and knowledge did I need to successfully complete this task?
- How does this assessment build on previous learning?

4. Review the arc of lessons that lead to this assessment. Use your Unit-at-a-Glance chart, or, if time permits, skim through the lessons:

- What ongoing assessment opportunities are there for students to demonstrate their progress toward meeting these same standards?

Chapter 6

Sources of Evidence in the Grades 6–8 Curriculum

Formative assessment opportunities are explicitly identified in the Ongoing Assessment section of each lesson. Within the lesson, this section is beneath the Daily Learning Targets section so that you can easily see how progress toward learning targets will be assessed throughout the lesson.

What follows are examples of the kinds of summative and formative assessments in the curriculum. This is not an exhaustive list, but it includes some of the more frequently occurring sources of evidence.

Summative Assessments

Mid-Unit and End of Unit Assessments

Unit assessments occur twice per unit. The format varies, from constructed response to selected response to culminating discussions or presentations. These summative assessments are on-demand and often mirror a format from previous lessons (e.g., the assessment is a note-catcher similar to one students have completed previously).

On-Demand Writing

Every module has an anchor writing standard—narrative, informative/explanatory, or opinion—and it is taught and assessed once over the course of the module. Students either write essays—to inform or to express a claim—or they write narratives. As a summative assessment, these writing tasks are independent and on-demand. Sometimes, but not always, these on-demand writing tasks serve as a draft for the scaffolded performance task.

Formative/Ongoing Assessments

Informal Checklists

Checklists are a tool to help you collect evidence of progress as you observe students working. They are designed to provide you with formative information that can inform instructional decisions going forward. The informal checklists in Grades 6–8 include:

- » Writing Process
- » Collaborative Discussion
- » Presentation of Knowledge and Ideas
- » Speaking and Listening Comprehension

Text-Dependent Questions

After reading Chapter 3, you know that text-dependent questions are an important part of close reads. However, those text-dependent questions are not usually counted as formative assessment evidence because they are heavily scaffolded. Students also complete text-dependent questions beyond close reading lessons. These are done independently while reading additional sections of text—after practicing during a close reading—and can serve as formative assessment evidence.

Writing Routines

Writing routines, such as exit tickets, note-catchers, and graphic organizers, are repeated multiple times in a unit, often coinciding with chapters of an anchor text. For example, the "Compare Text to Film: *Farewell to Manzanar* note-catcher" is used repeatedly throughout Units 1 and 2 of Grade 8, Module 4. As students make their way through the book, they watch corresponding sections of the film adaptation and analyze how the film stays faithful to and departs from the text. Students focus their analysis on how the film portrays significant ideas from the text, including the ways in which the main character and her family members are impacted by internment. This work helps to prepare students for the literary argument essay they will write in Unit 2. Exit tickets are used frequently at all grade levels to help students synthesize their learning from lessons. Figure 6.2 shows an exit ticket from Grade 8, Module 1.

Figure 6.2: Grade 8 Sample Exit Ticket

Grade 8: Module 1: Unit 1: Lesson 10

Exit Ticket: Analyze Point of View:
Summer of the Mariposas, Chapter 8

RL.8.1, RL.8.6

Name: Anna _____ Date: _____

Directions: Read chapter 8 of *Summer of the Mariposas*, then answer these questions.

Reread page 135 from "Feeling the blood rushing . . ." to ". . . I couldn't even talk."

Part A
What can the reader infer from her description that Odilia herself does not know? (RL.8.6)

The petit's are filled with something that are making her feel weird.

Part B
What effect does this create? (RL.8.6)

This creates a feeling of su

Grade 8: Module 1: Unit 1: Lesson 10

Part C
Which line from the text best supports your response? (RL.8.1)

"I looked around for a phone in the room but I couldn't see one. I was just about to ask Cecilia if she even had one when the tray of petit fours started making it's way around the room again."

Part D
How does the author use narrator's point of view to create the effect in this scene? Use details from the text to support your response. (RL.8.6)

The author uses Odilia's point of view to create suspense that something serious is happening. The text says, "I knew I had to do something, call someone, but my mind was suddenly blank and I couldn't think what it was I needed to do." This gives suspense to the text as the reader knows she is being drugged but they must wait for her to realize they have been drugged.

Chapter 6

Tracking Progress Forms

Tracking Progress forms are self-assessments that students in Grades 6–8 complete after each summative assessment (see Figure 6.1). To complete these forms, students review their assessment for evidence of mastery of standards and add sticky notes to their work to point to this evidence. After students track their own progress, the teacher then reviews and adds to the form. At the end of the year, students review previous tracking progress forms and work to recognize the progress they've made throughout the year. Tracking progress forms include the following:

» Reading, Understanding, and Explaining New Texts
» Opinion Writing
» Informative Writing
» Narrative Writing
» Research
» Collaborative Discussion

★ What about the Performance Tasks?

Technically, the performance tasks at the end of every module are neither formative nor summative assessments. They are not formative since they come at the end of the module, concluding students' learning about the module topic and the literacy skills they have built over eight or nine weeks. However, they are also not summative because they are heavily scaffolded to help students create high-quality work, and so are not a strong measure of what students can do independently. For these reasons, we do not recommend analyzing performance tasks with the same lens you might use to analyze assessments.

Of course, performance tasks can give you amazingly rich insight into what your students are capable of with support and scaffolding. Therefore, each module offers guidance on looking at students' performance tasks through the lens of the attributes of high-quality student work (authenticity, complexity, craftsmanship) discussed in Chapter 4A. Consider, for example, the questions that follow, which help teachers consider the attributes of high-quality student work when assessing the performance task for Grade 6, Module 4:

» Complexity: Did the students carefully consider what accomplishments are most important to share with their audience? Do the text and illustrations reveal an understanding of the abilities and interests of an elementary-age audience? Do students use thoughtful, precise, and appropriate vocabulary and grammatical structures to convey their ideas?

» Craftsmanship: Is the text carefully crafted to appeal to a younger audience? Are the characteristics of narrative nonfiction present in the writing? Is the text edited for conventions and aesthetics and presented in a professional manner? Are the illustrations carefully drawn or culled from online sources to accurately and meaningfully reflect the events described in the text? Did the students draw from the criteria for an effective children's picture book to create a book worthy of publication in the school library? During class presentations, did the students appropriately adjust their language (i.e., their wording, volume, and intonation) to share their work with a larger audience?

» Authenticity: Were the students careful to conduct accurate research from credible sources and to paraphrase their findings responsibly? Did students internalize the roles of author, illustrator, and editor, understanding the connection between their work and the tasks of those who work in these occupations? Does student work reflect an understanding of the need to lift up the stories of those who have historically gone unrecognized?

For more resources on analyzing high-quality student work, see Models of Excellence: The Center for High-Quality Student Work (www.modelsofexcellence.ELeducation.org).

▶ NOW THAT I HAVE COLLECTED THE EVIDENCE, HOW DO I SCORE IT?

Knowing which sources of evidence are worth collecting and analyzing is one important step toward creating usable data. Next, it is important to score that work in ways that make progress toward standards clear and that will be useful to you when creating sets of data. To look at student work and its alignment to standards objectively, it is useful to use a systematic and consistent process. In the curriculum, each module includes an Assessment Overview and Resources, which includes the assessments themselves and a variety of resources such as writing rubrics if applicable, checklists, and sample student responses at varying levels of proficiency. The scores you generate will help you compose data sets that you can analyze further to create an action plan for adjusting your instruction.

Often, especially for formative assessments (e.g., responses to questions on sticky notes; exit tickets), no tools are provided to support scoring student work. One of the best and simplest ways to approach scoring a collection of student work like this is to ask yourself the same question(s) about each student's work. This will allow you to gather all of the evidence from a group of students into data that you can use to adjust instruction if necessary, just as you would if you were using a rubric.

For ongoing formative assessments, what follows is a simple set of questions you can ask yourself:

1. What does this piece of student work indicate in terms of this particular student's progress toward the daily learning target?

2. What might this particular student need next?

3. Across this collection of student work, what patterns (of successes or struggle) am I noticing?

Figure 6.3: Sample Summary from Grade 7, Module 1

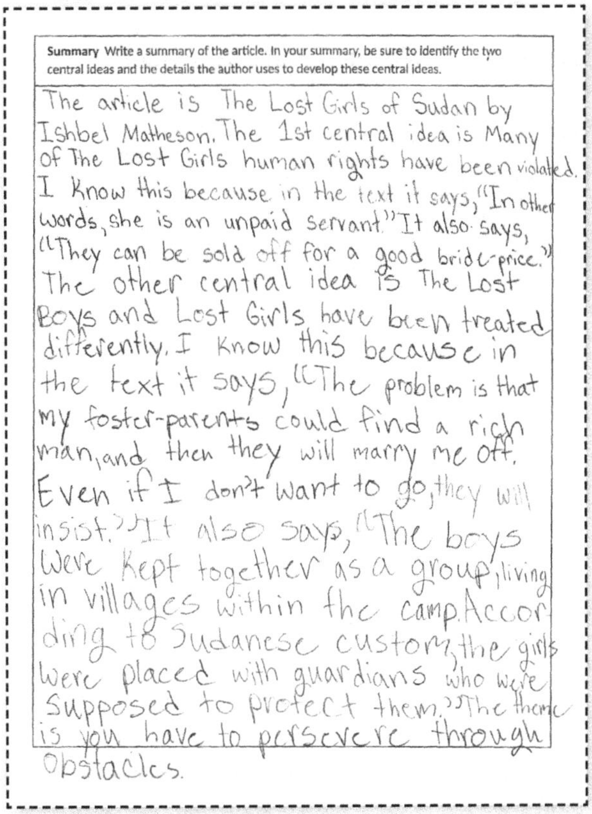

Summary Write a summary of the article. In your summary, be sure to identify the two central ideas and the details the author uses to develop these central ideas.

The article is The Lost Girls of Sudan by Ishbel Matheson. The 1st central idea is Many of The Lost Girls human rights have been violated. I know this because in the text it says, "In other words, she is an unpaid servant." It also says, "They can be sold off for a good bride-price." The other central idea is The Lost Boys and Lost Girls have been treated differently. I know this because in the text it says, "The problem is that my foster-parents could find a rich man, and then they will marry me off. Even if I don't want to go, they will insist." It also says, "The boys were kept together as a group, living in villages within the camp. According to Sudanese custom, the girls were placed with guardians who were supposed to protect them." The theme is you have to persevere through obstacles.

What does the work in Figure 6.3 tell us about this student's progress?[1]

1. What does this piece of student work indicate in terms of this particular student's progress toward the daily learning target?

   - Response: The standard that underpins the learning target for this writing sample (*I can write an objective summary of "The 'Lost Girls' of Sudan" article.*) is RI.7.2: *Determine two or more central ideas in a text and analyze their development over the course of the text; provide an objective summary of the text*. Based on this sample summary, this student has identified the two central ideas in the text and has used *some* details from the text as evidence that these are central ideas, but she doesn't go far enough to identify how the author develops the central ideas. The student doesn't make connections among the quotations or attempt to comment on their importance to the overall piece. Instead, they read like a string of disconnected pieces of evidence. Beyond this, there are many pieces of evidence from the text that could have been used to support the central ideas that the student did not use. Finally, in the first part of the lesson, students discuss the difference between a central idea—in informational texts—and a theme—in literary texts; this student seems to have confused those terms and added her thoughts on the theme of this informational text as a conclusion to the piece.

2. What might this particular student need next?

   - Response: This student could use support making meaning from the quotes in the text. Although she has pulled strong quotes to make her points, it is not yet clear that she fully understands how the quotes support the central ideas. Putting the quotes into her own words and explaining how they make her points would be good preparation for writing the summary. Not shown here is the students' note-catcher, which is incomplete. A completed note-catcher with greater interpretive "commentary" from the student may have helped her make connections among her pieces of evidence. Also, reminding her of the differences between the terms *central idea* and *theme* would support her ongoing development of these important concepts.

---

1. Note: For an individual student, only questions 1 and 2 apply.

Chapter 6B:
How Do I Turn Evidence into Usable Data?

Once you have scored each piece of student work, you are ready to begin thinking about the patterns you see and how those patterns will inform your instruction. Based on students' progress, what will you keep doing? What will you do more of, do less of, or do differently? What adjustments can you make to help more students reach standards? In short, how will you turn all of that evidence into usable data?

As a reminder, to be considered usable data, evidence must meet three criteria:

1. It must be systematically collected (e.g., you collect and score each student's work, versus "I feel like students are starting to get it").

2. It must be organized to aid its analysis (e.g., you create a spreadsheet to record all scores, versus a pile of completed assessments that are not organized in any way).

3. It must be based on a valid and reliable assessment.

For the most part, the ongoing formative assessments described in Chapter 6A, such as note-catchers and text-dependent questions, will not meet all of the criteria to be considered data. This is largely because you won't have time to systematically collect the data or organize it to aid analysis. There will be times, however, when you will want to pause on a formative assessment and turn that evidence into usable data, just as Ms. Ocampo did with the evidence from her students' Language Dives in the Snapshot in Chapter 6A.

▷   There's no sense collecting data if it doesn't inform actionable steps with direct benefit to students.

Formative assessments are a critical scaffold to help you prepare your students for the mid-unit and end of unit assessments, which is how you will assess their progress toward mastery of standards. Think of these assessments throughout the curriculum as rungs on a ladder your students are climbing. At the top of the ladder is mastery of standards. The information you glean from looking at your students' work and asking questions about what it shows about their

Chapter 6

progress on these lower rungs will ensure that you can adjust your instruction if necessary so that they can keep climbing.

We'll begin Chapter 6B by looking more closely at summative assessments in the curriculum and how evidence from these can be turned into usable data. We'll then look at evidence from formative assessments and explore under what circumstances you might want to analyze these more systematically. Finally, we'll conclude by unpacking more about what we mean by *usable* data. How can you use it to differentiate instruction to meet the needs of all of your students?

★ Using a Team Approach

It's important to consider how you will structure this work. In many schools, generating and looking at data happens collaboratively, through data-inquiry teams (or a similar structure by a different name). A collaborative structure supports teachers to analyze student work, build sets of data, and create specific action plans for changing their teaching practice to support all students' success.

Sheela Webster, principal of the World of Inquiry School in Rochester, New York, notes that her school's data inquiry teams, which involve all teachers, shift the focus of data from blaming teachers to supporting students. "In the past," she says, "it was very difficult to have conversations around data without it becoming a personal attack." The school put in place regular data team meetings with an instructional specialist who is the keeper of the data, and, says Webster, "the data now belongs to the child, and it's not the teacher's fault... We come together, know who this child is as a learner, and talk about instructional practice moving forward."

If your school doesn't have an official structure like this in place, we recommend that, at the very least, you sit down with a colleague or team, ideally with an instructional leader at the table, to set up systems for this work. As a team, you can look together at student work to assess progress and create structures to collect evidence and ensure that it becomes usable data. Making the data usable is key to this work: There's no sense collecting data if it doesn't inform actionable steps with direct benefit to students.

▶▶ Video Spotlight 6.1

In "Schoolwide Structures for Using Data with Students," Sheela Webster, principal of World of Inquiry School in Rochester, New York, discusses the value of data inquiry teams as a schoolwide structure.

https://vimeo.com/57527837

▶ WHEN AND HOW SHOULD I ANALYZE THE EVIDENCE FROM SUMMATIVE ASSESSMENTS SO THAT IT BECOMES USABLE DATA?

At each grade level, students complete a total of twenty-four summative assessments per year (four modules x six assessments per module: three mid-unit and three end of unit). This means that students complete a summative assessment approximately every week and a half. The frequency of these assessments offers you a great deal of evidence to turn into usable data.

The reality, however, is that you are unlikely to have time for a systematic analysis of all of that evidence, so how can you decide which of it to focus on?

> *"Using the right data to pinpoint exactly what students know and can do so that I choose the right next steps helps me avoid just putting a bandaid on a cut artery."*

Teacher
Atlanta, Georgia

Choosing Evidence for Analysis

Each assessment generates information about student progress that can help you sharpen instruction and scaffold the success of all students. It's information to grow on, as well as information to go on. Keeping in mind that you won't necessarily have time for a deep analysis of the evidence generated from every assessment, you will want to make some choices about how to focus your energy. One way to do this is by reviewing your curriculum map and looking for assessments that meet the following criteria:

» The standards assessed are key standards of focus for your students (determined by performance on a pre-assessment or previous assessment). For example, if your students are struggling with reading informational text, choose an assessment for analysis that includes at least one Reading: Informational Text standard.

» You feel that your students have had enough practice to gain the context of the module topics and to practice the skills taught before being assessed. The curriculum builds in this time, which you can see in the Unit-at-a-Glance chart in the Unit Overview (this chart will help you see how a series of lessons leads up to an assessment). But you may feel that your students need more practice before you spend time analyzing the evidence from their assessments.

» The assessment requires students to demonstrate skills that they will need again on future assessments.

» The assessment allows you to compare data points and identify trends over time. For example, the Mid-Unit 1 Assessment in Grade 7, Module 1 includes vocabulary questions. Students' ability to use a range of strategies to determine word meanings is a data point that can be measured and tracked over time.

Now, examine your assessments against the preceding criteria, and highlight those that you want to focus your energy on for deeper data analysis. Record your findings in a grid like that in Table 6.1.

Table 6.1: Assessing Your Assessments for Further Analysis

Assessment	Assessment	Assessment
Description/How it's Scored	**Description/How it's Scored**	**Description/How it's Scored**
Why is it optimal?	**Why is it optimal?**	**Why is it optimal?**

(Note: You may also be able to use a grid like this to assess formative assessments for further analysis.)

Organizing the Evidence

Each module in the curriculum includes an Assessment Overview and Resources, which includes the assessments themselves and a variety of resources such as writing rubrics if applicable, checklists where you can record your entire class's progress toward mastery of standards (see Figure 6.4) or where students can track their own progress against rubrics, and sample student responses. These tools are tailor-made for you to take evidence of progress and turn it into usable data that can help all students meet with success. We'll look at the important steps in this process in the pages that follow.

Figure 6.4: Grade 6, Module 2, Unit 3 Assessment Collaborative Discussion Checklist

End of Unit 3 Assessment Part II: Fishbowl Discussion Recording Sheet

Standards Assessed: SL.6.1a, SL.6.1b, SL.6.1c, SL.6.2

(For Teacher Reference)

Grade 6: Collaborative Discussion Checklist		
Discussion Topic: How do habits of character help people solve critical problems?		**Date:**
Students prepare for, and participate effectively in, conversations and collaborations on Grade 6 texts and topics.		
Comprehension and Collaboration		
CCSS	**Criteria**	**Student Initials**
SL.6.1a[1]	Comes to discussions prepared, having read or studied required material.	
SL.6.1a	Explicitly draws on preparation by referring to evidence on the topic.	
SL.6.1b	Follows rules for collegial discussions.	

(Note: Checklist is for example only. It may look different from actual curriculum materials.)

Identifying the Patterns and Trends that Can Inform Instrction

Tools like the checklist in Figure 6.4 will help you identify trends and patterns. Perhaps you will notice that nearly all of your students show an understanding of the content and use vocabulary that reflects this understanding, but that most students are struggling to provide a sense of closure in their writing. This is helpful and actionable information that can guide your planning for future lessons that you know will have more opportunities for practice writing paragraphs.

As you review sets of data like this, keep in mind these questions:

» In general, what do the students farthest from the standards most need to learn next?

» What is a generalizable "critical move" that could move the students who are close to meeting the standards into the next level? (You may want to revisit the Teaching Notes in the particular sequence of lessons, particularly the How It Builds on Previous Work and Down the Road sections.)

» What instructional choices did you make that led to the success of the students meeting the expectation?

» What qualities does the work of the students exceeding the standards most exhibit?

» Finally, choose an "actionable" issue from the trends (e.g., a common challenge) that you can address to help students make meaningful improvement.

Table 6.2 shows how a Grade 7 teacher answered these questions after students completed an assessment in Module 1 in which they analyzed theme and wrote objective summaries of a text. In this example, the teacher noticed a trend of students having trouble determining the most important details from the text to show support of the theme.

Table 6.2: Asking and Answering Questions Based on Data

Questions to Ask Yourself	Sample Answers from Grade 7, Module 1
In general, what do the students farthest from the standards most need to learn next?	*how to find the best evidence to support an emerging theme in a text*
What is a generalizable "critical move" that could move the students who are close to meeting the standards into the next level? (You may want to revisit Teaching Notes in the particular sequence of lessons.)	*more emphasis on key details when analyzing theme; comparing and contrasting key details with less significant ones*
What instructional choices did you make that led to the success of the students meeting the expectation?	*providing common themes in literature to support students' analyses; utilizing note-catchers on which students can track most important evidence of theme within a given section as well as how the author has developed the theme over time*
What qualities does the work of the students exceeding the standards most exhibit?	*the ability to not only identify theme, but also to provide evidence and analyze the development of the theme over the course of the text*
Finally, choose an "actionable" issue from the trends (e.g., a common challenge) that you can address to help students make meaningful improvement.	*Provide multiple options of evidence and have the class work on sorting most important details from minor details and then explain their sorting decisions to their peers.*

Creating an Action Plan Based on the Data

Looking at data is only as valuable as the actions that result from your analysis. If you don't change your approach to instruction, you are likely to get the same results again and again. So, the next step in the data analysis cycle is to create an actionable plan for your classroom. Ideally this work will be done in teams. The Results Meeting protocol described in the box that follows is a useful tool to help you and your team analyze data in your classroom and across classrooms. If you are unable to do this work in a team, you can still work through the protocol on your own. You'll note a suggested amount of time for each step; as with any protocol, there's no perfect amount of time for any given part, but we do recommend aligning as a group on how long you'd like to devote to each step, and reevaluating along the way as needed, keeping grounded in the big-picture purpose.

Results Meeting Protocol[2]

Purpose

The goal of the results meeting is to analyze with your data inquiry team (grade level or department team) the results of the most recent assessment and determine an action plan that meets the needs of students in your grade/department.

Materials

Student data recorded on a checklist (see "Pre-work"), Results Meeting protocol note-catcher (see Table 6.3), student assessments, assessment rubric, chart paper, markers

Time

Part I, 40 minutes; Part II, 45 minutes (Note: This protocol can be done as two separate protocols/sessions.)

Pre-work

Before engaging in a Results Meeting protocol, you will need to score your students' assessments and record the scores on a checklist.

Protocol Roles

Recorder (to record notes on chart paper); facilitator; timekeeper

Part I: Analyzing Student Data to Identify a Focus Standard (40 minutes)

Analyze: Individually read the checklist to determine areas of strength and struggle and trends related to student performance on standards. Record your individual findings on the note-catcher. (15 minutes)

Discuss and record on chart paper: Where did students do well? (5 minutes)

» Go around: Each person on the team names two areas in which they noticed students did well and cites evidence from the checklist.

» Group members ask "What evidence do you have?" as needed.

---

2. Informed by Bambrick-Santoyo, P. (2010). *Driven by Data: A Practical Guide to Improve Instruction.* San Francisco, CA: Jossey-Bass.

» The recorder takes notes on chart paper.

Discuss and record on chart paper: Where did students struggle? (5 minutes)

» Go around: Each person on the team names two areas they noticed in which students struggled and cites evidence from the checklist.

» Group members ask "What evidence do you have?" as needed.

» The recorder takes notes on chart paper.

Discuss and record on chart paper: What are the trends in the data? (5 minutes)

» Go around: Each person on the team names the top trend they noticed.

» The recorder takes notes on chart paper.

Discuss: Of the struggles identified, which should be prioritized (i.e., which standard)? (10 minutes)

» Open discussion: The team comes to an agreement about the top challenge to focus on right now.

» The recorder circles the selected challenge on the list on the chart paper.

Part II: Acting on Student Data to Increase Achievement on a Focus Standard (45 minutes)

Sort (5 minutes): Physically place the student assessments into three piles based on the standard of focus: *met* or *exceeded* the standard of focus, is *approaching* meeting the standard of focus, is *not approaching* meeting the standard of focus.

Analyze (20 minutes): Each member of the team will now focus on one particular group of students. In pairs or alone, analyze the student work in your pile, focusing on the following questions and using the learning targets from Module Lessons as a guide.

» Student work: What are the trending strengths in your students' work? (Refer to specific skills.)

» Student work: What are the trending areas of struggle in your students' work?

» Unit arc: Based on the Unit-at-a-Glance chart (in the Unit Overview), will your group have an opportunity to revisit these standards? If so, in which lesson? If not, what are some high-leverage moves you can make to meet their needs?

» Unit arc: Based on the Unit-at-a-Glance chart, will your students be reassessed on this standard in the next assessment? If not, how will you assess their progress on the focus standard?

Share (10 minutes): Each group will have 3 minutes to share their notes about their pile of student work, focusing on their suggestions for reteaching and reassessment.

Reflection (4 minutes): Which "high-leverage next steps" are most realistic, most helpful, and most effective?

» Silent think/write time: Each person silently assesses which solutions are doable/effective (1 minute).

» Each person on the team has 30 seconds to share their reflections.

Consensus and delegation (6 minutes): Which actions will teachers on our team take?

» Based on the reflections shared, the team discusses and comes to an agreement on a plan and dates for reteaching and reassessing the focus standard for each group of students.

» The recorder writes the agreed-upon actions on the chart paper.

Table 6.3: Results Meeting Note-catcher

	Notice	Evidence
Class strengths		
Class challenges		
Trends		
Standard(s) of focus		
High-leverage next step/ action plan		

The most important outcome of a Results Meeting protocol is a plan to support students who may need additional scaffolding or help to meet standards. Identifying feasible solutions is key. Once you have identified a feasible solution to an area in which students need improvement, consult your curriculum map and flag where skills and activities associated with this trend are targeted in future lessons. What new or different activities, grouping strategies, or supportive materials will you need to prepare in advance?

▶ WHAT ABOUT EVIDENCE FROM FORMATIVE/ ONGOING ASSESSMENTS? IS THAT WORTH ANALYZING AND TURNING INTO USABLE DATA?

Your main focus for systematically collecting and analyzing evidence of student progress will be the summative assessments in the curriculum. However, formative assessments offer a great deal of information about student progress, and there will be times when you'll want to take a closer look.

It's important to pause here in the midst of this chapter about evidence and data to talk about judgment. As a teacher, you use your judgement all day long. Your students steer you in unexpected directions each day, and your judgment, based largely on your experience in the classroom, is what keeps things rolling. There's nothing wrong with using your judgment to guide you to the evidence you should analyze in a more systematic way.

Trust your instincts, and use your judgment. If your students' discussions seem to be missing important understandings you had hoped they would have, if their opinions are not backed up by evidence, or if you simply feel that a lesson didn't go well, it's time to hit the pause button. Gather their note-catchers or exit tickets or whatever ongoing assessment evidence was generated during the lesson, and dig into some analysis. The Snapshot that follows is an excellent example of a teacher trusting her instincts. When teacher Bess Pinson noticed that her students were struggling with summarization, she started to do some digging into their previous assessments to see what she could discover that would help her better support them, not just in her class, but in all of their content-area classes.

At Lead Academy in Greenville, South Carolina, sixth-grade teacher Bess Pinson was excited for Module 1 on Greek Mythology. Students love *The Lightning Thief*, and she anticipated that their enjoyment of the text would provide great motivation as they did foundational work for the grade. When she unpacked the module, she could see that a lot of the work students would do in the module would hinge on their ability to determine theme and summarize, as laid out in CCSS RL6.2: *Determine a theme or central idea of a text and how it is conveyed through particular details; provide a summary of the text distinct from personal opinions or judgments*. This standard shows up in the first several lessons of both Unit 2 and Unit 3.

Ms. Pinson could see that the mid-unit assessments in Units 2 and 3 both required students to summarize. In Unit 2, the work they'd do identifying themes in myths and the novel (which would lead in the mid-unit assessment to the more significant skills of comparing and contrasting themes) would depend on students' ability to summarize what they'd read. In Unit 3, their work of planning a narrative would require strong understanding of all the myths they'd read so far.

Ms. Pinson knew that identifying theme was complex work for sixth-graders, but after reviewing the scaffolding in the lessons in Units 2 and 3, she felt confident that would give her students enough support to succeed with that abstract thinking. Yet she had already noticed issues of comprehension in her class, and, as she says, "I thought summaries would be a way to guide them to focus only on the information that mattered." So she chose to home in more on the second part of the standard: summarizing.

Ms. Pinson checked with the fifth-grade teacher to see whether she could access any module assessment data about how her current students performed with CCSS RL5.2 or RI5.2 toward the end of their fifth-grade year. She learned that in Grade 5 Module 4, the first half of Unit 2 also includes a lot of work with this standard; students' analysis of the contribution of multimedia in the mid-unit assessment hinges on their skills of summarizing and determining theme in the first few lessons.

Ms. Pinson was glad she asked because, as it turned out, the previous year, in fifth-grade, her current students had struggled quite a bit with summarizing. Looking at the evidence, two clear patterns emerged: students were either providing so much information that it was no longer a summary, or providing too little, and it read more like a gist. (Note that the main data source she had was their written summaries. But her fifth-grade colleague confirmed that students had struggled summarizing orally as well.)

Since Ms. Pinson knew she had a bit of time before Unit 2 launched their work on this standard, she decided to gather data from another source to help her be maximally strategic in planning her instruction: NWEA MAP. Supported by Sarah Mitchell, the school's instructional coach, Ms. Pinson hypothesized that there were two likely reasons students might not be able to summarize: they might not comprehend the text well enough to be able to summarize it, or they might comprehend the text, but simply not know what a summary (written or oral) should include (perhaps confusing it, as plenty of adults do too, with gist statements or paraphrases).

Those are very different reasons, and indicate different ways to provide support. Using MAP data helped Ms. Mitchell and Ms. Pinson focus on which students needed what kind of support.

Because MAP gave them an idea of student's reading levels, they were able to look at the Lexile® measures of what they'd be reading in the module (including the myths provided by EL Education) and see which students might benefit from what they came to call "comprehension frontloading." "We used 'Flex Time,' our school's intervention period," reflects Ms. Mitchell, "to build in opportunities to read out loud, and added scaffolds for unfamiliar vocabulary. We shifted pre-reading to homework. We were really cognizant of the Lexile® measures of myths, and used the differentiated ones in the curriculum, grouping kids by MAP score. Ms. Pinson also involved the school's Special Education department, as all of her students with IEPs for reading were reading below the Lexile® measure of the texts in this instance. For those students, they did frontloading work on comprehending the text in their pull-out period."

Ms. Pinson also added some more work with summarizing into Unit 1. She and her students made an anchor chart with criteria for a summary (in the curriculum, this is built into Unit 2, but Ms. Pinson had previewed that unit, identified this key scaffold, and chose to introduce it a little sooner based on the student needs she'd identified).

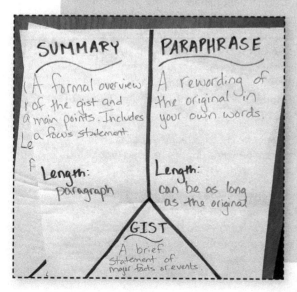

Using an exemplar from Grade 4 for clarity and accessibility, Ms. Pinson's class constructed a criteria list.

Then when they read from *The Lightning Thief* in class, in addition to the work of finding the gist, analyzing point of view, and preparing for their text-based discussion, her class would take a beat to talk through or write a summary, and check it against their criteria. At first they did this as a class. When students began writing summaries on their own, Ms. Pinson used her phone to quickly snap photos of student work, cast those up onscreen, and lead brief discussions about how the summaries reflected the criteria on their anchor chart. Eventually, Ms. Pinson included summarizing for homework.

Because students' struggles to summarize risked holding up their ability to progress to other skills, and because this was true both in ELA and across content areas, Ms. Pinson worked with her grade-level colleagues to align on clear expectations for a sixth-grade level summary. In math class, students had been summarizing what they'd learned that day; in social studies, students had been summarizing their own notes. As a group, the teachers realized that they also were unclear on the elements of a summary, and so were having trouble assessing what they got from students. Ms Pinson advocated amongst her grade-level colleagues for common terminology and expectations, so the work would feel more authentic and consistent for students.

Teachers aligned as a group on the requirements for a summary and how it differs from a gist or paraphrase, and made anchor charts to hang in math and social studies classrooms.

Just as they'd done in ELA class, students became accustomed not just to writing summaries, but self-assessing and receiving feedback about how well their summaries matched the agreed-upon criteria.

Once the grade level aligned on what a summary was, and drilled into assessment data to see which students needed that "comprehension frontloading" to give them access to practicing the skills of summarizing, Ms. Pinson saw steady improvements in the summaries students wrote about the curriculum texts. Her colleagues saw improvements on the content-area summaries, and their success has encouraged them all about what's possible when a grade-level team aligns on expectations about reading and writing. Ms. Pinson is planning to repeat the process for other high-leverage concepts and skills in the curriculum, and knows that in order to fully address RL6.2, students needed not only to be able to summarize, but also to keep digging into the first part of the standard: "determine theme."

In addition to your in-the-moment judgment, another indicator that a formative assessment is a good one for you to analyze further is students' past performance. If they struggled in a particular area on their mid-unit assessment and a subsequent lesson gives them a chance for further practice, that's a good time to look more closely at formative assessment evidence from that lesson.

In either case, ask yourself the questions described in Chapter 6A:

1. What does this piece of work indicate in terms of this particular student's progress toward the daily learning target?

2. What might this particular student need next?

3. Across this collection of student work, what patterns (of successes or struggle) am I noticing?

When working to turn evidence of individual students' progress into usable data, it's especially important to focus on question 3. After identifying patterns, you can ask yourself an additional question:

4. What might groups of students who are struggling with this learning target need to reach success? How can this understanding inform my instruction going forward?

A simple way to think about what each group of students needs is to sort work into piles: work that is *beginning*, *developing*, *proficient*, or *advanced* for the given target/standard. From there you can consider upcoming lessons or interventions and what opportunities there are to differentiate instruction to better address students' needs.

▶ HOW CAN I USE DATA TO DRIVE DIFFERENTIATION AND BEST SUPPORT MY STUDENTS?

Carol Ann Tomlinson, one of the leading experts on differentiated instruction, describes the difference great teachers make by seeing "humanity in every child; model[ing] a world that dignifies each child; and mak[ing] decisions to support the welfare of each child[3]." Recognizing and describing the strengths and challenges of your students allows you to tailor (i.e., differentiate) your instruction to meet their needs. Students' strengths and challenges are not static, however; students learn and grow all the time, and their struggles in one area (e.g., writing) do not necessarily mean that they will struggle in others (e.g., reading comprehension). This is why usable data, based on formative and summative assessments, is so important. Data allows you to select different instructional approaches and paths depending on the varying and changing needs of the students in your classroom.

After analyzing data for trends, you can select differentiated approaches that allow each student to work toward the same high standards. Sometimes a differentiated approach will be useful for one student, a small group of students, or your entire class. You want to be sure that the strategy you implement serves the right student(s) and doesn't impede those who are already succeeding.

---

3. From keynote speech at the EL Education National Conference, 2011

As we described in Chapter 5, the curriculum has been designed from the outset, based on the principles of Universal Design for Learning, to be supportive of students with varied learning needs. Also, extensive supports for ELLs, such as Language Dives, are woven into every lesson to give students full access to the curriculum. Beyond these pillars of the design, considerations for differentiation are offered throughout the curriculum to best support all students. The Teaching Notes section of every lesson and the Teacher's Guide for English Language Learners for each module provide specific suggestions.

However, despite the best-laid plans, sometimes students will need additional scaffolding and support. Table 6.4, which first appeared in Chapter 3B and was built-out in great detail in Chapter 5A, highlights differentiation options to consider based on the needs of your students.

Table 6.4: Scaffolding Options

	Scaffolding Options
Lesson calls for reading chunks of the text independently	» For students who might get overwhelmed by seeing the whole text on a page, format the text in "bite-sized" pieces (e.g., one paragraph at a time on index cards or one page as a separate handout).
	» Have students read with a buddy.
	» Have small groups read with you or another teacher (or via technology).
	» Provide structured overviews for some sections of text.
	» Predetermine importance for selections of text, and highlight those.
	» Reformat texts to include more embedded definitions or even picture cues.
	» Provide the text to students in a clear format, either on a handout or displayed clearly via technology.
Lesson calls for answering questions	» Start with concrete text-dependent questions before moving to the abstract.
	» Tackle small sections at a time.
	» Once students have tried the task, provide additional modeling for those who need it.
	» Provide sentence stems or frames.
	» Use a highlighter to emphasize key ideas/details in the text.
	» Modify graphic organizers to include picture cues or additional step-by-step directions.
	» Post directions and anchor charts.
	» Provide "hint cards" that give students more support with text-dependent questions (students access these only when they get stuck).
	» Indicate where students may find key information in the text or on an anchor chart by marking with sticky notes or highlights.
	» Give options for responding to questions with discussion before writing.
	» Use the lesson's Work Time for guided work with the teacher.

Lesson calls for writing	» Modify graphic organizers to include visual cues or additional step-by-step directions.
	» Provide sentence starters and sentence frames.
	» Use discussion, including Conversation Cues, to help students orally rehearse their answers before responding in writing.
	» Model writing using a similar prompt or a different section of the text.
	» Use the lesson's Work Time for small group guided work with the teacher.
	» Use the lesson's Work Time for conferring with individual students.
Lesson calls for collaborative work	» Review norms for collaboration in advance and after group work.
	» Have small groups work with a teacher.
	» Form heterogeneous pairs (strategic partnerships).
	» Monitor specific students more strategically (e.g., seat them closer to a teacher).
	» Provide (and model) structured roles for group members.
Other literacy or intervention time	» Offer additional practice with Speaking and Listening standards (e.g., oral reading, speaking with expression) and grammar rules.
	» Offer additional writing practice.
	» Pre-read with students the text used in the lesson.
	» Have students read additional (easier) texts on the same topic.
	» Have students reread texts used in lessons.
	» Provide additional quality read-alouds, including via technology.
	» Pre-teach critical vocabulary.
	» Engage students in word study (e.g., structural analysis of specific words from the text).
Homework	» Provide students with read-alouds via technology (e.g., audiobooks).
	» Provide visual cues or additional directions.
	» Provide sentence starters or sentence frames.
	» Provide video or slides of class examples on a website.
	» Modify expectations of quantity.

Considering the Needs of English Language Learners

Chapter 5C offers an extensive description of the curriculum's supports for ELLs. Here we expand on that information with a few specific considerations for looking at ELLs' work for evidence of meeting learning targets. In addition to some of the general questions to ask yourself (described in Chapter 6A), consider these additional questions and differentiation options for ELLs:

» If assessment data and checklists reveal that the student is not yet meeting learning targets related to reading, does this reflect the student's *reading* level or the student's *English language* level? Although a student beginning to learn English may indeed "struggle" to read English accurately and fluently, they may be a strong reader in their home language. Determining the cause of the struggle is important for planning the right next steps in supporting ELLs.

- Considerations for differentiation:
  ○ If the student is literate in a home language, ask them to read something in the home language for a teacher (or hired translator) who also speaks that language and informally assess their fluency and accuracy.

  ○ Preview key story elements and vocabulary before the student reads.

  ○ Encourage the student to reread the text after they read related comprehension questions.

» If assessment data and checklists reveal that the student's performance on a task is inconsistent with their abilities (as demonstrated previously), were the instructions for the task represented in a clear and comprehensible way for students who are learning English? ELLs may benefit from additional scaffolds when receiving instructions.

- Considerations for differentiation:
  ○ Read assessment questions aloud to students.

  ○ Model the task and "think aloud" as you go.

  ○ Allow students to discuss the task in home languages before they complete the task independently.

  ○ Check for comprehension by inviting students to summarize the instructions for the task.

» If assessment data and checklists reveal that the student is not yet meeting learning targets related to writing, did the student have enough opportunities to talk before they were expected to write? As we know from Chapter 4, engaging in discourse before writing is an important scaffold for ELLs. Was the student given enough time to write? Writing in a second language may require more processing time. Before drawing too many conclusions from data, ensure that these scaffolds were in place prior to writing.

- Considerations for differentiation:

  ○ If the student can write in their home language, have a teacher (or hired translator) who speaks the same language informally assess a written artifact for strengths in the home language.

  ○ Provide think time.

  ○ Provide oral processing time to plan writing with a teacher or peer in English or in the home language.

  ○ Model a sample written response, and "think aloud" as you go.

  ○ Provide sentence frames.

» If assessment data and checklists reveal that the student is not yet meeting learning targets related to speaking and listening, did the student have sufficient think time? Were they asked probing questions to engage their thinking? Because ELLs may need additional language processing time, it may be difficult for them to participate in conversations even if they have mastered the content and are able to express their ideas.

- Considerations for differentiation:

  ○ Provide additional think time.

  ○ Use Goal 1 Conversation Cues to elicit more information and to promote equity (Conversation Cues are described in detail in Chapter 5C).

  ○ Empower students to advocate for themselves when they need more time to think or when they would like something repeated.

When determining appropriate action steps based on your analysis of the work of ELLs, a good place to begin is with the specific details in the lesson: the language proficiency standards listed for each lesson in the Teacher's Guide for English Language Learners, and the ELL supports marked with black triangles in the lessons. Identify which support you can integrate into your instruction to help students take ownership of the learning target and make progress. Consult with an English as a second language specialist to help identify individual students' strengths in English language development and to plan appropriate support for each student.

Chapter 6C:
Habits of Character Connect Students' Growth as Learners to Their Growth as People

As one of our three dimensions of student achievement, mastery of knowledge and skills is clearly a focus of our language arts curriculum, and our path to help students succeed in this area has been detailed throughout this book. High-quality student work, another dimension of student achievement, took center stage in Chapter 4, particularly in 4C, where we explored how models, critique, and descriptive feedback help strengthen student writing within and beyond the curriculum. Here we turn to the third dimension, character, which we call habits of character in the curriculum.

You may wonder why we have chosen to highlight habits of character in a chapter about assessments, evidence, and data. On the surface, it may not seem like it fits. However, for us, character development is as important an "outcome" for students as mastery of standards (albeit much harder to measure!). Additionally, one-third of our framework for character is about helping students *work to become effective learners*. One of the best ways we know to do that is to engage students in the assessment process. In this way, habits of character are both a means to help students master knowledge and skills and an important end in themselves.

▷ ... habits of character are both a means to help students master knowledge and skills and an important end in themselves.

Three aspects of character are identified in our Dimensions of Student Achievement. Table 6.5 illustrates how each of these is taught in the curriculum. The right-hand column describes in student-friendly language some of the particular habits the curriculum works to grow.

Table 6.5: Habits of Character in the Curriculum

Aspect of Character	Habits of Character (in student-friendly language)
Work to become effective learners: develop the mindsets and skills for success in college, career, and life (e.g., initiative, responsibility, perseverance, collaboration).	» I take initiative. This means I notice what needs to be done and do it. » I take responsibility. This means I take ownership of my work, my actions, and my space. » I persevere. This means I challenge myself. When something is hard, I keep trying and ask for help if I need it. » I collaborate. This means I can work well with others to get something done.
Work to become ethical people: treat others well and stand up for what is right (e.g., empathy, integrity, respect, compassion).	» I show empathy. This means I try to understand how others feel. » I behave with integrity. This means I do the right thing even when it is hard. » I show respect. This means I treat myself, others, and the environment with care. » I show compassion. This means I notice when people are sad or upset and reach out to help them.
Work to contribute to a better world: put learning to use to improve communities (e.g., citizenship, service).	» I take care of and improve our shared spaces. » I use my strengths to help others grow. » I apply my learning to help our school, the community, and the environment.

In the pages that follow, we will explore the first aspect of our character framework: *work to become effective learners*. Specifically, we will address why it is so important to engage students in the assessment process, both as an end in itself (helping them develop lifelong habits of effective learners) and as a means to helping them master the literacy standards that the assessments in the curriculum measure. We will then explore how the other two aspects of our character framework—*work to become ethical people* and *work to contribute to a better world*—are an explicit focus of the curriculum.

▶ HOW WILL ENGAGING MY STUDENTS IN THE ASSESSMENT PROCESS HELP THEM BECOME MORE EFFECTIVE LEARNERS?[4]

The most important assessments that take place in any school building are seen by no one. They take place inside the heads of students, all day long. Students assess what they do, say, and produce, and decide what is good enough. These internal assessments govern how much they care, how hard they work, and how much they learn. They govern how kind and polite they are and how respectful and responsible. They set the standard for what is "good enough" in class. In the end, these are the assessments that really matter. All other assessments are in service of this goal—to get inside students' heads, raise the bar for effort and quality, and foster a growth mindset (i.e., a belief that learning comes from effort and that making mistakes is a part of how we learn).

---

4. This section is excerpted in part from the introduction to our 2014 book *Leaders of Their Own Learning: Transforming Schools through Student-Engaged Assessment*.

Engaging students in the assessment process is effective because it draws on these internal self-assessments that occur naturally for them. Unfortunately, students and teachers often don't know how to tap into this level of assessment and learn how to capitalize on it. Students frequently have widely varying internal standards for quality and aren't clear about what "good enough" looks like. Some students have internalized a sense that they don't have a value or voice in a classroom setting and that anything they do will be inferior to the work of the "smart kids." In other cases, they believe they have only one chance to do something and begin to work from a place of compliance and completion rather than working toward quality through a series of attempts.

Teachers frequently fall into the trap of simply saying "try harder" without giving students specific targets, feedback, time to revise, and a purpose for doing quality work. What students really need are tools and support to self-assess and improve their own learning and the motivation to do so. Knowing where they're headed and how to get there engenders responsibility and empowers students to take ownership of their learning. We also know that students from historically underserved groups do best when teachers explicitly communicate high expectations and a clear belief that the student is capable of reaching them. Unless students find reason and inspiration to care about learning and have hope that they can improve, excellence and high achievement will remain the domain of a select group.

▷ What students really need are tools and support to self-assess and improve their own learning and the motivation to do so. Knowing where they're headed and how to get there engenders responsibility and empowers students to take ownership of their learning.

Putting Students in the Driver's Seat as Leaders of Their Own Learning

Often when we think of an assessment, whether formative or summative, we think of it as something that is done *to* students, rather than something done *with* students. A big part of our approach to assessment at EL Education is to reframe it as something that students do *with* their teachers. If we give students the tools to understand where they are headed with their learning, help them track progress along the way, and then debrief with them not only *what* they learned but *how* they learned it, we put them in the driver's seat. After all, students are the ones who are in control of their learning, not us. If they feel motivated to persevere when the going gets tough because they understand where they are headed and why, that will take them much further than our encouragement or admonishments.

Our curriculum is designed to build in students a sense of ownership over their progress, changing the main goal of assessment from evaluating and ranking students to motivating them to learn. From goal-setting and reflection to learning targets and tracking progress forms, students become leaders of their own learning, motivated internally to succeed. They learn the language of standards and metacognition, identify patterns of strengths and weaknesses, become self-advocates, and assess their own work.

Helping students be purposeful and skillful in their ability to reflect on what and how they learned is at the core of becoming a self-directed learner and thus is essential for college and career readiness. Reflection is built into every lesson in our curriculum, ensuring that students develop the skills to reflect deeply and concretely, beyond vague statements of preferences, strengths, and weaknesses.

Motivating Students to Persevere through Challenges

In our curriculum, compelling topics, combined with meaningful tasks, collaboration with peers, and assessment practices that support students to do work that they are proud of, motivates them to step up to challenges.

Research suggests that student perseverance, grit, and self-discipline correlate strongly with academic success (Blackwell, Trzesniewski, and Dweck, 2007; Duckworth and Seligman, 2005; Dweck, Walton, and Cohen, 2011; Good, Aronson, and Inzlicht, 2003; Oyserman, Terry, and Bybee, 2002; Walton and Cohen, 2007). This will not surprise teachers or parents—it is common sense. But whether students bring these "noncognitive" strengths to a given task is deeply dependent on the degree to which students see alignment between what they care about and what they are asked to do. When they don't see that alignment, they have no reason to work hard.

When we see a student frequently declining to work hard on academic tasks, we often label them as "disengaged." It is worth noting that the behaviors we end up seeing and interpreting as "disengagement" emerge from the complex constellation that is that student's particular set of life experiences, both inside and outside of schools buildings. It is learned behavior, habitual, not inherent.

Kindergartners tend to come to school excited to learn. In the course of their schooling, however, some students become doubtful that they can thrive in a school environment. Their test scores and grades may have made this clear to them, or the frequency with which they are called out or punished for behavior that seems normal to them, or that other students display with impunity. We know, though, that test scores do not give the full picture of what students can do, and we know that students of color are disproportionately likely to experience school discipline (while not being more likely to actually misbehave).

So many factors influence whether a student believes school is a place where they can succeed. Our curriculum reflects the idea that students deserve to learn through work that matters to them and the world. It is our experience that when students have an opportunity to engage with a compelling topic and work through meaningful tasks in collaboration with their peers, they are motivated to step up to the challenges of that topic and those tasks in order to do work that they are proud of. These experiences, too, are habit forming, and can send students into their high school years with the mindsets that will help them succeed there and beyond.

Collaborative, meaningful work and high expectations helped these students at Propel Schools in Pittsburgh step up to challenges. Here, seventh-graders share their ebooks from the Module 2 performance task with third-graders.

▶ HOW ARE THE OTHER ASPECTS OF CHARACTER (*WORK TO BECOME ETHICAL PEOPLE* AND *WORK TO CONTRIBUTE TO A BETTER WORLD*) TAUGHT IN THE CURRICULUM?

The first part of our framework for fostering habits of character is helping students become effective learners. One way we do this is by engaging them in the assessment process, as previously described, but there are many ways in which this is a focus in our curriculum. In kindergarten, this may mean something as simple as asking students to take responsibility when cleaning up; in our Grades 6–8 curriculum, we ask students to consider questions like "how does the practice of collaboration support the development of academic mindsets like "I belong in this community?" We also focus strongly on helping students be collaborative learners (see Chapter 2C).

Beyond our emphasis on helping students become effective learners, our curriculum gives them authentic opportunities to learn and practice each aspect of our framework for character (see Table 6.5), including *work to become ethical people* and *work to contribute to a better world*. Our curriculum is unique in that it integrates an intentional focus on developing students' habits of character within the context of content-based English language arts (ELA) lessons. No curriculum is values-free; every curriculum either explicitly or implicitly addresses how students are expected to behave, in addition to what they are expected to learn. We choose to be explicit about character strengths and how teachers can foster them.

At all grade levels, the curriculum is designed to give students authentic opportunities to understand how character is a part of—not separate from—their academic work. We don't tell students to "have good character," but instead give them chances to learn about or demonstrate good character and then reflect on it, often in the context of academic lessons. For example, students read about people (real or fictional) who embody certain habits and serve as compelling models for students' own aspirations. In Grade 6, students read about the hidden figures of space science: the "West Computers," who were the first black women hired by NASA and whose talents and perseverance helped land human beings on the moon. Learning the stories about the personal strengths behind their remarkable contributions may inspire students to contribute to their own communities. Students practice aspects of character as they work independently, collaborate with peers, and care for one another and their classroom. They reflect on habits of character individually as they evaluate their work, set goals for themselves, and engage in the assessment process with their teachers.

★ Connecting the Curriculum's Habits of Character to Existing Character Frameworks

Many common frameworks are used to help educators think about the development of character in the classroom: character education, social-emotional learning, nonacademic factors, and the social curriculum are common examples. According to the U.S. Department of Education, the development of character is about helping "students and adults understand, care about, and act on core ethical values." We have our own language and approach to developing habits of character, but these can and should complement, not replace, existing frameworks, language, and routines for promoting social-emotional learning in your school.

For example, some schools focus on the five core competencies identified by the Collaborative for Academic, Social, and Emotional Learning (CASEL), or others might be using Second Step, Ruler, or Leader in Me. Schools may have codified specific character words or habits to focus on (e.g., *self-discipline* or *kindness*). You can certainly continue to use these words; when using our curriculum, you can simply help students connect the language used (e.g., *perseverance*) to how your school may already talk about character (e.g., *tenacity*). Such connections will expand students' academic vocabulary and enrich their understanding of these important concepts.

Work to Become Ethical People

In Chapter 3A, we detail the complex considerations that went into our choice of texts in the curriculum. In addition to choosing texts that ensure students will have the opportunity to meet ELA standards, we also prioritized texts that give students the opportunity to practice habits of character. We looked for texts that would offer students a chance to read, think, talk, and write about the human experience and reflect on how their actions impact others.

Every module has a habit of character focus that is woven into the lessons. As we designed the curriculum, we ensured that this habit of character focus was connected to the module topic, texts, and tasks so that students have an authentic and coherent experience. In Grade 8, Module 1, working to become an ethical person is the habit of character that is emphasized throughout Unit 1. Students practice *respect, empathy*, and *compassion* as they respond to one another's ideas and skills in written work and in discussions. Students also focus on working to become ethical people as they analyze ways in which characters in their anchor text, *Summer of the Mariposas*, show *compassion, empathy, integrity*, and *respect* in their actions. In particular, students look closely at Odilia's empathy and compassion for her sisters, and identify ways in which she demonstrates this throughout their journey. Students also find evidence of the compassion and empathy that La Llorona has for Odilia and her sisters, as she continually offers guidance and support on their journey. Students have the opportunity to think about the sisters' empathy and compassion toward one another, and any growth they show over time.

Work to Contribute to a Better World

The third part of our character framework is about contributing to a better world. Helping students consider their place in the world and how they can be of service is a part of the K–12 school experience for many students. In our curriculum we build off of this ethic by weaving service into ELA lessons so that students can put their learning to use to improve their communities.

Grade 7, Module 4 is a good example of how the curriculum helps students contribute to a better world. In Unit 3, students *use their strengths to help others grow*, informing others about the problem of plastic pollution and the steps they can take to help reduce pollution. Throughout the module, students have read texts, watched videos, and conducted research into the problem of plastic pollution and the possible solutions. For the performance task, students share their learning with an audience beyond their classroom by creating a brief documentary clip. Creating this clip is important because plastic pollution presents an urgent and real problem, and the ability to think through solutions, act on them, and share progress with others is crucial in addressing it. Students work in groups to write a documentary script and create a storyboard to plan their documentary clips. Then, for the performance task, students work in triads to film and edit their documentary clips with the purpose of sharing their message with their peers and a larger audience.

Creating work for an authentic audience motivates students to meet standards and engage in revision. Through the process, they develop *perseverance* and realize that they can do more than they thought they could. This particular example of fostering habits of character is also a nice example of another dimension of student achievement: high-quality student work. The performance task for this module allows students to create high-quality work based on their deep knowledge of plastic pollution. Using the literacy skills built throughout the school year; knowledge built in the module; and cycles of drafting, critique, and revision, students are able to create a high-quality product (the documentary clip) that showcases their learning for the year.

Table 6.6 includes additional specific examples of how the curriculum integrates habits of character into the daily life of the classroom.

Table 6.6: Developing Students' Habits of Character in the Grades 6–8 Curriculum

Structures and Practices in the Curriculum	Explanation and Example
Provides structures that empower students to participate in a collaborative community; fosters a sense of belonging	Students consider how to collaborate effectively. For example, students in all grades co-create a Discussion Norms anchor chart which they use to anchor their collaborative conversations (e.g., "I ask questions to better understand what people are saying"; "I make comments that contribute to the discussion").
Teaches the language of character explicitly and authentically in the context of lessons (not as a stand-alone "character curriculum")	Students learn how to talk about their interactions. For example, in Grade 7, Module 1, students do a collaborative challenge (stacking cups) to practice speaking and listening. During the Closing and Assessment portion of the lesson, they reflect on how they used *initiative* (a habit of character) to complete the challenge.
Devotes time for students to regularly set and reflect on individual goals; students see they can succeed at this work	Students own their own learning, regularly self-assessing. For example, after the End of Unit 1 Assessment of Module 1 in Grades 6 and 7, students reflect on their performance during the assessed collaborative discussion and set individual goals on a Track Progress form. Each student then briefly confers with the teacher to reflect on progress and set a specific goal for the next week.
Devotes time for students to regularly set and reflect on group goals	Students frequently "step back" and consider how their interactions are going and what could be improved. In Grade 6, Module 4, Unit 3, students work on writing a collaborative essay in pairs. In Lesson 3 they reflect on the strengths and challenges of a collaborative writing process.
Includes intentional grouping and protocols, so students interact with a wide variety of peers	Collaboration is a critical life skill explicitly named in the Speaking and Listening standards. In the curriculum, protocols—simple discussion routines—develop students' ability to have collaborative conversations with diverse peers.
Fosters collaboration as students work to create high-quality work; students see that this work has value to them	High-quality student work is one of our dimensions of student achievement. Collaboration is a key means to this end. For example, in Grade 7, Module 4, students work in groups to write a documentary script and create a storyboard to plan their documentary clips. For the performance task, students work in their triads to film and edit their documentary clips with the purpose of sharing their message with their peers and a larger audience.
Builds students' self-direction and independence	The curriculum helps students be leaders of their own learning. For example, students often set goals before engaging in an assessment and then reflect on their progress toward those goals after the assessment.
Builds students' ability to give and receive feedback that is kind, specific, and helpful	Students regularly critique one another's work, and they learn and practice how to give feedback. For example, in Grade 6, Module 1, students pair up and give each other one "star" (positive feedback) and one "step" (suggestion) on their draft Compare and Contrast essays, then revise.

Challenges students to connect their learning with the broader world and help solve real problems	Students are most engaged when doing real work that matters. In Grade 7, Module 4, students take on the challenge of thinking about a solution to plastic pollution. In Unit 3, students delve deeper into their chosen areas of intervention in the life cycle of plastic and choose a personal action to respond to the issue. Actions might include using less plastic or recycling more, communicating with officials, or researching an invention. Students form triads with classmates who have chosen the same category of action plan and determine how to coordinate their personal actions to be used in their documentary clip.
Allows students to make connections with the human condition and see other points of view through repeated reading of texts	In Grade 8, Module 3: Voices of the Holocaust, students learn about a terrible time period in history, and remember the voices of victims, survivors, and upstanders. They read multiple texts, including a graphic novel and poems, to develop their ability to determine and track themes, understand the development of characters, and identify and track the development of central ideas. This supports their work in Unit 3 when they write narratives to honor the memories of those who served as upstanders during the Holocaust.
Puts students in the role of experts	In Grade 7, Module 2, students learn about epidemics in many forms: historical and current, medical and social. They also focus on social and cultural responses to epidemics to develop a model of how best to respond to challenging circumstances. In Unit 3, students choose an epidemic that concerns them or their community, research the epidemic, and write and record a podcast script to convey the information they learned about the epidemic, including the story of the epidemic; the scientific and social ideas surrounding the epidemic; the tools, mindset, and character habits; and the lessons learned from the epidemic.
Helps students see and celebrate how their ability is growing with their effort	Growth mindset permeates the curriculum. For example, after each assessment, students track their own progress toward learning targets and reflect on their next steps.

The Relationship between Habits of Character and Academic Mindsets

In her work "Academic Mindsets as a Critical Component of Deeper Learning," Camille Farrington suggests that one of the most basic foundations for increasing student achievement is the development of four academic mindsets ("the psycho-social attitudes or beliefs one has about oneself in relation to academic work"):

» I belong to this academic community. (Connection)

» I can succeed at this. (Confidence)

» My ability and competence grow with my effort. (Perseverance)

» This work has value to me. (Relevance)

In explicitly addressing the habits of character described in Table 6.6 through the use of our curriculum, teachers can actively help develop these mindsets. When students develop a sense of belonging and engagement in an academic setting that engenders a sense of confidence, they are more likely to grow to become effective learners and ethical people. And contributing to their community helps students see firsthand the value of their work and feel satisfaction in their efforts.

EL Education believes that to prepare students for success in college, career, citizenship, and life, we must embrace a broader and deeper vision of what high achievement means. Good test scores are just a starting place. Mastery of knowledge and skills, character, and high-quality work are all critical for success.

Chapter 6:
Instructional Leadership

We believe that impactful instructional leadership involves cycles of action and reflection. Here we offer questions for reflection, indicators of progress, and resources as you support teachers in *using evidence effectively*.

Table 6.7: Chapter 6 Quick Guide for Instructional Leaders: Planning for Using Evidence Effectively

Questions for Reflection
» What support does your staff need to understand the difference between evidence and data? Are they prepared to select evidence of student progress that is worthy of further analysis (i.e., worth the time to turn it into usable data)?
• Are systems and structures in place to help teachers organize and analyze data so that it can inform their instruction? For example, have you prioritized time during staff or team meetings for teachers to look at student work together? How might your instructional coach support this work?
• What support do teachers need to feel confident in knowing what they are seeing and hearing when they look at student work and listen to student conversation? What additional learning do they need to help them do this work effectively? For example, should you model the process of looking at student work and identifying what it tells you about student progress toward mastery of particular standards? Would this help your teachers develop consistent schoolwide practices? What do your teachers need most to be successful with this practice?
» What support have you given teachers to identify when and how to scaffold students who are struggling toward mastery of standards? What else do they need?
• What best practices have you observed among those teachers who can respond to the needs of students (based on data) in ways that don't bog down their pacing? How can you ensure that all teachers can learn similar strategies?
» Have you messaged the importance of habits of character? If not, why not? What are your own beliefs about how important habits of character are both as a means to help students succeed with this curriculum and as an end in themselves?

Indicators of Progress

» Staff are not feeling overwhelmed by the amount of evidence of student progress (e.g., formative/ongoing and summative assessments) generated by the curriculum. They feel confident in their ability to select which evidence is worthy of deeper analysis.

Not Yet True   *Somewhat True*   *Very True*

» Whole staff and team meetings have time dedicated to looking at student work together and calibrating analysis. Instructional leaders support teachers in this work.

Not Yet True   *Somewhat True*   *Very True*

» Teachers use Curriculum Maps and the Unit-at-a-Glance charts to determine if and when students will have additional chances to work toward mastery of standards. They are able to strategize what they will need additional time to reteach and when they will do it (e.g., during built-in flex time). They stay on pace with lessons overall.

Not Yet True   *Somewhat True*   *Very True*

» Teachers consistently use data and pieces of student work to make instructional decisions.

Not Yet True   *Somewhat True*   *Very True*

» Teachers understand the array of differentiation options available for students who need additional scaffolding, based on data analysis. They know how to scaffold students in ways that don't take away their access to high-level texts and high-level thinking.

Not Yet True   *Somewhat True*   *Very True*

» Teachers support students to consistently self-identify goals and clarify how they will be working toward those goals.

Not Yet True   *Somewhat True*   *Very True*

» Teachers commit to engaging students in the assessment process. They ensure that students understand their learning targets and check their progress, and they make time for students to reflect on their learning. Even when time is tight, they don't skip time for students to reflect and track their progress.

Not Yet True   *Somewhat True*   *Very True*

» A focus on habits of character has allowed the curriculum to come to life in classrooms. Students are continually improving their abilities to work collaboratively, show respect for one another and their space, and connect their effort to their success.

Not Yet True   *Somewhat True*   *Very True*

Resources and Suggestions

» Resources available on our curriculum website (Curriculum.ELeducation.org):

• Assessment Overview and Resources (for every module)

• Checklists

• Writing rubrics

» Resources available on the main EL Education website (ELeducation.org):

• Videos: https://eleducation.org/resources/collections/your-curriculum-companion-6-8-videos

- PD Packs
    - Using Data
    - Collaborative Culture
    - Leaders of Their Own Learning
- Professional Learning Opportunities (or email pd@eleducation.org)

» EL Education books that deepen understanding of the practices in this chapter:

- *Leaders of Their Own Learning: Transforming Schools through Student-Engaged Assessment*

- *The Leaders of Their Own Learning Companion: New Tools and Tips for Tackling the Common Challenges of Student-Engaged Assessment*

» Book: *Driven by Data: A Practical Guide to Improving Instruction by Paul Bambrick-Santoyo*

» Website: Models of Excellence: The Center for High-Quality Student Work: resources available for teachers ready to do more in-depth analysis of student work (modelsofexcellence.ELeducation.org)

- Better World Day Projects from the 2017–18 school year (https://modelsofexcellence. eleducation.org/exhibits/better-world-projects)

» Website: The EL Education Character Framework: What does EL Education mean when it says character? (https://characterframework.eleducation.org/)

Chapter 6: Reflecting on Progress: Helping Students Grow as Learners and People

Chapter 6A: How Will I Know if My Students Are Making Progress?

Chapter 6B: How Do I Turn Evidence into Usable Data?

Chapter 6C: Habits of Character Connect Students' Growth as Learners to Their Growth as People

Instructional Leadership

▶ Frequently Asked Questions

Chapter 6:
Frequently Asked Questions

How should I record student grades? Does the curriculum have a progress monitoring system?

Our approach to assessment is standards-based, meaning that systems and structures within the curriculum are designed to reflect students' progress on each standard, versus giving letter grades or grading in more generic categories such as "writing." If your school already uses a standards-based grading system, it should be fairly easy for you to use that system for recording student grades from the curriculum. If not, you will likely need to develop your own systems for mapping scores from our rubrics, for example, onto your existing grading structure. EL Education currently does not have an official progress monitoring system for the curriculum. However, as is evident in this chapter and throughout the book, we have many resources in place to help you score student assessments and organize data.

I'm overwhelmed by the idea of analyzing my students' work. Is it really that important?

To thoughtfully and consistently analyze student work does take time, and you may feel overwhelmed by the pressure to cover material and stay on pace. This pressure may cause you to keep plowing through instead of pausing to take stock of how your students are making progress. This is not a good tradeoff. If you skip the step of looking closely at students' work in order to cover ground, you lose your most important lever to boost student learning: close understanding of how each student is doing and what they need to work on next.

What should I do with evidence of student progress that I have decided not to analyze?

One option is to help students use their work to develop portfolios that show their progress toward mastery of standards and growth over time. Portfolios are a great way to deeply engage students in the assessment process. Helping them curate and analyze their own work as sources of evidence is valuable learning for them. Another option, harkening back to Chapter 4C, where we talk about using models as a way to help students identify the criteria for quality work, is to begin collecting your own models. In subsequent years, you can use actual models of student work from the curriculum, which will be powerful for your future students.

My school leaders haven't structured professional learning time to allow teaching teams to gather to analyze data. Do you have any suggestions for how to do this work more independently?

First, we would encourage you to keep advocating with your school leaders for why you feel it would be more powerful to do this work in teams and the potential benefits you see both for teacher practice and student outcomes. But if that is not your current situation, you can still start by doing the work on your own or with a colleague who is willing to devote some time to working with you. Document your process and the impact it is having on your ability to meet students' needs. If your school leaders see the impact this work is having for you and your students, they are more likely to consider schoolwide structures. If a schoolwide structure is still not realistic, consider bringing your ideas for this work to team or grade-level meetings. You can start by having each team member bring in a sample or collection of student work for analysis and using the Results Meeting protocol. If you are the only teacher in your grade, you can do this in vertical team planning meetings or ask to include student work analysis in coaching sessions.

If my analysis of data shows that students need additional practice, how can I find time to reteach lessons or parts of lessons?

Before considering how you will find time to reteach, look at your Unit-at-a-Glance chart or Curriculum Map to see if there are already opportunities to address student needs built into upcoming lessons. Very often, standards will "spiral" in and out of lessons over the course of the module(s) and you will find that students are not expected to master a given standard the first time they encounter it. That said, some students may need additional intervention to master standards. Refer to Chapter 5A for extensive guidance.

I love the curriculum's focus on habits of character, and I'm interested in putting more emphasis on how students can contribute to a better world. What else can I do beyond the lessons in the curriculum?

At all grade levels, contributing to a better world is an explicit focus of each module. Often, after students have had a chance to build knowledge about a compelling topic in the first two units of a module, they will have the opportunity to take action in Unit 3 (typically connected to the performance task). Students creating an Audio Museum to act as witnesses to a long-unrecognized period of American Indian boarding schools is one example. Each Module Overview also has a section called "Optional: Community, Experts, Fieldwork, Service, and Extensions." This is a good place for you to start thinking about opportunities for students to contribute to a better world (e.g., service) beyond their ELA lessons but in a way that is connected to the module topic. For example, during Module 3, eighth-graders might volunteer to record stories from community members who have historical links to the Holocaust and write reflections on how they can be upstanders in their own communities. These optional (but no less important) extensions of the modules are opportunities to give students holistic learning experiences. Refer to Chapter 5B for more information on extensions of this type.

I love the curriculum's focus on habits of character, but I'm not sure if I should be "grading" student's growth in terms of character.

Our curriculum doesn't take a position on or provide resources for grading habits of character, largely since schools' grading systems are often already very complex, and schools may already have an existing approach to character. However, many schools in the EL Education network and beyond do grade certain aspects of character (sometimes called habits of scholarship or habits of work) that are in the "effective learners" category and have measurable components (e.g., I complete my homework on time) within a standards-based grading system. We do not suggest trying to grade students on their ethical character (e.g., compassion, respect), as it is difficult to quantify those habits and they may be most importantly exhibited when we are not watching students. However, students can certainly collect evidence of showing strong habits in ethical character.

Paramount to any effort to assess character is that character targets have clear criteria for success and are practiced, formatively assessed, self-assessed, and reported separately from academic grades. One of the easiest places to start with this work is the *work to become effective learners* aspect of our character framework. It can be powerful for students to see how their academic progress correlates with their progress toward the following criteria:

> » I take initiative. This means I notice what needs to be done and do it.
>
> » I take responsibility. This means I take ownership of my work, my actions, and my space.
>
> » I persevere. This means I challenge myself. When something is hard, I keep trying and ask for help if I need it.
>
> » I collaborate. This means I can work well with others to get something done.

Perhaps as part of your process of developing norms with your students, you could consider working with them to develop a rubric that will help them understand what it means to meet these criteria. This would provide you with a powerful vehicle not only to assess habits of character, but also to build and reinforce a positive classroom culture.

References

Abedi, J., & Linquanti, R. (2012). Issues and opportunity in improving the quality of large-scale assessment systems for English language learners. Stanford University. Retrieved from http://ell.stanford.edu/sites/default/files/pdf/academic-papers/07-Abedi%20 Linquanti%20Issues%20and%20Opportunities%20FINAL.pdf

ACT. (2006). Reading between the lines: What the ACT reveals about college readiness in reading. Retrieved from https://www.act.org/content/dam/act/unsecured/documents/ reading_summary.pdf

Adams, M. (2010–2011). Advancing our students' language and literacy: The challenge of complex text. *American Educator, 34*(4), 3–11.

Adams, M.J. (2009). The challenge of advanced texts: The interdependence of reading and learning. In E. H. Hiebert (Ed.), *Reading more, reading better: Are American students reading enough of the right stuff?* (pp. 163–189). New York, NY: Guilford Press.

Aspen Institute (2018). Pursuing social and emotional development through a racial equity lens: A call to action. Draft paper. Retrieved from https://assets.aspeninstitute.org/content/ uploads/2018/03/Pursuing-Social-and-Emotional-Development-Through-a-Racial-Equity-Lens_FINAL_Mar19.pdf

Baldwin, R.S., Peleg-Bruckner, Z., & McClintock, A. (1985). Effect of topic interest and prior knowledge on reading comprehension. *Reading Research Quarterly, 20*(4), 497–504.

Bambrick-Santoyo, P. (2010). *Driven by data: A practical guide to improve instruction.* San Francisco, CA: Jossey-Bass.

Barnes, D. (1976). *From communication to curriculum.* Harmondsworth, UK: Penguin.

Beach, R., & Friedrich, T. (2006). Response to writing. In C.A. MacArthur, S. Graham, & J. Fitzgerald (Eds.), *Handbook of writing research* (pp. 222–234). New York, NY: Guilford Press.

Berger, R., Rugen, L., & Woodfin, L. (2014). *Leaders of their own learning: Transforming schools through student-engaged assessment.* San Francisco, CA: Jossey-Bass.

Berger, R., Strasser, D., & Woodfin, L. (2015). *Management in the active classroom.* New York, NY: EL Education.

Berger, R., Vilen, A., and Woodfin, L. (2020). *The leaders of their own learning companion: New tools and tips for tackling the common challenges of student-engaged assessment.* San Francisco, CA: Jossey-Bass.

Berger, R., Woodfin, L., Plaut, S., & Dobbertin, C. (2014). *Transformational literacy: Making the Common Core shift with work that matters.* San Francisco, CA: Jossey-Bass.

Berger, R., Woodfin, L., & Vilen, A. (2016). *Learning that lasts: Challenging, engaging, and empowering students with deeper instruction.* San Francisco, CA: Jossey-Bass.

Blackwell, L.S., Trzesniewski, K.H., & Dweck, C.S. (2007). Implicit theories of intelligence predict achievement across an adolescent transition: A longitudinal study and an intervention. *Child Development, 78*(1), 246–263.

Blakemore, S.J. (2018). *Inventing ourselves.* New York, NY: PublicAffairs.

Blevins, W. (2001). *Teaching Phonics and Word Study in the Intermediate Grades.* New York: Scholastic.

Bloodgood, J.W., & Pacific, L.C. (2004). Bringing word study to intermediate classrooms. *Reading Teacher, 58*(3), 250–263.

Brookhart, S. (2008). *How to give effective feedback to your students.* Alexandria, VA: ASCD.

Bunch, G.C., Lotan, R., Valdés, G., & Cohen, E. (2005). Keeping content at the heart of content-based instruction: Access and support for transitional English learners. In D. Kaufman & J. Crandall (Eds.), *Content-based instruction in primary and secondary school settings* (pp. 11–25). Alexandria, VA: Teachers of English to Speakers of Other Languages.

Bunch, G., Kibler, A., & Pimentel, S. (2012). Realizing opportunities for ELLs in the Common Core English language arts and disciplinary literacy standards. Stanford University. Retrieved from http://ell.stanford.edu/sites/default/files/pdf/academic-papers/01_Bunch_Kibler_Pimentel_RealizingOpp% 20in%20ELA_FINAL_0.pdf

Cervetti, G.N., Jaynes, C.A., & Hiebert, E.H. (2009). Increasing opportunities to acquire knowledge. In E.H. Hiebert (Ed.), *Reading more, reading better: Solving problems in the teaching of literacy* (pp. 79–100). New York, NY: Guilford Press.

Cervetti, G.N., & Hiebert, E.H. (2015). The sixth pillar of reading instruction: Knowledge development. *Reading Teacher, 68*(7), 548–551.

Chall, J. (2005). *Diagnostic assessments of reading, 2nd ed.* Austin, TX: PsychCorp, A brand of Harcourt Assessment, Inc.

Clark, C., & Rumbold, K. (2006). Reading for pleasure: A research overview. National Literacy Trust. Retrieved from http://files.eric.ed.gov/fulltext/ED496343.pdf

Cohen, G.L., Steele, C.M., & Ross, L.D. (1999). The mentor's dilemma: Providing critical feedback across the racial divide. *Personality and social psychology bulletin, 25*(10), 1302–1318.

Collier, V., & Thomas, W. (2004). The astounding effectiveness of dual language education for all. NABE *Journal of Research and Practice, 2*(1), 1–20.

Council of the Great City Schools. (2019). English Language Learners in America's Great City Schools: Demographics, Achievement, and Staffing. Retrieved from https://www.cgcs.org/site/default.aspx?PageType=3&DomainID=4&ModuleInstanceID=834&ViewID=6446EE88-D30C-497E-9316-3F8874B3E108&RenderLoc=0&FlexDataID=4112&PageID=1.

Cunningham, A.E., & Stanovich, K.E. (1997). Early reading acquisition and the relation to reading experience and ability 10 years later. *Developmental Psychology, 33*, 934–945.

Duckworth, A.L., & Seligman, M.E.P. (2005). Self-discipline outdoes IQ in predicting academic performance of adolescents. *Psychological Science, 16*, 939–944.

Dweck, C.S., Walton, G.M., & Cohen, G.L. (2011). Academic tenacity: Mindsets and skills that promote long-term learning. White Paper. Seattle, WA: Gates Foundation.

Edreports.org. (n.d.). Grades 6–8 summary of alignment and usability. Retrieved from http://www.edreports.org/ela/reports/series/engage-ny.html

Emmer, E., Sabornie, E., Evertson, C.M., and Weinstein, C.S., eds. (2013). *Handbook of classroom management: Research, practice, and contemporary issues.* New York: Routledge.

Farrington, C., Johnson, D.W., Allensworth, E., Nagoaka, J., Roderick, M., Williams Beechum, N., & Seneca Keyes, T. (2012). Teaching Adolescents to Become Learners: The Role of Noncognitive Factors in Shaping School Performance: A Critical Literature Review. Chicago: University of Chicago Consortium on Chicago School Research.

Ferlazzo, L. (2015). "Culturally responsive teaching": An interview with Zaretta Hammond. *Classroom Q & A with Larry Ferlazzo.* Retrieved from https://blogs.edweek.org/teachers/classroom_qa_with_larry_ferlazzo/2015/07/culturally_responsive_teaching_an_interview_with_zaretta_hammond.html

Ferris, D.R., & Hedgcock, J.S. (2013). *Teaching L2 composition: Purpose, process, and practice.* New York, NY: Routledge Press.

Garcia, O. (2009). *Bilingual education in the 21st century: A global perspective.* West Sussex: UK: Wiley-Blackwell Press.

Garcia, O., & Walqui, A. (2015). What do educators need to know about language as they make decisions about Common Core standards implementation? In G. Valdés, K. Menken, & M. Castro (Eds.), *Common Core bilingual and English language learners* (pp. 47–50). Philadelphia, PA: Caslon Publishing.

Gay, G. (2000). *Culturally responsive teaching: Theory, research, and practice.* New York, NY: Teachers College Press.

Gibbons, P. (2010). Classroom talk and the learning of new registers in a second language. *Language and Education, 12*(2), 99–118.

Gilkerson, J., & Richards, J.A. (2008). The LENA Natural Language Study. The LENA Foundation. Retrieved from https://www.lena.org/wp-content/uploads/2016/07/LTR-02-2_Natural_Language_Study.pdf.

Gilkerson, J., Richards, J.A., Warren, S.F, Montgomery, J.K., Greenwood, C.R., Oller, D.K, Hansen, J.H.L., & Paul, T.D. (2017). Mapping the Early Language Environment Using All-Day Recordings and Automated Analysis. *American Journal of Speech-Language Pathology, 26* (2), 248–265.

Goldstein, J.S. & Tlusty, M.F. (2003). Substrate determinants and developmental rate of claw asymmetry in american lobsters, homarus americanus. *Journal of crustacean biology, 23*(4), 890–896.

Gomez, K., & Zywica, J. (2008). Annotating to support learning in content areas: Teaching and learning science. *Journal of Adolescent & Adult Literacy, 52*(2), 155–164.

Good, C., Aronson, J., & Inzlicht, M. (2003). Improving adolescents' standardized test performance: An intervention to reduce the effects of stereotype threat. *Journal of Applied Developmental Psychology, 24*, 645–662.

Hayes, D.P., Wolfer, L.T., & Wolfe, M.F. (1996). Sourcebook simplification and its relation to the decline in SAT-Verbal scores. *American Educational Research Journal, 33*, 489–508.

Hiebert, E.H. (2012). Core vocabulary: The foundation for successful reading of complex text. Text Matters. Text Project, Inc. Retrieved from: http://textproject.org/assets/Uploads/Text-MattersCore-Vocabulary.pdf

Himmele, P., & Himmele, W. (2011). *Total participation techniques: Making every student an active learner.* Alexandria, VA: Association for Supervision & Curriculum Development.

hooks, b. (2000). *Feminist theory: From margin to center.* Cambridge, MA: South End Press.

Israel, E. (2002). Examining multiple perspectives in literature. In *Inquiry and the literary text: Constructing discussions in the English Classroom.* Urbana, IL: NCTE.

Juel, C. & Deffes, R. (2004). Making Words Stick. *Educational Leadership, 61*(6).

Kintsch, E., & Hampton, S. (2009). Supporting cumulative knowledge building through reading. In S.R. Parris, D. Fisher, & K. Headley (Eds.), *Adolescent literacy, field tested: Effective solutions for every classroom* (pp. 47–57). Newark, DE: International Reading Association.

Kuhn, M.R., Schwanenflugel, P.J., & Meisinger, E.B. (2010). Aligning Theory and Assessment of Reading Fluency: Automaticity, Prosody, and Definitions of Fluency. *Reading Research Quarterly, 45*(2), 230–251.

Ladson-Billings, G. (2006). From the Achievement Gap to the Education Debt: Understanding Achievement in U.S. Schools. *Educational Researcher, 35*(7), 3–12.

Landauer, T.K., & Dumais, S.T. (1997). A solution to Plato's problem: The latent semantic analysis theory of acquisition, induction, and representation of knowledge. *Psychological Review, 104*(2), 211.

Liben, David. (2010). "Why text complexity matters" in Common Core state standards for English language arts and literacy in history/social studies, science, and technical subjects. Appendix A: Research supporting key elements of the standards. National Governors Association Center for Best Practices, Council of Chief State School Officers: Washington, DC.

Mathematica (2019). EL Education schools and teacher professional development. Retrieved from https://www.mathematica.org/our-publications-and-findings/projects/el-education-schools-and-teacher-professional-development

McNamara, D.S., & O'Reilly, T. (2009). Theories of comprehension skill: Knowledge and strategies versus capacity and suppression. In A.M. Columbus (Ed.), *Advances in psychology research, volume 62*. Hauppauge, NY: Nova Science Publishers, Inc.

Michaels, S., & O'Connor, C. (2012). Talk science primer. Cambridge, MA: TERC. http://inquiryproject.terc.edu/shared/pd/TalkScience_Primer.pdf. Based on Chapin, S., O'Connor, C., & Anderson, N. (2009). Classroom discussions: Using math talk to help students learn, grades K–6 (2nd ed.). Sausalito, CA: Math Solutions Publications.

Moss, C., & Brookhart, S. (2009). *Advancing formative assessment in every classroom*. Alexandria, VA: ASCD.

Nagaoka, J., Farrington, C., Ehrlich, S., & Heath, R. (2015). *Foundations for young adult success: A developmental framework*. Chicago, IL: The University of Chicago Consortium on Chicago School Research.

Nagy, W., & Anderson, R. (1984). The number of words in printed school English. Reading *Research Quarterly, 19*, 304–330.

Nagy, W., Anderson, R., & Herman, P. (1987). Learning word meanings from context during normal reading. *American Educational Research Journal, 24*, 237–270.

National Center for Education Statistics. (2012). The nation's report card: Vocabulary results from the 2009 and 2011 NAEP reading assessments. Institute of Education Sciences, U.S. Department of Education, Washington, DC.

National Equity Project (2019). Why Equity? Retrieved from https://nationalequityproject.org/about/equity

National Governors Association Center for Best Practices, Council of Chief State School Officers. (2010). Common Core state standards. Washington, DC: Author.

National Governors Association Center for Best Practices, Council of Chief State School Officers. (2010). Common Core state standards (appendix A). Washington, DC: Author.

National Institute for Literacy. (2001). Put reading first: The reading building blocks for teaching children to read. Retrieved from https://lincs.ed.gov/publications/pdf/PRFbooklet.pdf.

Nelson, J., Perfetti, C., Liben, D., & Liben, M. (2012). Measures of text difficulty: Testing their predictive value for grade levels and student performance. Council of Chief State School Officers, Washington, DC.

O'Connor, R.E., Swanson, H.L., & Geraghty, C. (2010). Improvement in reading rate under independent and difficult text levels: Influences on word and comprehension skills. *Journal of Educational Psychology, 102*(1), 1–19.

Olsen, L. (2010). *Reparable Harm: Fulfilling the Unkept Promise of Educational Opportunity for California's Long Term English Language Learners*. Long Beach, CA: Californians Together.

Oyserman, D., Terry, K., & Bybee, D. (2002). A possible selves intervention to enhance school involvement. *Journal of Adolescence, 25*, 313–326.

Rasinski, T. (2004). Creating fluent readers. *Educational Leadership, 61*(6), 46–51.

Rasinski, T. (2006). Reading fluency instruction: Moving beyond accuracy, automaticity, and prosody. *The Reading Teacher, 59*(7), 704–706.

Rasinski, T.V., Padak, N.D., McKeon, C.A., Wilfong, L.G., Friedauer, J.A., & Heim, P. (2005). Is reading fluency a key for successful high school reading? *Journal of Adolescent & Adult Literacy, 49*(1), 22–27.

Recht, D.R., & Leslie, L. (1988). Effect of prior knowledge on good and poor readers' memory of text. *Journal of Educational Psychology, 80*(1), 16–20.

Rodgers, C.R., & Raider-Roth, M.B. (2006). Presence in teaching. *Teachers and Teaching: Theory and Practice, 12*(3), 265–287.

Staehr Fenner, D. (2013). Overview of the Common Core state standards initiatives for ELLs. TESOL International Association.

Stanovich, K.E. (1986). Matthew effects in reading: Some consequences of individual differences in the acquisition of literacy. *Reading Research Quarterly, 2*(4), 360–407.

Stanovich, K.E. (1992). Speculations on the causes and consequences of individual differences in early reading acquisition. In *Reading Acquisition* (pp. 307–342). Hillsdale, NJ: L. Erlbaum Associates.

Stanovich, K. & Cunningham, A.E. (1993). Where does knowledge come from? Specific associations between print exposure and information acquisition. *Journal of Educational Psychology, 85*(2), 211.

Stiggins, R.J., Arter, J.A., Chappuis, J., & Chappuis, S. (2006) Classroom assessment for student learning: Doing it right—using it well, 1st edition.

Tedick, D., & Wesely, P. (2015). A review of research on content-based foreign/second language education in U.S. K–12 contexts. *Language, Culture, and Curriculum, 28*(1), 25–40.

Tomlinson, C.A. (1997). What it means to teach gifted learners well. National Association for Gifted Children. Retrieved from: https://www.nagc.org/resources-publications/gifted-education-practices/what-it-means-teach-gifted-learners-well

United Nations Educational, Scientific and Cultural Organization. (1996). Universal Declaration of Linguistic Rights. Declaration presented at the World Conference on Linguistic Rights, Barcelona, Spain.

Vermont Writing Collaborative. (2008). *Writing for understanding: Using backward design to help all students write effectively*. Vermont: Author.

Vermont Writing Collaborative. (2017). *The writing for understanding workbook*. Unpublished manuscript. Vermont: Author.

Walqui, A., & Van Lier, L. (2010). *Scaffolding the academic success of adolescent English language learners: A pedagogy of promise*. San Francisco, CA: WestEd.

Walton, G.M., & Cohen, G.L. (2007). A question of belonging: Race, social fit, and achievement. *Journal of Personality and Social Psychology, 92*, 82–96.

Weaver, C. & Bush, J. (2008). *Grammar to enrich and enhance writing*. Portsmouth, NH: Heinemann.

Weaver, C., McNally, C., & Moerman, S. (2001). To grammar or not to grammar: That is not the question! *Voices from the Middle, 8*(3), 17–33.

Webb, N.L. (2005). Web alignment tool. Wisconsin Center for Educational Research. University of Wisconsin-Madison. Retrieved from: https://static.pdesas.org/content/documents/M1-Slide_19_DOK_Wheel_Slide.pdf

Whipple, G.M. (1925). Report of the national committee on reading. Bloomington, IL: Public School Publishing.

Wiggins, G. (2012). Seven keys to effective feedback. *Educational Leadership, 70*(1), 10–16.

Wiliam, D. (2014). The right questions, the right way. *Educational Leadership, 71*(6), 16–19.

Williams, J.P., Stafford, K.B., Lauer, K.D., Hall, K.M., & Pollini, S. (2009). Embedding reading comprehension training in content-area instruction. *Journal of Educational Psychology, 101*, 1–20.

Wong Fillmore, L., & Fillmore, C. (2012). What does text complexity mean for English learners and language minority students? Paper presented at the Understanding Language Conference, Stanford, CA.

Zong, J. & Batalova, J. (2015). The limited English proficient population in the United States. The Migration Policy Institute. Retrieved from https://www.migrationpolicy.org/article/limited-english-proficient-population-united-states

Index